Ethical
Arguments
for Analysis

Ethical Arguments for Analysis

BRIEF EDITION

Edited by
Robert Baum
Rensselaer Polytechnic Institute

Holt, Rinehart and Winston
New York   Chicago   San Francisco
Dallas   Montreal   Toronto   London   Sydney

Cover drawing by Dana Fradon; © 1975 The New Yorker Magazine, Inc.

Library of Congress Cataloging in Publication Data

Baum, Robert, 1941–   comp.
  Ethical Arguments for analysis.

    Abridgement of the 2d ed.
    1. Ethics——Case studies.   I. Title
BJ1031.B332   170   78–10770
ISBN: 0–03–045011–x

Preface to Second Edition

Although every effort has been made to retain all of the features which instructors found useful in the first edition of *Ethical Arguments for Analysis*, there have been a number of changes made in this new edition which have been designed to increase its utility as a primary or supplementary text for a variety of courses, including ethics, logic, rhetoric, and politics. The Introduction has been completely rewritten to provide a sample analysis of an argument similar to most of those included in the fourteen sections, and a number of exercises have been supplied at appropriate points in the Introduction to assist in relating the discussion to the concrete examples contained in the rest of the book. All of the dated examples from the first edition have been dropped, and the total number of items included in this edition is almost double that in the first edition. The examples have been organized into fourteen new sections designed to bring out important points of difference and similarity between various arguments. The section introductions, which also are entirely new and include exercises, not only call attention to central issues unifying the arguments in a given section, but they also assist the student in relating the arguments in one section to those in other sections.

The key features of this book are the "unretouched" arguments drawn from everyday sources and the relatively neutral context in which they are reproduced. This format was proven in the first edition to be extremely flexible; it permits the instructor to use these materials in a variety of ways in a variety of courses. Although the first edition of this book was originally conceived of as a supplementary text for ethics courses, I and a number of other users have found it to be at least as useful in logic and other courses. In particular, it can be used to illustrate the ways in which the same argument in ordinary English can be translated into different logical systems (e.g., syllogistic, propositional, and predicate logics), often with strikingly different results, in contrast to arguments which have been rewritten or even specially written for use in conjunction with a chapter in a logic text on the propositional calculus which cannot be used very well in conjunction with the chapters on the syllogism or the predicate calculus. Even when translating into the same system, a class of students will sometimes come up with twenty or more different ways of translating or symbolizing a single argument out of everyday English. In addition, the arguments in this book provide concrete evidence that few if any arguments which are found in the "real world" resemble the artificial arguments in textbooks. In ethics courses, students will often show how a specific argument could actually be interpreted in terms of several quite different ethical theories. In brief, I and many others have found that the use of the materials in this book in a variety of classroom contexts has provided significant new insights not only for our students but also for ourselves. In this regard, anyone who is using this book for the first time should be prepared for the unexpected. This may make life for the instructor somewhat more difficult, but it also provides a richer, more stimulating intellectual adventure for both the instructor and students.

I cannot begin to name the literally hundreds of persons who have helped make this new edition a reality. I can only express my thanks and appreciation in blanket form to the many instructors who have taken the time to share their experiences in using the first edition and who have offered helpful suggestions for this edition; to the students in my classes who provided much of the inspiration for struggling through some of the more tedious tasks required for pulling this all together; to the copyright holders and members of the editorial staff at Holt, Rinehart and Winston who assisted in securing and keeping track of the reprint permissions; and to the colleagues who have read and commented on various portions of the text. The one person who must be singled out by name for her innumerable contributions—both tangible and intangible—to the completion of this project, is my wife Gail.

January 1976   R. J. B.

Preface to Brief Edition

This brief edition of *Ethical Arguments for Analysis* has been prepared particularly for the large number of instructors who wish to use it as a second or supplementary text in a variety of courses including Ethics, Logic, and Rhetoric. The original second edition has been shortened by more than one-third—primarily by deletion of arguments which closely resemble other arguments which have been retained and arguments which have become dated.

Two chapters of the original edition (4 and 14) have been deleted in this abridgment, but a number of significant arguments from each have been retained and relocated in other chapters. No new arguments have been added to this edition.

Troy, New York
July 11, 1978

R.J.B.

Contents

Ethical
Arguments
for Analysis

Introduction

It is a basic fact, for which this book provides substantial documentation, that in the course of a normal lifetime every human being is confronted with countless decisions and choices. A few examples should be sufficient for making it clear exactly what are being referred to as "decisions and choices".

A small child is faced with the choice of one of 47 different flavors of ice cream available at the local ice-cream parlor.

A high school athlete has to choose from among 43 colleges and universities which have offered attractive scholarships.

A philosophy professor has to assign a grade to a student who worked very hard in the course but did not do well on the exams or papers.

The members of the admissions committee of a medical college must select 100 persons to be admitted to next year's class from among the 5000 applicants.

A young married couple has to decide which of hundreds of houses and apartments they will buy or rent as their first home.

A corporate executive has to choose one person to be the manager of an important new project from a list of 25 candidates.

A registered voter is confronted with the choice of voting for or against a new bond issue or not voting at all.

Even while recognizing that we do in fact make such decisions and choices on a regular basis, we must also admit that we often make them in a reflexive or mechanical way, without being any more conscious of it than we normally are of breathing or of our heart beating. There are also instances that each of us can cite when we are conscious that a decision is being made (by us), but it is still being made in a mechanical, or at best arbitrary, way. But there are also times and circumstances in which each of us has stopped and thought over the situation, carefully considering the pros and cons of alternative courses of action before making our decision as to which course of action to follow. When it comes to decisions concerning questions such as what career to pursue, or whether or not to begin a family, some people spend significant portions of their lives "thinking things over" before committing themselves to a final course of action (or inaction, which is always an alternative).

Often, in the process of making a decision, we discuss the pros and cons of the alternative courses of action with friends and relatives. And after having made a choice, we often justify and/or defend our decision when circumstances demand it. We also praise or criticize others' decisions, offering our own reasons for agreeing or disagreeing with their choices. The presentation of reasons for our agreement with or opposition to a particular decision comprises what is commonly known as the process of "argumentation." And in so far as we put forward certain statements in support of another statement to the effect that one of a set of alternative courses of action is better or worse than another, we can be said to be presenting an argument in support of that judgment.

The term "argument" has several different meanings in everyday English usage. The type of situation to which this term is most frequently applied is exemplified by a highly emotional dispute between a husband and wife about whether or not to buy a new car, or a quarrel between a teenager and his or her parents over their imposition of a curfew for dates on weekends. A similar and also commonly encountered case to which the term "argument" can be applied is the cool, articulate discussion between formal debate teams. While the examples contained in this book might sometimes share the features of these types of cases, we will be concerned primarily, if not solely, with the fact that they satisfy a more technical and restricted definition of the term "argument", namely the formal, logical definition that *an argument is a set of statements, one of which is designated as a conclusion and the remainder of which are asserted as evidence, supporting or implying the truth of the conclusion.*

The mere presentation of an argument in support of a judgment that a particular decision is good or bad is not in and of itself adequate justification for accepting that judgment, insofar as only a few of the literally infinite number of possible arguments really provide any significant support for their conclusions. Consider the following examples:

It was right for Joe to cheat on the exam because he doesn't like applesauce.
It was right for Joe to cheat on the exam because he didn't have time to study for it.
It was right for Joe to cheat on the exam because the moon is made of blue cheese.

Each of the above statements comprises an argument insofar as each involves the presentation of some reason in support of the claim that it was right for Joe to cheat. The third example is clearly a very bad argument, in that the reason provided in fact gives no support whatsoever to the conclusion; the assertion that the moon is made of blue cheese is in fact false, and even if it were true it bears no logical relation whatsoever to the assertion that Joe did the right thing. The first two examples may be somewhat better arguments insofar as their premises could be true (Joe may indeed dislike applesauce and he may not have had time to study for the exam), but it is still not at all clear what logical relation may exist between either of these premises and the conclusion concerning the rightness of Joe's decision to cheat. In brief, not every argument provides us with the same (or even any) justification for accepting the conclusion; it is necessary that an argument provide actual support for the conclusion before it can be judged to be a *good* argument.

Our basic concern in this discussion is with choices and decisions, and with distinguishing good decisions from bad ones. However, since a judgment concerning the goodness or badness of a decision normally must be supported by an argument, and since there are both good and bad arguments in support of any particular judgment, our discussion must be moved to the more abstract level of evaluating arguments. It is hoped that the connection between our discussion of good and bad arguments and our primary concern with distinguishing good and bad decisions is sufficiently clear. In simplest terms, the connection is that a good argument in support of a judgment that an action or decision is good (or bad) normally is sufficient grounds for believing that the action or decision is in fact good (or bad). A bad argument in support of any judgment provides us with no grounds for believing anything at all about the goodness or badness of the action or decision being judged.

Before proceeding to a discussion of the criteria and procedures for distinguishing good arguments from bad ones, it is necessary to impose an important restriction on the scope of our discussion. In brief, we are *not* concerned in this book with the evaluation of *all* possible kinds of choices and decisions; we are only concerned with those choices and decisions which can be classified as "moral" or "ethical." Although it would certainly be useful at this point to provide a precise definition of the term "moral decision," it is unfortunately impossible to do this, since there are a number of different definitions of the term, most of which are incompatible in one way or another with the others. All that we can do here is provide a rough indication of the general area which for the purposes of this book will be considered as falling within the definition of "moral decision" or "ethical decision." (In this book we shall use the terms "moral" and "ethical" interchangeably.)

Most dictionaries define a moral decision as a decision made on the basis of an appeal to a set of moral rules or principles, or as a decision made by an appeal to one's conscience. Unfortunately, since the definitions provided for "moral principles" and "conscience" appeal back to the concept of moral decision (for example, one definition of "conscience" is "the faculty of mind used for making moral choices"), we are simply led in circles without ever gaining a clearer understanding of the basic concept of moral decision. An alternative procedure for defining "moral decision" is to simply provide examples, and that is the procedure we will use in this book. However, we must make it clear from the beginning that there is much room for disagreement over what does and what does not qualify as a moral decision, and some of the examples contained in this book have been selected precisely to provide examples of cases over which there is much disagreement as to whether they do indeed involve moral decisions. This issue is discussed further in the introduction to Section 7.

EXERCISES

1. Examine the examples in Sections 1, 7, and 13 of this book. Classify each example as involving what *you* consider to be (a) clearly a moral decision, (b) possibly a moral decision, or (c) clearly not a moral decision. Compare your classifications with those of several other persons. Try to determine the reasons for any differences that might appear between your classifications and those of someone else.
2. Using the examples which you classified in the previous exercise, try to formulate a definition or set of criteria for distinguishing in general between moral and nonmoral decisions. Compare your definition with those of several other persons and analyze any differences.
3. Apply the definition which you formulated in Exercise 2 to the following statement to determine whether this statement is true or false (by your definition): "The decision to consider a particular issue as a moral issue is itself a moral decision." (In other words, is it a moral decision, by your definition, to decide to consider, for example, the killing of a dog as a moral issue?)

The remainder of the discussion in this Introduction will be devoted to matters which should be of assistance in the development of the skills necessary for distinguishing good moral arguments from bad ones, which for reasons already discussed will also be of assistance in distinguishing good moral decisions from bad ones. Thus, even though our discussion will be formulated in terms of distinguishing good moral *arguments* from bad ones, it should be understood throughout that we are also concerned with distinguishing good moral *decisions* from bad ones.

For the most part, each of us is normally able to identify a good or bad argument for what it is without much conscious effort. On a purely intuitive level, most people would probably agree that a good argument is one in which all of the premises are already known to be true with a reasonable degree of certainty and in which the premises are related to the conclusion in such a way as to transmit the certainty of the premises in whole or part to the conclusion. In a somewhat more precise formulation, one basic requirement for a *good* argument is that it must be one for which it is the case that if the premises are true, Although this general definition may appear to be relatively simple and straight- then the conclusion is true or highly probable, and the premises are in fact true. forward, it is unfortunately the case that many arguments which we encounter in everyday life are such that it is not at all easy to determine whether they are good or not. Most of the ethical arguments included in this book have been selected precisely because they are not easily evaluated (although some of them at first glance may seem to be obviously good or bad). It is almost always the case that even if most people intuitively judge a particular argument to be "obviously" good, there remains the possibility that someone will not agree and may even feel that the same argument is "obviously" a bad one. In order to resolve such differences of opinion concerning the quality of a particular argument, it is necessary to have a good understanding of the nature of arguments and of the many factors which are relevant to their being good or bad. This kind of understanding cannot be acquired solely by reading an abstract theoretical discussion about analyzing arguments; rather, this understanding must be gained by actually applying the general concepts to concrete examples of the type provided in this book.

EXERCISES

4. Read through all of the arguments in one of the sections in this book. Relying on your own intuitions, label each argument according to the following 1–5 scale. (Remember, you are to evaluate the argument, not the decision being discussed in the argument.)

> 1–Very Good
> 2–Good
> 3–Indeterminate
> 4–Bad
> 5–Very Bad

5. Compare your evaluations of these arguments with those of several other persons. Discuss two or three arguments for which your evaluations differed the most to try to determine the reason(s) for the differences. Try to resolve these differences and come to an agreement concerning these arguments.

The process of distinguishing good moral arguments from bad ones (and thus of distinguishing good moral decisions from bad ones) is far from being a simple one. It is for this reason that the cartoon on the cover of this book contains a real element of truth, although its humor derives from its more obvious element of error. Most people would agree that there are no human beings who have some special innate faculty or insight which enables them to distinguish good moral choices from bad ones in a way that other people cannot. But there are in fact persons who have developed certain basic skills so that they can progress further towards the identification of good and bad decisions than persons who have not developed these skills. No medical doctor can cure all illnesses, nor can he or she keep anyone alive forever. However, the combination of basic skills acquired through formal training in medical school and the practice and experience gained from applying this knowledge to real situations during the internship and residence periods is normally sufficient to assist doctors in mastering the art of medicine, which enables them to cure many more illnesses and extend lives longer than can persons who have not had similar training and practical experience. Thus an analog to the cartoon on the cover might be a case where a person is asking for someone who can tell him or her how to live forever or how to cure a presently uncurable disease. We smile at this because we recognize that it is a request for what we now consider to be impossible; but this does not mean that we consider the practice and training of doctors and medical researchers to be a foolish enterprise. We are willing to accept the fact that while they cannot now provide solutions to the "problems" of indefinite prolongation of life or a cure of lung cancer, they are able to treat many problems in a way that most people would consider to be a significant improvement over the way they were treated a century ago and over the way persons without special training could treat them even today. In a like manner, a person with formal training and skills developed through careful practice should be able to deal more effectively and intelligently with difficult ethical decisions than a person without such training. They are not able to distinguish a good decision from a bad one at a glance any more than a physician is able to diagnose an illness at a glance. But a person with the proper training and experience should know what procedures to follow which will most likely lead to a determination of what is the morally right decision in a given situation, even if in many cases it is not possible to adequately complete all of these procedures. But all of this is much too abstract for adequate comprehension and is certainly not persuasive. So we will leave this discussion about the utility of this study and proceed to the study itself. After we have provided sample analyses of several examples, the utility of the study should be more clearly apparent.

To bring our discussion down to more concrete terms, we will use the following argument as the subject of a sample analysis. The argument is not intended to be particularly good or bad, but it is designed to enable us to identify many of the basic factors involved in evaluating most moral arguments.

It was morally wrong for Susan to write Tom's term paper for his ethics course, because helping someone else to cheat is as bad as cheating oneself. And history has shown that when one performs even a small act of dishonesty this can lead to ever more harmful acts, in addition to encouraging others to commit similar wrongs. When too many members of a particular society commit acts which are harmful to other members of that society, it ultimately leads to the destruction of that society, which is certainly reason enough for Susan not to write Tom's term paper.

We will now proceed to evaluate this argument. Remember, if we are able to show that this is a good argument, then we will have reason to believe that it was indeed morally wrong for Susan to do what she did; but if we show that the argument is bad, or even fail to show that it is good, then we will not have adequate reason to believe that Susan's choice was either good or bad. In other words, while a good argument provides justification for accepting its conclusion as true, a bad argument simply fails to provide adequate evidence for the truth of the conclusion. It must be emphasized that a bad argument does not prove that the conclusion is false. A bad argument is bad precisely because it proves *nothing at all*.

The process of analyzing arguments is not a simple linear one; there is no fixed and absolute sequence of steps through which we can mechanically move in such a way that we will automatically wind up with a definite determination of the quality of the argument. Thus, we must begin this analysis by making it as explicit as possible that the procedures used here are to be taken as a "model" procedure only in a very limited way. The sequence in which various points will be discussed should not be interpreted at all as the only possible one, or even as the best one, insofar as many of the steps can be performed simultaneously when they are not being written down as we have to do here. While most if not all of these points should be considered during the analysis of most arguments, there are many other kinds of factors that need to be considered in the analysis of this and other arguments which we simply cannot go into here, although we will try to give some indication of where one can find a more detailed discussion of such factors in the course of our own analysis.

For our present purposes, it is appropriate and useful, but not absolutely necessary, to begin our analysis by trying to identify the conclusion of the argument we have selected as our sample. Probably most persons (whose native language is English, of course) would agree that the conclusion is expressed by the first part of the first sentence, that is, "It was morally wrong for Susan to write Tom's term paper for his ethics course." While this might be considered by many to be simply intuitively obvious, there is a more specific and concrete bit of evidence that this is the case, namely, the word "because" following the sentence. Frequently, *but not always*, the appearance of the term "because" (or "since" or any one of several other words) indicates that the sentence immediately preceding the word is the conclusion of an argument, and that the sentence immediately following (and perhaps other sentences as well) expresses a premise of that argument. Unfortunately, these indicator words are also used in other ways which have nothing whatever to do with arguments, so we cannot rely on their appearance as a guarantee that a particular sentence expresses the conclusion or premise of an argument. In the end, we usually have to rely on our "intuition" or our "feel" for the language for identification of the conclusion of an argument.

But in many cases, including our example, the problem of identifying the conclusion of a moral argument is even more difficult and complex than this. Even though we may agree that the sentence "It was morally wrong for Susan . . ." expresses the conclusion of this argument, it is not entirely clear what the precise wording of the conclusion should be. Is the conclusion really that it was wrong for Susan to write Tom's term paper, or is it instead that it was wrong for Susan to help Tom cheat? While this may seem to be a relatively minor or even trivial question, it does have some significance for the overall evaluation of this argument.

It is also important to recognize that insofar as this is being presented as a *moral* judgment there must be some choice or decision involved, and it is not at all clear from the conclusion as given what the alternatives were from which Susan chose. For example, did Susan know that she was writing this paper so that Tom could submit it for his ethics course or did she perhaps believe that she was doing this for some quite different purpose? And even if she knew that Tom was going to submit it for his course, what options were open to her? If Tom had been pointing a gun at her head, and the option was to not write the paper and get shot, this would significantly affect the evaluation of the entire argument and ultimately the evaluation of the act itself. Likewise, it may be that Tom had saved Susan's life at a previous time and Susan felt herself to be in great debt to him, and if she did not write the paper she would be failing to repay this debt. Thus, it is important that the statement of the conclusion of a moral argument should include an explicit statement of the alternative choices which could have been made. The conclusion in our example should not merely say that it was wrong for Susan to write Tom's paper; it should specify that it was wrong for Susan to have done this instead of one or more of the alternatives that were available to her.

Although most arguments fail to adequately spell out in the conclusion the alternatives to a given course of action, these alternatives are often discussed in the premises in a way which is adequate for enabling us to fully formulate the conclusion for the purposes of analyzing it. Thus, if our example had contained some mention of alternatives in the premises (e.g., a premise such as "If Susan had not written Tom's paper, then she would have been failing to repay her debt to him for having saved her from a shark at the beach the previous week"), the argument as a whole would have been strengthened considerably, and it would have been both easy and reasonable to add this information to the statement of the conclusion. Insofar as no indication is given anywhere at all in the argument of the options open to Susan in this case, the argument is weaker than if these alternatives were explicitly stated.

Not only is some information left out of the statement of the conclusion in some arguments, but it is not uncommon for the conclusion to never be explicitly stated at all. An argument in which some part is not explicitly stated is known as an "enthymeme," and in such cases it is normal procedure to simply try to supply the missing elements of the argument in as reasonable a manner as possible. Consider the following version of our example:

> Helping someone else to cheat is as bad as cheating oneself, and Susan did help Tom to cheat when she wrote his ethics term paper for him. And history . . . .

Although it is not explicitly stated in this version, it is sufficiently clear that the intended conclusion of the argument is that Susan was wrong to write Tom's paper (or to help him to cheat). In such cases, it is necessary for the person analyzing the argument to make explicit in the most reasonable way any and all information which is implicit in the original argument. To analyze an argument should not be the same as to attack it. The purpose of analysis is to identify the strengths as well as the weaknesses of an argument, and to correct its weaknesses as much as possible in order to lead to a determination as to what is the best choice to make in a particular situation. Because the primary aim of our analysis is positive rather than critical, it is necessary to rely on a basic rule which we will refer as the "Principle of Charity." The Principle of Charity is simply the quite reasonable rule that *we should always make every effort possible to interpret an argument in the way which makes it as strong as possible.* For example, we could have interpreted the enthymeme above as not even expressing any argument at all insofar as it has no conclusion, but this would clearly have violated the Principle of Charity. It would not be an unreasonable application of the Principle of Charity to interpret the lack of mention of alternative courses of action in our sample argument as an implicit assertion that none of the possible options available in this specific case involve any special overriding obligations, such as keeping a promise or preserving one's life, which might be relevant to the basic judgment concerning the rightness or wrongness of Susan's act. Wording to this effect might even be explicitly included in our reformulation of the conclusion, although it would have to be kept clearly in mind that we certainly do not have conclusive evidence that this is in fact the case. An argument which states explicitly all of the available courses of action for a given case is generally a better argument than one in which some of the options are only implicitly identified.

Our discussion thus far has focused on an example in which the conclusion is a judgment about a specific decision made by a particular individual. However, an examination of the arguments reprinted in the following pages reveals that many of them have conclusions which involve generalizations about kinds of action (e.g., Abortion is wrong.) or judgments concerning events where the agent is not clearly identified, (e.g., The Vietnam war was morally wrong.). We must therefore digress from our example for a moment to discuss such conclusions.

For the purposes of this book, we will consider arguments with general conclusions as subordinate arguments which are such that they can be used as components of any number of other arguments with conclusions about specific cases. Thus an argument with the conclusion "Abortion is wrong" can be taken as part of a set of premises such as "Dr. Jones performed an abortion on Mary Doe" in support of the specific conclusion "It was wrong for Dr. Jones to perform an abortion on Mary Doe." We will see a little bit later in the discussion of our sample case that the argument concerning Susan and Tom contains several implicit premises which are general conclusions of subarguments in the overall argument. We will therefore wait to discuss these general conclusions in that context.

A conclusion such as "The Vietnam war was wrong" is not a generalization of the type just discussed, since there is precisely one event being talked about— or at least that appears to be the case. The problem with a conclusion such as this is that it is not at all clear what decision by what agent is being categorized as wrong. Since an action cannot be appropriately classified as right or wrong unless there are alternative courses of action open to the agent, it is necessary that both the agent and the choices be known in order to make an adequate determination of the rightness or wrongness of the action being judged. If, as some historians have argued, major events such as wars are the product of forces in society over which no individual has any control at all, then it would follow that it is simply improper, or an incorrect use of language, to assert that the Vietnam war was morally wrong. We cannot go into the whole set of issues related to the question of "historical determinism" here. Instead, we shall simply reiterate that all conclusions with inadequate identification of the alternative courses of action should be reformulated to make the agent and the choices explicit where this is possible. Thus, for example, the conclusion of the Vietnam argument could be reformulated as a judgment concerning Lyndon Johnson's options at the time he took the Gulf of Tonkin resolution to Congress or at the time he made the commitment to send as many as 500,000 troops to Vietnam rather than pulling out the relatively few troops that were then there. Of course, one could also place the responsibility on the members of Congress, or on the Secretary of State, or on other persons who had other options. But the main point to be made here is that we are not even dealing with a moral argument if the conclusion is not general and also is not concerned with a decision for which there were at least two real options available to some agent. The problem of identifying the agent for complex cases such as the Vietnam war is just one issue related to the evaluation of moral arguments that we will not be able to discuss in sufficient detail in this Introduction, although it will be touched on in the introductions to several of the following sections of this book.

It is not possible in the space limitations of this discussion to detail all of the factors which should be taken into account in the single task of identifying and formulating the conclusion of an argument, but we must make it clear that this is indeed a complex process which has not been completely presented here. For example, we have not adequately discussed complex arguments which contain arguments within arguments, and thus multiple conclusions (only one of which, of course, is the primary or final conclusion) which must be sorted out before the final conclusion can be identified. Thus, although we are now going on to discuss some of the other tasks involved in the evaluation of moral arguments, it should not be assumed that our treatment of the procedures for identifying and formulating conclusions has been in any sense complete.

In summary, the identification and complete formulation of the conclusion is a necessary and critical, although not necessarily first, step in the evaluation of an ethical argument. If after making every reasonable effort (in compliance with the Principle of Charity) one is still unable to identify or formulate the conclusion of an argument, one then has adequate grounds for judging the argument to be a bad one. However, if one has adequately identified and formulated the conclusion and then considers the conclusion to be false, this is not an adequate reason for rejecting either the conclusion or the argument. In order to reject an argument whose conclusion is (or can be) properly formulated, it is necessary to identify some other weakness in the argument. If no other weakness can be found, then it would be irrational to reject the argument as a bad one simply because one believes that the conclusion is false.

EXERCISES

6. Select one argument from each of the sections of this book that appears to you intuitively to be a good one, and one argument from each section which appears to be a bad one. Identify, where possible, the main conclusion of each of these arguments. (Remember, some arguments are enthymematic and the conclusions are not explicitly stated.)
7. Classify each of the conclusions identified in the previous exercise as (a) a judgment concerning a particular decision or choice made by a specific individual; (b) a judgment concerning a particular event in which the agent and/or the alternative choices is (are) not adequately specified; (c) a general judgment concerning a type of action rather than a specific case.
8. Determine whether there are any adequate grounds for judging any of these arguments to be bad ones solely on the basis of your consideration of their conclusions.

Even using the Principle of Charity we were not able to provide a formulation of the conclusion of our sample argument which contains any indication of the options which were open to the agent (Susan) in this particular case, so we already have identified one weakness in it. However, insofar as every argument has weaknesses of one kind or another, we shall continue using this example for the remainder of our discussion of some of the other significant factors related to the goodness or badness of a moral argument.

In addition to identifying and adequately formulating the conclusion, it is also a necessary and critical part of any analysis to identify and properly formulate the premises offered in support of that conclusion. The consideration of the premises is not normally a sequel to the identification of the conclusion, insofar as the argument must usually be considered as a whole before the conclusion can be properly identified and formulated. In the case of enthymemes in which the conclusion is implicit, it is necessary to conduct a particularly thorough and detailed analysis of the premises before even trying to formulate the conclusion. We shall also see later that there are a number of other considerations that have to be made before or during the process of identifying and reformulating the premises of an argument.

Referring back to our sample argument, it might not seem unreasonable to assume that all of the statements other than the conclusion were asserted as being in some way supportive of the conclusion, and thus all of them can be considered as premises. Unfortunately, such an assumption is all too often quite mistaken. It is not uncommon to discover in a lengthy editorial that only a few of the many sentences actually express premises which in any way support the conclusion. However, it is not always easy to determine whether or not a particular statement is an essential premise of an argument, and we certainly cannot rely solely on our intuitions as to whether or not a specific statement is essential. The inclusion of totally irrelevant premises in an analysis may complicate things a little and create some extra work, but it will not distort the ultimate result of the analysis. If the argument is basically good, our analysis will show it to be such even if some of the premises are unnecessary. On the other hand, if an essential premise is omitted, any analysis will result in a negative evaluation, even if the original argument was a good one. Thus, since it is better to include too many statements than to leave out an essential premise, we will always follow the rule (which is really a corollary to the Principle of Charity) *that no statement should be discarded in the analysis of an argument unless it can be demonstrated conclusively that it is either redundant or irrelevant.*

Using this rule, the first step in the identification and formulation of the premises of a moral argument is to list the premises as stated in the original argument. The explicitly stated premises of our sample argument are as follows:

1. Helping someone else to cheat is as bad as cheating oneself.
2. History has shown that when one performs even a small act of dishonesty this can lead to ever more harmful acts, in addition to encouraging others to commit similar wrongs.
3. When too many members of a particular society commit acts which are harmful to other members of that society, it ultimately leads to the destruction of that society.
4. This is certainly reason enough for Susan to not write Tom's term paper.

Each of these seems reasonably clear and comprehensible at first glance. The most natural next step would appear to be the determination of whether or not these premises need to be reformulated in any way or whether any implicit or "suppressed" premises must be made explicit. But in order to do this properly, it is necessary to perform several other tasks first (or if it is possible, simultaneously). These tasks include, but are not necessarily limited to, testing the argument for validity or inductive strength and ascertaining the truth or degree of probability of the premises. We shall thus wait to consider any changes in or additions to the premises until we have discussed some of the other factors in the evaluation of moral arguments.

EXERCISES

9. For each of the arguments selected for Exercise 6, list each of the explicitly stated premises in a numerical sequence as was done with the sample argument. Identify any of the premises which are vague or ambiguous and try to reformulate them to remove the vagueness and ambiguity.
10. On a purely "intuitive" basis, try to determine what implicit or suppressed premises need to be made explicit in each of these arguments.

It was indicated earlier in this discussion that in the simplest and most general terms, a "good" argument is one which is structured in such a way that *if* its premises are true, *then* the conclusion must be true or at least highly probable, *and* all of the premises are in fact true. An adequate elaboration of this general definition would require an entire book and/or course on formal logic, and it is certainly to be recommended that anyone truly interested in the analysis of ethical (or any other kind of) arguments should take a logic course or at least study a basic logic text.*

While it is obviously not possible to give a complete discussion of the formal logical factors required for the analysis of ethical arguments here, we will try to provide some elaboration of the intuitive concepts presented thus far. First we must distinguish between two logically different types of argument—inductive and deductive. A valid deductive argument is one which is such that if all of its premises are true, then it is logically impossible for its conclusion to be false. In other terms, a valid deductive argument is such that its conclusion is in some way implicitly (or explicitly) contained in its premises. An ancient example of a valid deductive argument is the following:

Socrates is a man.
All men are mortal.

Therefore, Socrates is mortal.

Any argument with the same *form* as this one is also deductively valid, even though its premises may not be actually true. (Remember, our definition stated only that "*IF*" the premises are true.) Thus, the following argument is also deductively valid:

* One such text is this author's *Logic*, Holt, Rinehart and Winston, 1975.

12

Socrates is an angel.
All angels are mortal.

Therefore, Socrates is mortal.

In this example, the premises are presumably false, but the argument is still valid. The argument could be proven invalid only if it could be shown that it is *possible* for some argument with the same form to have true premises and a false conclusion. The following example is invalid, even though its premises and the conclusion are all true.

Socrates is a mortal.
All men are mortal.

Therefore, Socrates is a man.

This argument can be proven to be deductively invalid by the following example which has exactly the same logical form, but which has true premises and a false conclusion:

Socrates is a mammal.
All horses are mammals.

Therefore, Socrates is a horse.

The presentation of just one argument with true premises and a false conclusion is sufficient proof that *all* arguments with the same logical form are invalid. However, the failure to construct an argument with a specific form with true premises and a false conclusion is not sufficient to prove that the argument is valid, since it is always possible that someone might come along at some future date with such an example. There are several different procedures which can be used to prove that a particular argument is deductively valid, but we cannot discuss them here; any basic logic text can be consulted by interested persons.

EXERCISES

11. Each of the following arguments is deductively invalid. Try to construct an argument with the same logical form but with true premises and a false conclusion to prove their invalidity.

   a. Some students work hard.   *only some*
      Tom is a student.

      Therefore, Tom works hard.

   b. If Susan worked hard, then she got an A in Ethics.
      Susan got an A in Ethics.

      Therefore, Susan worked hard.

   c. If many students register for Ethics, then it must be a good course.
      Not many students registered for Ethics.

      Therefore, Ethics must not be a good course.

d. Some people are ethical.
   Some people are wealthy.

   _____

   Therefore, some people are ethical and wealthy.
e. Apple A obeys the law of gravity.
   Apple B obeys the law of gravity.   *induction*
   Apple C obeys the law of gravity.

   _____

   Therefore, all apples obey the law of gravity.

The reason for distinguishing between the two different kinds of argument—inductive and deductive—is that bad (invalid) deductive arguments can still be very good inductive arguments. The last argument in the above exercise is an example of an argument which is deductively invalid but inductively good. A good inductive argument is one for which if the premises are true then it is highly probable that the conclusion is also true, but the possibility always remains that the conclusion is false. The main reason for this difference in certainty between deductive and inductive arguments is that for a valid deductive argument it is always the case that all of the information in the conclusion is also contained in some way in the premises, while for an inductive argument there is always some information in the conclusion that is not contained at all in the premises. Readers interested in learning more about the procedures for distinguishing good inductive arguments from bad ones are again referred to a basic logic text.

For both inductive and deductive arguments it is also the case that in order to be "good" they must not only have a certain logical form but they must also have "true" premises. Of course, even in the sciences there are very few (if any) statements which are considered to be absolutely true and certain. Most statements with which we normally deal are only what would be considered as highly probable. Thus, while it is certainly not as good as an argument with absolutely true premises, an argument with highly probable premises and a good deductive or inductive logical form is also a good argument. In applying the Principle of Charity to the reformulation of any arguments we must always do this in such a way as to give it both the best logical form and *also* the most highly certain premises. This often requires making trade-offs, as in a case where in order to put an argument into a deductively valid form we must add a highly dubious premise, but if we use only highly probable premises then the argument must be put into a not very strong inductive form. Let us now work with our sample argument again with these additional factors in mind.

EXERCISES

12. Examine each of the arguments as formulated in Exercise 10. Label them as either "inductive" or "deductive." If an argument has one or more subarguments, label each subargument as well.
13. Evaluate each of the arguments as reformulated in Exercise 11. In particular, check to see if reformulating a deductive argument as an inductive one, or an inductive one as deductive would strengthen or weaken each argument,

keeping in mind that the overall quality of an argument is a function *both* of its logical form *and* of the plausibility of its premises.

In looking at the four premises as listed on page 11 and the conclusion, it appears on the surface that there is little if any logical connection between any of the premises and between the premises and the conclusion, since the conclusion is about the wrongness of Susan writing Tom's ethics paper, the first premise is about cheating, the second premise is about history, dishonesty, and so on, and the third premise is a generalization about causes of the destruction of societies. There are very few key terms in the different statements which can act as a "logical glue" to hold the argument together. Thus, we must try to reformulate some or all of these statements to make explicit any connections which may exist between them, or else add some additional premises which would also tie them together.

The connection between the first premise and the conclusion is quite clear, even if it is not explicit. It is certainly implicit in this argument that in writing Tom's paper, Susan was helping Tom to cheat. This connection can be made explicit by adding a premise:

5. In writing Tom's ethics paper, Susan was helping Tom to cheat.

It is also necessary for logical purposes to make explicit the assertion that Susan did in fact write Tom's paper. Thus,

6. Susan wrote Tom's term paper for his ethics course.

Elaborating and reformulating this a little bit more in a way which seems to be entirely within the spirit of the original argument, we can construct the following *valid* deductive argument:

7. Cheating is wrong.
1. Helping someone else to cheat is as wrong as cheating oneself.
5. If Susan wrote Tom's ethics paper, then Susan helped Tom to cheat.
8. If Susan helped Tom to cheat, then Susan did wrong.
6. Susan wrote Tom's ethics paper.

Therefore, Susan did wrong (by writing Tom's ethics paper).

Although in this form the argument is deductively valid, it is not a very good argument for several reasons. As we have already noted, it is not a good *moral* argument because the alternative courses of action are not spelled out in the conclusion or in the premises. The argument is also weak in the above form since the first two premises are somewhat questionable, and even a valid argument cannot provide more certainty for its conclusion than is possessed by any of its relevant premises. The second premise is weak in several ways. For example, is helping someone else to cheat if one is not aware that one is doing so as bad an act as knowingly cheating oneself? And is helping someone else to cheat as repayment of a debt as bad as cheating oneself for purely selfish reasons? At best, this premise requires some additional support if it is to lend any significant support to the conclusion. At worst, it is a false statement resulting from a careless oversimplification and overgeneralization of a set of complex, concrete realities. The first premise can be subjected to similar criticisms, but insofar as a subargument is presented in support of this premise, we will analyze the subargument before making a final judgment on the first premise of the main argument as formulated above.

The subargument offered in support of the premise that cheating is wrong consists of a sequence of inductive and deductive arguments based on an interpretation of human history. Insofar as the original argument is formulated using a "can," the Principle of Charity requires that our reformulation be in less than absolute terms. The following would appear to be a sympathetic and reasonable rendition of the subargument, although of course it is only one of a number of possible versions that could be constructed.

7a. In the past it was often (or usually or generally) the case that when a person performed a small act of dishonesty it led to the performance of ever more harmful acts.

7b. In the past it was often (or usually or generally) the case that when a person performed a small act of dishonesty it led to the performance of similar acts by others.

7c. Therefore, in the future it will often (or usually or generally) be the case that when a person performs a small act of dishonesty it will lead to the performance of more harmful acts by many people.

7d. It is generally the case that when too many members of a particular society commit acts which are harmful to other members of that society, it ultimately leads to the destruction of that society.

7e. Any act which leads to the destruction of a society is wrong.

7f. Cheating is a small act of dishonesty and therefore will lead to the destruction of a society.

---

7. Therefore, cheating is wrong.

Steps 7a, 7b, and 7c, which represent an "unpacking" of the original premise 4, comprise an inductive argument. The two premises of this inductive argument involve questions of historical fact which are probably still quite open to debate even among experts. The more strongly they are stated ("generally" is much stronger than "often") the more doubtful they become; but as their formulation is made weaker, less support is provided for the conclusion of the main argument. But this is not the most serious problem here, because as long as the conclusion of the inductive argument is not formulated in absolute terms (i.e., that it is *always* the case that a small act of dishonesty leads to the performance of more harmful acts by many people), then there is no strong logical connection between it and the rest of the subargument in support of the conclusion that cheating is wrong. The crucial premise in this subargument is one which we supplied, 7e, one which was not present in the original argument, but which we added under the Principle of Charity as a premise which seemed to be implicit in, or at least in the spirit of, the original argument and which appeared to be necessary for the argument to be in its strongest form. It is not uncommon in analyzing arguments to carry out procedures which intuitively seem to strengthen an argument, only to discover on closer analysis that these changes themselves have to be changed. This is in part what was being referred to earlier when we warned that the analysis and evaluation of ethical arguments is a complex and difficult task, one that certainly does not follow any simple, straightforward mechanical procedure.

The subargument which we are currently discussing can be strengthened somewhat by weakening the premise which we added (7e) to the effect that "Any act which leads to the destruction of a society is wrong" by qualifying it to now read "Any act which *can* lead to the destruction of a society is wrong." This strengthens the subargument because in this form it can be logically combined with the other premises, and one other premise to be added which asserts that "Any act which has ever occurred in the past is an act which *can* occur," to yield the conclusion that cheating is wrong. Unfortunately, even though this argument is logically stronger than what we started with, it is still vulnerable to a variety of other criticisms, especially those directed at the basic reasonableness of several of the added premises (which seem to be necessary for logical purposes). For example, the new premise "Any act which can lead to the destruction of a society is wrong" is not at all easy to evaluate in terms of its truth or probability, insofar as almost any act whatsoever could be classified as wrong under this stipulation. Is there any act at all for which it could not be said that under some circumstances or other the act *can* "lead to" the destruction of a society? Responding to such criticisms might be characterized more as a kind of "fine tuning" of the argument rather than anything very serious, but this is still a part of the process of evaluating moral arguments which cannot be entirely ignored.

Questions such as those of which acts are such that in fact they "can lead to" the destruction of a society are questions of historical fact or even of scientific theory insofar as they are concerned with the identification of causal connections between events. However, the premise "Any act which can lead to the destruction of a society is wrong" is essentially a moral judgment or principle concerning the wrongness of a general type of act. Just as the procedures and criteria for evaluating the logical structure of an argument require at least an entire book or course for even an introductory presentation, so also the procedures and criteria for evaluating basic ethical principles and theories are such that no adequate discussion of them can be presented in the limited space available here. All that we can do here is to point out that there are several different types of moral theory. Some of these theories are such that they provide procedures or criteria for generating general principles of the type "Cheating is wrong." In addition to the theory illustrated by our example concerning the judgment of a general type of act in terms of its relation to the destruction or survival of a society (which is a variant of a type of ethical theory known as "utilitarianism"), other principle-generating theories include some based on religious assumptions (e.g., whatever God—or the Bible—says is right is right) or political bases (e.g., whatever the majority of the members of a society says is right is right). The most obvious question now would seem to be that of determining which of the alternative rule-generating theories is the best or "correct" one. But there is an alternative factor which must also be considered at this point in our analysis and that is the fact that most if not all of these rule-generating theories share a basic weakness. The problem they all face can be stated simply; its solution, if it has an adequate one, is certainly not an obvious one. In brief, each of these theories is capable of generating a multiplicity of rules which are such that it is not impossible, or even uncommon, for two or more of them to come into direct conflict in specific real situations. For example, the ethical theory based on the survival and destruction of a society can also generate rules such as "Breaking promises is wrong" and "Not repaying debts is wrong," and it is not difficult at all to conceive of situations in which these rules could directly conflict with the rule "Cheating is wrong," that is, a situation in which the only choices are to cheat or break a promise or not repay a debt. Different rule-generating ethical theories deal with this kind of difficulty in different ways which we cannot elaborate on here. We can only refer the interested reader to an introductory ethics text or course.

The alternative to a rule-generating ethical theory is what is commonly referred to as an *act* theory, a theory that rejects the need for any formal set of intermediary rules of the type provided by the rule-generating theories. Thus, under an act theory, the rightness or wrongness of a particular action must be determined directly (by some kind of direct intuition or perception, as when we determine the color or smell of a flower) or by appeal directly to the ethical theory itself, which may include some kind of a universal principle for judging all kinds of action. Some of the different kinds of universal principles include the Golden Rule ("Do unto others. . . .), the Principle of Utility ("An act is right if it produces the greatest amount of good for the greatest number of people," or any of numerous variations of this), an Egoistic Principle ("An act is right if it produces the greatest good for me"), and some kind of principle involving motivation ("An act is right if it is done out of good motives"). Once again, it is impossible to begin to discuss the relative strengths and weaknesses of the various act theories of ethics here. It is necessary, however, to point out that each theory does have strengths and weaknesses, just as do the various rule theories. The relative merits of the various kinds of ethical theory have been debated since the beginning of recorded history, and the fact that a large number of different theories are appealed to in the arguments reprinted in this volume is a clear indication that among the general population no consensus has yet been reached concerning which of them is the best.

EXERCISES

14. Examine the arguments as you formulated them for Exercise 13. Identify the premise (or premises) which states the ethical theory being appealed to in the argument. Try to determine whether this is an act or rule theory. (Note: If only a single specific rule is being appealed to, such as "Cheating is wrong," and no other references are made to any general rule-generating principles, you can assume that this ultimately rests on some kind of a rule-generating theory which has not been explicitly stated in the argument. Also, if no ethical rule or theory is explicitly contained in the premises at all, then you can assume that the argument is assuming an act theory which involves

some kind of direct perception or intuition of the rightness and wrongness of particular concrete acts.)

15. Consider the arguments as labeled in Exercise 14. Identify all of those which seem to you to appeal to "good" ethical theories. Now try to determine whether the theories you have classified as good ones have anything in common. Are they all rule-generating or all act theories? If they are all of the same general type, do they all appeal to the same specific theory? (Note that it is quite likely that you will disagree with the conclusion of some arguments even though you agree with the basic moral premises, insofar as there are many other factors which could result in the derivation of different conclusions from the same moral premises.)

Although we are far from finishing a complete analysis of our sample argument, we are going to end our discussion of it at this point. The primary intent of our discussion has been to illustrate certain basic considerations involved in the analysis and evaluation of moral arguments in general, and to make it as clear as possible that this can be a very difficult and complex process. We shall now provide a brief summary of the kinds of factors relevant to the analysis of ethical arguments which we have discussed, and then we will conclude by placing all of this in a more balanced perspective with regard to the ways in which analyses of ethical arguments are relevant to everyday decision-making processes.

The following listing of factors to be considered in the analysis and evaluation of ethical arguments is in no way intended to be complete either in substance or detail. These are at most some of the more important and significant factors, and it must be recognized that there are many other factors which are more or less frequently relevant to the evaluation of particular arguments. It is also hoped that the preceding discussion of the sample argument has made it clear that a simple task description does not always mean that the task is simple. For example, it is easy to stipulate that the main conclusion should be identified and clearly and precisely formulated; it is all too often the case in dealing with actual arguments that this can be a very lengthy and complex task. In part, this complexity is the result of the requirement to adhere to the Principle of Charity, that is, to always try to interpret and formulate an argument in its strongest possible form. Since the strength of an argument is a function of the relation between the premises and conclusion, we cannot really know what formulation of a conclusion will make an argument stronger or weaker unless we already have some idea what the premises are. This also serves, therefore, as a reminder that the following list should not be understood to represent any kind of a fixed, necessary order for considering the specified factors. In actual practice it is not uncommon and often is even necessary to consider several factors simultaneously and/or to go from one to another and then back again to the first in some kind of a cyclic pattern. With these disclaimers and warnings, we now present the following list of significant factors in the analysis and evaluation of moral arguments:

- Identify and reformulate as necessary the main conclusion of the argument.

- Identify and reformulate as necessary the premises of the argument, making explicit any implicit premises.
- Determine whether the argument is most appropriately and strongly formulated in an inductive or deductive form.
- Identify and evaluate (using these same procedures) any subarguments offered in support of premises.
- Test the main argument for deductive validity or inductive strength.
- Make explicit the options or alternative courses of action which are open to the agent.
- Identify the different kinds of premises, that is, those which are definitions, those which are statements of scientific fact or theory, metaphysical theory, ethical theory, and so on.
- Determine the degree of truth or plausibility of each of the premises.

This listing is not only not complete, it is also of questionable value with regard to our main concern—the determination of which actions are right and which are wrong in concrete situations. Even if we have carried out all of the above tasks in compliance with the Principle of Charity, we still may not have reached a determination as to whether or not the argument is a good one or a bad one, that is, whether or not the argument provides reasonable grounds for our acceptance of the conclusion as true. This determination requires the consideration of several factors which are not part of the argument itself, which we will now comment on briefly.

In order to determine whether or not a moral argument provides reasonable grounds for accepting the conclusion as true, it is first necessary to determine *who* is presenting the argument to *whom* for *what purposes* under *what conditions*. A moral argument presented by one person to another under one set of conditions for a specific purpose might be a very good one in that context, but the same argument might not be as good if any one of these conditions is changed. (It must be emphasized that the quality of an argument is not completely correlated with the moral quality of the act being judged. The fact that an argument in support of the judgment that a particular act is right is a good argument in one context but not so good in another context does not necessarily mean that the same act is both right and wrong.) Let us go back to our sample argument to illustrate several points about determining the goodness or badness of moral arguments.

When we first presented the argument concerning Susan's writing of Tom's ethics paper, we gave no indication of who was presenting the argument to whom for what purposes under what conditions. For illustration, let us consider several different circumstances which could have surrounded this argument. First, let us assume that this argument is being expressed by the dean of students at Susan's college after a brief hearing to determine whether or not Susan should be expelled or suspended. Susan had been asked during the hearing whether she had in fact written the paper which Tom had submitted for his ethics course, but she had not been asked nor allowed to say whether or not she knew when she gave it to Tom that he was going to submit it for the course, and she was not asked or allowed to explain her reasons for doing it. Insofar as the person presenting the argument (in this case the dean) could easily have obtained this information before making a final judgment but in fact did not obtain it, and given that this information is quite relevant to the argument for reasons mentioned in our earlier discussion, we would have to consider this as a relatively weak argument. Notice that in evaluating this argument (and this holds for any other moral argument as well), it must be compared to other possible arguments. *It is only insofar as we can specify other arguments which could have been presented under the existing conditions, and then can show that at least one of these is better than the argument which was actually presented, that we can justify a judgment that a moral argument is not a good one.* There is no absolute scale against which one can profitably measure the quality of a moral argument (even though there may be such a scale against which one can evaluate actions). Thus we can only judge that the dean's argument under these conditions was not a very good one because we are able to specify another argument which could have been formulated under the same conditions which would have been better.

For contrast, let us now assume that the same argument was being presented by Ann Landers or a similar person in a newspaper column, in response to an anonymous letter from someone who identified herself as Susan's best friend and who provided only the information included in the argument, that is, that Susan wrote a paper which Tom submitted for his ethics course. Now certainly the columnist could have avoided making a judgment at all on the grounds that not enough information was provided. However, a moment's thought should be sufficient to make it clear that on that condition no such advice columns could ever be written about anything, since it is always possible to demand more information regarding any case whatsoever no matter how much information has already been provided. In this case, then, given that no other details of the case are available, the only possible better arguments would be ones which appeal to different ethical theories than the sample argument *and* which give stronger support for the ethical theory being used. The question about the need for support for the ethical theory being used is dependent on the extent to which the intended audience can be assumed to share this theory with the person giving the argument. If it is reasonable to believe that the audience does indeed accept the theory on which the argument is being based, then it is not necessary to provide the lengthy subarguments which might otherwise be required to support the premise expressing the ethical theory, and the argument as presented is a good one.

This topic can be put into an illuminating perspective by noting that arguments in support of different ethical theories have been under continual discussion, evaluation, and refinement since at least the beginning of written history, and this process is still continuing. It is the analysis of arguments in support of various ethical theories that comprises a significant part of the subject matter in basic ethics texts and courses. It should be clear that it is therefore impossible, in most concrete situations in which an individual must make an ethical decision, for that person to provide a complete argument in support of the ethical theory being used as the basic premise of the main argument. Thus, in evaluating an ethical argument we should not automatically require that some kind of a "complete" justification be provided for the ethical theory being used. Instead, we only need to determine whether an *appropriate* justification has been provided. An "appropriate" justification is one which is based on a careful consideration of both the nature of the audience (i.e., whether, and to what extent, they already accept the theory being used) and the time available in the specific situation.

This last criterion, the time available, is one that we have not really dealt with yet, and even though we are discussing it last, it is really one of the most important factors in the evaluation of any ethical argument. As already indicated, arguments in support of various ethical theories have been under discussion for literally thousands of years. Some individuals, both saints and philosophers, have spent their entire lives trying to provide the best possible argument in support of particular ethical theories. But when an ordinary person is confronted with an ethical decision he or she usually does not have such an abundant amount of time in which to reason things out. Certainly a pregnant woman cannot spend 12 years, or even 12 months, deciding whether or not to have an abortion. A student who is suddenly and unexpectedly confronted with an opportunity to cheat on an important examination may not even have 12 minutes to think things through. It is an inherent feature of all moral arguments that the failure to make a decision itself involves a moral decision—the decision to not act or to maintain the status quo. The pregnant woman who spends 10 months thinking about whether or not to have an abortion has in effect made the decision to not have the abortion. The student in the exam who takes a week to determine whether or not to take advantage of a momentary opportunity to cheat has in fact made the very real decision not to cheat—at least not at this time on this test. Thus, it is necessary in evaluating any moral argument to carefully consider the time factor before judging the argument to be good or bad. A valid deductive argument with highly plausible premises, with a detailed analysis of all of the contextual factors and all of the alternative courses of action—in brief, a very good argument by almost all of the standards we have identified in our discussion— could easily take several hours, days, or even longer to formulate and reason through. Such an argument would obviously not be a very good one in a situation in which one has only a few minutes to think things through and make a decision. Thus, any set of criteria for good moral arguments must contain some recognition of the fact that an argument, to be "good" (at least in the very important sense of being useful), should be one which can be thought through in the time available in the circumstances of the specific case involved.

EXERCISES

16. Reevaluate the arguments which you have been analyzing in Exercises 6 through 15, applying not only the basic criteria listed on pages 19–20, but also the comparative factors just discussed. In particular, try to construct an alternative argument which is a "better" one when considered in the same context (time, audience, etc.).

17. For each of the arguments used in Exercise 16, change the contextual factors in such a way that a) the same argument in the new context is relatively better than it was in the original context, and b) the same argument in an-

other context is weaker than it was in the original context. Try this for different contextual factors, e.g., change the time available for making the decision, the audience, the factual information available, and so on.

18. Apply the instructions for Exercises 16 and 17 to the arguments which you originally evaluated on a purely intuitive basis in Exercise 4.

In concluding this all too brief and incomplete discussion of the rudiments of moral reasoning and the evaluation of ethical arguments, we should take a moment to reflect back on the points made earlier with respect to the "message" of the cartoon on the cover of this book. It will be remembered that we considered an analogy between medicine and ethics, and it was suggested that just as a physician is not able to diagnose and cure all illnesses even though he or she is able to treat many cases more effectively than the person with no medical training, so also a person with training in analyzing and evaluating ethical arguments is able to do this much more effectively than someone with no such training even though there will always be some cases which he or she will not be able to handle adequately. It is hoped that the intervening discussion has given the reader some indication of the kinds of skills which must be developed in order to improve one's ability to deal adequately with ethical arguments. It is especially hoped that one element of the analogy is now more easily appreciated, namely the need for practice on concrete cases as part of the training process. Just as the mastery of the art of medicine requires a great deal of supervised work with real patients, so also the development of the skills needed for analyzing ethical arguments requires a great deal of practice on "real" arguments. A thorough knowledge of anatomy, endocrinology, chemistry, and so on is quite helpful and perhaps even essential in order to be a good physician; but "book-learning" in and of itself is not sufficient for a person to be a good physician. Likewise, a thorough knowledge of formal logic, ethical theory, and other subjects is important, if not essential, in order to be able to properly analyze and evaluate ethical arguments; but this knowledge by itself is not adequate to guarantee that a person can provide a good evaluation of an argument.

It is to provide one of these additional requirements—practice on real cases —that this book is primarily intended. But it cannot be emphasized too strongly that this book in and of itself can provide little if any assistance to persons wishing to develop the basic skills of analyzing and evaluating ethical arguments. It is best if one's study using these examples is done with someone who is more advanced in these skills, and it is also useful to do it in conjunction with other "beginners" from whom it is possible to gain much insight as to the variety of perspectives from which any given case can be viewed. It should also be noted here that one must bring more than one's intellect to this enterprise, just as in medicine. Although these arguments are to all appearances just words on paper, it must be remembered that all of them were originally formulated by real persons who had a deep personal interest in the issues involved. Thus, we must try to use our imagination, in addition to our intellect, to try to place ourselves in the position of the kinds of persons most intimately involved in the cases being discussed. No words can convey strongly enough the need for compassion, empathy, and other human resources in the analysis and evaluation of moral arguments, but it is hoped that some of the cases among the hundreds contained in the following pages will strike close enough to each reader's personal experiences and concerns that this need will be felt and recognized directly in those cases and then transferred to the other more remote cases.

In summary, we should consider briefly the truly fundamental question of the value of this whole enterprise. Is it really better to make moral decisions on the basis of thoughtful and intelligent deliberation, or would we be just as well-off making moral decisions without really thinking about them at all? It is hoped that the reader will attempt to answer this question on the basis of actual experience, waiting until after he or she has made an effort to improve his or her skills along the lines outlined in the preceding pages to make any judgment as to whether these skills are in fact worth developing or not. Certainly any judgment not based on such first-hand experience would not be as good or as well-justified as a judgment based on such experience.

Finally, it is necessary to make several comments on the criteria used for selecting and arranging the arguments in this volume, insofar as the complexity of the arguments and issues involved implies that there is no single "right" way of selecting and organizing the examples. Many different criteria were used in the selection of these arguments, and it is likely that there are other criteria that could have also been used. One of the most important factors in the selection of these examples of moral reasoning was to include arguments from as wide a variety of sources as possible. In fact, the following pages contain items from large and small publications across the United States as well as from several foreign countries, from left-wing and right-wing political groups, from the "establishment" (the Supreme Court, major corporations, several presidents and congresspersons), from a variety of religious sects, and from "just plain folks." A number of arguments from earlier historical periods dating back to the United States colonial period are also included to add a temporal dimension to a variety of current issues.

The general topics of the arguments were also selected using several different criteria. Some topics were included because they represent very frequently debated moral problems while others were included precisely because they are not commonly encountered; some topics were included because they are intrinsically very interesting to most people, while others were used because it was judged that they *should* be studied, even though at first glance they might not appear to be very interesting or significant.

With regard to the grouping of arguments in sections, this too could have been done in different ways, and any argument in any one of the following sections could probably have been reasonably assigned to one or more of the other sections insofar as each argument touches on several different issues. Some of the more significant connections between arguments assigned to different sections are pointed out in the section introductions and exercises.

Although every effort has been made to provide at least one example from each side for topics over which there is significant disagreement, in some cases this proved to be impossible for various reasons. Balance of pro and con arguments on any single topic was only one of the factors taken into account in the selection of arguments, and the lack of this kind of balance on some topic should in no way be interpreted as reflecting the biases of the editor on that topic. Given the emphasis in this Introduction on the need to consider all alternative arguments before making a judgment about the goodness or badness of any single argument, it should be clear that only one argument on a given topic should be sufficient to require the evaluator to think through all possible arguments on both sides of that topic.

SECTION 1

Interpersonal Relations

The arguments comprising this section deal with a variety of situations which confront many of us at different points in our lives—at school, at work and in the marketplace. For the most part the cases discussed in the selections in this section are concerned with actions involving two specific individuals, such as a doctor and patient, a thief and victim, a teacher and student, two friends, or two fellow-workers. This is indeed the level at which most moral decisions are made, and because it is the area with which we are probably most familiar it has been placed at the beginning of this book.

On the surface, cases involving only two persons would seem to be relatively simple in comparison to those involving larger numbers of persons, but this is not necessarily always true. In fact, it is often the case that certain emotional and other factors come into play in situations involving two individuals which are not present in cases involving many parties.

In cases of theft it is not always clear who the affected parties are, especially in contemporary society, and sometimes a thief uses the fact that it is difficult to identify a specific victim as part of a justification for the theft. For example, the thief might argue that the individual from whom he or she stole was probably insured so the "victim" didn't really lose anything. And it is certainly not easy to assess what the cost was to whom when we begin to distribute the loss among all of the stockholders and policyholders of the insurance company. Theft from a large chain store or a corporation involves similar complications. But the burden of proof still rests on the thief to prove that the difficulty of determining the loss resulting from the theft to any specific individual in any way makes the basic act itself any less wrong.

It must also be recognized that even when one individual can be identified as the only one directly affected by a particular act, it is almost always the case that the act indirectly affects other persons, sometimes in relatively significant ways. For example, one of the figures in the Watergate affair, Egil Krogh, Jr., admitted that he authorized the break-in of a psychiatrist's office to obtain the file of the man who transmitted the classified Pentagon Papers to the press. The person directly affected by this act was the psychiatrist who was the victim of the theft, but it is not difficult to see that the act also violated certain rights of the doctor's patient. To pursue the implications of this act even further, it could be argued that this act set a precedent which weakened the system of government in the United States and thus indirectly had some effect, however small, on all citizens of the country.

EXERCISES

1. Identify the individuals *directly* involved in each case discussed in the arguments in this section. Are any of the cases such that the action affects (directly or indirectly) only one individual?
2. To what extent can the same moral principles be applied to the cases of a thief stealing a car from an unknown person, a doctor overcharging a patient, and a student with wealthy parents collecting welfare payments and food stamps?
3. Examine the arguments in Section 9 concerning euthanasia and the arguments in Section 2 concerning the use of drugs (including cigarettes). To what extent do those arguments involve some consideration of persons indirectly affected by the acts under discussion?

*dishonesty ok enriches job
, doesn't cost much
because less turnover
higher morale
consumer pays for employee theft

utilitarianism / bad arguments*

A Little Larceny Can Do a Lot For Employee Morale

by Lawrence R. Zeitlin

The dishonest worker is enriching his own job in a manner that is very satisfactory (for him). This enrichment is costing management, on the average, $1.50 per worker per day. At this rate, management gets a bargain.

Toolbox. The important word is *control*. Properly utilized, controlled employee theft can be used as another implement in management's motivational toolbox. As in the case of most motivational tools, costs and conditions of utilization must be carefully studied. (Ethically, of course, it would be more desirable for management to motivate employees by means other than inviting them into lives of petty crime. It is traditionally considered better to have workers directing their energies toward furthering the course of the business rather than toward satisfying their individual larcenous desires.)

Before deciding to minimize or eliminate employee theft, management should ask itself these four practical questions:

1. How much is employee theft actually costing us?

2. What increase in employee dissatisfaction could we expect if we controlled theft?

3. What increase in employee turnover could we expect?

4. What would it cost to build employee motivation up to a desirable level by conventional means of job enrichment or through higher salaries?

Cost. Setting aside ethical and emotional considerations, management may decide that the monetary cost of enforcing honesty is too great.

I do not advocate abandonment of the traditional responsibilities of management, but I suggest that management adopt a more realistic and certainly less hypocritical attitude to business "honesty" and publicly recognize that there is benefit to be obtained by utilizing employee theft as a motivational tool. ↻

☐ Zeitlin justifies peoples' stealing because they are bored. This is fallacious thinking for several reasons. First: it's like saying, "I'm bored so I'm going to cut off your arm. Shall I cut it off here, or here?" Second: it encourages people to destroy the necessary interdependence among all of us; whereas, we need more and more to encourage and foster dependable healthy relationships. Third: he is advising these persons to hurt themselves by becoming more callous, less sensitive, amoral (if he doesn't concede that stealing is actually immoral) like the very "machinery" they're bucking. Fourth: he underestimates industrial psychologists (I hope). Surely he and they can use their ingenuity to think of constructive alternatives (i.e. profit-sharing, alternating jobs) to help meet the needs he says cause the stealing. . . .

Ellen Smith

Normal, Ill.

Above left, reprinted from *Psychology Today*, June 1971. Copyright © Communications/Research/Machines, Inc.
Above, courtesy of Ellen Smith (Mrs. Ralph L.), Normal, Ill.

wrong A copy copyrighted materials
write loss income

Multiplied Theft
good argument / golden rule

The widespread availability of photocopying machines provides another means of stealing—as if there weren't already enough ways to break the eighth commandment. The problem involves the laws of copyright, established to protect the rights of individuals to monetary income for their labors. Writers, composers, and illustrators, for example, support themselves and their families not by creative work itself but by *selling* the product of their creativity. Moreover, their income is usually a few cents on each sale; it's the large number of copies sold that enables them to make a living.

But the culprits—those who would never think of stealing another's tangible property, or who would never think of taking copyrighted material and typesetting it, printing it, and selling it for themselves—misuse the photocopying machine. They will buy, for example, one copy of an anthem for the choir to sing, and then photocopy enough copies for every choir member to have his own. No conscientious person should engage in such an obviously illegal action.

But there's one other culprit: the highly unrealistic state of copyright law in view of modern developments in photocopying and information storage and retrieval systems. According to copyright law it is a violation either to make one photocopy of one page of a thousand-page tome or to make a hundred copies of an entire piece of music. Until the writers, publishers, consumers, lawmakers, and other interested parties come up with a rational, equitable, enforceable set of laws to bring copyright and technology into reasonable alignment, individuals and groups should avoid photocopying multiple copies or single copies of significant portions of a work without permission. We will be glad, however, to give you permission to reproduce without payment as many copies of this particular editorial as you wish! □

Above, copyright 1971 by *Christianity Today*; reprinted by permission.

Above right, courtesy of Ann Landers and Field Newspaper Syndicate.

DEAR ANN LANDERS: I need the advice of an adult who doesn't know me. Please don't let me down. Last night I was at my girl friend's house. (We have been best friends ever since third grade. We are both 14 now.) She made me promise I would never tell a soul if she let me in on her big secret. After I promised, she took a key out of a hiding place and opened a cedar chest. She started to show me her "fun stuff." I nearly keeled over. This girl has shoplifted at least $300 worth of merchandise. What scares me is that she has plenty of money and can buy anything she wants.

Another, queer thing, Ann, there wasn't one article in that chest that she can use. She has dozens of packages of fish food and she has no fish—needlepoint canvasses and thread and she doesn't even know how to sew. She has shoplifted an electric heating pad, carpenter tools, fishing equipment, corn and bunion plasters—the craziest stuff you can imagine. The price tags are on everything. She likes to look at this junk and recall the fun she had getting it out of the store.

I now know there is something wrong with her, but I don't know what to do about it. I have promised not to tell, but maybe I should—for her own good. Please advise me, Ann. I am—SCARED SICK

DEAR SS.: A promise is a promise. You must not betray your friend. But you must somehow get across to her that she is sick and needs help. If she gets caught she could be in serious trouble. She must tell everything and asked to be taken to a doctor.

In the meantime, here's a word for you. DON'T go shopping with this girl. If she is caught stealing and you are with her, you could be in trouble, too.

ALL THIS BIG DEAL ABOUT WHITE COLLAR CRIME—WHAT'S **WRONG** WITH WHITE COLLAR CRIME?

WHO ENJOYS HIS JOB TODAY? YOU? ME? **ANYBODY?** THE ONLY SATISFYING PART OF ANY JOB IS COFFEE BREAK, LUNCH HOUR AND QUITTING TIME.

YEARS AGO THERE WAS AT LEAST THE HOPE OF IMPROVEMENT—EVENTUAL PROMOTION—MORE IMPORTANT JOBS TO COME. ONCE YOU CAN BE SOLD THE MYTH THAT YOU MAY MAKE PRESIDENT OF THE COMPANY YOU'LL HARDLY EVER STEAL STAMPS.

BUT NOBODY BELIEVES HE'S GOING TO BE PRESIDENT ANYMORE. THE MORE PEOPLE CHANGE JOBS THE MORE THEY REALIZE THAT THERE IS A DIRECT CONNECTION BETWEEN WORKING FOR A LIVING AND TOTAL STUPEFYING BOREDOM.

SO WHY **NOT** TAKE REVENGE? YOU'RE NOT GOING TO FIND **ME** KNOCKING A GUY BECAUSE HE PADS AN EXPENSE ACCOUNT AND HIS HOME STATIONERY CARRIES THE COMPANY EMBLEM.

TAKE AWAY CRIME FROM THE WHITE COLLAR WORKER AND YOU WILL ROB HIM OF HIS LAST VESTIGE OF JOB INTEREST

If he hollers, let him go

Employes Who Snitch

by TIMOTHY H. INGRAM

No one likes a fink—yet our initial revulsion at snitching and our concept of employe loyalty may need serious revision. Clearly the employer has the right to expect a reasonable amount of loyalty from his employes, and to demand confidentiality in everyday business, in contract negotiations, trade secrets, client and personnel lists, and the like. But there are areas of concern to the public—as, for example, uncovering frauds, thefts, and serious improprieties—which require that the informer not be muzzled by employer censorship.

Moreover, the corporate hard-hats holding a "Your company, love it or leave it" attitude are depriving themselves of a useful mechanism for reform, capable of correcting an institution's seemingly unlimited capacity for organized error. Snitchers, in fact, are often a firm's *most* loyal members, for it takes a greater degree of attachment to stay with a firm and to protest than it does to "opt out," by remaining silent or moving on.

Above, from *The Progressive*, January 1971. Right, from *Time*, January 6, 1975.

Stealing Cars Is a Growth Industry

By PETER HELLMAN

EVEN the thieves are able to justify their work. A veteran, very professional thief who lives in New Jersey reasons, "What I do is good for everybody. First of all, I create work. I hire men to deliver the cars, work on the numbers, paint them, give them paper, maybe drive them out of state, find customers. That's good for the economy. Then I'm helping working people to get what they could never afford otherwise. A fellow wants a Cadillac but he can't afford it; his wife wants it but she knows he can't afford it. So I get this fellow a nice car at a price he can afford; maybe I save him as much as $2,000. Now he's happy. But so is the guy who lost his car. He gets a nice new Cadillac from the insurance company—without the dents and scratches we had to take out. The Cadillac company—they're happy too because they sell another Cadillac.

"The only people who don't do so good is the insurance company. But they're so big that nobody cares *personally*. They got a budget for this sort of thing anyway. So here I am, a guy without an education, sending both my kids to college, giving my family a good home, making other people happy. Come on now—who am I really hurting?"

Above, from the *New York Times* magazine, June 20, 1971.

The Sultan of Swag

Looking for a bargain? Try Vincent Swaggi's store, where merchandise is stacked to the ceiling: household goods, toys, shoes, sweaters, suits, radios, electric toothbrushes, records, film, perfume, wigs, even ballet slippers. Ignore the department-store price marked on most items. Swaggi will give you "a real steal." But watch yourself. What you are reaching for is likely to be really stolen goods.

Swaggi offers no apologies. Says he: "The way I look at it, I'm a businessman. Sure I buy hot stuff ... but if I don't buy it, somebody else will." So the fence goes about his business, cunningly aware that good citizens and good thieves share a common goal: getting something for almost nothing.

31

Store tag-switcher too honest to steal

Los Angeles Times Service

LOS ANGELES — In the privacy of department store dressing rooms and the confusion around merchandise tables, people who would not think of stealing are taking the price tags off cheap items and putting them on more expensive ones.

With the desired object in hand the switcher marches up to the register to buy, not steal.

If the clerk does not notice the change, the switcher has successfully added his version of Phase III to President Nixon's wage and price controls.

If he is caught, he simply says, "That's just the way I found it."

Dr. John Steiner, a sociology professor at California State College at Pomona, with the help of three students, has done a preliminary study on price tag switchers.

So far he has found that switchers are usually middle class persons, with very strong moral codes that will not allow them to steal.

Although there is no age limit on switching, it usually does not begin until the late teens (before that, youths are more inclined to shoplifting).

Switchers seem to come upon the practice on their own and usually work alone.

Some young tag switchers are politically motivated.

"They are upset about (what they believe are) the exploitative practices of large corporations, and feel the only way to fight against it is to reduce exploitation to a minimum — to what they feel is a fair exchange," Steiner said.

Older tag switchers see their act as compensation for unreasonable prices, he said.

"They feel their budget is at a certain level and they don't want to exceed it so they compromise by lowering prices," Steiner said.

In addition to higher prices, the tag switcher also feels victimized by the disparity between regular prices and sale prices (why can't the store sell the item at sale prices all the time?) and psychologically manipulative advertising, Steiner said.

Through advertising, nonessential items are presented as indispensable commodities and the tag switcher develops a psychological need to own, he said.

Most tag switchers will not tamper with the prices of necessities, Steiner said, but will concentrate on luxury items like cosmetics, sporting and household goods, records and electronic equipment and expensive food items.

The tag switcher sees himself as a "cavalier derelict" — a dispenser of "instantaneous self-serviced justice," Steiner said.

Anything for a Grade

In the fall quarter at the University of Denver, Michael Rock, visiting professor from Bennington College, Vermont, strode into his principles of economics class, made a surprise announcement. "You people have won," he declared. "I'm going to sell grades.

Grades will go to the highest bidder. If you people are so happy with the free market process, why don't we just let the market system dictate who gets what?"

Another professor was called in to auction off the grades without prejudice.

While several students objected to the auction—some even complained to the dean and the department chairman—approximately 90 percent of the class participated. Professor Rock collected almost $2000, averaging $85 for an A in his course, $55 for a B, $35 for a C. Rock accepted promissory notes from most of the students, but one insisted upon giving him $80 in cash. Another student, observing the absence of several friends who were obviously cutting class, bought up extra C's and D's, tried to make a few bucks by advertising them in the school paper.

To the shock of many students who'd ceased studying for their class final and burned their term papers, Rock announced on the last day of class that his auction was a hoax.

Wailed one incredulous student: "That can't be. You're an authority figure. We've all accepted you as an authority figure and what you told us as true."

Rock says now that he wishes he hadn't done it. Why then did he conduct his phony auction? Largely, he explains, because he was annoyed at the uncritical acceptance of the free enterprise system by his students and some of the comments they had written on their examinations. "I had hoped," he says, "that we wouldn't be able to pull it off. Particularly after what I tried to do in the class for nine weeks."

(handwritten annotations at top of page:) plagiarism is ok / provides a service / must be market for it

(handwritten annotation, upper right:) But students not getting an education / People relying on them may be hurt

Doctoral Dissertations For Sale

Students Clamor for Ghosted Research Papers

By Richard S. Johnson
FROM DENVER

"Nota: We do not condone Plagiarism."

This mocking legend, its pretentious use of a Latin word and its deliberate misspelling suggesting pseudoscholarship, is inscribed on a sign in the offices of a Denver ghost-writing company that expects to sell more than $100,000 worth of term papers, masters' theses, and doctoral dissertations during this academic year.

The company, Research and Educational Associates, Ltd. (REA), was formed here last Feb. 1 and already has 500 student clients. It has hired business managers to open offices in East Lansing, Mich.. where there is a 100,000-student population, and in Cleveland, Chicago, and Washington, D.C., all cities with major universities. Its founders also are negotiating with a prospective business manager in Tucson, home of the University of Arizona.

If all goes well, REA's founders expect to double or even triple this expansion before the third academic quarter begins next spring. Moreover, they see in academic ghostwriting a base for a potential multimillion-dollar business in providing information and literary services.

REA is a limited stock company with five youthful shareholders: Charles Johnson, Robert Pike, Paul Relyea, Marge Smith, and Larry Groeger. Johnson, a 30-year-old former college teacher, began the business part-time a year ago, when he was working on a Ph.D. degree at the University of Denver, "because I was tired of being a ribbon clerk in a department store."

The research and writing is supervised by Groeger, 20, an undergraduate philosophy major at Denver's Metropolitan State College. Groeger cheerfully admits that REA stole its misspelled slogan from a Boston group that he says grossed more than $250,000 last year ghosting for Harvard students. But REA's sights are already higher than that, Groeger says: This year it'll offer the first nationwide academic ghost-writing service.

Volume in the Denver area alone during the 1971 spring term was sufficient to convince REA's officers that they can gross a minimum of $100,000 by May 1972. And that should be, they think, a modest beginning.

'Absolute Security'

Yet, says Groeger: "We're not out to make it rich. We operate as a service. We all have a human-resources orientation." REA says that a client needn't sign a contract, and that the company doesn't permit clients to remain dissatisfied—particularly since the value of word-of-mouth advertising is obvious. Groeger says that REA guarantees absolute security of its records and anonymity for its clients.

Groeger can recall only one client whose experience with an REA-produced paper was unhappy. The student ordered a paper for a graduate seminar in philosophy, but "the subject was a very sophisticated one and he didn't understand the paper," Groeger says. "Others in the seminar shot him down." After that, REA began counseling clients on the various possible interpretations of "their" papers.

One of his favorite former college teachers takes a dim view of his occupation, Groeger says. So does his mother. But he himself finds no ethical problems in helping students plagiarize their way to academic degrees.

"Early in life I saw that the real ethos of America is, 'Anything you do is okay if you don't get caught,' " he explains. "I became acquainted with bureaucratic discrepancies in the university, and I saw the double standard that pervades the real world of politics and business." To Groeger, trading deals and favors isn't a moral or ethical matter; it's "just the way the world operates."

'You've Ruined My Week End'

Despite his criticism of the academic establishment, Groeger is considering teaching at the university level some day. He says that some of his philosophy teachers at Metropolitan State College here understand and sympathize with his ghostwriting activities.

But Groeger's department chairman, Dr. William E. Rhodes, didn't know of REA's existence until a reporter asked about it. "You've ruined my week end," he groaned. "I'm the last one to know, apparently."

Dr. Rhodes says that he is "totally unsympathetic" with academic ghostwriting and that he will debate its ethics with Groeger. "It poses a profound moral and ethical problem, both for Larry and his customers—and even more so for members of the faculty who would countenance this." Plagiarism, Dr. Rhodes adds, "undercuts the whole notion of a free and responsible society.

"I would oppose just as much a secret-police agency in the college" to stop plagiarism, Dr. Rhodes continues. "All of this would destroy the integrity of a free and responsible community."

Term Paper Mills: A Booming Business

By M. J. WILSON
(Newsweek Feature Service)

"WHY SHOULDN'T I buy a term paper?" says a student at New York University. "I'm an English major, assigned a paper on physics, a subject I don't know anything about, and don't want to know anything about."

"Even if I write a paper myself," says a University of Maryland coed, "the professor isn't going to read it. How can he? He's got about 300 people writing papers for him. He'll just farm it out to some graduate student."

Term-Paper Hustlers

Meanwhile, the entrepreneurs are in some disagreement over the ethics of their work. Warren claims that customers use his products only as reference sources. "Listen," he insists, "I've taken surveys of 400 of my clients, and the overwhelming majority say that they don't plagiarize." One professor cites the case of a senior she confronted who confessed "four years of successful plagiarism, parental pressure and a conviction of his intellectual incapacity for college." Richard Mari, 26, a former technical writer for General Dynamics who heads Quality Bullshit, says that plagiarism is the whole point. "The kids have so many term-paper assignments now that they're an obstacle to a degree rather than a learning technique. As long as we're operating to help people, the business is not only justifiable, it may even be commendable."

Reprinted by permission from *Time, the Weekly Newsmagazine.* Copyright Time, Inc., 1971.

DEAR ANN LANDERS: Our 12-year-old son is selling his homework and my husband thinks it is just terrific. He keeps saying, "That kid will make it big one of these days."

Albert has fixed prices (from what I gather when he talks on the telephone.) He gets a dime for an arithmetic assignment and 25 cents for a book review. The boy is doing a very good business. He bragged at dinner tonight that he has saved up $21.

I think this is disgraceful but whenever I open my mouth I am shou ted down. My husband insists that Albert has ingenuity, is smart and is making his brains pay off. If I am wrong, please tell me. If my husband is wrong, please tell him. I'm beginning to doubt my own sanity.

— CHICAGO MOTHER

DEAR MOTHER: You are not wrong and I hope you'll keep talking.

In this age of tax-chiseling, padded expense accounts and political pay-offs, it's a small wonder a kid would take to selling his homework. Someone should explain to the boy that it is admirable to help friends with their homework by showing them how to do it. But a person who sells "help" is supporting dishonesty in them and behaving dishonestly himself.

The 'test' of morality

Morality: Knowledge of moral principles; quality of character; moral wisdom; righteousness; virtue.

That's what Webster says.

We've been "wallowing in Watergate" for over a year now and perhaps there is some truth to the allegations that Americans are too preoccupied with the scandals in Washington.

On the other hand, developments unrelated to Watergate have recently come to light which, although not as sensational, are equally as shocking.

Cheating seems to have become a part of some of our greatest American institutions.

Indications of this began filtering out of our military academies, moved to the high school Regents examinations, down to the leadership of the American Boy Scouts—and now we have reports that there may be cheating in the statewide nursing tests.

The State Education Department has begun an investigation into the reports of cheating last February in the nursing exams. A spokesman said, "We have received reports of irregularities in the nursing examination...and these reports are being investigated."

Quite obviously, we have no intention here to indict those thousands of young and dedicated people who have studied long and hard to reach the stage where they are eligible to take the state exams.

Another 15,000 prospective nurses will be taking the tests next week and the state spokesman said there is "no reason to believe security has been breached." We certainly hope he is right.

But actually that is not the point. If someone is determined to cheat, he can usually find a way to do so.

It therefore becomes a matter of individual morality. If someone makes the test answers available to the student, does that make it necessary for him to accept them? We don't think so.

But apparently there is a kind of rationalization by the individual when he discovers — or thinks he has discovered — that most of the students are cheating, so why shouldn't he? He'll just be left behind, so the thinking goes.

Tighter security may be the answer. But if it is, there is indeed something wrong with today's morality.

The Albany (N.Y.) "Times-Union," July 6, 1974.

Have Adults Corrupted the Soap Box Derby?

Ski-boot manufacturer Robert B. Lange, Sr., of Boulder, Colo., wrote to his local Jaycees last week—not about skis or boots or business, but about cheating in the Soap Box Derby.

Lange's allegations about widespread use of prohibited but commonplace tricks for winning cast a cloud over the renowned race. Lange told the Jaycees, sponsor of Boulder's local Soap Box

---

This account was prepared from reports by correspondents Peter Geiger in Akron and Richard S. Johnson in Denver.

Derby, that there was nothing uncommon about the electromagnetic device that gave his nephew a boost to become this year's national Soap Box Derby winner—and that also caused the youth to be disqualified two days after the race.

Lange, whose son won the race last year in a different car, admitted in his letter that he had advised his nephew and ward, Jimmy Gronen, 14, to cheat in the All-American Soap Box Derby in Akron, Ohio, by installing a battery-powered electromagnet in the nose of his gravity-driven racer. The electromagnet provided an advantage for Jimmy by drawing has car toward a metal restraining plate that is dropped forward to the track surface at the start of the downhill race. Jimmy won, but he was disqualified after officials discovered the magnet.

'Mistake in Judgment'

"I knew that this was a violation of the official Derby rules," Lange wrote, noting that he made a "serious mistake in judgment." But he said he felt that "to be competitive" his nephew needed one of the "speed gimmicks in widespread use." He maintained that "the Derby rules have been consistently and notoriously violated by some participants without censure or disqualification." Derby officials declined to comment on the allegations.

Among the violations that officials in the national competition have failed to see, according to Lange:

"Some cars are built by professional adult competitors who get lightweight drivers known as 'chauffeurs' to drive the cars.

"Metal and other substances are used extensively as ballast.

"Unofficial tires and axles and altered official tires and axles are used.

"Magnetic noses and other fast-start aids are employed."

Lange's six-page letter "reads like *The Prince*," Machiavelli's classic on political power, says Boulder County District Attorney Alex Hunter. Last week Hunter charged Lange with two counts of contributing to the delinquency of a minor, a misdemeanor, in connection with the Derby cheating. No charges were planned against Jimmy, who was disqualified before receiving the winner's first-place trophy and $7,500 college scholarship.

"The cars are too sophisticated," Tom Jenkins, 45, a United Rubber Workers Union business agent told The National Observer. Each year Jenkins spends his two weeks' vacation as chief of the racecourse service area's volunteer repair crew. Says Jenkins: "The boys and girls [aged 11 to 15] couldn't build these cars. There's no question in my mind about that. Some of them are quite professional looking. I have to agree with Lange: The professionals have taken over. Sixty per cent of the cars in the All-American were never touched by the boys. I'm very serious about this. You'd be surprised how many kids can't even change a wheel. . . .

Immoral to make more per hour than your patient; psychologist devaluing other in his panel; he feels better

ONE-MAN DEFLATION

... A psychologist cuts fees, and smiles.

By Daniel Henninger

Rita Flynn, an Observer reader in Spokane, Wash., wrote recently to tell us about something her husband had done, something she thought worthy of notice:

Jim Flynn, a practicing psychologist in Spokane, is lowering his prices.

Until last December the fee for Flynn's services was $35 an hour. Then he sent a letter to his customers, as he prefers to call them, saying in part:

Comment

"At the same time that I was raising prices in a dizzying dance with all the inflationary forces rampant in our nation, another part of my mind was deciding that my fees were unfair, immoral, and at this time in our nation's needs, unpatriotic."

Though he has 11 children to support, Flynn dropped his hourly fee to $30 and instituted Tuesday as "workers' day." On that day he would treat anyone for an hourly fee equal to his or her own hourly wage.

Had Flynn flipped? I telephoned him to find out.

"I've been in sort of a reflective period for several years," said Jim Flynn, who has been practicing in Spokane for about 20 years, 10 years in a state hospital and the past 10 in private practice.

Fear of Degrading

Flynn had been impressed by some of the things happening in the women's movement. But he considered the flip side of feminism, male consciousness. He finds men more difficult to treat than women; many don't even want to come in to see him.

"I got to thinking here I am charging 35 bucks an hour, and a guy who's earning, say, 5 or 10 bucks an hour in some way or another had to come to terms with that. Does he have to say that Flynn is three or four times the better man than he is? Here I'm trying to help these guys, and yet I'm doing something that could be degrading to them."

Flynn was thinking about himself too. His private psychology practice has made him pretty well off, and though he occasionally wondered about the rightness of his large income, there always seemed sufficient reason to justify it: a big family, all the time spent in graduate school running up debts to earn his degree.

The doubts persisted: "I realized the position I was playing in my family because I was earning so much dough," he said. "Because I was funding all of them, it gave me a power and authority that dwarfed the others. I've got cute kids. But, for instance, one of them said he wanted to be a psychologist but he couldn't because he couldn't be as good as I was, and hell, I'm sure he'll be better."

Finally, Jim Flynn laid it on the line in his letter: "I have come to the conclusion that charging what the traffic will bear or going along with prevailing rates may not be a defensible way to live."

He lowered his rates and eliminated many of the debts owed him. "Some of the people who owed money had finished with me and were hacking away at it 5 bucks a month," he said. "I started to feel like an economic bully."

PROFESSIONAL MORALS.

No man has a right to practice his profession in such a way as to encourage personal vice in those whom he serves, or wrong-doing towards individuals and the community. This is a very simple proposition, to which no respectable man in any profession will presume to make objection. If there ever lived a professional villain of whom a professional vilifier could say : "This is he who made it safe to murder, and of whose health thieves asked before they began to steal," he could only be saved from universal execration by a natural doubt of the justice of the sarcasm and the candor of its author. Theoretically, there are no differences among decent men on this subject, when it is placed before the mind in this way. It is one of those simple, self-evident propositions, about which no man would think of arguing for an instant. Up to the bar of this proposition one can bring every act of his professional life, and decide for himself whether it be legitimate and morally good. We repeat it,—*No man has a right to practice his profession in such a way as to encourage personal vice in those whom he serves, or wrong-doing towards individuals and the community.*

The great cities are full of men who have achieved remarkable skill in the treatment of a certain class of diseases, and other dangerous or inconvenient consequences of a bestial social vice. No matter how often their patients may approach them, or how vile they may be, or how successfully they may scheme against the peace and purity of society, or what form the consequences of their sin may assume, these professional men take their fee, and do what they can to shield the sinners from the effect of their crimes. Whatever they may be able to do professionally to make it safe for men and women to trample upon the laws of social purity, they do and constantly stand ready to do. Yet these men have a defense of themselves which enables them to hold their heads up. They are physicians. It is their business to treat disease in whatever form it may present itself. It would be impertinent in them to inquire into the life of those who come to them for advice. They are not the keepers of other men's consciences. They are men of science and not of morals. It is their business to cure disease by the speediest and best methods they know, and not to inquire into character, or be curious about the indirect results of their skill. Such would be their defense, or the line of their defense ; yet, if it can be seen or shown that their professional life encourages vice in the community, by the constant shield which it offers against the consequences of vice, the defence amounts to nothing. If a debauchee or a sensualist of any sort finds impunity for his excesses in the professional skill of his physician, and relies upon that skill to shield him from the consequences of his sin, be they what they may, his physician becomes the partner of his guilt for gold, and a professional pander to his appetites. He may find professional brethren to defend him, but before the unsophisticated moral sense of the world he will be a degraded man, and stand condemned.

There are such men in the world as professional pardoners of sin. There are men in priestly robes who, on the confession of a penitent, or one who assumes the position of a penitent, release him professionally from the consequences of his misdeeds. Unless history has lied, there have been men among these to whom the vicious have gone for shrift and pardon for a consideration, and received what they went for, on every occasion of overt crime when the voice of conscience in their superstitious souls would not be still, and who have retired from the confessional ready for more crimes, from whose spiritual consequences they have intended and expected to find relief in the same way. It is not necessary to charge such desecration of the priestly office upon any one. We have no reason to believe that in this country such things are common ; but we know that priests are human, and that there have been bad and mercenary men among them. It is only necessary to suppose cases like this, to see that a priest may, in the exercise of his professional functions, become the partner of the criminal in his crimes, a friend and protector of vice, and a foe to the purity and good order of society. He can set up his professional defense, and find professional defenders, perhaps ; but any child, capable of comprehending the question, will decide that he is degraded and disgraced.

What is true, or may be true, of these professions, is true of any profession. Nothing is more notorious than that there are lawyers who are public nuisances—who encourage litigation, who are universally relied upon by criminals for the defense of crime, and whose reputation and money have indeed been won by their ability to clear the guilty from the consequences of their wrong-doing. Between these low extremes of professional prostitution and the high ground occupied by the great mass of legal men, there are many points where self-interest, united with incomplete knowledge, is powerful to lead the best minds into doubtful ways, and engage them in the support of doubtful causes or the defense of doubtful men. It is freely admitted that the best lawyer may find questions of personal morality and professional propriety in his practice that are hard to settle, and that may conscientiously be settled incorrectly ; but no lawyer needs to question whether it is right for him to strengthen the position of a notorious scamp, especially if that scamp is known to be a corrupter of the law by all the means in his power, and a wholesale plunderer of the people.

From *Scribner's Monthly*, 1871.

Dear Ann Landers:

Something has been preying on my conscience and I need to know what to do about it.

As a secretary I make out my boss's expense account reports. I am aware that he puts down false expenses and charges personal expenditures to the business.

I have a strong sense of morality and feel this is wrong. I realize the practice is rampant, but still it doesn't make me feel any better about doing it.

If I confront him he will probably tell me it's none of my business. Is it? (P.S. He is a V.P. and has hundreds of people under him.) Sign me

—Guilty Conscience.

Dear G.C.:

Confront Mr. Chiseler and ask him to give his expense account work to another secretary, or do it himself. (P.S. Have some job prospects lined up before the confrontation. You may be handed your walking papers. If your competence matches your integrity, you have nothing to worry about. You'll do just fine. Bravo, Lady.)

Right, from "The Secretary's Dilemma" by B. J. Phillips, in *Ms.* magazine, March 1975.
Above, courtesy of Ann Landers, Field Newspaper Syndicate, and *The Atlanta Journal*.
Below, from *The Autobiography of Benjamin Franklin*.

I grew convinced that *truth, sincerity* and *integrity* in dealings between man and man were of the utmost importance to the felicity of life, and I formed written resolutions (which still remain in my Journal book) to practise them ever while I lived. Revelation had indeed no weight with me as such; but I entertained an opinion that tho' certain actions might not be bad *because* they were forbidden by it, or good *because* it commanded them, yet probably those actions might be forbidden *because* they were bad for us or commanded *because* they were beneficial to us, in their own natures, all the circumstances of things considered. And this persuasion, with the kind hand of Providence, or some guardian angel, or accidental favourable circumstances and situations, or all together, preserved me (thro' this dangerous time of youth and the hazardous situations I was sometimes in among strangers, remote from the eye and advice of my father) without any *wilful*, gross immorality or injustice that might have been expected from my want of religion. I say *wilful* because the instances I have mentioned had something of necessity in them, from my youth, inexperience, and the knavery of others. I had, therefore, a tolerable character to begin the world with; I valued it properly and determined to preserve it.

What about the Wall Street secretary who knows that her boss has decided to manipulate the price of a stock? Unless the Securities and Exchange Commission catches it, that's business as usual on Wall Street. "It happens every day," said Margie Albert, onetime brokerage-house secretary, now union organizer of office workers. "Sometimes when they had a stock they knew was going to be good because they were going to push it to clients and make it good, they'd cut the secretaries in on it, arrange for the employees to buy some shares. Look, corporate life is shot through with corruption like this. What's a secretary supposed to do? Complain? She'd just lose her job. She's not the one who makes the decisions."

No, she isn't the one who makes the decisions. Yes, Ann Landers agrees, she would probably lose her job. And while it may be easy for me to risk someone else's job with my theories, I believe she should complain. If she is the Wall Street secretary, she should complain to the SEC for the sake of thousands of people who will be financially hurt (and you better believe that means the small investors). Complain for the sake of her dignity. They allow her to know because they think it's safe for her to know. She is, after all, just a secretary. She is identified with her function, not with the rational, judging, moral mind that is hers also. Secretary as Dictabelt, something you turn on when you want, turn off when you want, as devoid of a will of her own as a machine. Complain to be a human being.

Rising Up Angry Funnies © by Aaron Fagen.

William Raspberry

The Unlearned Lesson of Watergate

When I met him last year, Ira Rosen —a Cornell University senior at the time—was disturbed over the number of bright, well-educated young men who managed to become involved in the Watergate scandals.

He thought he knew why. "It's the educational system," he said. "It's geared toward cheating because of the pressure to succeed."

Rosen was still disturbed when I had lunch with him the other day— this time because so many of his contemporaries seem to have learned so little from the Watergate experience.

The unlearned lesson, as he sees it, is that once you start rationalizing actions that you know to be immoral or unethical, it is very difficult to stop.

Rosen, who is a reporter intern for columnist Jack Anderson, said he recently interviewed 45 congressional interns and asked them this question:

"Where would you draw the line if you were asked by your congressman or senator to do something that you believed to be morally or ethically wrong?"

Only about half of these brightest and best said they would refuse the assignment outright. The others gave various versions of: "It depends."

One Senate intern said she would "do whatever my senator asked, because that's my job." Another said "I'd do it and sweep it under the rug, because that kind of thing goes on all the time." Rosen said the two interns, both women, indicated they would do their bosses' bidding even if they knew the act to be legally wrong.

On the other hand, one young woman thought that "waiting in the unemployment line would be a viable alternative to doing something which

I think to be ethically or morally wrong," Rosen reported. Another, in her second year as intern to a conservative Republican, said she was prepared to quit her job last year if her boss had asked her to act in support of President Nixon.

In general, however, Rosen said he found that the interns he talked to would have more misgivings about working for a legislator whose politics they disagreed with than about assignments of questionable ethics or legality.

It is all very distressing to Rosen, who thinks he would have little trouble making the moral choices, even at risk of losing his job. "If you continue saying yes, yes—if you continue along the lines of rationalization—where do you stop?" he insisted.

Rosen later acknowledged that it might not be as easy as all that.

He's absolutely certain that he wouldn't help to arrange a bribe for a senator or engage in illegal acts for him. But he might: tell a telephone caller (falsely) that the boss was out; obey a direct order to mail a congressman's private material in franked envelopes; write letters that seemed to imply support of a measure that the congressman intended to vote against, and do other misleading things short of lying outright.

Rosen was acknowledging that the line between right and wrong doesn't always stay put.

Congressional interns seldom get asked to do things which, if discovered, would create scandals. Assignments like that come much later, after you've already proven your reliability and trustworthiness by telling small lies and countenancing bigger ones. They bring you along slowly, and after

awhile you're willing to do nearly anything that isn't flagrantly criminal— and later maybe you'll do that, too.

Take Rosen's advice and avoid that first white lie, and maybe you'll never get the big stuff because you'll never get promoted from office boy.

But that's too cynical. Probably most of the questionable actions are not those that involve personal greed or ambition but those that involve shortcuts to an important goal: passing an important bill, electing a singularly worthy candidate, protecting an important official from scandal so he can be free to go on doing important things.

That is what produces Watergates. What is less clear is what it takes to produce people like Archibald Cox, Elliot Richardson and William Ruckelshaus, who had sufficient faith of their own moral conviction to say no to a desperate president.

Suppose their attitude had been more widespread. Suppose Robert Bork had said "no" to the firing of Archie Cox, too, and the man under Bork, and so on. Would that have brought the government to a halt? Or would it merely have halted the cover-up?

You'd think that the tough moral stance of a few honest men might inspire some of us and that the devastating consequences of dishonesty might instruct the rest of us. Such are supposed to be the "lessons of Watergate."

But the lessons aren't quite so clear as Ira Rosen would have them. Not to the congressional interns and not to straight-arrow men like Gerald Ford and Frank Church, who so soon after Watergate, can agonize over how much of the truth about CIA crimes is in the public interest to cover up.

Buzhardt Hits Standards As Too High

HILTON HEAD, S.C., March 10 (AP)—Americans demand too much moral accountability of their public officials, according to J. Fred Buzhardt, a key figure in former President Nixon's Watergate defense.

"Would you rather have a competent scoundrel or an honest boob in office?" asked Buzhardt in an interview with the Charlotte Observer.

"You can make a strong argument that for a President in this day and time you don't want a babe in the woods. He's got to deal with some pretty rough-and-tumble people."

Buzhardt, who was primary attorney for Nixon in the Watergate affair until he suffered a heart attack last summer, said the country would have been better off if Nixon had not been forced to resign.

He said he does not consider President Ford a "babe in the woods," however.

The public and the media have set an unrealistic moral standard for government, resulting in a lack of public confidence, Buzhardt said.

Above, © The Washington Post, June 26, 1975.
Left, courtesy of The Associated Press.

SECTION 2

"Victimless Crimes"

The cases discussed in the arguments in this section belong to a general category sometimes referred to as "victimless crimes." The implication of this title is not that the acts included in this group have no detrimental effects on anyone at all, but that they cause no harm to anyone other than the person(s) performing the act. The use of the term "crime" in this title makes explicit the fact that the question of greatest concern about these acts is that of whether or not they should be illegal. However, as with many other cases involving the question of legalization or prohibition of an act, there is also a significant moral question at a more basic level. The basic ethical question with regard to the so-called "victimless" crimes is that of whether an individual has a moral right to do things which could lead to his or her own ill health or death. In this regard, the question is almost indistinguishable from the moral question concerning the justifiability of suicide (see Section 9).

It is important to note in this context that any suggestion that any act is "victimless" in the sense just explained must be examined very critically. Although the poet's line that "No man is an island" has become almost a cliché, it must also be recognized that it appears to be very insightful and factually true. It is certainly to be hoped that the death or illness of any individual will have some emotional impact on other persons. In any case, economists, sociologists, and others have provided detailed descriptions in recent years of the ways in which the illness and/or death of any individual has measurable economic and social impacts. Some of these impacts may be positive, but many of them are negative. Thus, we should be very cautious before accepting any claim that a particular act which may be detrimental to the agent(s) has no negative impact whatsoever on any other parties.

Most of the arguments in this section deal with questions related to the use of drugs (in the broadest sense of that term). A critical element in the discussion of this topic is the issue of logical consistency, an issue raised by almost all factions. An example of the appeal to the principle of consistency is the question "If you don't object to alcohol, why do you object to marijuana?". The only satisfactory answer to such a question is the identification of some morally relevant difference between the use of alcohol and the use of marijuana. However, it must be recognized that even if no relevant difference can be identified, this indicates at most that their moral worth is the same. It must still be ascertained whether this moral value is positive or negative, whether they are both good or bad. Also, the whole set of questions concerning the legalization or prohibition of either or both requires the consideration of numerous other factors.

EXERCISES

1. Compare the arguments in this section with those in Section 6 concerned with gun-control legislation. Are there any significant differences between the arguments in the two sections on the two sides of the legalization/prohibition question other than those resulting from the difficulty in identifying victims in the cases in this section?
2. Compare the arguments in this section with those in Section 9 dealing with the question of suicide. Is there any difference in the cases other than that of the degree of certainty that the death of the agent will result from the act being discussed?
3. To what extent could any of the arguments in this section be applied to the question of censorship of pornography as discussed in the arguments in Section 5?

WOMEN AND WINE.

WOMAN has never been associated with wine without disgrace and disaster. The toast and the bacchanal that, with musical alliteration, couple these two words, spring from the hot lips of sensuality, and are burdened with shame. A man who can sing of wine and women in the same breath, is one whose presence is disgrace, and whose touch is pollution. A man who can forget mother and sister, or wife and daughter, and wantonly engage in a revel in which the name of woman is invoked to heighten the pleasures of the intoxicating cup, is, beyond controversy and without mitigation, a beast. "Dost thou think, because thou art virtuous, there shall be no more cakes and ale?" Ay, cakes and ale, if you will, but let it be cakes and ale. Let not the name by which we call the pure and precious ones at home be brought in to illuminate a degrading feast.

Of the worst foes that woman has ever had to encounter, wine stands at the head. The appetite for strong drink in man has spoiled the lives of more women—ruined more hopes for them, scattered more fortunes for them, brought to them more shame, sorrow, and hardship—than any other evil that lives. The country numbers tens of thousands—nay, hundreds of thousands—of women who are widows to-day, and sit in hopeless weeds, because their husbands have been slain by strong drink. There are hundreds of thousands of homes, scattered all over the land, in which women live lives of torture, going through all the changes of suffering that lie between the extremes of fear and despair, because those whom they love, love wine better than they do the women they have sworn to love. There are women by thousands who dread to hear at the door the step that once thrilled them with pleasure, because that step has learned to reel under the influence of the seductive poison. There are women groaning with pain, while we write these words, from bruises and brutalities inflicted by husbands made mad by drink. There can be no exaggeration in any statement made in regard to this matter, because no human imagination can create anything worse than the truth, and no pen is capable of portraying the truth. The sorrows and the horrors of a wife with a drunken husband, or a mother with a drunken son, are as near the realization of hell as can be reached in this world, at least. The shame, the indignation, the sorrow, the sense of disgrace for herself and her children, the poverty,—and not unfrequently the beggary,—the fear and the fact of violence, the lingering, life-long struggle and despair of countless women with drunken husbands, are enough to make all women curse wine, and engage unitedly to oppose it everywhere as the worst enemy of their sex.

And now what shall we see on the New-Year's Day, 1871? Women all over the city of New York — women here and there all over the country, where like social customs prevail—setting out upon their tables the well-filled decanters which, before night shall close down, will be emptied into the brains of young men and old men, who will go reeling to darker orgies, or to homes that will feel ashamed of them. Woman's lips will give the invitation, woman's hand will fill and present the glass, woman's careless voice will laugh at the effects of the mischievous draught upon their friends, and, having done all this, woman will retire to balmy rest, previously having reckoned the number of those to whom she has, during the day, presented a dangerous temptation, and rejoiced over it in the degree of its magnitude.

O woman! woman! Is it not about time that this thing were stopped? Have you a husband, a brother, a son? Are they stronger than their neighbors who have, one after another, dropped into the graves of drunkards? Look around you, and see the desolations that drink has wrought among your acquaintance, and then decide whether you have a right to place temptation in any man's way, or do aught to make a social custom respectable which leads hundreds of thousands of men into bondage and death. Why must the bottle come out everywhere? Why can there not be a festal occasion without this vulgar guzzling of strong drink?

Woman, there are some things that you can do, and this is one: you can make drinking unpopular and disgraceful among the young. You can utterly discountenance all drinking in your own house, and you can hold in suspicion every young man who touches the cup. You know that no young man who drinks can safely be trusted with the happiness of any woman, and that he is as unfit as a man can be for woman's society. Have this understood: that every young man who drinks is socially proscribed. Bring up your children to regard drinking as not only dangerous but disgraceful. Place temptation in no man's way. If men will make beasts of themselves, let them do it in other society than yours. If your mercenary husbands treat their customers from private stores kept in their counting-rooms, shame them into decency by your regard for the honor of your home. Recognize the living, terrible fact that wine has always been, and is to-day, the curse of your sex; that it steals the hearts of men away from you, that it dries up your prosperity, that it endangers your safety, that it can only bring you evil. If social custom compels you to present wine at your feasts, rebel against it, and make a social custom in the interests of virtue and purity. The matter is very much in your own hands. The women of the country, in what is called polite society, can do more to make the nation temperate than all the legislators and tumultuous reformers that are struggling and blundering in their efforts to this end. At any rate, if they will try, they shall have SCRIBNER'S MONTHLY to help them.

From *Scribner's Monthly*, 1871.

Legalized Pot

HERE IS ONE small cheer for legalizing marijuana. Rah for *cannabis sativa*, pot, grass, Mary Jane.

Two rahs would be too many, because the principal reason for legalizing the happy-time weed is quite similar to the reason for repealing the prohibition against alcoholic beverages four decades ago. Both marijuana and alcohol seem to cause more trouble when they are illegal than when they become legal.

No one can argue compellingly that Americans become better persons by drinking Martinis, as President Nixon does, or by drawing pot smoke into their lungs, as many young and not-so-young people are doing in defiance of the law. Outside of occasional medicinal use—marijuana now is being tried as a relaxant for terminal cancer patients—there is no strong, positive reason for legalizing either drug.

But a positive reason is not really necessary. A strong negative reason against the grass ban will do. The argument for marijuana rests on such a negative reason and on one indisputable fact: Large numbers of human beings *will* use psychoactive drugs like pot and alcohol.

Today, marijuana is being smoked by great numbers of Americans. Most of them know, or at least guess, that grass is not as dangerous to them as alcohol is. As psychiatrist Lester Grinspoon of Harvard says in his new book, *Marihuana Reconsidered*, marijuana is "among the least dangerous of the psychoactive drugs." He points to the "curious fact" that Western society sanctions the use of tobacco and alcohol, though both cause tissue damage in humans. Marijuana does not. Nor does it lead to addiction. The question of whether pot leads to harder drugs is in dispute, but most authorities can find no real cause-and-effect relationship. President Nixon chose to ignore these findings last week when he said that legalizing marijuana would be "detrimental" to young people, because pot "is only a half-way house to something worse." Like Martinis?

Those who smoke grass also know they are violating the law, and are "criminals" subject to stiff jail sentences. This "punitive, repressive approach," argues Dr. Grinspoon, leads young pot smokers to view their society as hypocritical. A pot high is banned; an alcohol high is not, even though it is more dangerous.

That is the real problem of the legal ban against grass. As young people turn on with pot, they tend to turn off the society at large.

Dr. Grinspoon offers a reasonable solution: Legalize marijuana under controls similar to those for alcohol. No one under 18 could use it legally. Marijuana's potency would be strictly controlled to reduce the chance of a "bad trip." The quality would be guaranteed, so the smoker would know that his grass was not laced with other drugs.

Over all, this could be about as effective as present controls over alcohol—not perfect, but better than it was. There still would be abuse of pot smoking as there is of alcohol drinking. But no more criminal arrests for getting a simple pot high, as there are no arrests for drinking a Martini at the White House.

—JAMES G. DRISCOLL

CRACKDOWN IS ESSENTIAL

The gravity of the drug problem in this country looms over us like the sword of Damocles. Millions of Americans use drugs. Thousands of others are profiting personally by the selling of drugs. Their crimes breed more crime until the shock waves reach every corner of our society.

We have become so inured to drug horror stories that little short of a drug-induced tragedy in our own homes can spur us to personal involvement. Nevertheless the problem is so pervasive that the personal attention of all of us will be required to solve it. The root causes of the problem are many and complex, but one of the basic causes is surely our attitude toward drugs in general.

It has been argued that the line between the legal use of drugs and the criminal use is thin at best, and that we are not certain always where it should be drawn. Where does it belong, for example, so far as the free and easy prescibing of antibiotics or sleeping potions is concerned?

Americans may not at times be able to see the problem in taking an occasional tranquilizer or pep pill. On the other hand they certainly can see the moral wrong in the use of amphetimines and other drugs by athletes. The thought that athletic performance is the result of a drug-produced distortion rather than natural perfection is bad enough. Worse is the fact that athletes are heroes to many persons in our society, young and old. Their personal use of drugs adds substantially to the general belief that there is nothing wrong about destroying one's mind and body for personal gain or psychological kicks.

There are many other areas where Americans can agree, we believe, that the use of drugs harms both the person using them or society, or both. A person drunk on marijuana behind the wheel of a car is no different than a driver who is drunk on alcohol, for example. A person so hooked on heroin or cocaine that he must steal thousands of dollars a week to support his addiction is a menace to others as well as to himself.

Drugs certainly do not have any place in the lives of young, immature people whose judgments and characters are not yet formed.

There are many other areas of agreement. Instead of focusing on the thin line of absolutes it is time that Americans attacked the drug problem with the broad brush of consensus.

If police, prosecutors, judges and an outraged citizenry will unite to stop the flow of narcotics into the United States of America, if they throw the book at the pusher and crack down on the addict, whether on the street in the classroom or on the football field, drug prevention will begin to have real meaning.

Subsequent argument over the thin line would be the frosting on the cake.

From *The Troy Sunday.*

Since marijuana is not a deterrent, no more than cigarettes, it seems inhumane that they *schlep* people and put them in jail with it.

> "Well, maybe marijuana's not *bad* for you, but it's a stepping stone. It leads to heavier drugs—heroin, etc."

Well, that syllogism has to work out this way, though: The heroin addict, the bust-out junkie that started out smoking pot, says to his cell-mate:

> "I'm a bust-out junkie. Started out smoking pot, look at me now. By the way, cell-mate, what happened to you? There's blood on your hands. How'd you get to murder those kids in that crap game? Where did it all start?"
> "Started with bingo in the Catholic Church."
> "I see."

Top left, from *The Essential Lenny Bruce.* Copyright 1967 Ballantine Books/A Product of Douglas Book Corporation.

Below , from *Psychology Today.*

Drug Abuse— Just What The Doctor Ordered

by J. Maurice Rogers

The image of the physician as expert and benign begins to evaporate when we see physicians pushing psychoactive pills whose consequences are not fully understood into patients whose problems require human, not chemical, solutions.

Ads. Doctors are strongly encouraged in their pill-for-every-problem syndrome by drug manufacturers who bombard them with advertisements in psychiatric and medical journals:

"WHAT MAKES A WOMAN CRY? *A man? Another woman? Three kids? No kids at all? Wrinkles? You name it . . . If she is depressed, consider Pertofane.*"

And:

"SCHOOL, THE DARK, SEPARATION, DENTAL VISITS, MONSTERS. THE EVERYDAY ANXIETY OF CHILDREN SOMETIMES GETS OUT OF HAND. *A child can usually deal with his anxieties. But sometimes the anxieties overpower the child. Then he needs your help. Your help may include Vistaril.*"

And this advertisement, which shows an attractive but worried-looking young woman with an armful of books, and describes the problems that face a new college student:

"*Exposure to new friends and other influences may force her to re-evaluate herself and her goals . . . Her newly stimulated intellectual curiosity may make her more sensitive to and apprehensive about national and world conditions.*" The headline reads: "TO HELP FREE HER OF EXCESSIVE ANXIETY . . . LIBRIUM."

Such advertisements redefine normal problems of living as medical problems to be solved by drugs. Most small children, of course, are at some time afraid of the dark or anxious about school. A person may become depressed after personal loss, upon facing a new job, having to adjust to new conditions, or upon experiencing impotence in the face of increasing social turmoil. But the advocacy of drugs for such problems is socially irresponsible.

POINT

SAFER: So-called "victimless crime" and how we should deal with it is one of those topics of conversation that people argue about. And if people argue about it, you can be sure so do Shana Alexander and Jack Kilpatrick. Here's Point/Counterpoint.

SHANA ALEXANDER: Jack, I've been forced to change my mind about drugs. Let anybody put anything he wants into his mouth or his veins. Make hard drugs as legal as alcohol. Let everybody take charge of his own bad habits, and I really think we'll all be better off. If addicts didn't have to steal, society would no longer have to spend impossible sums trying to protect people from addicts. As for protecting addicts from themselves, from destroying themselves, I no longer think that's society's job. What finally persuaded me was the record here in New York State. Two years ago Governor Rockefeller put through the toughest drug law in the country. Selling just one ounce of the hard stuff means a mandatory prison term of at least 15 years. It can mean prison for life. Yet, even this brutish escalation of punishment to barbarous levels has had no effect whatever, neither on drug addiction nor on drug-related crime. I conclude you cannot protect people from themselves. Therefore, I would remove the penalties from all victimless crimes, not only drugs. Also gambling, drunkenness, prostitution, homosexuality, and so on. If these activities lead to violent crime, prosecute the thief, the mugger, the rapist, but put public safety ahead of public morals. You'll charge me with endangering the safety of children, but kids learn by example, Jack. Make each person free to take pot, to take cocaine, to take rat poison, and you begin to make him responsible for his own acts. That's got to be better, Jack, for us and for our kids.

COUNTERPOINT

JAMES J. KILPATRICK: Up to a point, Shana, I share your libertarian theories. I too believe an individual has a right to mess up his own life, so long as he does no harm to others. But there is such a thing as society or community or the commonweal - a body of moral conviction developed over many centuries out of law and religion, and I believe it cannot wisely be distained. In libertarian theory, laws against prostitution should be repealed. A woman's body is her own, and she can sell it if she wants to. But I believe society has a right to say prostitution is wrong, it's degrading, and if it can never be eliminated it should not be implicitly approved. It's the same with hard-core pornography. As a writer, I'm troubled by legal censorship. I don't like it. But I believe the community has a right to say hard-core pornography is wrong, it pollutes, and it subtly eats at the fabric of our life. You make persuasive arguments for legalized heroin, but maybe society has a right to say, out of its collective wisdom and experience: Heroin is a terrible evil; we ought not to make it easy for the weak to surrender to addiction. What I am suggesting, Shana, is that we should not flinch from setting standards of right conduct, of virtue, of public good and public evil. And we ought to shun the notion that the drunk, the drug addict, and the whore, even if they do not demonstrably harm others, do not affect others - for they do. For better or for worse, a community is influenced by each of its members. Saints and sinners, we are touching atoms. So, ask not for whom the bell tolls, Shana, it tolls for thee and me, and for all of you out there.

Left and right page from the CBS News broadcast *60 Minutes*, September 11, 1975.

SOUNDING BOARD

One Person's Opinion on a Several-Sided Subject

It's a sin to smoke

YVONNE GOULET

It is a sin to smoke. My certainty of this fact came after reading Kevin Axe's "Sounding Board" article in the November issue of U.S. CATHOLIC entitled "It's Sinful Not to Vote." Mr. Axe's thesis was that not voting shows lack of concern for the welfare of one's fellowman and, therefore, violates the law of love.

It is, I believe, this same law of love that smoking violates (as well as its more explicit formulation in the Fifth Commandment).

I'm convinced that smoking is a sin from considering 1) the nature of smoking; 2) the new understanding of the nature of sin.

Smoking, which has proved to be harmful in a variety of laboratory tests, is sinful, I believe, because it deprives the smoker of 1) health; 2) eventually, life itself. Moreover, it deprives others of comfort, security, health, and sometimes, in the case of stillborn infants and deaths of newborn babies, of their lives. Before elaborating, however, I would like to consider briefly the nature of sin.

In post-Vatican II theology, sin is falling short of the mark, making the wrong choices. As Marc Oraison says in his book, *Morality For Our Time*, "This is our sin: to fail to respond to the demand of love. We spend our entire lives either not responding at all, or not responding enough, or responding only indirectly. We are sinners all the time."

Although some will say that smoking, even if wrong, is trivial compared to worldwide problems of poverty, war, and injustice, I submit that it is precisely the immediacy of smoking that makes its sinfulness so crucial. It is easy to be filled with zeal for abstractions: harder to confront evil literally at one's fingertips.

. . .

The law of love involves three persons: God, our neighbor, ourselves. Smoking sins against all three:

Only God, according to moralists, has direct dominion over creation. We are only stewards of our bodies; by persistently injuring our bodies, we assume dominion over them, thereby displacing God.

We offend ourselves by smoking in that 1) we curtail our ability to function at peak efficiency (according to the same government report mentioned earlier, "clinical studies involving healthy young men have shown that cigarette smoking impairs exercise performance especially for many types of athletic events and activities involving maximal work capacity."); 2) Smokers further offend themselves by increasing seven-fold their susceptibility to lung cancer and to other respiratory and cardiovascular disease (Surgeon General's report).

Smokers violate love of neighbor by 1) causing discomfort to others by polluting shared air; 2) causing physical damage to those with allergies or other respiratory ailments; 3) endangering the lives of unborn children they may be carrying; 4) endangering the financial and emotional security of those who depend upon them; 5) giving bad example to children and young people who may be influenced to smoke.

A recent example of point two, above, is a situation I know of personally. A child with cystic fibrosis has parents who are chain smokers. The child, with diseased lungs, is forced constantly to breathe polluted air in her own home. How can her parents be blameless?

. . .

Those who profit from the sale of tobacco products, I believe, are guilty of a grave sin against the common good. As Paul Hanly Furfey says in his book, *The Morality Gap*, "For the sake of their profits, the tobacco moguls have had no scruple about sending tens of thousands of their fellow Americans to a premature death."

Others who share culpability are doctors who, by smoking themselves, give bad example to their patients, or who, for the sake of profit, fail to warn a patient of the dangers of smoking while accepting his money for treatment.

Since in many cases, the civil authority can pass legislation to protect some citizens from others, I believe steps should be taken to prohibit smoking in public places and perhaps to provide for fines for those who violate those laws. I am against total prohibition because 1) The freedom of smokers to self-pollute should be respected, (although, as suggested by a delegate to the U.N. World Health Organization, restricted to consenting adults in private); 2) It won't work.

Finally, one anti-smoker spoke recently of the need for church leaders to provide direction and good example in this area. He derided a priest who, while preaching about the evil of masturbation, puffed eagerly on a cigarette. I agree that such hypocrisy creates a credibility gap.

Then not wrong & myph

I am an anesthesiologist, and daily I have to administer anesthesia to chronic smokers and nurse them through their post-operative period. Fifty percent of those who have smoked a package a day for 10 years have chronic bronchitis.

You know how smoking has crippled someone when you try to get them to cough up their secretions after they have had abdominal surgery and they *must* cough, or be a prime target for pneumonia.

When one sees a smoking colleague get one coronary after another until he is almost dead, one needs little more proof that nicotine constricts arteries and damages tissues.

There is no question that, morally, smoking is a sin. Grave sin.

The problem is that smoking is an addiction. We Americans love freedom, yet so readily give it up to tobacco and other drugs. One wonders why.

Robert H. Irwin, M.D.
Berkeley, California

A silly subject.

Steven Wilson
Ashland, Oregon

This whole bit of trivial rot smells like the "hard sell" Baptist approach of several generations ago: No smoking, drinking, dancing, etc. Why don't you address the real issues that are polluting this nation?

C. Romano
Kailua, Hawaii

Smoke regularly, but hope to quit eventually. As I have done with alcohol. Quitting both are too much right now.

Have just begun to realize the full impact of smoking, the imposition on others, etc. So, awareness comes first, hopefully actions come later.

Name Withheld
Fox River Grove, Illinois

It seems to me that should we agree with Ms. Goulet, we might in the near future be confronted with the question, "Is it a sin to eat eggs?"

There is sufficient scientific evidence pertaining to the relationship of the ingestion of food with a high cholesterol content and heart attacks. Can we not say, therefore, that eggs cause heart attacks like smoking causes lung cancer?

Mary C. Wittingham
Louisville, Kentucky

This topic can be expanded to almost any extent and both sides deserve defense.

Smoking is no more a sin than wearing high-heel, spike-type shoes. These also are dangerous to your health and they destroy the property of others. Have you seen hardwood floors after a woman has walked over them in spike high heels?

Charles M. Fischer
Paducah, Kentucky

As I am not perfect, I am not overly hasty in condemn a smoker his habit. But to smoke in my presence is thrusting a habit upon me which I disapprove of. I find it hard to be a judge, but harder still to be a silent victim. If one must smoke, do it alone or with other smokers. It does not negate the sin, but, to me at least, it definitely lessens it.

Sara Ann Sieland
Troy, Michigan

As a non-smoker and a researcher, I still cannot reach the conclusion that smoking affects health (e.g., cancer).

The correlation cited by the Surgeon General indicates an association between the two but not a cause-effect relationship.

Some smoking may be sinful, but Ms. Goulet tends to view it as an absolute, i.e., all smoking is sinful. That kind of theology and code of morality has done Catholicism much damage in the past and has little place in today's theology.

Joe Gavin
Philadelphia, Pennsylvania

"It is a sin to smoke" may be a puritanism of the next phase of history which we shall have to bear. The medical evidence against smoking will never be great enough to make the command against it absolute, because smoking simply does not have to be a craze or frequency for people who care; and there will always be those few blessed and wise, so free of the Devil, the World, and the Flesh, that they will have no part in promoting extremism for the sake of Salvation. Maybe moralistic laws for an age can be formulated in a more knowing manner, without tending to warp the precise truth.

James Peter Lorge
Milwaukee, Wisconsin

I can't disagree with anything Ms. Goulet said; step by logical step one finds oneself agreeing; but then, in the end, I don't agree. Isn't there something to be said for the quality of life over quantity? Most of life's little pleasures are sooner or later found harmful. Personally, I don't wish to live to be 95 anyway! One would have to live in a sterile box to avoid all the dangers of plain, ordinary, risky living.

Joanne Willette
Delavan, Minnesota

There is a moral responsibility here somewhere, it seems to me. If one really loves neighbor as well as self, then there would be more responsibility and concern by all Christians for our neighbor's well-being. Can one honestly believe that he does not care what might happen to himself and be called morally responsible? No one is an island. If one cannot tolerate cigarette smoke, there are fewer and fewer places he can go.

Lora Jakoubek
Janesville, Wisconsin

Hey, Let the Lady Smoke!

By Abigail Van Buren

DEAR ABBY: I am a smoker. I know all the hazards, but I enjoy smoking and will not give it up. I resent all the reformed smokers who have quit for whatever reason and preach to me to quit smoking.

I respect all the "No Smoking" signs. I do not smoke while I am in an automobile with others. I smoke while I am in my office, my home or with friends.

I do not drink. I hate heavy drinkers and detest drunks, yet I am constantly being exposed to drunks. On a long plane ride, for instance. I sat next to a woman who drank all the way. She was so loaded when we landed that she had to be helped from the plane.

Bars, restaurants, theaters, etc., serve liquor, but they want to put up "No Smoking" signs.

I protest!

I would like to see every eating place with a "No Smoking" sign stop serving liquor and beer so I won't have to be around drunks. Also, airlines should have a separate section for drinkers, just as they do for smokers.

I am not asking people to stop drinking: "I'm just asking that the drinkers drink with each other and leave us sober people alone."

Mrs. T.S.

You make a valid point. But while obnoxious drunks are no pleasure to encounter, they do no violence to your lungs and the environment. Smokers do.

This Space Available

Broadcast cigarette ads have been banned. It won't end there—that's not the way of governments. Further federal interference was augured by the Surgeon General last month: "Nonsmokers have as much right to clean and wholesome air as smokers have to their so-called right to smoke, which I would redefine as a right to pollute." He specifically mentioned airplanes and restaurants (it won't end there) as public places where smoking should be banned.

Now, to our knowledge, everyone has the right *not* to smoke, whether subjected to an advertisement or not; nor is anyone denying nonsmokers the right to stay away from restaurants. Could it be, then, that the government is getting at the problem, not of "rights," but of pollution? Then why pick on cigarettes and not, say, airplanes or cars? If health is the issue, why not ban television (it causes scurvy of the mind), or saturated fats, or the Pill, or the Surgeon General?

The anti-tobacco evangelism is a neo-Puritan substitute for moral fervor: when no one any longer believes in sin, something new must be found to condemn. But morality, having connections with higher things, does not take kindly to such arbitrary treatment.

Moved by this higher morality, we repeat our willingness to run cigarette ads in our pages. And some of us, as Christians, will do penance for the sins of the state by not giving up smoking for Lent.

Top, courtesy of Abigail Van Buren, syndicated newspaper columnist, "Dear Abby." Above from *Triumph*, publication of the Society for the Christian Commonwealth, 278 Broadview Avenue, Warrenton, Virginia 22186, February 1971.

Smoking and the Public Interest

THE LOGIC of conservative thought often eludes me, so I wasn't suprised the other day to see columnist James J. Kilpatrick inveigh against Government efforts to warn people about the perils of smoking.

Years of "intensive" educational programs "have had little effect on the smoking hab-it," wrote the affable pundit from Virginia, a tobacco-growing state. Health warnings on cigaret packages and in printed advertisements are "ignored," he contends, adding that "most smokers die from causes apparently unrelated to smoking.

"There may be lessons in all this, in terms of the power of government to control the personal habits of the people," he argues. "Men have smoked for 500 years, and whole platoons of Surgeons General are not likely to dissuade them now."

Well, *some* have been dissuaded, as Kilpatrick's own data attest: "Per capita consumption in 1963 amounted to 217 packs; last year it was 205 packs." The number of smokers has climbed from 50 million to 52 million since 1964, but public health officials estimate that, without the warnings, there would be 75 million today. At least 10 million have quit the habit.

Hence, there no doubt has been less business for farmers, tobacco companies, advertising agencies, broadcasting networks, cowboy actors, chest surgeons, hospitals, mortuaries, cemeteries, and fire departments.

But Kilpatrick's central concern seems to be over the wisdom and propriety of Uncle Sam's involvement in the smoking-and-health issue. He infers that the Government is engaged in a futile, wasteful, and undemocratic war against smoking, and thereby is infringing on the right to use or sell tobacco products.

Nonsense. The Government is merely insisting that potentially harmful products be labeled as such and that publicly owned broadcasting channels not be used to advertise them.

Why should any fair-minded person object to that? What could be more in the public interest?

One is tempted to wonder how Kilpatrick would react if, say, his car were mortally wounded from straying into an unmarked pothole around Scrabble, Va. It's doubtful that all would remain serene around the Virginia highway department.

Really, governments should go further and ban smoking in all public places. The right to gulp tobacco fumes doesn't include a right to befoul air breathed by others.

If Kilpatrick and his right-wing brethren are the champions of personal liberty they profess to be, they should take up that cause forthwith.

—*MORTON C. PAULSON*

Reprinted with permission from *The National Observer*, copyright Dow Jones & Company, Inc., 1974.

Sexual Morality

The area of human relations involving sexual practices is one of the areas (abortion is another) where conflicting judgments concerning the rightness or wrongness of specific acts often reflect deep-seated metaphysical differences in addition to or instead of basic moral differences. In any case, the moral considerations in this area are often secondary to problems related to different metaphysical assumptions and/or perceptual frameworks of different individuals.

Some people figuratively, if not literally, "see" the world in terms of a grand dichotomy between mind and matter; mind is identified with the morally good, matter with evil. Accordingly, these people reason that things mental ought to dominate over the material (evil) body. In specific contexts this very general and abstract way of approaching experience manifests itself in adherence to rigid and narrow codes of sexual morality which embody the metaphysical belief that the resistance of bodily desires is the resistance of evil. Other persons who do not share this type of world view often perceive sexual desires as morally neutral or even as good. Such people have little sympathy or use for strict or narrow codes of sexual morality.

A related set of issues which are also more matters of different metaphysics or ways of seeing than they are matters of morality are the questions concerning what is "natural" and what is "unnatural." There are many people who do not necessarily accept the mind(good)/matter(evil) dichotomy as spelled out above, but who do perceive certain kinds of acts as being natural and others as being unnatural, with the associated assumption that natural acts are good and unnatural acts are morally bad. This generates disagreements not only with persons who do not associate natural acts with goodness and unnatural acts with evil, but it also involves serious disagreements, among the persons who accept this assumption, over which acts are in fact natural and which are unnatural.

An examination of the arguments in this section provides evidence of the difficulties to be encountered in trying to reconcile conflicting arguments concerning sexual morality. Persons who hold different positions on this topic often cannot even adequately communicate with one another until they are able to perceive the world in different ways, and they cannot fruitfully argue the moral issues involved until they bridge the wide metaphysical gulf that separates them. This is just one further confirmation of the warning given in the Introduction to the effect that the analysis and evaluation of ethical arguments is a very difficult task which requires much more than formal training in ethical theory alone. The fact that metaphysical beliefs manifest themselves in morally significant ways makes it imperative that we try to understand both our own and other metaphysical systems, as the first step to evaluating them as well as to evaluating specific moral arguments.

EXERCISES

1. Examine the arguments in Section 8 concerning abortion as well as the arguments in this section. To what extent are the arguments against abortion, which are based on the assumption that a soul enters the body at the moment of conception, similar to the arguments concerning sexual morality, which are based on the assumption that bodily desires are evil? Is it possible to consistently accept one of these positions and reject the other?
2. Compare the arguments in this section concerning homosexuals with the arguments in Section 4 about women and racial minorities. In what ways, if at all, are the basic *moral* premises different?
3. Identify which acts or situations in this section appear to be "natural" and which appear to be "unnatural." Try to formulate a general definition of "natural" which is consistent with your classification of these acts and situations. Then apply your definition of "natural" to the cases of euthanasia discussed in Section 9 to determine whether modern medical techniques for prolonging bodily functions are natural or unnatural by your definition.

A Matter Of Morals

It is sometimes said that you should not try to legislate morality.

If this premise were to be accepted then it should also follow that you should not try to legislate immorality.

Yet this is exactly what Senator Roy M. Goodman of New York City is doing in a bill he has introduced in the legislature.

The bill would repeal a section of the Education law that states any article or medicine for the prevention of conception has to be sold in a registered pharmacy or hospital.

The law further states that such devices can not be advertised or displayed.

Finally, and most significantly, it states that it is a misdemeanor to sell these devices to a minor under the age of 16.

If this bill of Senator Goodman were to be passed and approved it would mean that contraceptive devices could be purchased by a 15-year-old at any candy store and just as easily as candy.

Senator Goodman's intent is to prevent the transmission of veneral disease. This is a technical and practical approach to a great problem. However in solving problems it raises more serious problems.

Whatever may be his contention the open display, the open sale of these devices is an open invitation and encouragement to young people to engage in a way of life that most people would not approve.

That many young people would engage in such practice without protection and therefore subject themselves to disease peril must be admitted but we find it hard to assume the "if-you-can't-beat-'em-join-'em" philosophy that says if this condition is to exist let's make it safe even if it isn't right.

The over-the-counter sale to a 15-year-old is a confession of moral bankruptcy and an invitation to immorality. Would the next step be to sell devices in vending machines in shopping centers?

Isn't there a moral approach, a deeper and more meaningful approach to this problem as well as the technical approach? How many bars does society let down, how many guidelines are abandoned for young people. Isn't there a point where one says this much and no more?

Certainly if this legal bar is let down by Mr. Goodman's proposal there will be still more bars let down. Society seems unable to draw a hard and fast line on ethical problems and there are times when nothing but a hard and fast line is proper.

The spirit of the Goodman legislation is to accept the fact of immorality but try to curb its consequences by making it safe.

It is in the home, with proper upbringing, where the problem should be eliminated before it starts. There are many homes that are not the proper setting but it would be even more regrettable to have over-the-counter invitation to immature youths.

Reprinted from *The Troy Times Record*, May 12, 1973.

Birth Control Subverts Morality

By THOMAS A. LANE

CBS Radio was reporting the Irish conflict over birth control. The message alleged that Catholics as well as Protestants were practicing artificial contraception in Northern Ireland and that the legal ban on contraceptives in Eire, adamantly supported by the Catholic Church, was a serious obstacle to reunion. If the Church would stop trying to dictate morality. . . .

The program recalled to mind the 1930 Lambeth Conference at which the Anglican Church abandoned its moral opposition to birth control and embraced the use of contraceptives for family planning. People of sensitive conscience then decided that the breach of the natural law would serve higher ends of conjugal harmony and population control.

We can now regard that decision with forty years of hindsight. A person may in good faith select a new course of action; but he should then be sensitive to the consequences of his decision. Has the Anglican Church realized its hopes of greater conjugal harmony and improved family life within the Church?

Any objective observer of Western Civilization must note the sharp deterioration of individual and family morality since 1930. As the religious rhetoric of peace and charity intensifies, the practice of both decays. Within the family, the true state of affairs is measured in the high divorce rate and the religiously disoriented children. Sexual promiscuity, illegitimacy, abortion and the drug culture illustrate the rejection of Christian moral influence.

There are other subversive influences shaping our society. However, I believe that a serious study of these decades would identify the Christian acceptance of birth control as the breach in the citadel of Christian family life. The Lambeth Conference merely accepted what had been a growing practice in the community; but that church sanction, approving what had theretofore been regarded as sinful, legalized the destruction of the Christian family.

It was a mistake to suppose that contraceptives could be used within the marriage contract without promoting their general use. If marriage was merely an arrangement for sexual gratification, men would try to devise better arrangements for that purpose. If parents could frustrate intercourse to prevent conception, why shouldn't their children do so?

In professing to set a new standard for married love, the Anglican Church set a new standard for all love. It invited the sex-is-fun syndrome of recent decades which hides from youth the truth that illicit sex is tragedy.

Illicit sex is tragedy for married people, too. When persons accept faithfully the duties of the married state, they harvest the rewards of nature fulfilled. When they cheat on nature, they build a burden of guilt. The first lie begets others. The sanctity of the marriage bond is undermined.

And when a church professing to teach the will of God to men sanctions what all men and women know to be wrong, it forsakes its true mission. It becomes merely another human judge of expediency, severed from eternity.

I suggest to the Protestants of Northern Ireland that they should re-examine their beliefs about birth control. They can see in the travail of our society the future of their own, unless they turn back. They should return to the pre-Lambeth morality of their church. They should look upon reunion with Eire as an accession of strength in which Protestants and Catholics will work together to preserve the Christian family.

In the world context, these considerations challenge our Anglican brethren to condemn the error of artificial birth control and to restore universal Christian adherence to the natural law. Honesty requires the action. The survival of Western Civilization urges it. This should be a first step of ecumenical reconciliation.

from *The Wanderer*, June 17, 1971.

Contraception: a male responsibility?

To the Editor:

Having recently undergone a vasectomy, I read Mrs. Westoff's article with great interest, but some dismay: after the recent essays on the single lifestyle and the modern family, I had hoped for a more complete and sympathetic treatment of the single person's point of view and reasons for wishing to be sterilized. Therefore, for what it may be worth in indicating the diversity of those reasons, I offer some account of my own thinking.

The two charges usually leveled at singles who wish to be sterilized are that they are doing it for spurious ideological reasons or for the sake of sexual freedom. At 33, I think my stock of youthful idealism is about exhausted, but my resolution not to have children was made in college, when I first realized the seriousness of the population problem. If that insight seems precocious, remember that Malthus had it two centuries ago, and it is one of the foundations of evolutionary theory. But the very enormity of the population crisis makes many of us in biology despair of a solution, and I seriously doubt that my renunciation of children is going to do any real public good: it is, so far as smothering the population bomb is concerned, a gesture. Thus I must agree with the charge that, unless and until greater numbers become sterilized, the idealism that impels a single person to this step is perhaps misplaced.

The charge that singles become sterilized to enjoy sexual license is less fair. Surely we have lived long enough with the idea of birth control and the consequent de-coupling of sexual enjoyment and procreation that we do not need to make such accusations! And in what way is it less acceptable for a single than a married person to enjoy sex without the fear of pregnancy? Sexual freedom is certainly a benefit of sterilization, but not—for me at least—the reason for being sterilized.

Rather, I think my main reason for choosing vasectomy comes from guilty sympathy with the women's movement: I believe contraception to be a male responsibility, because so many of the women I know have had some difficulty with their means of birth control, whether mechanical or hormonal. As a biologist, I find endocrinological manipulations repulsive, and while there may be some risks to me from vasectomy, these seem no higher than those associated with female contraceptive techniques — and there is no compelling argument why I should not be as willing to take such risks as my female partners.

A friend of mine in the women's movement has pointed out that there is a sense in which vasectomy may be the ultimate put down of women. As a bisexual who once regarded himself as exclusively Gay, I am particularly sensitive to this criticism; but, on the contrary, I feel that my relationships with women have improved with the issue of children removed: I can see my one-time exclusivity as a form of voluntary sterilization, a way of coping with my adolescent terror of heterosexuality.

Much is made of the regrets a sterilized person may have if she or he does marry and desires children later on. The happy experience of couples who have (for one reason or another) chosen artificial insemination or adoption ought to offset such regrets. We should none of us be so in love with our own genes, or rather gene-combinations, that we object to these alternatives.

Yet, reproduction is the only form of immortality one can be certain of, however weak a simulacrum of eternity the unlikely persistence of a few linked genes may be. Vasectomy or tubal ligation is thus, in a way, a mild form of suicide; and it is in these terms that I can most appreciate the distress that sterilization causes some people. For this reason I urge a more helpful attitude towards singles who wish to be sterilized. Perhaps because I am lucky enough to live in a university community, I encountered very little resistance to my decision to have a vasectomy, or delay in its implementation. This intelligent cooperation in such a serious personal matter is very important if we believe that voluntary sterilization is right—whether we think it right for public reasons, or for the personal growth of the individual.

JOHN A. W. KIRSCH
Assistant Professor of Biology,
Yale University
New Haven

Letter to the editor of *The New York Times Magazine* by John A. W. Kirsch, Assistant Professor of Biology, Yale University, June 28, 1974.

THE ETHICS OF ADULTERY

In *The Playboy Forum*, a lady from Wichita, Kansas, inquired about PLAYBOY's readers' opinions on mate swapping and asked, "When both partners consent, is adultery immoral?" In the old days, people turned to religious authorities to find out what was moral or immoral. More recently, they have been asking psychiatrists and political theorists. Now, in true democratic fashion, the Wichita housewife wants to poll PLAYBOY's readers. This lady and her husband are already indulging in spouse swapping and are apparently enjoying it, but if the *Forum* published many letters telling her the practice is evil, I wonder, would she stop it?

In my opinion, to ask whether or not a given act, such as mate swapping, is moral is to pose a meaningless question. There are those who still believe that some supernatural monarch has decreed a code of rules by which we must live, but they are on ground only slightly less unsound than those who still reject evolution. Nor can any modern-minded atheist or agnostic prove, philosophically or scientifically, that any set of secular rules or obligations is superior to the individual's own desires. Modern ideologues may tell us we have a duty to humanity, society, reason or revolution till they are blue—or red—in the face, but they are human, like everyone else, and why should one man's code bind another?

People such as your mate-swapping correspondent feel that their personal decisions must be guided by some higher rationale. They need reassurance that there is something more important backing their decisions than their own feelings. But individual feelings are the most important thing there is. Religions, philosophies and ideologies are, in a sense, illusions: They have only such size and power as we assign them.

We must recognize that ethical codes are but convenient (and, too often, inconvenient) fictions. By doing so, we can then make decisions on reasonable, realistic bases, while also giving proper dignity to our genuine feelings. We can end the idolization of abstract principles for which too many people are willing to murder others and be killed themselves ("Better dead than Red" —that sort of thing). To realize that each man is a law unto himself is to arrive at an irreducible basis for libertarian thought—the most valuable and needed viewpoint in avoiding the pitfalls of right- or left-wing totalitarianism.

Therefore, I suggest to the lady from Wichita one rule that eliminates the need for all others: "Think for yourself."

Dion O'Glass
New York, New York

Light from the Eternal City

Pope Paul VI . . .

Lust Of The Flesh Leads Man Away From God

Everyone knows what is meant by "flesh" in moral language. It refers to everything connected with undisciplined sensuality; that is, that dangerous interplay of physical sensibility in conflict or in complicity with spiritual sensibility, animal pleasure, voluptuousness, the body in the grip of passion that draws the soul to itself and lowers it to its own instincts, captures it and blinds it, so that, as St. Paul says, "the unspiritual man does not receive the gifts of the Spirit of God" (1 Cor. 2, 14). We do not think there is any need of explanations in this connection. It is so much discussed today, too much, perhaps. It is a rare thing today for the novelist not to pay his sorry tribute, with a few pages at least, to some folly of the senses, or to some Dionysiac rapture, with which the world of literary culture is pervaded, as is that of pleasure-loving dissoluteness, pursued by anguish. Psychoanalytical studies on human instincts, and particularly on neuropathology and sexuality, have given a scientific language to the common empirical experience of erotic passions. They have even been exalted as real new discoveries of man.

SHUN TEMPTATION

And the recommendation follows by itself: we say it to the Father in the usual prayer: "lead us not into temptation"! Let us apply it to ourselves, as if to grant this supreme prayer. We must defend ourselves from the tyrannical temptation of the flesh, if we wish to live the paschal mystery. Inwardly and outwardly; in our hearts, above all, from which come the good and the evil of which we are capable (cfr. Mt. 15, 19; 2 Tim. 2, 22); and in our surroundings. Today men are concerned with ecology, that is purification of the physical environment in which man's life takes place. Why should we not be concerned, too, with a moral ecology in which man lives as a man and as a son of God? This is what we recommend to you, with our Apostolic Blessing.

Above, from *The Wanderer*, April 15, 1971.

DEAR ABBY
BY
ABIGAIL VAN BUREN

A friend of mine recently died and left a pretty young widow. The brother of the man who died is married, and he told me himself that he has been doing "double duty" and acting the part of a husband to this widow, if you know what I mean. He says the Bible says it is all right. I can't find anything in my Bible that gives approval to such scandalous goings on. If you can, I wish you would tell me where it is. Thank you.

A FRIEND

DEAR FRIEND: Your friend went back to the Old Testament. In Deuteronomy 25:5. "If a brethren dwell together, and one of them shall die, and have no child, the wife of the dead shall not marry a stranger: her husband's brother shall go unto her and perform the duty of a husband. And the firstborn which she shall beareth shall succeed in the name of his brother which is dead that his name shall not be put out of Israel."

Your friend is using this passage to suit his own purpose. The Deuteronomic Law no longer applies. But the Seventh Commandment does.

DEAR ABBY: It is so difficult to know what is morally right and what is morally wrong these days. What used to be considered wrong 25 years ago is suddenly "right." How is a person supposed to know how to behave?

BIG DILEMMA

DEAR BIG : Let your conscience be your guide. For some strange reason, we now have about 20 million laws trying to enforce the Ten Commandments.

Courtesy of Abigail Van Buren, syndicated newspaper columnist, "Dear Abby."

DEAR ABBY: Your outdated advice to the woman whose husband wanted her to have sex with other men really irked me. I'd have advised her to ask her husband why he wanted to share her. If it was because he didn't love her and wanted to get rid of her, then I fully agree, she shouldn't put up with it. But, did you ever stop to think that maybe the husband enjoyed her so much in bed that he wanted to show others what a great wife he has? Or it's possible that his sexual enjoyment may really be heightened if she has sex with other men?

Please don't call this perverted, or say that this man needs a psychiatrist. He doesn't need one. Read the sex manuals. This is an accepted sex practice and is widely accepted nowadays.

SEE THE LIGHT

DEAR SEE: I'm sorry I cannot agree with you. No man in our culture who truly loves his wife wants her to have sex with other men. If his own sexual enjoyment is heightened by such a need, it suggests either that he may have unconscious homosexual feelings or that he consciously or unconsciously has a need to degrade his wife.

George F. Will

'Prostitution Should Be Decriminalized'

World's oldest nuisance, government, should abandon the counterproductive fight against world's oldest profession. Prostitution should be decriminalized.

This is not apt to happen soon, given the instinct of state legislators to recoil in horror from any idea that has only reason on its side. But the reasons for decriminalizing prostitution are impeccably conservative, involving respect for privacy, liberty, the Constitution, the law and the police.

As Justice Louis Brandeis said, the Constitution confers on all citizens "as against the government the right to be let alone—the most comprehensive of rights and the right most valued by civilized men." That right to privacy should not be infringed unless a powerfully compelling state interest is served by doing so.

Because prostitution is private sexual conduct between consenting adults, the state should not proscribe it unless the state can demonstrate that it involves substantial harmful public consequences. But the harmful public consequences associated with prostitution are either unaffected by attempts to proscribe it or are produced by those attempts.

Prostitution is immoral, but it is not a threat to the fabric of society. Disrespect for the law is such a threat, and anti-prostitution laws foster such disrespect. The laws do not work, and they usually involve violations of three provisions of the Constitution.

Anti-prostitution laws invariably violate the right to privacy, a right implicit in First Amendment values and given explicit constitutional rank in a Supreme Court decision a decade ago dealing with private sexual activity.

Anti-prostitution laws, usually in their words and invariably in their applications, violate the equal protection provision of the Constitution by discriminating against women. In five states the laws apply only to women, not to their customers. Even where the laws are cast in sexually neutral language or where "patronizing a prostitute" also is a crime, the pattern of enforcement is discriminatory.

Prostitutes' customers rarely are arrested, and when they are arrested it usually is only to induce them to testify against prostitutes. For example, in 1968 New York City arrested 8,000 prostitutes, but only 112 customers, and only two of the customers were convicted.

Because neither prostitutes nor their customers complain to the police about prostitution, it is not easy for the police to make prostitution arrests. So male police officers frequently pose as customers or female officers pose as prostitutes, in order to lure prostitutes into soliciting or to lure men into propositioning. These police practices should be considered illegal entrapment and violations of the constitutional guarantee of due process.

Such behavior degrades the dignity of the police profession. And it is expensive. In 1971 San Francisco spent $375,000 processing 2,000 prostitution arrests. It costs Seattle about $1 million annually for prostitution arrests and trials.

It is estimated that only 5 per cent of the nation's more than a quarter of a million prostitutes have venereal diseases. (The rate for high school students between the ages of 15 and 19 is estimated to be at least three times that high.) The VD rate is low among prostitutes because they know a lot about the problem. Of course, even a rate of 5 per cent is a public health problem, but as long as prostitutes are liable to criminal sanctions, they will be reluctant to risk seeking regular treatment.

And criminalizing prostitution tends to make criminals out of policemen as well as prostitutes.

Prostitution, banned nearly everywhere, exists nearly everywhere, and it often pays for its existence with graft that corrupts the law enforcement machinery. Seventy per cent of all women in prison today were first arrested for prostitution, and many say they've learned about "real crime" while in prison. Indeed, many turned to "real crime" because prostitution arrest records made it difficult for them to find more respectable employment.

To the extent that solicitation by prostitutes is a public nuisance, it can be regulated by statutes concerning street solicitation for commercial purposes. In any case, prostitutes tend to isolate themselves. They know when and where customers are apt to congregate.

Obviously anti-prostitution laws are not the most important of the many laws that infringe freedom while serving no legitimate state interest. But every repeal of such a law helps instill in our rulers the habit of repeal. If that habit spreads, government will appear less foolish and will be less harmful.

© *The Washington Post*, August 26, 1974.

Label wrong all along, says author of change

by DAVID L. AIKEN

WASHINGTON—The psychiatrist who prepared the rationale for the American Psychiatric Association's removal of homosexuality from its list of disorders admits that it shouldn't have been there in the first place.

Dr. Robert L. Spitzer, a member of the APA's Task Force on Nomenclature and a psychiatrist at New York's Columbia University College of Physicians and Surgeons, said he felt homosexuality never met the criteria for defining a condition as a disorder: That it cause continual discomfort and interfere continually with ability to function in society.

Instead, he said, the main reason homosexuality was in the list of disorders was simply that society disapproved of it. This, he said, "is not in my view a scientific basis for having a nomenclature."

The primary reason for the APA's turnabout, he admitted, was persuasion from the gay activist movement. Here is a transcript of the interview:

Persuasive Arguments

ADVOCATE: What were the most salient arguments that the Gays used to convince you personally that homosexuality should be taken out of the nomenclature?

SPITZER: I guess the most salient arguments were that if one thought about it clearly, one could not merely use the criterion that the object choice by itself constituted an illness. They forced me to rethink what are the grounds for a condition being considered a psychiatric disorder.

On reflecting on that, it seemed to me that, with the exception of homosexuality, all of the conditions in the nomenclature did meet one of two criteria: Either they were regularly associated with subjective distress—the person was pained in some way—or they regularly led to generalized impairment in functioning—difficulty working, difficulty with friends.

Homosexuality just did not regularly lead to either of those conditions. So one might feel that it was not optimal sexual development, as many psychiatrists, I think, will continue to feel. But it just does not meet the criteria for being considered a psychiatric disorder.

ADVOCATE: Does this decision to change signify that times have changed and the APA is changing with them, or were you wrong all along?

SPITZER: I would have to say we were wrong. Since this is not getting wide circulation, I can say that. Of course, in some sense a mental disorder is whatever the profession says it is, but I think one can have certain criteria which make more sense than other criteria. The old criterion really was, anything that society very much disapproved of was grounds for being in the nomenclature. Society continues to disap-prove of homosexual behavior, although certainly not to the extent it did, but that is not in my view a scientific basis for having a nomenclature. So I would have to say, yes, it never should have been there, by itself.

ADVOCATE: Will the APA's decision help change the attitudes of society toward homosexuality?

SPITZER: I think so, and I guess you people have been telling us all along that it will . . . . Of course, psychiatry doesn't have the same currency that it did 10 or 20 years ago. I don't know how much people even care what psychiatrists have to say, but to the extent that they still do, it will have some effect. My impression is that people are not that interested in what psychiatrists have to say anymore.

ADVOCATE: Do you now agree with the slogan, 'Gay is Good'?

SPITZER: No. I haven't joined the homosexual activists movement. If that means that homosexuals should not hate themselves for being homosexuals, I would say, 'Fine, no one should hate themselves for being what they are.' To the extent that psychiatry has in the past made homosexuals hate themselves—which I think it has—to the extent that we're stopping that, I'm very delighted.

Gay Rights

At least ten American cities have now adopted one or another measure designed to assure the so-called civil rights of homosexuals and other deviants, and such legislation is now under consideration in New York City.

In its key passages, the New York bill contains the following language: "A city agency is hereby created with power to eliminate and prevent discrimination in employment, in places of public accommodation, resort or amusement, in housing accommodations, and in commercial space, because of race, creed, color, national origin, sexual orientation, or physical handicap, and take other action against discrimination because of race, creed, color, sexual orientation, or national origin, as herein provided." Such other action, for example, includes enlisting "the cooperation of the various racial and ethnic groups, community organizations, labor organizations, fraternal and benevolent organizations, and other groups, including those devoted to the eradication of prejudice based on a person's sexual orientation." The bill, it is important to note, describes discrimination based on a person's "sexual orientation" as resulting from "prejudice, intolerance, [or] bigotry."

The language of this bill, reflecting the avowed goals of various "gay liberation" organizations, would make homosexuality merely another lifestyle in the eyes of the law, and would both break down social resistance to it and stigmatize such resistance as "bigotry."

A similar measure, it is interesting to note, was recently put to the test of a referendum in Boulder, Colorado, and the voters rejected it by an overwhelming majority. If that expression of ordinary human feeling constituted prejudice, then it was prejudice in the Burkean sense of the word: the intuition of norms and assumptions that lie at the roots of Western civilization.

Though to some it may seem quaint to appeal to Scripture for the illumination of an ethical problem, nevertheless it will not be denied that Scripture is profoundly involved with the assumptions of the West. Scriptural insights can hardly be rejected lightly, within the spirit of the West. And it will be noted that both the Old and the New Testaments begin with *families*. When God perceived Adam's loneliness in the Garden, He did not choose Eve over a catamite by the toss of a coin. It will also be noted that both the original family in the Garden and the Holy Family of the Gospels are direct divine creations. The repetition of that pattern at the commencement of key founding documents of the West can hardly be supposed accidental.

It suggests that the family "was there from the beginning," at least so far as Western civilization is concerned; that the family is fundamental to the civilization of the West.

The religious foundations, the laws, the customs, and the ordinary human feeling of the West all testify to, support, and even celebrate that ethical fact. If custom and prejudice refuse to establish homosexuality and other deviations as the full equals of the family, then they reflect those root civilizational assumptions.

In actuality, discreet homosexuals probably suffer a minimum of discrimination. These homosexual "rights" bills are, accordingly, really a form of ideological assault, rather than humanitarian measures. They strike, and they mean to strike, at fundamental ethical assumptions. But that, you may have noticed, is true more often than not of liberal measures.

Above, reprinted with permission from *National Review* (June 7, 1974), 150 East 35th Street, New York, N.Y. 10016.
Below, courtesy of National Organization for Women.

NOW Res. 144—NOW Literature—Sexuality and Lesbianism: Passed

Whereas, women have the basic right to develop to the maximum their full human sexual potential, and

Whereas, diversity is richly human and all women must be able to freely define and to express their own sexuality and to choose their own life style, and

Whereas, NOW's public relations and communications have omitted references to the unified efforts of women of traditional and diverse sexual experience, and

Whereas, Lesbians have formed a caucus in NOW to communicate openly, without fear and hostility, and

Whereas, the threat traditionally felt from Lesbianism must no longer be a barrier to open communication between all people, and

Whereas, we recognize that women are all oppressed by one common oppression, and therefore, surely we must not oppress one another for any reason;

Therefore be it resolved that a statement adopting the sense of this resolution be included in all appropriate NOW publications and policy statements; and,

Be it further resolved that NOW actively introduce and support civil rights legislation designed to end discrimination based on sexual orientation and to introduce with legislation to end discrimination based on sex the phrase "sexual orientation" in areas such as, but not limited to, housing, unemployment, credit, finance, child custody and public accomodations. (Submitted by Sexuality and Lesbianism Workshop)

WORDS WE LIVED BY...

The following is excerpted from the *Ladies' Guide,* a popular reference book of the 1890s.

EFFECTS OF SOLITARY VICE IN GIRLS

The victim of this evil habit is certain to suffer sooner or later the penalty which nature invariably inflicts upon those who transgress her laws. Every law of nature is enforced by an inexorable penalty. This is emphatically true respecting the laws which relate to the sexual organs.

Wide observation has convinced us that a great many of the backaches, side-aches, and other aches and pains of which girls complain, are attributable to this injurious habit. Much of the nervousness, hysteria, neuralgia, and general worthlessness of girls originates in this cause alone.

The period of puberty is one at which thousands of girls break down in health. The constitution, already weakened by a debilitating, debasing vice, is not prepared for the strain, and the poor victim drops into a premature grave.

SIGNS OF SELF-ABUSE IN GIRLS

Mothers should always be on the alert to detect the first evidences of this vice in their daughters, since later nothing but almighty power seems competent to loosen its grasp. The only positive evidence is detection of the child in the act. A suspected child should be watched under all circumstances with unceasing vigilance.

[But] aside from positive evidence, there are other signs which may lead to the discovery of positive evidence.

• *A marked change in disposition.* When a girl who has been truthful, happy, obliging, gentle, and confiding, becomes peevish, irritable, morose, and disobedient, she is under the influence of some foul blight.

• *Loss of memory and loss of the love for study.* The nervous forces are weakened, giving place to mental weakness and inactivity.

• *Unnatural boldness in a little girl.* If she has previously been reserved, this is just ground for the suspicion of secret vice.

• *A forward or loose manner in company with little boys.* Girls addicted to this habit are guilty of the most wanton conduct.

• *Languor and lassitude.* In a girl who has possessed a marked de-

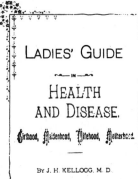

LADIES' GUIDE

— IN —

HEALTH AND DISEASE.

Girlhood, Maidenhood, Wifehood, Motherhood.

By J. H. KELLOGG, M. D.

gree of activity and energy, this should give rise to earnest solicitude on the part of the mother for the physical and moral condition of her child.

• *An unnatural appetite.* Sometimes children will show an excessive fondness for mustard, pepper, vinegar, and spices. Little girls who are very fond of cloves are likely to be depraved in other respects.

• *The presence of leukorrhoea.* Self-abuse occasions a frequently recurring congestion of the parts, together with the mechanical irritation accompanying the habit.

• *Ulceration about the roots of the nails.* This especially affects one or both of the first two fingers of the hand, the irritation of the fingers being occasioned by the acrid vaginal discharge.

• *Biting the fingernails.* The irritation of the fingers, which gives rise to the habit of biting nails, grows out of the irritable condition of the nails mentioned above.

• *The expression of the eyes.* The dull, lusterless eye, surrounded by a dark ring, tells the tale of sin.

• *Palpitations of the heart, hysteria, nervousness, St. Vitus's dance, epilepsy, and incontinence of urine, giving rise to wetting the bed.*

HOW TO CURE VICIOUS HABITS

The habit of self-pollution is one which when thoroughly established, is by no means easily broken. The victim of this most terrible vice is held in the most abject slavery, the iron fetters of habit daily closing the prisoner more and more tightly in their grasp. The effect is to weaken the moral sense perhaps more rapidly than any other vice, until there is little left in the child's character to which an appeal can be made.

The mother should first carefully set before the child the exceeding sinfulness of the habit, its loathsomeness and vileness, and the horrible consequences which follow in its wake. But in most cases, the evil is not so easily mastered. The little girl should be kept under constant observation every moment of her waking hours. Care should be taken that the child does not feign sleep for the purpose of gaining an opportunity to avoid observation.

It is much more difficult to cure this soul-destroying vice in girls than in boys. They are seldom as ready to confess their guilt as are boys, and then are less easily influenced by a portrayal of its terrible consequences. Sleepless vigilance must be coupled with the most persevering patience.

In obstinate cases, severe means must be adopted. We were once obliged after every other measure had failed, to perform a surgical operation [clitoridectomy] before we were able to break the habit in the case of a girl of eight or ten years who had become addicted to the vice to a most extraordinary degree.

SECTION 5

Censorship

The mention of the word "censorship" probably calls up in many people's minds thoughts about pornography, a topic which has been widely discussed and debated in the United States for several decades as the Supreme Court and various legislative bodies have attempted to come up with workable definitions and legal sanctions. But, as the examples in this section serve to remind us, censorship is really the act of preventing public dissemination of any kind of idea or image, and at various times in various societies attempts have been made (very often quite successfully) to censor almost every conceivable kind of idea and image. The problems here, as with gun control, abortion, and drugs, are at several levels which must be kept quite distinct in the analysis and evaluation of arguments. One level is that of the basic rightness or wrongness of specific acts (e.g., the classic case of shouting "Fire!" in a crowded theater) and another quite different level is that of whether or not legal sanctions should be imposed against persons for disseminating particular ideas or images. The arguments in this section address a variety of these issues at both levels, sometimes mixing the two in a way which makes it difficult or impossible to separate them in a clear and precise manner.

The question of censorship often overlaps other basic ethical questions, as is evidenced by many of the examples in this section. For example, it is generally agreed that in most situations telling lies and untruths is morally wrong. But what about fairy tales and other stories which have traditionally been a part of almost everyone's childhood? Is it wrong to tell untrue stories to small children? And if so, should this be legally prohibited by the state? This question may seem almost absurd to some readers, but some very serious debates over it have taken place recently in some schools, as indicated in the first item in this section. Other ethical issues which come into consideration in discussions of censorship range from professional responsibility (of journalists, teachers, scientists, etc.) to protection of one's country (for example, Daniel Ellsberg argued that his "leaking" of the classified information known as the Pentagon Papers was for the good of the country).

EXERCISES

1. Compare the cases of journalistic censorship discussed in this section to determine what basic questions, if any, are common to all of them, and also to identify significant differences among the cases. Are matters such as the nature of the audience (high school students versus adults) or the nature of the subject matter (prostitution, national security, death) "significant" factors in distinguishing cases or not?
2. Examine the excerpts from the opinions in the Supreme Court ruling on pornography to determine the extent to which the arguments of the court might be different from the kinds of arguments that are commonly given by "ordinary" people in everyday situations. Can one formulate a clear distinction between law and ethics on the basis of this comparison?
3. Examine the arguments concerning censorship of sexual materials and those involving violence to see what differences if any exist between them. Is it possible to use the same moral premises to justify the censorship of one kind which would at the same time permit the publication and dissemination of the other kind?

Textbook Banners Busy

By John Mathews
Washington Star Staff Writer

Should Montgomery County kindergarten, first- and second-grade children be told that owls and elephants are wise, that wolves are cruel or that a whale spouts water and a bear hibernates in winter?

Should the school system keep showing a decade-old black and white film ("What is a Concerto?") featuring a young-looking Leonard Bernstein conducting an orchestra with no black or women members?

Or should county students have access to "Mommies Are For Loving," a book some consider "sexist," or to a film, "The Magic Balloons," which shows a young boy smoking, stealing and swimming without supervision.

In each case, Supt. Homer Elseroad or a review committee of teachers, librarians and subject specialists have said "No!", backing complaints of parents who objected to the books and films.

The decisions, made last month, represent a new twist in the continuing nationwide controversy over textbooks and other classroom materials.

Last year, Montgomery and Prince Georges counties' and other school systems were facing citizen complaints — often from conservative organizations — about obscenity, profanity and sexual content in books such as Eldridge Cleaver's "Soul on Ice," or Claude Brown's "Manchild in the Promised Land."

"Now, it's a whole new ballgame," says Frances C. Dean, coordinator of Montgomery's Division of Evaluation and Selection. Individual parents are now objecting to the accuracy and truthfulness of books and films, their contemporary value, sexist content or their moral messages.

A parent, for example, raised questions about the accuracy of animal behavior depicted in the popular early grade book "Animals Everywhere," and its use of anthropomorphism — the attribution of human qualities to animals.

After consulting a mammalogist at the U.S. Fish and Wildlife Service, the teacher committee recommended withdrawing the book, because of "its many misleading or inaccurate scientific statements," including descriptions of owls and elephants as "wise," wolves as "cruel," and statements that a whale spouts water and a bear hibernates.

An unnamed dissenter on the committee (school officials do not reveal review committee members or the names of parents who lodge complaints) said the decision on the book could lead to banning even "Peter Rabbit," since there is a "certain amount of stereotyping of animals" in most children's books.

"Animals Everywhere" does not present itself as "an absolutely scientifically true book," the objector added, noting the cover which shows a boy petting a tiger and a goat, while a cat smiles. "Obviously, the tiger is not ferociously eating them," the dissenter wrote.

Dr. Alfred Gardner, the mammalogist who was questioned on the telephone by a member of the review committee, was much less concerned with inaccuracies in the book than the teacher reviewers. "For teaching purposes, you often hedge the truth and avoid answering all questions," he said in an interview. "As far as anthropomorphic language," he added, "we always think of animals in terms of whether they are soft or nice or dangerous."

But, Dr. Gardner added there were debatable issues of accuracy in the book. "There is no way to tell whether owls or elephants are wise. That's definitely anthropomorphic," he said. Wolves, he added, "are really no more cruel than a human who scales a fish while it's still alive and flopping around."

He said also that whales actually spout air and not water, although the pressure causes water above the whale to be displaced in a geyser effect. Bears do not actually hibernate, which is scientifically defined as a metabolic state of torpor in which body temperature is lowered and physical activity is greatly reduced. Bears, he said, actually enter a state of extended sleep, which is often interrupted.

The teacher committee generally approved the Bernstein film on the concerto, although it acknowledged that there were no blacks or women in the orchestra, and as a music supervisor observed about the decade-old film, "I am sure Mr. Bernstein would be pleased to maintain the youthful countenance seen in this film — unfortunately, only the content is ageless!"

The charge of sexism against the elementary-age book "Mommies Are For Loving" was rejected by the teacher committee. Despite passages, like "Mommies are for saying No . . . and drying tears and scrubs in tubs . . . . Mommies are for lots of things but best of all Mommies are for loving," the committee decided the book was "harmless" and depicted a typical, although not exclusive, role of the mother in a family unit.

"The Magic Balloons," a fantasy film for kindergarten to sixth grade depicting a young boy encountering balloons which magically become real people, things and experiences, was rejected. The committee objected to "examples of antisocial and unsafe behavior: stealing, unsupervised swimming and boating, unsupervised living, dangerous driving."

Elseroad agreed with the committee decision to bar "The Magic Balloons" film, but disagreed with the teachers on the other items. He ordered a ban on "Mommies Are For Loving," which the teachers wanted retained despite the sexist charge, and ordered the Bernstein film removed on grounds it is outdated.

On "Animals Everywhere," the superintendent also overruled the teacher committee. Rather than taking the book off the shelves, Elseroad ordered that it continue in use, but that no new copies be purchased unless the publisher changes statements the committee considered inaccurate.

Mrs. Dean, the county book evaluation head, wrote Doubleday and Company Inc., the publishers, stating the committee objections. She got an answer from a sales manager, who noted that in 21 years "Animals Everywhere" by Ingri and Edgar Parin d'Aulaire has sold more than 150,000 copies and was issued in paperback three years ago.

"He said nothing about our objections, so I guess they don't plan to make any changes," Mrs. Dean said.

James J. Kilpatrick

A willful exercise in intellectual dishonesty

The MacMillan Publishing Company delivered itself the other day of a policy statement expounding "today's egalitarian standards." The statement sets forth guidelines for textbooks that are to govern its authors and illustrators henceforth.

The purpose is "to maintain sexual and racial balance in every item we publish."

The company's statement is likely to be received in most quarters, publicly at least, with the kind of fulsome and dutiful praise extended by Pravda to the utterances of Mr. Brezhnev or, for that matter, by the American Conservative Union to the utterances of Mr. Reagan.

In the popular view of "today's egalitarian standards," MacMillan has said and done the right thing: The publishers have confessed their sins, repented, and embarked upon a new life. They are born-again egalitarians. A holy spirit moves within them.

Permit, if you will, a dissenting view. MacMillan's guidelines ought to be denounced for what they are: a willful exercise in intellectual dishonesty. The company is insisting that its textbooks depict society not as it is, but as the publishers, in the fantasies of their "newly raised consciousness," would like it to be.

Their purpose in producing textbooks is not primarily to teach, to inform, to instruct, or to educate, but to propagandize for a new social order.

The guidelines begin with a preface of Dr. Matina S. Horner, president of Radcliffe College. She speaks for those who are struggling for a "more egalitarian society."

The achievement of such a society is hampered by the "tyranny of the norm," which is to say, by a tyranny that seeks to enforce upon young people irrelevant, innacurate, and outdated stereotypes about the roles they are expected to play.

Dr. Horner would abolish such norms. Through a process of education to counteract the stereotyping, she would rid society of false notions, for example, of what is manly or womanly. In the new egalitarian society, a woman who exhibited "competition, independence, intellectual competence, and leadership" no longer would be regarded as a victim of mental instability.

MacMillan's editors are r'aring to go. They offer examples of their new publishing philosophy. Because more than one-half of the population is female, illustrators should see that females are represented appropriately hereafter.

In the bad old days of textbook illustration, a drawing might have appeared of "mother sewing while dad reads." Under the new egalitarian standards, MacMillan wants a drawing of "mother looking at her desk while dad reads or clears the dining room table."

In the sinful past, an unregenerate illustrator, his consciousness not yet raised, might have depicted "mother bringing sandwiches to dad as he fixes the roof." No more! New textbooks will depict "mother fixing the roof."

Once a textbook might have shown "boys playing ball, girls watching." Such innacurate, irrelevant and outmoded depictions are now condemned. MacMillan decrees "both sexes playing ball; sometimes boys watching a girls' team play."

MacMillan is not bothered by intellectual fraud: "We are more interested in emphasizing what can be, rather than the negatives that still exist. ... The fact that black persons do not yet hold a proportionate share of executive positions should not prevent us from depicting a sizable number of blacks as executives."

Now, for the record, there is, of course, much in MacMillan's position that is admirable. It is perfectly true that for generations our textbooks ignored Negroes, depicted feathered Indians in tepees, put blankets on indolent Mexicans, and consigned darling little lily-white girls to the endless baking of cherry pies.

It is altogether desirable to abandon or to modify practices both cruel and stupid.

But the wrong is not corrected, it is merely reversed and compounded, by imposing educational policies depicting a fantasy world. Are we to imagine a baseball team consisting of three white girls, two black girls, three white boys, and a Chinese shortstop?

Children are wiser than we think. Looking at such an illustration, children will not say, "What a beautiful egalitarian ideal!" They will say, "What a fake!"

"HOP IN WE'RE JUST KILLING TIME TILL NEXT CLASS"

DEATH SKETCH — This cartoon by student cartoonist Brian Basset is critical of reckless student driving. Basset resigned from the staff of Langley High School student newspaper in Northern Virginia after the paper decided not to publish his drawing. (AP)

DEATH SKETCH RULED 'TOO PERSONAL'

Teenage Cartoonist Quits Over Publication Dispute

WASHINGTON (AP) — The cartoonist of a high school newspaper in nearby northern Virginia has resigned because the paper refused to publish a drawing bitterly criticizing reckless student driving.

It had been scheduled to appear in the newspaper of Fairfax County's Langley High School last Friday along with an editorial on the subject and a tribute to a Langley student who was killed last month in an automobile accident during school hours.

THE CARTOONIST, Brian Basset, 17, refused to change the cartoon, which depicted five students picking up a black-clad, sickly-carrying grim reaper as a hitchhiker. He also refused to change the caption: "Hop in . . . we're just killing time till next class."

"Basically I was doing humorous editorials, but death is a strong issue and I wanted the cartoon to have impact," said Basset, the son of newspaper cartoonist Gene Basset.

John Bussey, 18, editor of the paper, said that after a close vote of the staff and considerable soul-searching, he decided to ask Basset to change the drawing because it would not be in good taste along with a memorial to Patricia Collier, 17, the student who was killed

"**THE CARTOON** was excellently done," he said, "but it could be taken the wrong way by a segment of the school who knew Patty, and by her family."

Huldah Clark, an English and journalism teacher who serves as faculty adviser to the tabloid paper, described the cartoon as "too personal, too soon and too strong," adding:

"It wasn't a right or wrong situation. There were good points on both sides, but there were reservations that the cartoon might be taken too personally."

Courtesy of The Associated Press.

Editorial

Society's evils unfit for News?

The **News** would like to take this opportunity to comment on some of the letters and conversations we have had with people concerning the prostitution article in the January 31 issue. Many people seem to have their own ideas of what the story really means and why we printed it.

Many people were upset with various aspects of the article and did not read it with the proper perspective. Some felt we were building up prostitution and trying to influence moral judgements. Others thought we "put down" a NT graduate. Still others were offended by the language used. We did not intend to condone or degrade prostitution. The article was simply an interview.

We believe the **News** gives fairly balanced coverage of both the good and bad aspects of NT. Not every graduate becomes as successful as Ann-Margaret and Sen. Charles Percy. No newspaper or news program shows only the good side of life. It is our obligation to print articles whether or not it agrees with the moral code of **some** of our readers.

The obscenity was not put in to purposely offend people or to gain attention to the article. It was merely part of the interview and was a direct quote. The girl chose to express herself in this manner, and we felt it would have detracted from the way she presented herself in the interview if we censored the obscenities.

Finally, many students are not as sheltered as some parents and teachers may believe. We considered the article worthwhile because it presented a new and interesting point of view. While we received several objections to the article, many readers enjoyed it. It was a side of society that is too often censored, but it is a realistic part of life that students will be exposed to sooner or later. It is far better that the student be exposed to this "evil of society" in a matter-of-fact manner. More harm comes from ignorance than knowledge. We are not our readers' rose colored glasses.

NEWS MEDIA

New Trier News

NT graduate talks about prostitution

by Clark Marlide

New Trier's News: Hooking the readers

High School Confidential

"When I first started," confided the 18-year-old prostitute to her interviewer, "my thinking was: guys can get it on, why can't I? And hell, I can get paid for it and they can't. I was 16 the first time I actually charged." If the interview had appeared in a girlie magazine or even a big-city newspaper, it would have lifted few eyebrows. But it happened to run in a recent issue of the New Trier News, the school paper of the New Trier East High School in the posh Chicago suburb of Winnetka. The interviewer was a 17-year-old senior and the happy hooker was a 1974 New Trier alumna.

Above, *New Trier News*, New Trier High School East, Winnetka, Illinois.
Right, from *Newsweek*, May 26, 1975.

Where responsibility lies

Right from *The Arizona Republic*, February 7, 1975.
Below, from The Arizona State University *State Press*, February 14, 1975.

An Arizona State University committee, composed of faculty and student members, has recommended that the State Press, an undergraduate publication, be placed directly under the office of the President.

The four-times-a-week newspaper is now run as an adjunct of the journalism department. It is financed in large part by a subsidy from student fees. The paper frequently criticizes the administration of the university, sometimes fairly, sometimes unfairly.

Max Jennings, a professor in the journalism department, is faculty adviser to the State Press. He described himself as concerned about the possibility of censorship if the committee's recommendations are followed. Prof. William E. Arnold, who was chairman of the committee, apparently has no such fears.

Obviously The Arizona Republic is as much opposed to censorship as anyone. All general circulation newspapers owe their very existence to the First Amendment, which guarantees a free press in this country.

But the rights of free speech and a free press don't apply to an undergraduate newspaper which is subsidized by fees that the students must pay. The First Amendment doesn't repeal the ancient adage that whoever pays the fiddler can call the tune.

If the State Press were published by students who sold subscriptions, solicited ads and paid their own bills, it would be as free to lambaste the ASU administration as The Arizona Republic is.

But so long as it accepts a subsidy from university funds, with the staffers being paid for what should be a learning experience, the State Press cannot expect to be a free agent.

The undergraduate paper is in fact an arm of the university. A wise administration would give it as much leeway as it seemed to deserve, but it would be foolish to let it remain a burr under the president's saddle.

The faculty-student committee recommendation is interesting in one respect. It shows an admirable reversal of the one-time campus attitude toward the administration.

The committee clearly understands that "academic freedom" does not give either professors or students the authority to publish a newspaper without assuming the responsibility that goes with publication.

Student newspaper has rights, prof says

By Wendy Johnson

A nationally known authority on constitutional law said an Arizona Republic editorial is "dead wrong" by saying the First Amendment rights of free speech and press do not apply to the State Press, an undergraduate newspaper partially subsidized by student fees.

William Canby Jr., ASU professor of law, was commenting on a Republic editorial appearing last week which said the State Press could be legally censored since it is partially funded by the university.

The editorial stated, "The First Amendment doesn't repeal the ancient adage that whoever pays the fiddler can call the tune."

In answer, Canby said, "Several cases, especially in Federal Courts, have upheld the rights of student editors against censorship of a university president, even when the newspaper was financed either by student fees or by direct state appropriations."

The Republic argued "If the State Press were published by students who sold subscriptions, solicited ads and paid their own bills, it would be as free to lambast the ASU administration as The Arizona Republic is."

Canby cited the case of Dickey (a student newspaper editor) vs. Alabama State Board of Education in which the state argued that if the state owned the newspaper, it had the right to prevent the student editor from criticizing the state. The Federal District Court overturned the case in favor of Dickey.

"Virtually every federal court that has considered it (the matter of censorship) has given student editors of college newspapers some sort of protection against censorship by administrative authorities," Canby said.

Canceled Debate

Roy Innis, executive director of the Congress of Racial Equality, is an advocate of black nationalism and a militant opponent of racial integration. Dr. William Shockley, a physicist who won the Nobel Prize for his role in invention of the transistor, is a vigorous exponent of the theory that genetic rather than environmental factors are primarily responsible for the disadvantaged position of blacks in a predominantly white society.

There is much in the views and ideologies of both men with which rational observers of American society have good reason to disagree. That very fact makes a public debate between these two controversial figures a matter of special interest, with a university campus an appropriate setting.

It is therefore a sad commentary on the state of intellectual tolerance in the academic community that, in response to pressure from the Black Law Students Association, a scheduled Innis-Shockley debate at Harvard has been canceled. The incident renders particularly relevant a warning issued last week by a group of prominent scholars from the United States and abroad. They concluded a four-day discussion in Venice on "The Crisis of the University" by noting that, even though overt violence and intimidation have diminished, "concessions to expediency are being made every day." Such concern is clearly justified when one of the world's leading universities finds it expedient to let free debate be stifled on its campus.

Thinking Out Loud

Permit me to debunk some of the favorite words and cliches of the liberals and left-wingers. One of these is the high-sounding phrase, "Academic Freedom."

Once it appeared to be a good word, when it seemed to give the teacher liberty to explore new horizons, and to teach within the limits of decency and respectability all available knowledge on any given subject, always careful to teach fact as fact, and theory as theory, and to point out and define the difference between the two.

"Academic freedom" was never intended to be divorced from moral responsibility; nor was it ever intended to challenge the existence of God Almighty, or His operations among the sons of men.

It was never intended to be an excuse for free thinkers to challenge the divine creation of man, nor to overthrow the law of God, nor to deny man's need of redemption, nor to teach infidelity.

"Academic freedom" is a misnomer if it seeks to operate outside of God's orbit, for man has no rights—not even the right to exist—outside the sovereign will of God.

But, alas, what has this so-called "academic freedom" come to mean in its present distortion? Never has a phrase been so corrupted or prostituted.

For many today who loudly demand the use of "academic freedom," mean, rather, "unrestrained license" to teach whatever they choose, with total disregard of the basic rights of those whom they teach, and regardless of the people who through their gifts, tax dollars, and sacrifices make possible the very existence of our schools and universities.

To them it means an unhindered, unrestrained, unsupervised license to teach, as they choose, infidelity, atheism, Communism, sex perversion, intemperance, anything — even the change of our form of government from a constitutional republic to a socialistic state.

Under the guise of this so-called "academic freedom" they presume to have the right to usurp the place of the parents, and teach doctrines and philosophies which will have the effect of completely changing the beliefs and the behaviour of our young people.

Under this damnable cloak of so-called "academic freedom" they presume to compel the society which supports them to completely refrain from interference with their program of humanism, and to arrogantly reach their slimy hands down your pockets for the funds necessary to subvert and corrupt your children. Not only so, but they are so lifted up with pride and vanity as to look with disdain upon any citizen who criticizes their licentious program.

If you dare to get in their way, they will brand you as a square, an ignoramous, an old fogey, a Puritan, a hater of arts and literature.

Although they boast of a supreme liberalism, when crowded into the corner they manifest the most pronounced spirit of bigotry. Their ideas, they think, represent the last word in intelligence; no other opinions, or philosophies, or religions are of any worth. All knowledge ends with them!

Well, I've got news for them. They are the biggest bunch of asinine parasites on the face of the earth. And so help me God, I shall continue to devote a good part of my life to exposing their hypocrisy. It is time that we begin to find out who the real phonies are in our society.

Dale Crowley in *The Capital Voice*, January 1, 1971.

A Resolution* Against Racism

The doctrine of racial supremacy is with us again. New studies claiming to demonstrate "scientifically" the old notion that black people are inferior have been rapidly spreading in professional literature, texts, and respectable popular magazines. Even more ominously, it is now being taught as fact in classrooms across the country.

The leading contemporary protagonists of this theory include Arthur Jensen (Berkeley), Hans Eysenck (London), Richard Herrnstein (Harvard), and William Shockley (Stanford). Basing their conclusions on the results of aptitude, achievement, and I.Q. tests, these theorists claim that black or other oppressed peoples are genetically endowed with less intelligence than the dominant group. They sweep aside the fact that tests of any oppressed group in a stratified society measure only that group's social rejection and not its relative intelligence. Jensen asserts: "There are intelligence genes, which are found in populations in different proportions, somewhat like the distribution of blood types. The number of intelligence genes seems to be lower, overall, in the black population than in the white." (*The New York Times Magazine*, 31 August 1969, p. 43). And Shockley claims, "Nature has color coded groups of individuals so that statistically reliable predictions of their adaptability to intellectually rewarding and effective lives can easily be made and profitably used by the pragmatic man on the street." (*Boston Sunday Globe*, 12 September 1971, Sect. A, p. 6).

Theories of racial inferiority are rendered untenable by the evidence of human history: every population has developed its own complex culture. Contrary to the supremacist view, the peoples of Africa and Asia have, at various times, produced civilizations far more advanced than those existing simultaneously in Europe. Moreover, the constant geographical shift of centers of culture is in itself proof of the equal capabilities of all peoples. It is nonsense to suppose genetic superiority wandering about the world.

The doctrine of racial inferiority is thus unscientific as well as socially vicious. Its sole claim to objectivity rests on a veneer of scientific techniques that covers distortion and false assumptions. Indeed, the current "master-race" ideas are once again being discredited in the scientific literature (cf. R. Lewontin, *Bull. Atomic Sci.*, March 1970; S. Searr-Salapatek, *Science*, 174: 4016; 178: 4058; C. Brace, *et al.*, *Anthropological Studies*, No. 8, Am. Anth. Assn.). Nevertheless, the generators of this new racism persist in their bigotry. Their theories, despite their academic garb, do not differ in their scientific character or their social effects from those advanced by American slave-owners, the Nazis, or the advocates of apartheid in South Africa. Racist ideas, if it were not for their political and economic role in justifying oppression and exploitation, would long since have joined phlogiston and geocentric theories of the universe in the mausoleum of science.

Our common human heritage has endowed all groups of people with equal intellectual abilities. Of course there are secondary physical differences. Nobody denies this. But they have nothing to do with intelligence. Research involving these differences must not be misused to support theories of racial inferiority.

Racist theoreticians have recently sought sanction and protection in the concept of academic freedom. This is a subterfuge. It is true that academic freedom protects the right to free inquiry and to the expression of controversial ideas. But it is not license to justify oppression. It was no more intended to protect racism than verbal assault or libel, with which racism has more in common than it has with free intellectual inquiry. Nor, in the light of all the evidence, can the ideology of racism be legitimately called "controversial" and open to debate. It is a false doctrine that serves only to facilitate brutalization and exploitation. Thus, because it is both socially pernicious and scientifically incorrect, its proponents forfeit any right to academic protection.

The use of the academy to further racist oppression must be halted. We therefore call upon our colleagues to:

1) Urge their university senates to adopt measures designed to eliminate classroom racism.

2) Urge professional organizations and societies, academic departments, and editors of scholarly journals to condemn and refuse to disseminate racist research.

3) Expose the unscientific character of racist ideas so as to deny them the appearance of legitimacy provided by academia.

4) Organize and support activities to eliminate racist practices and ideas wherever they occur.

Courtesy of the Committee Against Racism.

John P. Roche

The right to be heard

I WAS RECENTLY asked how I felt about an invitation by a nearby university to a spokesman for the Palestine Liberation Organization: there was some feeling that his talk might constitute a "provocation."

My reply was that I consider the PLO to be a bunch of ideological gangsters, but that if its speaker appeared (unarmed) he deserved to be heard, and anybody who tried to break up the meeting or shout him down should be tucked in the slammer.

Recently, however, Ronald Ziegler has been put through the mill at Boston University's School of Public Communication. Originally the student assembly unanimously voted to invite him to lecture on the "use and abuse of power" at a $2,700 fee.

The dean then intervened, protesting the fee. In fairness, he did add that he would defend Ziegler's right to speak -- for nothing. The faculty unanimously supported this suggestion and, when the matter returned to the student government, the latter disinvited Ziegler.

The nub of the attack was that by paying Ziegler, the school was endorsing the whole "immoral" Watergate sequence.

What is raised by this assault on Ziegler is the whole question of double-moral book-keeping. Let me say, for starters, that I think the student assembly was out of its mind to invite Ziegler to talk at a School of Public Communication. It is comparable to inviting a color-blind individual to lecture on the French impressionists. Ziegler's specialty was non-communication.

Second, the $2,700 fee is mind-boggling. I believe the original offer was inane.

However, once the invitation was out, it seems to me that the dean and his faculty behaved in a quite outrageous fashion. One can make a case — number of conservatives do — that the faculty and administration of a school should act ideologically in *loco parentis* to the students, effectively straightening the children out when the little dears go astray. But the liberal view, as I understand it, is that the students are not to be treated as *non compos* infants, that they have wide areas of free choice, and that customarily in a liberal institution one of these areas is who they want to listen to on issues of the day.

Between 1968 and 71 it was hard to turn around without finding some left-wing militant whooping up the campus revolution. In my personal judgment a number of them were taking "immoral" positions and collecting substantial sums in the process.

To this, a conservative (like, I presume, the dean of Boston University's School of Public Communications) will replay, "why don't you take your morals seriously?" I do, but I also have a haunting sense of fallibility and deep suspicion of obsequious piety.

One of the students at the school, commenting on the decision, said, "we have a chance to tell the entire country that we don't want a deceitful person to speak from a public platform. No one in America had a say in the pardon of Nixon, but this is our opportunity not to pardon Ziegler."

I suppose it's uplifting to have students with such a prophetic afflatus, but this sinner's reaction is simply to gag.

Arrogance, Not Freedom, Tested

Before he became disillusioned by the misbehavior of the media of his day, Thomas Jefferson said that if he were forced to make one choice only, he would select a free press over government.

If the New York Times, the Washington Post and the Boston Globe are sustained in their thesis that they can at their own discretion publish any top secret documents that they can acquire, the nation may face a Jeffersonian choice.

Freedom of the press is really not the issue that the three newspapers have brought before the nation as the federal government seeks to recover top secret documents that were stolen from the Pentagon files.

No responsible person is against freedom of the press or the legitimate right of the public to know the decisions of its governments. By the same token, no responsible citizen challenges the principle that some things that government does must be kept secret in order to protect our nation.

Thus the willful publication of stolen, secret material must be considered in another light, particularly in view of the current newspaper tactics. When the New York Times was enjoined from further publication after publishing three articles, the Washington Post printed the next two. When the Washington Post was enjoined, the Boston Globe presumably completed the series. At no time did any of the newspapers make contact with the government to urge regular procedures to de-classify the material. None of them yielded to the pleadings of the federal government to stop publication. The material, for example, could readily have been paraphrased if principles of free press alone were the issue. Instead volumes of secret data were published verbatim — an act which could be of value to an enemy.

Clearly the challenge is to the institution of government itself. What the three newspapers are saying is that the judgment of the press —

and that could be anybody with a mimeograph machine — supersedes that of the elected and appointed representatives of the people.

Moreover, those newspapers are saying that the means justifies the end — that if they regard their goals as moral, they can break the law to attain those goals. In this respect, their argument is little different than that used by the anarchists who take to the streets. A comparable principle would be that false testimony and tainted evidence could be used in court so long as it results in the guilty being punished.

Reason alone dictates that this concept cannot be sustained if the United States of America is to survive. If the United States could no longer have secrets, or if stolen secrets were fair game for dissemination, there would be no United States government — probably no free press either.

Above from *The San Diego Union*, June 23, 1971.
Below, courtesy of Mike Peters.

JUST LOOK AT THESE HEADLINES..... NIXON ADMITS HEDGING ON TAXES....

OUTRAGEOUS....

NIXON ADMITS KNOWING ABOUT WATERGATE HUSH FUND....

APPALLING....

NIXON LAWYER PLEADS GUILTY TO SELLING AMBASSADORSHIPS....

THAT DOES IT...

IM SICK OF HOW THE PRESS IS DAMAGING THE PRESIDENCY.....

PETERS—DAYTON DAILY NEWS

75

The Right to Know vs. Rubies

THE WORD from Boston is that the Justice Department is trying to get an indictment against Neil Sheehan, the New York Times reporter who first wrote the story of the Pentagon papers. The charge being sought is that Sheehan knowingly transported stolen property across state lines.

There may be a technical point of law involved, but in equity and intent this is blatant nonsense.

This is not to say that Sheehan or any other newspaperman is immune from prosecution for violating the law. As Tom Winship, editor of the Boston Globe, said when his newspaper published the Pentagon papers, he was prepared to bear the consequences, whatever they might be. This was the same position taken by civil rights leaders in the South who knowingly broke state laws. They were willing to go to jail to demonstrate to the nation that the state laws were in violation of the Constitution.

To get a conviction against Sheehan, Justice is going to have to prove first that a crime was committed, and then that Sheehan did it. Assuming that Sheehan did what he is suspected of doing, Justice is still going to have trouble proving a crime.

Were the documents stolen? We don't know. They were certainly copied, but that's different. Documents aren't like a ruby necklace, nor was copying them like infringing on a copyright, which denies to its owner something of value.

A theft implies a victim. Who was the victim? The answer is that there wasn't any.

The papers were the result of work done at government expense. The papers belong to the people. And what Sheehan did was not take the papers from the people, but the precise opposite. He and his presumed accomplices took copies of the papers from those who were hiding them from the people and delivered them to their rightful owners.

If anyone could be said to own them more than anyone else, it might be Robert McNamara, who commissioned them while secretary of Defense. Mr. McNamara is on record that the papers should have been given to the public long before.

It is interesting to note that Mr. Sheehan is apparently not to be charged with violating national security, which was the first reaction from the Nixon administration. The reason is simple: Experts from Dean Rusk, secretary of State at the time, on down say that no security was violated.

To argue that Mr. Sheehan committed no crime and violated no security in this case is not to provide the press with an absolute blanket of privilege. We recognize the necessity for some government secrecy and we recognize the dangers to security. On the whole, the media's record is exemplary. It is far better, for example, than the record of government officials who pepper their memoirs with classified material to justify their stewardship.

If anything, this is the issue which Sheehan has raised. The people have the right to know the people's business, not just that part of it some bureaucrat wants them to know. With common sense, publication of the papers will lead to sensible use, rather than abuse, of classification codes. This in turn will better serve the public interest.

From the *Detroit Free Press*, July 17, 1971.

WHAT IT'S LIKE TO BROADCAST NEWS

by WALTER CRONKITE

I don't think it is any of our business what the moral, political, social, or economic effect of our reporting is. I say let's get on with the job of reporting the news—and let the chips fall where they may. I suggest we concentrate on doing our job of telling it like it is and not be diverted from that exalted task by the apoplectic apostles of alliteration.

If it *happened*, the people are entitled to know. There is no condition that can be imposed on that dictum without placing a barrier (censorship) between the people and the truth—at once as fallible and corrupt as only self-serving men can make it. The barrier can be built by government—overtly by dictatorship or covertly with propaganda on the political stump, harassment by subpoena, or abuse of the licensing power. Or the barrier can be built by the news media themselves. If we permit our news judgment to be colored by godlike decisions as to what is good for our readers, listeners, or viewers, we are building a barrier—no matter how pure our motives.

Above, courtesy of Walter Cronkite and *Saturday Review*, December 12, 1970.

IT IS YOUR BUSINESS, MR. CRONKITE

by IRVING E. FANG

I disagree with Mr. Cronkite. It *is* the journalist's concern to consider the consequences of his work, just as it is the physician's, the attorney's, the minister's, the professor's, and indeed every professional man's concern.

Above courtesy of Irving E. Fang and *Saturday Review*, January 9, 1971. Dr. Fang is an associate professor in the School of Journalism and Mass Communication at the University of Minnesota. A TV newsman for nine years, he is author of a textbook, *Television News*, published by Hastings House.

The distinction between the journalist judging an individual story on its merits and the journalist ignoring the impact of news upon his audience is obviously far more than hairsplitting. To cite one example, riot news was once reported on television newscasts purely on its merits as news. But it soon became evident that the impact of riot news on television viewers—including the rioters themselves—was so great that television news departments trimmed their sails. Broadcast journalists had to make the effects of riot news their business. They did so voluntarily, behaving as responsible members of our society. To ignore the effects of this news would have been unacceptable, and everyone knew it.

From *The Rat/Underground Press Syndicate.*

Overemphasis of sex and violence on television will
be a deterrent to your child. Why? In the formative
years, what he sees now, later on he will do. He will
ape the actions of the actor.

Good logic. Correct. If so, your kid is better off watching
a stag movie than *King of Kings*. Mine, anyway. Because
I just don't want my kid to kill Christ when he comes
back. And that's what's in *King of Kings*—but tell me
about a stag movie where someone got killed in the
end, or slapped in the mouth, or heard any Communist
propaganda. So the sense of values would be, the morals:

"Well, for kids to watch killing—Yes; but *schtup-
ping*—No! Cause if they watch *schtup* pictures,
they may do it some day."

Above, from *The Essential Lenny Bruce.*
Copyright 1967 Ballantine Books/A Product
of Douglas Book Corporation.

Vonnegut's Otherworldly Laughter

by BENJAMIN DeMOTT

● Youthcult holds that the attempt of the elders to hide the prevalence of brutality from the young (and from themselves) is both criminally evasive and doomed to failure. Vonnegut says the same. At the end of *Mother Night* Howard Campbell, on trial for genocide, receives some junk mail from Creative Playthings pitching for toys that prepare kids for life and help them to "work off aggression." Campbell answers:

I doubt that any playthings could prepare a child for one millionth of what is going to hit him in the teeth, ready or not. My own feeling is . . . [against] bland, pleasing, smooth, easily manipulated playthings like those in your brochure, friends! Let there be nothing harmonious about our children's playthings, lest they grow up expecting peace and order, and be eaten alive. As for children's working off aggressions, I'm against it. They are going to need all the aggressions they can contain for ultimate release in the adult world . . . . Let me tell you that the children in my charge. . . . are spying on real grownups all the time, learning what they fight about, what they're greedy for, how they satisfy their greed, why and how they lie, what makes them go crazy, the different ways they go crazy and so on . . . .

From *Saturday Review*, May 1, 1971.

Whose morality?

The backlash, as we all know, is against sexual permissiveness. But a backlash implies a return to a different norm. What are we proposing to return to? This is the first question to examine if we are to make sense of a moral controversy that has already been rumbling on for years and looks like keeping its point for a good many years to come. Is there some more healthy, stable, and satisfying morality to which we can return? To the morality of the interwar years? To the Edwardians or the Victorians? Hardly anyone is seriously proposing that, partly because even a strict theologian nowadays allows that there is no unchangeable moral code that can be summarised in a decalogue, and partly because we know that Victorian morality was a fraud, sweeping prostitution and pornography into dark corners.

Indeed what we are still experiencing now is an overdue backlash against Victorianism and its hangover into the twentieth century. The reaction against permissiveness today is more accurately described as a counter-backlash.

That sex should be exciting so much argument is not surprising, for we find ourselves in a situation without precedent. The old taboos were securely based as a defence against the risk of pregnancy. The development of effective contraception has altered the context and consequences of extra-marital sexual relations and has made loving and responsible sexual relationships possible outside marriage. For those who do not acknowledge the religious prohibitions it seems arbitrary and unnecessary to deny the place of sex in extra-marital love. With the disappearance of the old taboos it has also become natural to talk openly of sex and sexuality and for the writer and artist to depict the sexual aspect of relationships explicitly. All this offends deep-seated convictions or prejudices in some people, but others ask what is the harm if this greater openness makes for greater fulfilment and personal happiness? Is it not a positive advance in the human condition?

We cannot be too sure, because this is virtually unexplored territory, and one where the experts — psychologists, sociologists, and educationists — disagree among themselves. It is good to take the sense of guilt out of sex. On the other hand every intimate personal relationship carries with it the risk of neurotic hang-ups. To recommend promiscuity as a form of self-education (to take an issue raging furiously at the moment) would seem to invite the misery of rejection, and emotional insecurity.

As for pornography, we cannot be too sure of that either. Probably it can deprave and corrupt. On the other hand, the bawdy and the erotic have a place in literature and the arts,

If we look for the enrichment of the individual personality most people would say that a more relaxed and knowledgeable enjoyment of sexual relationships is a plus point on that test. This is no Sodom and Gomorrah we live in even though there may be fringe extravagances. There is some virtue in having a rather more easy-going, open-minded, and plain-speaking society than we have had in the past.

Above, from *The Guardian*, London, May 15, 1971.

The Busybody Factor

Buttinskies Make the Culture Scene

By Clifford A. Ridley

Depending on where you sit, the art business may or may not be running low on people of talent, imagination, and daring. Of one commodity, however, it has no dearth. It is up to its ears in busybodies.

Coming from a critic, that may seem an odd complaint. But I will submit in self-defense that my brethren and I are all yap and no bite—that while we breed preferences and proposals by the gross, we really have neither the inclination nor the power to compel anyone to do much about them.

Others are not so reticent.

Consider, for instance, the ABC television network, which determined some 10 days ago that Chicago Seven defendants Hayden, Hoffman, Davis, and Rubin are apparently so inflammatory that they can't be heard without an immediate rebuttal. Lacking such "balance," the network pulled a Dick Cavett interview with the quartet off the air.

Well, one's first reaction is that the ABC assessment will surely come as news to the Messrs. Hayden, Hoffman, Davis, and Rubin, who are about as effective or, as interested in overthrowing the Government these days as I am. One's second reaction is that ABC is running awfully scared. Hey, guys, haven't you heard? Agnew quit!

One-Sided Demand?

"There's nothing in the fairness doctrine about balance of views within a program," Cavett was quoted as saying. "On the other hand, I have an agreement with the network that such balance will be supplied." That, I suspect, was probably a mistake, but Cavett says he was properly skeptical during this particular show—and anyway, he wants to know, where were the equal-timers during his interview with Jerry Ford earlier this year?

A silly episode, and no mistake. Chalk one up for the busybodies.

Comment

Bury the Bard?

Finally, in Minneapolis, a local rabbi last month deplored the Guthrie Theatre's inclusion of *The Merchant of Venice* in its current repertory, saying, "It's time we did away with all stereotypes." From his remarks, it's clear that the rabbi is no hothead—he's a longtime supporter of the Guthrie—but in this context I fear that he, too, is a busybody.

There's no gainsaying, of course, that there are elements of anti-Semitism in Shakespeare's Shylock, but there's also no gainsaying that for all its biases *The Merchant* is a great play (perhaps, even, because of them), illuminating the human heart and mind in language that is entrusted to but a sacred few. Putting the matter simply, you don't ignore great art, however hard it makes you swallow—and an awful lot of it does, when you think about it.

You can explain it in the context of its time, you can warn folks who might be offended not to come, you can candidly acknowledge that in some respects its creator was a crackpot, but you don't ignore it. We are not yet so well endowed with the truth and beauty that great art provides that we can afford to consign any of it to the dustbin. And I doubt we ever will be.

Hey, everybody! Lay off, huh?

Excerpts From Pornography Opinions

MILLER v. CALIFORNIA
Opinion by Burger

We acknowledge, however, the inherent dangers of undertaking to regulate any form of expression. State statutes designed to regulate obscene materials must be carefully limited. As a result, we now confine the permissible scope of such regulations to works which depict or describe sexual conduct.

That conduct must be specifically defined by the applicable state law, as written or authoritatively construed. A state offense must also be limited to works which, taken as a whole, appeal to the prurient interest in sex, which portray sexual conduct in a patently offensive way, and which, taken as a whole, do not have serious literary, artistic, political or scientific value.

The basic guidelines for the tryer of fact must be: (a) whether "the average person, applying contemporary community standards" would find that the work, taken as a whole, appeals to the prurient interest; (b) whether the work depicts or describes, in a patently offensive way, sexual conduct specifically defined by the applicable state law, and (c) whether the work, taken as a whole, lacks serious literary, artistic, political, or scientific value.

A Rejected Concept

We do not adopt as a constitutional standard the "utterly without redeeming social value" test. That concept has never commanded the adherence of more than three justices at one time. If a state law that regulates obscene material is thus limited, as written or construed, the First Amendment values applicable to the states through the 14th Amendment are adequately protected by the ultimate power of appellate courts to conduct an independent review of constitutional claims when necessary.

PARIS THEATER CASE
Opinion by Burger

It should be clear from the outset that we do not undertake to tell the states what they must do, but rather to define the area in which they may chart their own course in dealing with obscene material.

We categorically disapprove the theory, apparently adopted by the trial judge, that obscene, pornographic films acquire constitutional immunity from state regulation simply because they are exhibited for consenting adults only.

Although we have often pointedly recognized the high importance of the state interest in regulating the exposure of obscene materials to juveniles and unconsenting adults, this Court has never declared these to be the only legitimate state interests permitting regulation of obscene material.

The states have a long-recognized legitimate interest in regulating the use of obscene material in local commerce and in all places of public accommodation, as long as these regulations do not run afoul of specific constitutional prohibitions.

In particular, we hold that there are legitimate state interests at stake in stemming the tide of commercialized obscenity, even assuming it is feasible to enforce effective safeguards against exposure to juveniles and to the passerby. Rights and interests "other than those of the advocates are involved." These include the interest of the public in the quality of life and the total community environment, the tone of commerce in the great city centers, and, possibly, the public safety itself.

As Chief Justice Warren stated, There is a "right of the nation and of the states to maintain a decent society."

But, it is argued, there is no scientific data which conclusively demonstrates that exposure to obscene materials adversely affects men and women or their society. It is urged on behalf of the petitioner that, absent such a demonstration, any kind of state regulation is "impermissible."

We regret this argument. Although there is no conclusive proof of a connection between antisocial behavior and obscene material, the legislature of Georgia could quite reasonably determine that such a connection does or might exist.

From the beginning of civilized societies legislators and judges have acted on various unprovable assumptions. Such assumptions underlie much lawful state regulation of commercial and business affairs.

Decision for Legislature

If we accept the unprovable assumption that a complete education requires certain books, and the well nigh universal belief that good books, plays, and art lift the spirit, improve the mind, enrich the human personality and develop character, can we then say that a state legislature may not act on the corollary assumption that commerce in obscene books, or public exhibitions focused on obscene conduct, have a tendency to exert a corrupting and debasing impact leading to antisocial behavior?

It is argued that individual "free will" must govern, even in activities beyond the protection of the First Amendment and other constitutional guarantees of privacy, and that government cannot legitimately impede an individual's desire to see or acquire obscene plays, movies, and books.

We do indeed base our society on certain assumptions that people have the capacity for free choice. Most exercises of individual free choice —those in politics, religion, and expression of ideas—are explicitly protected by the Constitution. Totally unlimited play for free will, however, is not allowed in ours or any other society.

Dissent by Brennan

If, as the Court today assumes, "a state legislature may act on the assumption that commerce in obscene books, or public exhibitions focused on obscene conduct, have a tendency to exert a corrupting and debasing impact leading to antisocial behavior," then it is hard to see how state-ordered regimentation of our minds can ever be forestalled.

For if a state may, in an effort to maintain or create a particular moral tone, prescribe what its citizens cannot read or cannot see, then it would seem to follow that in pursuit of that same objective a state could decree that its citizens must read certain books or must view certain films.

However laudable its goal —and that is obviously a question on which reasonable minds may differ—the state cannot proceed by means that violate the Constitution.

Even a legitimate, sharply focused state concern for the morality of the community cannot, in other words, justify an assault on the protections of the First Amendment. Where the state interest in regulation of morality is vague and ill-defined, interference with the guarantees of the First Amendment is even more difficult to justify.

In short, while I cannot say that the interests of the state—apart from the question of juveniles and unconsenting adults—are trivial or nonexistent, I am compelled to conclude that these interests cannot justify the substantial damage to constitutional rights and to this nation's judicial machinery that inevitably results from state efforts to bar the distribution even of unprotected material to consenting adults.

I would hold, therefore, that at least in the absence of distribution to juveniles or obtrusive exposure to unconsenting adults, the First and 14th Amendments prohibit the state and Federal governments from attempting wholly to suppress sexually oriented materials on the basis of their allegedly "obscene" contents.

From *The New York Times*, June 22, 1973.

Movie Mailbag

'Decent Americans Hail Supreme Court Rulings'

To THE EDITOR:

YOUR symposium concerning the new Supreme Court ruling on obscenity (Aug. 5) is a fine example of unbalanced reporting.

How about an article devoted to the millions of decent Americans who are hailing the ruling as a step toward rebuilding the moral fiber of our country?

In this war between good and evil, we must learn to recognize who our enemies are and what weapons they use. Key words and phrases such as "censorship," "freedom of speech," "art," "vigilantes," "puritans," "book burners" and "blue noses," are being used as weapons by those forces which are out to destroy every last vestige of decency and good taste, thus bringing about the moral destruction of our nation.

Motion-picture producers, writers and artists with high moral standards do not fear the new decision simply because they would never stoop to the depths of degeneracy. It is only those who are morally deficient who fear the decision. They feel restricted within the framework of decency because the evil inclinations within them have overpowered the good. If they would recognize the fact that God gave them the power to reach greater heights in their thinking and actions so that mankind could be elevated rather than degraded, the turmoil within them would subside and they would find reconciliation within that framework which they now find so confining.

A careful study of the Preamble to the Constitution would reveal to them that it is inconceivable that our forefathers, being fully aware that it was internal moral decay which caused the collapse of nations, would advocate freedom as a vehicle for the filth, vice and corruption which would lead our country to a similar fate.

Pornography does not help to form a more perfect union, nor does it help to promote the general welfare simply because it appeals to the lower, animalistic instincts in man. To cater to such instincts is not "freedom," it is sheer slavery because man becomes a slave to his passions and impulses rather than their master. When man becomes a slave unto himself, he loses the proper perspective and control, thus losing the very values which go into the making of a civilization.

DIANA RONALD
N.Y. Diocesan Chairman
Women for Decency
Catholic Daughters of America
Pound Ridge, N. Y.

Above, letter to the editor of *The New York Times*, courtesy of Diana Ronald, Pound Ridge, New York, September 9, 1973.

'Rulings? Not Mine'

By MELVIN VAN PEEBLES, *author and director.*

MY shiftless behind must have slept through the whole thing. NEW OBSCENITY RULING!!!??? Lord, Lord, new rulings and here me I haven't never even run into no relevant *old* obscenity laws.

What obscenity rules? You still can and always could show and do all the most really big obscenities on the old silver screen you wanted—from shuffling niggers rushing to massa with a mint julep, to triumphant superblacks winning with the help of law and order (massa disguised behind a badge), to Tonto getting done in (long on nobility but short on victory).

You can deal, do, show, say all and anything you please about spics, coons, wops, broads, honkeys, wasps, yids, gooks, slopes, imperialism, gangsterism, Watergate games, pacification, reallocation, megatons, methadone, and so on —what obscenity laws? We are free to deal with all the big-time perversions any way we please (with impunity, so the saying goes).

There are no obscenity laws to speak of, unless maybe you mean that pet preoccupation of some of the mainstream folks obsessed with restraining glimpses of PEOPLE DOING IT and associable genitalia. The topsy-turviness of their priorities is a clue to where their heads are. The absurdity of a mentality that puts pubic hair over laissez-faire, sex over self-hate-fostering stereotypes — that's insanity!

When Third World folks and disenfranchised youth are struggling for perspective on their existence, to have some folks pushing their pet coital obsession and coming on righteous behind it, to boot — that's obscenity. New rulings, Old rulings, Whose rulings — not mine.

Fred Douglass laid it out a long time ago when he said the master ain't got no laws, national or local, a slave oughta feel duty bound to respect.

The Court and Obscenity: A Dissent

'How Can the Librarian Be Sure?'

♦ The U.S. Supreme Court last week reaffirmed 5-to-4 its decision of last June that the question of what is obscene must be defined according to local community standards. The Court upheld one lower-court obscenity conviction, dismissed appeals in two convictions, and sent eight other obscenity cases back to lower courts for review under the June guidelines. Those guidelines provided for the states to punish printers or sellers of magazines, books, or films "which appeal to the prurient sexual conduct in a patently offensive way and which, taken as a whole, do not have serious literary, artistic, political, or scientific value." As he had last June, Justice William O. Douglas dissented, and last week he was joined by Justices Potter Stewart, Thurgood Marshall, and William Brennan. Here are excerpts from the Douglas dissent:

EVERY AUTHOR, every bookseller, every movie exhibitor, and perhaps, every librarian is now at the mercy of the local police force's conception of what appeals to the "prurient interest" or is "patently offensive." The standard can vary from town to town and day to day in an unpredictable fashion. How can an author or bookseller or librarian know whether the community deems his books acceptable until after the jury renders its verdict? The meaning of the standards necessarily vary according to each person's idiosyncracies. The standards fail to give adequate notice and invite arbitrary exercise of police power. The evil is multiplied because of the danger to First Amendment values of free expression. "Bookselling should not be a hazardous profession" [a quotation from an earlier High Court decision].

If the magazine in question were truly "patently offensive" to the local community, there would be no need to ban them through the exercise of police power; they would be banned by the market place which provided no buyers for them. Thus it must be the case that some substantial portion of the public not only found them not offensive, but worthy of purchase.

How can the bookseller or librarian be sure which of the publications on his shelves are offensive to the majority? Perhaps he will be safe if he sells only publications with a certified history of broad appeal, thus attempting to "steer wide of the unlawful zone." Yet there are many who deem some magazines offensive and even lingerie advertisements in the Sunday papers. A bookseller or a librarian can never know if some jury will find those views representative of the community. A movie exhibitor in Georgia has just found himself convicted under the state's obscenity laws for showing a film [*Carnal Knowledge*] which received much critical acclaim, and an Oscar nomination for the female lead. We deal here with criminal prosecutions under which a man may lose his liberty. Our Constitution requires fair notice so that the law-abiding can conform their conduct to the requirements of the law.

Above, from *The National Observer*, November 3, 1973. Copyright Dow Jones & Co., Inc.

A FOUR-LETTER WORD FOR THE OBSCENITY RULING

The Supreme Court has spoken and, by a 5-4 decision, has taken another tortuous twist in the perpetual attempt to obliterate "obscenity"—which nobody has yet been able to define, except in the dictionary.

This latest effort is really a beaut.

Now every Tom, Dick and Harriet in every hamlet, city and suburb, county and state can and will produce his own judge, jury and decision. Commented Michigan Attorney General Frank Kelley: "Now prosecuting attorneys in every county and state will be grandstanding, and every jury in every little community will have a crack at each new book, play and movie."

And magazine, speech, TV program, radio program and Kiwanis Masters of Ceremonies' jokes.

Despite the kidding that greeted Justice Stewart's observation on obscenity—to wit, "I can't define it but I know it when I see it"—I think I agree with him. In studying Latin (it took me three years to pass Caesar, so my translations might be questioned), I recollect that it didn't take me or my classmates long to locate the "dirty" parts. Ditto *Macbeth* and other required Shakespeare plays.

But this new—I'm tempted to say "current" because I don't see how it can long stand as a guide—decision entitles coffee-klatching collections of housewives to posse down to the local newsstand and get the local police or the area prosecutor seeking reelection to arrest the newsstander for his *Playboy* or any periodical with an "objectionable" picture or word in it.

Books? Every one describing or discussing the fact that storks don't bring all the babies can be the subject of suit by anyone anywhere.

It's hard for people generally to understand that when those of us concerned with a free press object and fight infringements of freedom of expression, we're not trying to defend some of the abuses and some of the explicit in obscenity. But putting up with a little of that to protect your rights under the Constitution to read or to see or to think what you like is vastly more important.

Protecting the young from exposure to pornography and other abuses is another question entirely. Protecting the public generally from public display of such is certainly, too, in order.

But no one forces an adult into a movie theater showing X-rated movies or into book stores to buy erotica.

It was a Justice of the Supreme Court widely considered one of the greatest ever to grace that great bench, Oliver Wendell Holmes, who was said to regale his colleagues with tales of his private collection of pornography. But his revered Supreme Court opinions dealt with the essence of justice, not the circumscribing of freedoms.

—**MALCOLM S. FORBES,**
Editor-in-Chief

Above, reprinted by permission of *Forbes Magazine* from the July 15, 1973 issue.

Censorship of Pornography?
YES

by REO M. CHRISTENSON

Unhappily, all of the major premises on which our society rests derive from the realm of intuition—the viscera. Can anyone *prove* that the family is a desirable institution? That higher education promotes human welfare? That technology makes men happier? That love is better than hate? That democracy is superior to dictatorship? None of these is provable. But this does not stop us from acting on our best judgment, knowing that all human judgment is fallible. If, then, the regulation of pornography comes down to a matter of visceral hunches, why should not the majority of viscera prevail?

Is "pornography" such an imprecise term that it lacks sufficient clarity to meet the "due process" test?

Current state laws could be updated and made more explicit if they were refined to forbid actual or simulated exhibitions of sexual intercourse or sexual perversion on stage or screen—or pictorial representations thereof in other media—when such exhibitions or pictorial representations are primarily intended for commercial entertainment rather than for education.

Censorship of Pornography?
NO

by A. S. ENGEL

Finally, I cannot seriously believe that Christenson can really be comfortable as the champion of visceral supremacy or of majorities armed with more feelings than facts. I need hardly remind him that those are the very conditions under which many a community has attempted to legislate its prejudices concerning race, or political belief, or religious favoritism. Simply because we cannot prove scientifically that atheists are headed for hell, although the majority has pretty strong feelings on the subject, does not entitle the majority to legislate its prejudices. Why we should now depart from that rule, which insists that majoritarianism be tempered by minority rights, is not made clear to me.

The Supreme Court on obscenity

The recent decision by the Arizona Supreme Court upholding the state's obscenity statute represents a necessary attempt to come to terms with reality.

The Court declared that there is indeed such a thing as hard - core pornography and that "we find it objectionable and illogical to hold . . . that hard - core pornography can be made publishable by inter-spacing it with items of alleged redeeming social value."

The unanimous opinion, written by Justice James Cameron, agreed with a Maricopa County Superior Court ruling that "I Am Curious (Yellow)" is obscene.

The thicket of legal and moral questions surrounding the subject of obscenity is formidable and complex. However, this is no excuse to regard the subject as incapable of definition.

Doubtless, some people would advocate a stamp of pornography being placed on practically any artistic work.

But these censorious sorts are far fewer today than the muddled but vocal legalists who claim there is no possible way to define hard - core pornography.

The Arizona Supreme Court, agreeing with a definition formulated by the New York Supreme Court, held that hard - core pornography "focuses predominantly upon what is sexually morbid, grossly perverse, and bizarre, without any artistic or scientific purpose or justification.

" . . . It is to be differentiated from the bawdy and the ribald . . . depicting dirt for dirt's sake . . . the blow to sense, not merely to sensibility," in the words of the New York Court.

This trenchant insight, we believe, should be of considerable assistance to prosecutors who have contended that obscenity guidelines have been unsatisfactory.

While pornography may be difficult to define, the State Supreme Court, in dealing with the issue, has not allowed itself to be paralyzed with the indecisiveness that argues there are no parameters to the obscene.

Top page, from *The Progressive*, September 1970.
Above, from *The Arizona Republic*, October 24, 1971.

Ask Them Yourself

Want to ask a famous person a question? Send the question on a postcard, to "Ask," Family Weekly, 641 Lexington Ave., New York, N.Y. 10022 We'll pay $5 for published questions. Sorry, we can't answer others

FOR GLORIA STEINEM,
journalist, women's activist

How do you feel about pornography? Don't you feel the smut peddlers degrade women by using them to make money?—Mary R. Burns, Fort Worth, Texas

● Yes, most pornography does degrade women because most of it is written from the traditional male viewpoint that women are objects to be used, and therefore humiliated, by men.

But I don't object to pornography as it is usually defined. There is nothing wrong with writing about sexual pleasure.

The problem is that very little sexual writing depicts women as autonomous human beings, with dignity and sexual rights of their own.

Perhaps, what I think of as "pornography" extends beyond glorifying sado-masochism in sex. It is *any kind of propaganda that urges finding personal pleasure in the physical pain or humiliation of another. That kind of "pornography" includes the glorification of war or any other violence against individuals.*

To me, for instance, both Joseph Alsop and the Marquis de Sade are pornographic writers. It's just that the Marquis had more imagination.

Says Pornography Incites To Sexual Crimes

In a recent article in **The Los Angeles Times,** Judge Macklin Fleming, California Court of Appeal, says it is the experience of most judges, chiefs of police and prosecutors that sexual crimes triggered by pornography are not rare.

Judge Fleming gave as an example a case where a man, excited by pornographic material, sought out a sexual victim and committed murder. In sustaining the murder conviction, the California Supreme Court said he had clearly set out to commit rape and that "he admitted that he became sexually aroused after viewing photographs of nude women in a magazine. . . ."

Judge Fleming wrote, "In the experience of must judges, prosecutors, and chiefs of police, such crimes are by no means rare, and at any given time society contains some sexually unstable persons who may be triggered to violence by exposure to sexually suggestive materials.

"I think any discussion of obscenity and pornography which ignores this connection is bound to be unpersuasive to the general public."

He went on to say, "The advertising effect of obscenity and pornography, that is, the power of explicit sexual materials to suggest and influence the conduct of stable persons, is more difficult to evaluate than the influence of such materials on unstable personalities, but if we start from the premise that society wishes to discourage and inhibit certain types of conduct (forcible rape, child molestation, incest, sodomy, bestiality, etc.), then a strong case can be made for the discouragement of materials which explicitly depict such acts or suggest the desirability of their performance."

*Hold on, you anti-smut crusaders. I know you have lots of "evidence" that persons arrested for sex crimes have had sexual materials in their possession. But the relevant statistic is not how many offenders read dirty books (no one really knows how many do), but whether people who read such books are more likely to commit crimes than people who do not. Before the obscenity commission was established, neither you nor anyone else had ever done extensive research on the subject. The commission tried, and one study done for it showed that adult sex offenders and "deviates" actually had *less* exposure to sexual materials during adolescence than a carefully matched control group. (Does that mean that we should require that obscenity be read?) But even if sex offenders *did* see more obscenity than the rest of us, that would only show a correlation, not a cause-and-effect relationship. It would be quite plausible that people who are perpetually inclined to sex crimes are, for the same reason, also excessively inclined to sexual materials. (Some people think that sexual materials often provide a harmless release for such persons.) Of course, sexual material may, now and then, trigger an act of violence (although no one, to my knowledge, has ever found such a case). But so may detective stories; *The Godfather*, the Bible, and who knows what else. We don't ban these things because a clear and present danger means a high degree of probability of harm, not a one-in-a-million possibility. If a freak possibility of harm from a book were enough, none of us would be able to read anything.

Top, courtesy of *Family Weekly,* September 19, 1971.
Above, from *The Wanderer*, February 18, 1971.

Above, excerpted from a footnote in "The Obscenity Muddle" by Paul Bender, In *Harper's Magazine*, February 1973.

SECTION 6

Gun Control

All of the arguments contained in this section are concerned with the subject of prohibition—not of alcoholic beverages, but of handguns or guns in general. The ethical questions arise at several different levels in any discussion of any kind of prohibition. One question is whether or not a particular type of act is right; in this case it is a question of whether or not it is right to own, carry, and/or in certain situations to actually use a handgun or other type of gun. But the ultimate ethical questions revolve around the moral rightness or wrongness of prohibiting under law, with the threat of arrest and punishment for failure to comply, one or more of these acts. There are many acts which many of us would agree are immoral, but which we would not want to see made illegal for one reason or another. And the question of gun control is not one for which there is anything approaching a consensus as to its rightness or wrongness, which raises the additional question of using the law to force the ethical beliefs of one segment of the population on the other segments. It should be noted in this regard that, insofar as any legal system exists at all, the *lack* of legal sanctions against gun ownership, possession, or use can be perceived as a use of the law (that is, of the legal system) against those who are opposed to guns.

The obvious analogy in any discussion of any kind of prohibition is of course the American experience with the prohibition of alcoholic beverages in the 1920s, a "grand experiment" whose failure is cited by many opponents of gun prohibition as proof that even if enacted, laws against gun ownership and possession cannot be enforced. But, as with all analogies and all inductive arguments, there is always a certain degree of uncertainty inherent in the very form of argument itself, and in this particular case there is a great deal of debate about the conceptual questions of the similarity of the two cases being compared (alcohol and guns), and ultimately of the basic prediction concerning the enforcibility of gun-control laws. However, there are many other analogies which can be and have been drawn in the discussion of this issue, and it is important to recognize that a preoccupation with this single analogy could lead to a failure to adequately consider a number of other relevant factors which are brought out in the examples in this section. For example, there is a radical difference in the very perception of the nature of handguns, so that while some people perceive them as being essentially a means for protecting one's life and property, other people perceive guns as being primarily a great threat to their lives and property. It is differences in perceptions such as this that are critical to the resolution of disagreements concerning gun-control legislation. Thus it might even be profitable to look for some parallels between this topic and the question of the legalization of abortion, where there are radical differences in perceptions of the essential nature of the fetus, ranging from perceiving it as a complete human being to seeing only a mere organic growth in the body of a woman.

As in any question concerning prohibition of some act, it is difficult to formulate it as a clear-cut ethical question. We can easily identify the ethical question in terms of one individual's act in a particular situation—that is, whether it was right or wrong for a specific person to use a gun in a certain situation—but what is the decision being made by what person when we talk in terms of prohibiting a general practice such as the ownership of handguns? This question provides the basis for a quite difficult exercise.

EXERCISES

1. Examine each of the arguments in this section to determine which ones if any are concerned with genuine ethical decisions and which ones are concerned with general ethical rules or principles. Is a conclusion such as "Owning a handgun should be made illegal" directly concerned with a concrete moral decision? Whose decision is it? What are the alternative courses of action?
2. Construct a list of the analogies used in the arguments in this section on both sides of the gun-control issue. Does any one kind of analogy seem to provide more support for one side of the debate than the other, or can each analogy be interpreted as supportive of both sides of the debate? Construct a list of additional analogies which might be useful in dealing with this topic.
3. Compare the arguments in this section with those in Section 2 concerning the legalization of various drugs (which have been prohibited) and the arguments in Section 8 concerning abortion (which was only recently made legal by a Supreme Court ruling). How could one remain logically consistent while arguing for the legalization of one of these practices and the prohibition of another? Is there any real difference between arguing against the prohibition of one act (if it is presently legal) and for the legalization of the same act (if it is already illegal)?

Food for thought: smoking and gun bans

Zealous advocates of legislation to ban handguns might give some thought to the ban on smoking in MBTA rapid transit trains.

Nonsmokers comply. Smokers who habitually obey regulations, from fear or because they prefer the values of an orderly society, also comply. Others smoke. The ban is, in fact, unenforced and unenforceable.

Now if society chose to put a policeman in every car of every train, the problem might be abated, at great cost and not without considerable unpleasantness. Society chooses not to, and we manage, somehow, to get along.

To put a policeman in every home, apartment and place of business to maintain continuous surveillance of such places might make a handgun ban enforceable. It is impossible to say, for sure. It is clear, however, that short of such drastic action a handgun ban would largely serve the interests of its promoters. Americans are just not that law abiding a people.

People who hate guns generally don't have them. Law-abiding gun owners would turn in their weapons. Everybody else would hide them. And once again the state would be making a fool of itself, authority would be flouted, and lawlessness would quite possibly increase.

Advocates of weapons bans prefer not to deal with the conflict of constitutional rights involved here. Searches and seizures in private homes certainly would be conducted by any competent agency to enforce the new law. Do we want to surrender our protection against such state intrusion for the possibly illusory advantages of questionable statutory protection against getting shot at?

Perhaps a better means of obtaining such protection might be a mandatory jail sentence — say 90 days — for any person convicted of carrying, on person or in vehicle, a concealed weapon—gun, knife, switchblade, sling-shot, etc.

One of the points the handgun ban advocates have failed to deal with satisfactorily is the presence on the Massachusetts statute books of very stiff laws, presumably reflecting legislative intention, against unauthorized possession of concealed weapons.

Maximum penalty, in fact, is 2½ to 5 years in State Prison for mere possession. Mimimum can be a suspended $50 fine. Judges have wide discretion in imposing sentences, and, since in most cases gun carrying is a charge in a prosecution involving a crime like robbery or assault and battery, the weapons possession becomes a subsidiary aspect of the case.

Under a recent US Supreme Court decision, police have authority to search suspects if they have reasonable cause to believe a crime has been committed or is about to be committed. A law requiring the jailing of persons found to be carrying concealed weapons would, I think, have public support.

DAVID B. WILSON

It also might be a good idea to cancel all gun permits in force and to require the holders to reapply. The police, in their own interest, ought happily to shoulder this burden. A deadline might be set after which all licenses now in force would be voided.

The argument is advanced that guns cause accidental deaths and woundings in private homes. This is, of course, true.

So also do stairways, defective flooring, the edges of carpeting, power tools, lawn mowers, gas stoves, axes, heating plants and medicine cabinets. Do you want some civil servant inspecting yours?

It seems to me that persons who wish to assume the risk of having guns in their homes ought to be permitted to do so. Else, why not ban fast cars, skiing, swimming, ocean sailing and other activities which produce a certain amount of injury and death every year? Is there any reason to believe that a government that has failed in so much else can really succeed in weapons control?

David Wilson is a Globe columnist.

Above, courtesy of *The Boston Globe* (February 19, 1974). Below, copyright 1975 by Herblock in *The Washington Post* (May 25, 1975).

"Fair enough—let's give them a cut out of what we take tonight"

PISTOL REGULATION

Its Principles and History
(Selected Extracts)

By

KARL T. FREDERICK, A. M.; LL. B.
(1881-1963)

To sum up: laws which attempt to disarm criminals by making it impossible for them to procure pistols or ammunition are inevitably bound to fail. Instead of accomplishing the desirable object of disarming the crook, they can accomplish little in that direction. Such laws, however, will disarm the law-abiding citizen and tend to make him helpless against the raids of the criminal. The legitimate uses of the pistol vastly outnumber its illegitimate uses in the approximate proportion of 98 to 2. Laws which seek to abolish pistols, consequently, are not only impractical, unworkable, and unenforcible but are, in addition, harmful to society because they place the honest man at a distinct disadvantage in the face of crime. They inflict injury upon the honest part of society, without interfering to any appreciable extent with the dishonest and criminal element of society. Their result is exactly the opposite of that which is intended.

Self-Evident Principles

In this study we should bear in mind certain principles which appear to be axiomatic and which we may state as follows:

1. A law which for any reason is incapable of accomplishing its object with reasonable success is harmful and undesirable.

2. A criminal statute which is intended to affect any considerable number of persons and which is not voluntarily obeyed by the great majority of that group is certain to fail. Laws depend chiefly for their effectiveness upon voluntary acquiescence.

3. Laws relating to pistols have but one legitimate general purpose, namely, to hinder or prevent the use of pistols in crimes of violence. (The legitimate and desirable uses of pistols have already been enumerated. They outnumber the improper uses in the approximate ratio of 98 to 2.)

4. A pistol law which is incapable of preventing the frequent use of pistols in crime, but which tends to prevent their use for self-defense or other desirable purposes, will inevitably defeat its own object. It will increase crime by decreasing the means for resisting crime.

The foregoing principles seem to be almost self-evident. But it is apparent that they are not appreciated, or that they are often overlooked. In the end, however, they cannot be ignored. Like the laws of nature they are almost inevitable.

Let Everybody Carry a Gun

By Morton C. Paulson

IN BALTIMORE, where flying lead seems to be as abundant as crab houses and marble steps, Councilman Robert L. Douglass fears for the safety of one and all. He is particularly distressed over the recent murder of a mother before the eyes of her 10-year-old son, and is urging all Baltimoreans to press Congress for stringent controls over firearms use.

If action isn't forthcoming, he asserts, "we ought to do the next best thing. We ought to legalize them [guns] so that everybody can carry them."

Since the nation's firearms policy is dictated by the National Rifle Association (NRA) rather than Congress, the outlook for reforms is less than salubrious. Thus, we are left with Douglass' one-man, one-gun alternative.

The idea of every citizen packing a rod, under the coat or on the hip, Dodge City style, may be unthinkable to some, but the proposition ought not be dismissed out of hand. A lot of people would benefit. The handgun business would boom. Lead mines would prosper, along with target ranges, powder makers, morticians, and the NRA. Unemployment would fall as factories from coast to coast turned to volume production of bulletproof vests and armor-plated cars.

Above, from an editorial by Morton C. Paulson in *The National Observer*, January 18, 1975

The clogging of traffic courts would diminish; many a fender-bender dispute would be settled right on the spot. Children could be expected to spend less time watching X-rated movies and more learning the manly art of the fast draw.

Noise pollution would increase, but population control would be significantly improved.

Finally, street crime might diminish as merchants and pedestrians fought back against gun-wielding thugs—unless, of course, the latter opted for heavier weapons. But that imbalance could be rectified too. Come to think of it, it doesn't seem fair that while machine guns are outlawed, only outlaws have machine guns.

WHY GUN PROHIBITION WON'T WORK

Gun owners are indebted to the U.S. Customs Service, a branch of the Treasury Department, for a clear if unintentional insight into how impossible it would be to banish guns from the U.S. as some anti-gun fanatics demand.

Customs, in a press release, reported a 260% increase in known cases involving illegal attempts to *export* weapons and munitions, not all of them firearms, from the country in fiscal 1974 over 1973.

Just as what goes up must come down, what can be exported illegally through our approximately 90,000 miles of continental and overseas land and sea borders presumably can be imported the same way. We are talking now of firearms, which certain idealists and others would eliminate just as some people attempted to eliminate alcoholic beverages half a century ago.

There can be little doubt that the 15,000 Customs Service employees, hard-working and conscientious though they may be, cannot begin to stop the flow of illicit firearms from this country to troubled parts of the world where underground forces are willing to pay fancy prices for guns. It was always thus. And so it will be here in reverse if the fanatics who want a Federal law to end private firearms ownership ever succeed.

Those in this country who disobey the laws and are willing to pay a high cash price will always be able to get guns. In sad and solemn fact, money appears to be able to buy anything, anytime, anywhere.

Trying to close some 90,000 miles of border to disarm 220,000,000 people obviously never will work.

So why prate about prohibiting guns?

In the urgent quest for crime control, the anti-gun element has come up with the wrong answer, firearms confiscation, but lacks the common sense to see it.

The real problem is exactly what it always was —law-breaking.

The only solution is the one which consistently used to work so well—a court system which serves justice instead of sometimes making an empty mockery of it. ∎

Above, from *The American Rifleman*, December, 1974.

Words Of Wisdom On Gun Laws

THE Governor of a great State and a Supreme Court Justice of another great State have, in public utterances, given the United States able guidance on firearms legislation and its effect. What they said, one in an annual message to the legislature and the other in a court decision, may aptly point the way to more practical, realistic thinking on gun laws—a kind of thinking that is much needed now.

First, take the annual message of Governor John Connally, of Texas, a man tragically close to one of the most shocking misuses of firearms of all time. From a proximity to stark realism that few other public spokesmen can approach, Governor Connally said this:

"I recognize that there is a great hue and cry in some areas of our country today for a gun registration law. I am not convinced that this is the answer to our problems for two principal reasons: (1) the criminal element could still obtain firearms illegally, and (2) many of our most dastardly and shocking crimes have been committed by individuals who would have encountered no difficulty in obtaining and registering firearms under even the most strict gun registration law recommended.

"I believe that we should hit hard at the unlawful use of firearms and concealed weapons rather than at the right of ownership."

As for firearms legislation in general, no one has a greater stake in America nor a deeper concern for national welfare than the 800,000 members of the National Rifle Association.

Citizens in the fullest sense of the word, a high percentage of NRA members have risked their lives for our country in past wars or stand ready in the full vigor of their youth to serve "as needed" in the near future. Many are now in Viet Nam, or in the National Guard or law enforcement agencies protecting Americans at home.

Neither citizens such as these nor the NRA, their organization, would put personal pastime with firearms ahead of the national welfare. The record in that respect is crystal clear. Many of the truly effective firearms regulations in this country, including 2 Federal statutes, were passed with NRA support and counsel. The NRA always has been and always will be ready to do what is best for America. It is first of all a patriotic organization of good conscience.

Therefore it must in good conscience recognize the sound advice of Governor Connally that "we should hit hard at the unlawful use of firearms"—something NRA constantly advocates—rather than experiment with gun laws that might disarm law-abiding citizens in the midst of a crime wave.

Nor can the NRA in good conscience forget that a statute like the Sullivan Law, or its 1966 counterpart in New Jersey, can give rise to a police ruling which, as Mr. Justice Aurelio so well stated, "is not in accordance with the American way of life."

(Permission is granted to reprint this editorial.
THE AMERICAN RIFLEMAN, *Washington, D. C., March 1967)*

Gun Deaths and Gun Laws

By Barbara J. Katz

I CAUGHT the news on a late-afternoon broadcast and felt sickened the rest of the day: A Miami couple who had fulfilled a demand to withdraw $50,000 from their bank account had been coldly, senselessly murdered by their alleged captor in a burst of submachine-gun fire as he spotted police tailing them.

How needless, I kept saying to myself. Why did he have to kill them? He must have been crazy!

And then I began recalling other recent bizarre gun deaths: the murder of Mrs. Martin Luther King, Sr., as she sat playing the organ in church, the shooting of a National Rifle Association lobbyist in an apparent case of mistaken identity, the self-slaying of a child playing "Russian roulette" with his sister, the killing of a youth by his father, who thought he was firing at a prowler. Were all these persons crazy? Are all the people involved in the hundreds of other gun deaths we hear about every year stark-raving mad?

No, it's not the murderers and the other killers who are crazy, I've decided. It's our society that's insane—for permitting virtually anyone to own a gun, with virtually no requirements for licensing, registration, or proper use and safekeeping. I, for one, am sick of reading about the latest grisly murder or the latest bizarre accidental gun death, and other people tell me the same thing.

But we might as well face one basic fact: Until we decide to enact meaningful gun control, and until we put sufficient pressure on our public officials to fulfill that resolve, the killing is going to continue. We'll continue clucking over the distressing news and wondering how anyone could do such a terrible thing—and the answer lies with ourselves.

Above, from an editorial by Barbara J. Katz in *The National Observer*, August 17, 1974. Below, copyright 1974, Universal Press Syndicate.

GARRY WILLS
Real Wyatt Earp Took Fewer Risks

There are a number of sheepish people who feel that a handgun in their drawer or closet somehow makes them more manly. Their arguments are rather pathetic. They feel that the police force is insufficient protection for them—and so make the lives of policemen more dangerous, their work more difficult, by holding out the constant menace that every man will become his own policeman in some Armageddon encouraged by their very belief in it.

The weird thing is that some policemen are gun addicts, as well—though the peril they live with is encouraged by the ready access to cheap guns, the large permanent floating stock being pushed out by sporting firms and mail order ads.

Movies and TV fantasy feed the old myth that "we" brought law and order to the old wild West with guns wielded by the good guys in self-defense against the bad guys. We neglect, too often, the bad guys who were selling guns to both sides to begin with—"cowboys" and Indians, settlers and herdsmen. The power of this myth to pervert reality is spectacularly exemplified in the story of Wyatt Earp.

Wyatt Earp "cleaned up" Dodge City, among other places—but not the way movie and TV screens have depicted that process. There were no high noon shootouts, barrooms full of gun smoke, or hasty checked motions to "draw" inhibited only by Wyatt's lightning speed.

What was there, then? A room for confiscated weapons, that's what. Wyatt Earp cleaned up Dodge City by making it illegal to wear a gun in the town. By gun control. Arrest was automatic, and Earp's three deputies were encouraged to be zealous by a supplement to their salaries—$2.50 for every arrest made. And one more thing: in Earp's own words, "Dead ones wouldn't count...Mayor Hoover had hired me to cut down the killings in Dodge, not to increase them." Earp had to kill one man in all his time at Dodge City, famed for its toughness.

And it was tough. But Earp's method tamed it. For a while, arrests on this charge ran about 400 per month (good pay for Earp himself and the deputies). But the lawmen worked themselves out of a job—within two years he had these arrests down to a slim 29 for the entire twelve-month.

So he moved on to clean up other towns. Sucessfully. And died in his bed at age 81. His method worked. All the "good" citizens did not fight it on the grounds that they were being disarmed, but crooks would not keep the law. Those who didn't were arrested.

There is at least one handgun for every eight persons in America—a constant temptation to the angered husband, drunk fighter, young bandit, curious child. Those determined to get a gun may be able to get it despite more stringent controls than we have. But crimes of passion or convenience would not have guns practically pushed into the hands of their perpetrators.

Yet when an eminent psychiatrist, Dr. Kent Robinson of Baltimore, first pointed out the significance of Earp's true history for the question of gun control, he got the usual spate of irrational letters from gun cultists.

If we stop listening to the swaggerers, one truth emerges—that the Wyatt Earp of history was more "manly" than the Wyatt Earp of legend, the mythical stalker of his mirror-selves with guns slung low. Civilization is not kid stuff. But gun games are—very deadly and dangerous kid stuff.

The City as OK Corral

IF, BY SOME unfortunate chance, you had been in the 3100 block of M Street NW at about 5 p.m. on Thursday afternoon, you could have seen some real action, some gunplay that might have reminded you of a western movie. It might also have helped illustrate why the proliferation of handguns in a modern society is a menace to us all.

As the police tell the story, a shopkeeper became suspicious of one of his customers. When the man ran onto the street, according to the police, the shopkeeper "picked up a white-handled revolver" and began chasing the customer down M Street. A plainclothes police officer happened along at about that time, his attention drawn to the spectacle of a man with a gun running in the streets. The shopkeeper turned, gun in hand, toward the police officer, and the policeman shot him. "Why did you shoot me?" the shop owner asked the officer, as he lay wounded on the sidewalk. "I didn't know you were officers. Why did you shoot me?"

Above, © *The Washington Post* (January 18, 1975).

The rights and wrongs of the actual shooting that took place will of course have to be sorted out by police officials, and possibly even by the courts. Our point concerns the proliferation of handguns and the danger they frequently pose to those persons who own them for their "protection." The sorry statistics show that three quarters of the people wounded by handguns owned by private citizens are friends, relatives or acquaintances of the owner. The notion that a privately-owned handgun protects is one of the most dangerous and enduring myths of our society. And the sad incident on M Street just provides one more example.

We think it is a timely example because this year Congress will again have an opportunity to enact comprehensive gun control legislation. This is a Congress that exudes confidence in its ability to do the people's business, and gun control should be prominent on its agenda. As former District Police Chief Jerry V. Wilson pointed out on these pages recently, every poll since 1938 has shown that a majority of the American people favor some sort of gun control. The problem has been a strident and well organized lobby, one that is also extremely well-financed. It has been able to block legislation because it can put pressure on those legislators who defy it—just because it is so well financed. Yet, a quarter of a million Americans are harmed each year in some way because handguns exist in such large numbers.

The answer in our view is readily apparent. We need a comprehensive law that licenses the use of handguns by those persons who can demonstrate a vital need for them; and the ordinary shopkeeper would hardly qualify unless he could show that vital need. All other handgun ownership by individuals would be illegal. People who use handguns for target practice or other sporting purposes would be required to deposit them with the local police and check them out when they planned to go target shooting. Collectors of antique guns could keep and display them as long as their guns were deactivated by removal of the firing pin. Those guns in existence would be purchased from their owners by the government in a manner similar to that once employed in Baltimore and suggested for the District.

Guns in a city are no joke, as the M Street shopkeeper discovered, and as thousands of other Americans find out—too late. The shopkeeper was fortunate in that he was not badly wounded. But during the summer, a youngster in Northern Virginia was killed by another teen-ager with a hefty .45 automatic after a violent dispute. The same fate awaited a woman executive at the hands of another executive who had just been fired. Whoever gets pleasure from the ownership of handguns must come to recognize that the current state of affairs is too high a price for the rest of us to pay.

Left, courtesy of The National Council to Control Handguns.

Murder in the Making

By W. A. Swallow

Giving a boy a gun is much like striking a match over an open gasoline tank. No mishap may occur, but the chances are all in favor of a big explosion. In the case of the gasoline one explosion will occur and it will be all over. The boy with the gun may cause a number of fatal accidents; he may grow up with the love of destruction instilled in his mind. Which, then, has the more lasting and devastating effect?

The only way to fight this evil is to dig right down to the source and extract the roots, not forgetting the branches on the way. Is it wise to create, in the minds of children of formative years a desire for warlike toys and instruments? Many people argue that a five-year-old with a toy gun cannot possibly do any harm, nor will he in later years have an overwhelming desire to play with real guns. In many cases this is no doubt true. I can remember, as a child owning an air rifle, but at the same time my parents cautioned me that I must never shoot it at anything alive or in any place where there might be the remotest possibility of doing any harm. I was one of the lucky ones — I heeded these warnings. Nothing happened to spoil my taste for weapons, but even at that it was the first and only gun I ever owned.

However, to get back to the subject, I would have been just as well off without the gun with the probabilities all in favor of being *much* better off. Let us give our children something better to do and think about than handling toy guns or any manner of lethal weapons.

We have fought several wars to end war. We thought by various measures, the League of Nations, the United Nations, general disarmament, treaties and whatnot that any future wars were most improbable. Needless to say, these measures fell down one by one and like Humpty-Dumpty, defied "all the King's horses and all the King's men" to put them back in workable condition. Both force and compromise have proved inadequate. The only thing left seems to be education and understanding. After all, the only reason we look down on other nations is because, in some ways, we fail to understand their national customs and manner of living.

From *Reverence for Life*, published by the New England Anti-Vivisection Society.

Education, then, seems to be our last resort. We may not live to see the day when nations are living in accord with each other, but we surely may plan toward that end and insure lasting peace for our children. Proper training in schools and homes will eradicate the thought of war; engender a better understanding of other countries. We must have something positive to give the youngsters. Unfortunately, it has always been true that children have liked best the games where wooden or tin soldiers were involved or, a little later, the actual playing at war with other children.

To perpetuate this ideal, toy manufacturers have put on the market toy guns, toy pistols, toy machine guns, cannon, tanks, airplanes, submarines, destroyers — everything possible that youth might want for its amusement. The first step toward peace-education is the abolition of such toys. That we are on the right road is evidenced by the mounting production of such peaceful toys as electric trains and various types of games. It seems that the yearning of all Americans for an improved standard of living is reflected in toys, reproducing the finest types of American housing, transportations, furniture, art and home making. These toys are keyed in with the desire of American parents to maintain peace. Indeed, it is a step in the right direction.

There is yet another phase of the gun peril, for one of the most popular games of youngsters is still the "cops and robbers" type. There are many factors which determine the source of these games — sensational news stories, moving pictures, radio and television are the principle ones which incite the desire to play at war or gangsters. Those are the roots at which we must strike. It is time our children learn not to make heroes of racketeers and gangsters. If a better example is set them they will respond.

It is but a short step from toy guns to real ones. Rifles, shot guns, even bows and arrows in the hands of minors can and do lead, not only to tragedy in hunting accidents but also inflict untold suffering on such animal targets as may come their way.

Let us all, then, do everything in our power to keep guns, even though they may be only toys, out of the hands of our children.

SECTION 7

Animals and Vegetables

The arguments in this section fall the closest of any in this book to the issue mentioned in the Introduction concerning what is and what is not a *moral* argument. There are indeed some people who would assert that none of the arguments in this section are ethical arguments at all insofar as they do not involve human decisions which have a direct impact on the welfare of other human beings. It is certainly true that the arguments in this section deal primarily with human decisions which directly effect only nonhuman living things. But it is also important to recognize that some people consider this to be irrelevant to the question of whether these are ethical issues insofar as their definition of ethics involves the concept of human decisions which affect the well-being of *any and every* living thing. Thus we are confronted with another level of ethical argument—in addition to those in the other sections which focus on the determination of the rightness and wrongness of various acts and those which focus on the question of making certain acts illegal—namely arguments concerning what in fact comprises the realm of ethical argumentation.

Beginning with the assumption that most people would agree that it is clearly morally wrong to kill another adult human being under most conditions (and possibly even under any condition), it is possible to move across the spectrum of life-forms to terminally ill, comatose adult humans and severely retarded and deformed human infants to human fetuses to dogs and other pets to ants and rats and then to living plants in an attempt to find a point where one can say that it is morally right (or no moral issue at all is involved) to terminate the life of an individual person, animal, or plant. The arguments in this section provide clear evidence that different persons locate that line at radically different points on the spectrum.

It must be pointed out that the arguments in this section are not all of the "all or none" type; some of them are quite clearly focussed on the question of trade-offs. For example, it is not necessary to assume that humans have no moral obligation towards animals in order to justify the killing and eating of animals by humans. Some people would argue that the killing and eating of nonhuman animals is necessary for the very survival of some humans, and that while it would be wrong otherwise to kill animals it is justifiable in order to save human lives. In effect, this argument asserts that when confronted with the choice between killing a nonhuman and allowing a human to die of starvation, it is right to kill the animal. But there are some interesting scientific questions that can be raised here regarding the claim that it is a fact of nutrition that some persons would die if some animals were not slaughtered. It is even asserted as a fact by some persons that the use of grains for the raising of animals bred expressly for the purpose of providing meat for human consumption involves an inefficient use of the grain, which in turn ultimately leads to the starvation of some poor people in other countries who would have lived if they had been given this grain instead. In this kind of argument, the question of the basic treatment of the animal is almost irrelevant and the main consideration is the feeding of one group of people at the expense of others. And this moves into the set of issues raised in the arguments in the section on international relations.

EXERCISES

1. Examine the arguments in this section to determine for which the basic issue is that of taking the life of a nonhuman living thing and for which the basic issue is the causing of unnecessary pain and suffering.
2. Examine the ways in which the arguments in this section have relevance to the questions of international relations discussed in Section 13.
3. Discuss whether there are any significant differences between the position that moral principles do not apply to the killing of nonhumans and the position that moral rules apply but these rules permit the killing of any nonhuman at any time.

SOUNDING BOARD

One Person's Opinion on a Several-Sided Subject

Let's stop keeping pets

JOHN MAHONEY

Pets are lovable, frequently delightful. The dog and the cat, the most favored of pets, are beautiful, intelligent animals. To assume the care for them can help bring out the humanity in our children and even in us. A dog or a cat can teach us a lot about human nature; they are a lot more like us than some might think. More than one owner of a dog has said that the animal under-stands everything he says to it. So a mother and father who have ever cared for pets are likely to be more patient and understanding with their children as well, and especially to avoid making negative, depreciative remarks in the presence of a child, no matter how young.

It is touching to see how a cat or dog—especially a dog—attaches itself to a family and wants to share in all its goings and comings. If certain animal psycholo-gists are right, a dog adopts his family in a most literal way—taking it for granted that the family is the pack of dogs he belongs to.

It is sometimes said that the cat, aloof and reserved except when making some demand of us, "takes all and gives nothing." But is that really true? A cat can teach us a valuable lesson about how to be contented, how to be serene and at ease, how to sit and contemplate. Whereas a dog's overwhelming affection and constant pleas for attention become, sometimes, almost a bit too much. Nevertheless it is the dog who can teach us les-sons of loyalty, gratitude, and devotion that no cat ever knew.

So there's plenty to be said in favor of keeping pets. But with all that in mind, I still say let's stop keeping pets. Not that a family should *exterminate* its pets. Very few could bring themselves to do that. To be practical, I am suggesting that if we do not now have a pet we should not acquire one; second, that if we now have a pet, we let it be our last one. I could never say that pets are bad. I am saying, let's give up this good thing—the ownership of a pet—in favor of a more imperative good.

The purchase, the licensing, the inoculations and health care, the feeding and housing and training of a pet—and I chiefly mean the larger, longer-lived pets—cost time and money. Depending on the animal's size and activity, it's special tastes and needs, and the standard of living we establish for it, the care of a pet can cost from a dollar a week to a dollar or more a day. I would not for a moment deny it is worth that.

Reprinted with permission from *U.S. Cath-olic*, 221 West Madison Street, Chicago, Illinois 60606.

But facts outside the walls of our cozy home keep breaking in on our awareness. Though we do not see the famine-stricken people of India and Africa and South America, we can never quite forget that they are there. Now and then their faces are shown in the news, or in the begging ads of mission and relief organizations. Probably we send a donation whenever we can.

But we do not, as a rule, feel a heavy personal responsi-bility for the afflicted and deprived for we are pretty thoroughly formed by the individualistic, competitive society which we live in—a society whose unwritten rule is, "I got mine, now let him get his." The first dime we ever made for raking grass or shoveling snow was ours to spend in any way we chose. No one thought of question-ing that. That attitude, formed before we had learned to think, usually prevails right through adulthood: "I made my money. I can spend it any way I like."

But more and more we are reading that the people of the "Third World" are resentful of us in the developed countries (with the United States far more developed than any of the others) for our grabbing up two-thirds of the world's wealth and living like kings while they scrounge all day for a yam and a bowl of rice—and die off at thirty-five or forty, provided they outlive the heavy scourge of infant mortality.

The money and the time we spend on pets is simply not our own to spend as we like in a time of widespread want and starvation. A missionary society advertises that for $33 a month they can give hospital care to a child suffering from *kwashiorkor*—the severe deficiency disease which is simply a starving for protein. Many a Boxer, Afghan, Irish Setter or Dalmatian requires at least that amount each month for his food and care. Doing without such a pet, and then *sending the money saved* to a creditable relief organization would mean saving a life—over the years, several human lives.

Children not suffering from such a grave disease could be fed with half that amount—not on a diet like ours, but on plain, basic, life-sustaining food such as unpol-ished rice, soy meal, powdered milk, and an occasional guava or mango. It is not unreasonable to believe that the amount of money we spend on the average pet dog could keep a child alive in a region of great poverty. To give what we would spend on a cat might not feed a child, but it would probably pay for his medical care or basic schooling. The point needs no laboring. That is all that need be said.

They're as much of concern to us as anyone.

The fate of the world's starving may seem very much outside the RSPCA's province.

The truth of the matter is quite the reverse.

Of course humanity must be fed.

And animals must be exploited in vast numbers if Man is to survive.

It's a fact that modern methods of intensive farming have done much to increase production.

Yet in facing up to a vital human right, we feel another is being denied.

The animals'.

As often as not, we make them into machines.

Piglets are frequently kept in total darkness.

Pigs can spend the whole of their productive lives confined in restrictive stalls.

Hens are crammed into battery systems.

Five-day old calves are kept in boxes for fourteen weeks, then taken out and slaughtered.

We believe there simply have to be alternatives.

Economically viable. So the hungry can be fed.

Yet humane.

It's a big job. And in our fight to help solve these problems, we need your support.

To help us find alternative methods of farming. Through our own contribution to research.

And to help us make more people aware. So we gain even more support.

Today tens of thousands of people will die in misery.

Today tens of thousands of animals will die in misery.

In overcoming one problem, we believe there's no reason for turning a blind eye to the other.

Hence this advertisement. But such advertisements are far from cheap.

Won't you help us by sending a donation?

Write to us here at the RSPCA, so we can continue to plead the animals' case.

In return we'll send you a leaflet detailing precisely what you can do to help animals.

Including those you wouldn't normally see.

RSPCA

Be human.
Show animals a little humanity. Too!

RSPCA (SE-S-1), 105 Jermyn Street, London SW1Y 6EG.

COMPASSION FOR ANIMALS

The beginning of ethical vegetarianism is the knowledge that other creatures feel, and that their feelings are very similar to ours. This knowledge encourages one to extend personal awareness to also encompass the sufferings of others. This is the essence of compassion—the feeling of the sufferings of others, and sympathizing with them, and doing all we can to change such sorry conditions.

Because we know in ourselves the feeling of pain and suffering, we refuse to be a party to inflicting such anguish upon others.

Because we can smell the urine-drenched straw in the livestock truck and see how the animals are packed in for transit (although they sometimes even fall and break their legs in the sudden stops and starts), we realize the grossly cruel conditions of servitude imposed by us upon these animals, and oppose that cruelty.

Because we know that mother cows love their young, and grieve when the calves are taken from them at birth to be fattened up for veal, we cannot in good conscience con-condone such practices. Indeed, a well-developed conscience dictates that we must stand in opposition to these brutal actions.

Ethical vegetarians oppose not only the killing but the whole assortment of cruelties, artificialities, debasements of humans and animals alike, that go with food-animal raising, shipping, and killing.

We recognize our moral obligation to actively work to correct such conditions, not by a dab of fresh straw here and there, but by doing away with the whole callous system of animal-killing for food.

This is done by refusing to create the demand which makes it profitable for a few, and by helping to educate other thoughtful people to the ethical and other benefits of a common-sense vegetarian régimen.

Left, from "Facts of Vegetarianism" published by the North American Vegetarian Society, Malaga, New Jersey 08328 (1975). Authors: Nellie Shriver, Dudley Giehl, Nat Altman, H. Jay Dinshah.
Right, letter to the editor of *The New York Times Magazine* by F. Brodie, December 12, 1974.

Letters

Cats and dogs eat too

While Maya Pines ("Meatless, Guiltless," Nov. 24) makes the obvious moral points with regard to eating meat in a world faced with unprecedented starvation, she only skirts an issue equally relevant which will have to be faced with the same moral poignancy. I refer to the tens of millions of dogs and cats in this country who consume three billion pounds of food yearly.

Humans can live healthful lives without meat; dogs and cats are carnivorous animals, they *must* have meat. Pet food has become this nation's largest single grocery item, with $2-billion in sales annually.

It seems almost certain that uncounted millions of people will, barring a miracle, starve to death in the near future. It also seems certain that while this is occurring, Americans will continue to feed millions of ecological sponges—the dogs and cats of this country—the meat they require.

Paradoxically, many of the "guiltless" vegetarians will feed the meat from herbivorous animals they didn't eat to other carnivorous animals. And millions of Americans will watch millions of other people die in living color while Morris the cat dines on chicken and Herman the dog gulps down chunks of beef.

FRANKLIN BRODIE
New York City

Dominion Challenged

To the Editor:

The National Observer is to be commended for its courageous publication of Peter Singer's "And Now It's Animal Lib." This review challenges the whole "dominion over the animals" interpretation of the Judeao-Christian philosophy.

How tragic that the Jew who is justifiably horrified by the treatment of his kin by Nazi Germany cannot see the cruelty involved in kosher slaughtering. And how ironic it is that the "loving Christian" who is encouraged to "feed the hungry," "care for the sick," "clothe the naked," etc. finds pleasure in "killing for fun and profit" by way of hunting, trapping, vivisection, fishing, etc.

If man is supposed to be made in the "image and likeness of God," shouldn't he realize that compassion and empathy cannot be limited to his own species, but should be extended to all living creatures, many of which cannot lobby for their own rights to "life, liberty, and the pursuit of happiness"? Perhaps the Judeao-Christian man would view the "animals were made only for man's use" doctrine from a different perspective if our planet were invaded by superhuman beings who regarded us as "animals."

MARSHA GRAVITZ

Fond du Lac, Wis.

Logical End

To the Editor:

As a marine biologist, I must take exception to the concept of treating animals as "equals." If this reasoning is followed to a logical end, we must not only treat all birds and animals as equals, but also all of the lower animals (snakes and lizards, fishes, insects, and spiders, and then even the single-celled protozoans, many of which are parasites).

Any taxonomist knows that all living organisms form a continuum. If it is wrong to poison squirrels or rats, then it would also be wrong to poison snails and ants. Likewise, if we find it wrong to kill snails and ants, then we must stop the wholesale murder of minute organisms when we chlorinate our drinking water. Are these small animals not entitled to equality simply because a microscope must be used to see them?

JOHN J. GEIBEL

Menlo Park, Calif.

Encouraging Inhumanity

I AM WRITING to protest an article in your women's pages, "Fur Conversions: Recycled Mink." Marji Kunz is a fine writer whose column is enjoyable and helpful, but I still must protest this particular piece.

She suggests having old coats made from the skins of animals made up into coats and jackets in today's styles. Thankfully, this is one way to avoid the needless killing of more animals. But with today's marvelous synthetics, no one else should have to use real fur certainly not for warmth as our ancestors had to do.

I feel that the wearing of the hide of any creature of God, whether it is domestically raised for slaughter or caught in traps which are, unfortunately, still legal in 48 of our "civilized" states— is grossly immoral. And it encourages more people to do so.

If every person who purchased a real fur or fur trimmed piece of clothing would take the time to contact their humane societies and find out the manner in which many of the animals died to obtain their skins, they would be too ashamed to wear the article.

LINDA SHAFFER

Mt. Clemens

Top left, letter to the editor of *The National Observer* by Marsha Gravitz, June 9, 1973.

Left, letter to the editor of *The National Observer* by John J. Giebel, June 9, 1973.

Above, reprinted with the permission of the *Detroit Free Press*, December 23, 1973.

Answers To Your Questions

(A page of brief but illuminating answers to some of the questions most often asked about vegetarianism.)

6) EXPERIMENTS INDICATE THAT PLANTS HAVE CONSCIOUSNESS; HOW DO VEGETARIANS FEEL ABOUT THIS?

Wonderful! Vegetarians have been battling for centuries against the cynical attitude that even the ANIMALS are unfeeling brutes; and vegetarian sages of India have taught plant-consciousness and the Universality of all Life, over the past thousands of years. So we are at last making progress in educating the public. Pioneering scientific experiments in this field were made half a century ago by a vegetarian, when Dr. Bose examined rudimentary consciousness in the plants, albeit a greatly different type from that in humans and animals. But we need no Crescograph or Polygraph to prove that ANIMALS are subject to the SAME feelings of pain and emotions as we are.

Still, vegetarians can easily live on those foods which do not require the killing, or even harming, of the plants. These would include ripe fruits & nuts, berries and melons, legumes, tomatoes, seeds, squashes and pumpkins, okras, cucumbers, and many other vegetables. Potatoes are dug from the ground after the plant has died. Most vegetables are annuals, harvested at or near the end of their natural life. But please bear in mind that animals must eat about ten times as much vegetable food to return to us one unit of food value as meat. Thus, even in terms of destruction of plant-life, we see a factor of 10 to 1. Obviously, the question of plant consciousness can only be a strong point FOR vegetarianism.

7) THERE IS SO MUCH CRUELTY TO PEOPLE; WHY DO YOU WASTE TIME ON ANIMALS?

Can we really separate cruelty to fellow man, to children, to animals, or to nature and the world? If we never learn compassion, pity, and mercy for the weak and defenseless, is it likely we will ever begin to treat our fellow man fairly?

ALL brutality and cruelty poisons and stifles the higher, finer nature in humanity; ALL kindness helps make a better world for all. Vegetarianism—and all it implies—is of the utmost importance and potential benefit for animal and human alike. Thus, there is no question of choosing between them.

From "Facts of Vegetarianism" published by the North American Vegetarian Society, Malaga, New Jersey 08328 (1975). Authors: Nellie Shriver, Dudley Giehl, Nat Altman, H. Jay Dinshah.

The Rights of Animals

By Brigid Brophy

If we are going to rear and kill animals for our food, I think we have a moral obligation to spare them pain and terror in both processes, simply because they are sentient. I can't *prove* they are sentient; but

---

"When factory farmers tell us that calves do not mind being tethered for life on slats . . . an echo should start in our historical consciousness."

---

then I have no proof *you* are. Even though you are articulate, whereas an animal can only scream or struggle, I have no assurance that your "It hurts" expresses anything like the intolerable sensations I experience in pain. I know, however, that when I visit my dentist and say "It hurts", I am grateful that he gives me the benefit of the doubt.

I don't myself believe that, even when we fulfil our minimum obligations not to cause pain, we have the right to kill animals. I know I would have no right to kill you, however painlessly, just because I liked your flavour, and I am not in a position to judge that your life is worth more to you than the animal's to it. If anything, you probably value yours less; unlike the animal, you are capable of acting on an impulse to suicide. Christian tradition would permit me to kill the animal but not you, on the grounds that you have, and it hasn't, an immortal soul. I am not a Christian and do not avail myself of this licence; but if I were, I should in elementary justice see the soul theory as all the more reason to let the animal live out the one mortal life it has.

From *The Sunday Times* (London), October 10, 1965.

Can You be Indifferent?

In January of 1970 the President of the United States promised the people "peace with nature." Yet, in the summer of 1970, men were sent forth to murder 60,000 sentient animals: 9,000 for Japan, 9,000 for Canada—and 42,000 ostensibly for the people of the United States.

As president of Friends of Animals, I, Alice Herrington, spent ten days on the Pribilof Islands, our Federal public territory, to observe and report on this massacre of seals. Hour after hour I watched helpless animals being driven inland a mile or more, until their lungs were bursting; watched the clubs being raised over and over as the seals were battered into insensibility. As my eyes watched, my mind recalled the litany of the bureaucrats, remembered their statements that this is mercy killing, done to save the seals from starvation and disease. And then I moved closer to the seals as they grouped together in terror. The men were killing only the healthy seals whose coats would gleam on fashion row. The seal with fish net imbedded in its fur was ignored after only one bash of the club—a bash which removed an eye. And I remembered these same bureaucrats' statement that only 15 out of every 100 seals born survives the first three years. And there they were, the 15 three-year-old seals nature wanted to survive, being crushed at that very moment by employees of the United States Government.

That individual man often engages his lust to kill is apparent. That our society, our government, condones murder for profit is abominable. And then the profit is only for the Fouke Fur Company which holds a monopoly contract with the government; the whole barbaric "program" is subsidized by the tax dollar of the American people.

If you are one who feels, one who recognizes that all life is bound together on this earth, won't you join and ask Congress to pass this law:

A. To permit the Aleut native on the Pribilofs to kill, for their own commercial profit, 18,000 seals per year; the sealskins—not the American dollars—to be delivered to Japan and Canada ...until 1975 when the current agreement to kill for those countries runs out.

B. To ban the import into the United States of all products, raw or finished, from marine mammals (seals, whales, walrus, polar bear, otters, etc.)

C. To direct the administration to initiate a truly international agreement to protect marine mammals.

As the prime consumer of the world's resources, we owe it to the world and the coming generations of all species not to abuse the world. Please join and write your representatives in the Congress today, asking them to sponsor this measure.

An advertisement in *The New York Times* courtesy of Humane Legislation, Inc.

Sixty years ago Congress passed a law to save the Alaska fur seal.

This year they're considering a law that could destroy it.

In 1911, a four-nation treaty was signed to save the Alaska fur seal from indiscriminate slaughter on the open sea, a method that had reduced the fur seal population to near extinction.

Alaska Fur Seals Increased 1,000%

As a result of the treaty, and with the careful guidance of the U.S. government, the Alaska fur seal population has grown from approximately 120,000 to 1½ million — an increase of over 1,000%.

In March, a Bill was introduced into Congress that would end the treaty, leave the Aleut natives, who are dependent on the harvests, jobless and with no practical alternative, and eventually return the Alaska fur seal to open sea killing — a method that is sure to complete the job it didn't sixty years ago.

What Is The Issue?

Why, you might ask, has such a Bill been proposed?

Because certain "conservation" organizations have succeeded in misleading many people into believing that what has been going on in the Pribilof Islands for the last sixty years is nothing but some kind of inhuman carnage.

Have all the knowledgeable conservationists and scientists involved in establishing and administering this fur seal program since 1911 been wrong?

Has it been wrong to have administered the fur seal program in such a way that the herd has grown from near extinction to 1½ million?

Has it been wrong that a four-nation treaty dependent on international cooperation has permitted this phenomenal growth?

Is it wrong to harvest animals surplus to the needs of the herd so that disease and starvation are minimized for the benefit of the great majority of the animals?

Is it wrong that man, through sound principles and programs, manages nature, to the benefit of man and nature?

Emotion Vs. Conservation

Because these organizations cannot attack the fur seal program on its record of successful wildlife management, they have resorted to innuendo and exploitation of emotions. How? By clouding the major issue of conservation with the issue of the harvesting method. Yes. The seals are clubbed. Because scientists have as yet found no other method that is more humane, quicker, or more efficient.

The $1,000 Misunderstanding

Which seals are taken? Mostly three- and four-year-old bachelor males. No baby seals are killed; no animals are ever skinned alive. And if anybody can produce an authentic photograph of a baby fur seal being killed on the Pribilof Islands as part of the annual U.S. commercial harvest, The Fouke Company will pay them $1,000.

Consider The Consequences

If this Bill is passed, the consequences will be disastrous.

The Aleuts, who have been dependent on the seal harvests for generations, will be without their livelihood and left with an alternative that is neither practical nor satisfactory to the Aleuts. Many others' jobs will be threatened, or eliminated. (Yes, the fur seal program is also a business — a business that supports a conservation program at no cost to the taxpayers. The United States receives a share, as do Japan and Canada. The state of Alaska gets 70% of the net proceeds from the Pribilof harvests, and the balance goes into a general treasury fund).

The greatest consequence, however, is for the seals. Most of their time is spent in international waters—and they can be preyed upon by any nation, using any method they care to use. Don't mislead yourself into believing others will practice good will if the treaty is ended. They won't. Many countries have commercial fishing industries — and the fewer seals around, the more fish.

Banning the importation of Alaska fur pelts into the U.S. will have little, or no, effect on world seal harvests. The majority of Alaska fur sealskins are sold to Europe, and they can just as easily buy from any of a number of other countries, or individuals, who would now be able to get into the act.

There is little doubt that the Alaska fur seal cannot survive a return to open sea sealing.

We Need Your Help

Think about it. And think about the long-range consequences of this Bill. Don't delude yourself into believing it's for a good cause, because its end is an evil one. And if it goes through, it's only the beginning. (We kill domestic animals and use their products in our daily lives—is that not also "immoral?")

If you're on our side, and the side of conservation and the Alaska fur seal, please write to your senators and representatives in Congress and protest the enactment of S.1315 and H.R.6554.

The Fouke Company, Route 1, Box 168, Greenville, S. C. 29611

An advertisement in *The New York Times*, courtesy of The Fouke Company.

Weep Not for the Lamb?

OH, PITY the poor, defenseless little baby seals! Block the heartless hunters from bludgeoning them brutally and mercilessly to death for mere profit and fashion! Stop the threat to still another irreplaceable species! Shouldn't we all shed tears for the poor baby seals?

I won't.

Not until it becomes more fashionable to bewail a far bloodier, far greater slaughter of the innocents than hardly anyone—not even the tenderest heart—speaks much of.

I speak of the lambs and calves who perish by the millions every year for you and me for our breakfast, lunch, and dinner.

I speak of the 500,000 sound, healthy adult animals—sheep, cattle, hogs—that suffer terror and death daily under the packing-house captive-bolt device that supposedly stuns, the electric prod that supposedly stupifies without burning. And there are the billions of chickens that die for you and for me every year by the implacable finger knife.

It would be nice to think that these animals and birds don't know what is happening. But their terrified squealing and bellowing in the slaughter pens engraves the memory.

And it would be nice, too, to think that their deaths are instantaneous and painless. But no one can be sure, despite Federal and state humane-slaughter laws, that the methods prescribed and in widespread use are in fact humane. Packers themselves acknowledge that the act of slaying meat animals is a problem that continues to defy resolution.

The fact is, almost all meat animals are stunned one way or another before they are killed. Baby seals are clubbed, as prescribed by law, because that's the most humane way anybody has so far devised—better than former practice, which included kicking, shooting, gaffing, and ripping open their bellies.

If clubbing seals is inhumane and should be stopped, so also should killing meat animals the way we do. And if no better way can be found, we should all embrace vegetarianism.

But it is safe to say that hardly any hogs, sheep, or cattle will be spared if our palates must suffer.

—JOE WESTERN

I believe I have omitted mentioning that in my first voyage from Boston to Philadelphia, being becalmed off Block Island, our crew employed themselves catching cod and hauled up a great number. 'Till then I had stuck to my resolution to eat nothing that had had life; and on this occasion I considered, according to my Master Tryon, the taking every fish as a kind of unprovoked murder, since none of them had or ever could do us any injury that might justify this massacre. All this seemed very reasonable. But I had formerly been a great lover of fish, and when this came hot out of the frying pan, it smelled admirably well. I balanced some time between principle and inclination till I recollected that when the fish were opened, I saw smaller fish taken out of their stomachs. "Then," thought I, "if you eat one another, I don't see why we mayn't eat you." So I dined upon cod very heartily and have since continued to eat as other people, returning only now and then occasionally to a vegetable diet. So convenient a thing it is to be a *reasonable creature*, since it enables one to find or make a reason for everything one has a mind to do.

Above, from the *Autobiography of Benjamin Franklin.*

☆ ☆ ☆

Seals and Lambs

Editor, The National Observer:

In regard to Mr. Western's editorial "Weep Not for the Lamb?" [Observations, March 29], there is a difference in lambs and calves we eat for food and sealskins we wear to keep up with fashion.

JOAN MOONEY

Washington, D. C.

☆ ☆ ☆

Call for Realism

Editor, The National Observer:

At last someone spoke out expressing my sentiments about the killing of baby seals.

I've had some experience with the economic side of this, so it doesn't seem like wanton killing of a defenseless baby. The parent seals are at sea—the baby is at hand. In most cases, subsistence and even existence of the hunter and his family are involved.

Having spent over a year in a coastal Eskimo village on the Seward peninsula, I've seen what takes place. The hunter takes the sealskin to the trading post, and usually before the actual cash involved leaves the area it has gone through four or five transactions. For these skins he gets food, clothing, fuel, lumber, shells, and other things necessary for his family.

Right, wrong, cruel — who is to say? Clubbing baby seals to death in order to eat, clothe, and keep warm is still a far cry above trophy killing by sportsmen or hunting deer by car lights or crocodile killing at night or the killing of great numbers of seals by early fur-company ship's crews.

Let us be realistic about this and not pick just one isolated group without knowing anything about the circumstances behind the slaughter.

As Joe Western wrote, "We might all embrace vegetarianism." But what about the theory that plants grow better if one speaks kindly of them? Surely this means they, too, have feelings which hurt when we pull up, pare, boil, fry, or chew them.

MALINDA CARROLL

Hyannis, Mass.

☆ ☆ ☆

Top left, from *The National Observer*, March 29, 1971.

Top right, letter to the editor of *The National Observer* by Joan Mooney, April 12, 1971.

Above right, letter to the editor of *The National Observer* by Malinda Carroll, April 12, 1971.

It's Open Season On Hunters

By JERRY KENNEY
Outdoor Editor of THE NEWS

HUNTERS this weekend are quietly moving through the painted autumn uplands of New York, stalking the lordly whitetail deer and the elusive black bear that for a short season are legal targets.

And stalking the hunters, but not quietly, are the seasonal crowd of ecologists, conservationists and other cause collectors to whom hunting is a bloody atrocity.

In New York alone, a half-million hunters will be on "binges of mayhem and murder," to hear the anti-hunting zealots tell it.

"Miserable cowards with a lust to kill," is how one so-called animal-lover described hunters on a radio program. Then she was permitted to express her wish that all of them be shot, too.

This bitter critic of hunting represents just one of several organizations that are determined to put an end to all game shooting.

They aren't opposed to killing steers, pigs, sheep, turkeys and other critters that are lured to the block by a man in a white, blood-spattered apron and an ax or hammer. And they aren't particularly upset that mink, beavers, raccoons and all those cuddly creatures have to be dispatched unceremoniously to provide warmth for some soft, pink bosom.

But the 17 million men and women who hunt for sport in this country have to go. This anti-hunting movement continues to grow even though its supporters have no concept of game management or what the ultimate outcome will be if they accomplish their goal.

It's easy to understand how the anti-hunters arouse the greatest amount of sympathy from the Bambi-lovers. Innocent, lovable, limpid-eyed creatures are pictured being slaughtered by ruthless hunters who will shoot anything that moves.

Unfortunately, there are a few creeps around the woods who fit this description. They take their share of horses, cows, dogs and chickens and they pepper farm houses, roadsigns and automobile tires. And every time one does, this transgression is blown all out of proportion and held to be typical of the hunting breed. But this charge is as unjust as tabbing every New York City cop a bribe taker.

The sport hunter does his damnedest to keep these characters out of circulation because they are his biggest threat. They keep the anti-hunting forces supplied with ammunition. But it's the only valid charge they have. Once they switch to the "hunters - exterminate - game - charge," they don't have a leg to stand on.

Game management professionals don't even like to use the term "hunting." It is hunting to us who tramp the woods and mountains. But, to them, killing animals is considered a harvest. Like any growing crop, game must be harvested or it will choke itself out of existence.

If deer and other game animals kept within the bounds of their habitats and obtained sufficient sustenance within that area, there would be no hunting. But there are no birth control pills out there, and doing what comes naturally can send any population completely out of control.

As the population increases, the habitat shrinks and the winter food supply disappears. The result is starvation and sick, weak deer. Additional starvation is likely in subsequent winters because the food supply is not replenished in one season, but may take from three to 10 years.

An unchecked game population is doomed, and this would have happened to the deer if sound game management hadn't been practiced long ago. The excess population must be harvested, and it's the hunter who harvests it. Hunters have taken over a million deer in New York in the last decade, but for every deer a hunter kills, there is still one that starves or dies a "natural" death.

Those who insist we should let nature take its course have never seen a deer starving, a doe trampling her fawn to get browse on a tree or dogs tearing at deer until their guts are dragging on the ground as they run.

Cars and trucks alone kill about 20,-000 deer every year in New York. Predators—wolves, wildcats and such—no longer are a threat to deer. But domestic dogs, the collies, poodles, beagles and mutts that are allowed to roam untended, are becoming one of the most serious threats to deer in the Northeast. It's so serious that game protectors shoot any dogs they find in the woods from October through April.

The dogs don't eat the deer. They just kill them, thus wasting a link in the food chain. Man is also a predator, and has been since the beginning of time. Most men do not have to hunt to eat today, but if they eat meat, someone has to kill it for them. So, when a hunter kills swiftly with an accurate, high - powered bullet, and makes good use of the meat, why should he be condemned?

Every hunter aims for a clean kill. Anything short of that lessens his chance of taking his prize. Everyone can't be a marksman, but with the quality of firearms and optics available today, hunters rarely wound animals and lose them.

A hunter's bullet is at least as humane as a slaughter house worker's ax, hammer or knife, and probably more so, but even the most dedicated of conservationists is seldom moved to tears by the sight of a succulent steak on his plate.

From The New York Daily News, November 21, 1971.

HUNTERS Make it "Dear"... not "Deer"
will you...won't you...can't you?

friends of animals, inc.   11 West 60th Street, New York, N.Y. 10023   Circle 7-8120

Rod Hunter, "Sports" Columnist
Echoes Sentinel
Stirling, New Jersey

Dear Mr. Hunter,

You suggest that hunters have a "reverance" for life. Is it then something akin to the reverence the Marquis de Sade had for women? We never thought of it that way but it seems to make sense.

To your astute observation that nature is "no Disneyland" may we add: nor is it a boudoir. We're not turned on by a show of masculinity which takes place in the forests through maiming or occasionally killing helpless animals. We like guys whose virility holds on better proving grounds.

But, credit where credit is due: You hunters certainly are potent with the politicians. Now you may enter a sanctuary and blast off. On December 19, the New Jersey Great Swamp National Wildlife Refuge will throng with 150 of you lucky lottery-winners, tested for sharp-shooting by your ability to pay $7.15 for a license to murder.

Please spare our minds as you spare our bodies and don't try to ennoble your psychotic behavior by claiming you are trimming the herd for the benefit of the herd (which you say consists of 400 deer). We've read your magazines where you admit to each other that it's fun... fun...fun...to kill...kill...kill.

The only herd that needs trimming is the herd of hunters. So please garb yourselves, you brave 150, in fawn color on December 19, and double your thrill... thrill...thrill.

Sincerely yours, For the Girls:

GRETCHEN WYLER

LAUREN BACALL

GLORIA DE HAVEN

ALI MacGRAW

JUNE HAVOC

PATRICE MUNSEL

SHEILA MacRAE

BETSY PALMER

JOANNE WOODWARD

Courtesy Friends of Animals, Inc.

In Defense of Deer Hunting and Killing

By Arthur C. Tennies
FROM CHENANGO COUNTY, N.Y.

"You hunt deer?" When I nodded, my shocked colleague went on to say, "Why my whole image of you has been shattered. How can you kill such beautiful creatures?"

And so would many others who view the deliberate killing of deer as brutal and senseless. Such people look upon the hunter as a barbaric hangover

Comment

from the distant past of the human race. To my colleague, the incongruity between the barbarism of hunting and normal civilized conduct was made more intense because I was a minister. How could I as a minister do such a thing?

I thought about that as I drove through the early morning darkness toward the southeastern part of Chenango County. It was a little after 5 a.m. I had gotten up at 4, something I only do in the case of an emergency or when I am going deer hunting. It was cold, the temperature in the 20s. With

Arthur C. Tennies is the associate executive director for Planning and Research for the New York State Council of Churches and Associate for Non-Metropolitan Ministries with the United Presbyterian Program Agency. He is author of a book entitled, A Church for Sinners, Seekers and Sundry Non-Saints, *published by Abingdon.*

the ground frozen, it would be too noisy for still hunting until the sun had had a chance to thaw the frost. So it would be wait and freeze. My first thoughts about why I would hunt deer had nothing to do with the supposed barbarism of it. I thought of the foolishness of it. Wait hour after hour in the cold, feet numb, hands numb, and small chance of getting a deer.

I was going to hunt on Schlafer Hill on the farm of Pershing Schlafer. My choice of a place to hunt had been determined by the party permit that three of us had, which allowed us to kill one other deer of either sex besides the three bucks that we were allowed.

I thought about the party system in New York, the way the state controlled the size of the deer herd. The state is divided into about 40 deer-management areas. The state biologists know how many deer each area can handle, how many deer can feed on the browse available without destroying it. If there are too many deer, they will kill the plants and bushes upon which they depend. The next step is starvation for large numbers. Since the deer's natural predators were wiped out by the first settlers, the only control over their numbers now is starvation or hunting. Thus, so many deer must be killed in a deer-management area. A certain number will be killed by motor vehicles. The biologists can estimate how many will be killed on the highways and also the number of bucks that will be killed. The surplus is taken care of by issuing a set number of party permits.

I have often marveled at the state biologists, their skill and knowledge in managing the deer herd. As I have pondered the problems of people—poverty, starvation, injustice, and all the others—and our frantic and often futile efforts to solve these problems, I have thought, "If only we could manage the problems of people as well as we can manage a deer herd."

The Great Difference

Then I realize the great difference between the two. People are not for being managed. We manage people only by robbing them of the right to choose—and the most brutal attempts to manage are ultimately frustrated by the obstinacy of human nature, its refusal to be managed. A handful of biologists may manage a deer herd and a handful of scientists may be able to put a man on the moon, but no handful of planners will ever manage the human race. And so I thought again, as the car rushed through the dark, that all of our modern management techniques would fail to come up with quick and perfect solutions to the problems of people.

It was Dead

I waited another hour. It was warmer now. Finally a deer appeared, a head above a rise. It started to come nearer. Then it stopped. Something was wrong. It decided to leave. As it turned, my gun came up and I shot. It lurched sideways, kicking and thrashing, disappearing under a pine tree. I walked to the spot. No deer. I went around the tree and there it lay. In a second it was dead.

I looked down at the deer, a button buck, and I thought: This is the way of nature, one creature feeding on another. Thousands of years ago our forebearers survived in just this way. They killed, gutted, butchered, and ate. Now we buy in a supermarket or order in a restaurant.

The first task was to gut the deer, kind of a messy process. I got my knife cut, turned the deer on his back, and slit him open. I spilled the guts out on the ground. I saved the liver and heart, even though the heart had been mangled by the bullet. I cut through the diaphragm and pulled the lungs out.

Back Up the Hill

Then I was ready to pull the deer back to the car. It was 3 p.m. when I got to the car. Time yet to hunt for a buck, so I dumped the deer into the trunk. Back up the hill, but no luck. As night came on, I got back to the car. I tied the deer on the top of the trunk and started for home.

As I drove toward home, I had a sense of satisfaction. I had fitted myself to nature's way and had been successful. For a few short hours, I had marched to the beat of nature's drum, not that of our modern world. At least for me, the barrier that we had built between nature and us could still be breached.

As I went to sleep that night I thought: "I suppose that no matter what I say, a lot of people will still never understand why I hunt deer. Well, they don't have to, but let only vegetarians condemn me."

By Arthur C. Tennies in *The National Observer*, January 18, 1975.

The Ethical Basis of Our Cause

That the anti-vivisection movement is essentially ethical in its inspiration — predominantly moral in its objective — cannot be too strongly emphasized. Its philosophy is not primarily utilitarian, but fundamentally humanitarian. Unfortunately, it has always seemed to me that a great number of its active exponents have narrowly limited the field of constructive action to the arena of controversies over the utility of the practices that they deplore. Hence much anti-vivisection literature tends to be largely confined to technical discussions over the scientific value of certain "discoveries," the efficacy of particular serums, the accuracy of various pretensions of certain members of the medical profession and the reliability and value of numerous statistical compilations. These resources are all valid enough when not given a prominence which tends to minimize or obscure considerations which seem to be of far greater importance and possessed of much wider human appeal. I believe the retardation of progress in America is due in no small measure to this misplacing of emphasis on basic principles.

We need no other major argument — and we can find no more persuasive one — against the torture of dumb life in the name of science, than its downright sinfulness. I believe that an ingrained reverence for the mystery and inviolability of life, howsoever manifested, and a profound compassion for all sentient creatures, to be the foundation of the cause we espouse. While, therefore, I am free to question the utility of much that is tolerated in the name of medical science, my abhorrence of cruelty in any form would remain unaffected even if the claims asserted in justification were proved to demonstration. I refuse to ignore the insistent prompting of ethical instincts in the formation of my judgments. I reject the necessity of debating an issue of utility when the moral considerations are to me overwhelmingly preponderant. I decline to compromise with that which I deem fundamentally wrong.

G. R. F.

From *Reverence for Life*, published by the
New England Anti-Vivisection Society.

SECTION 8

Abortion and Sterilization

Like those in the previous section, the arguments in this section involve consideration of the boundaries of the realm of morality; but the arguments in this section involve one issue which did not appear at all in the previous section, the question of when *human* life begins. The discussion of whether or not certain treatment of nonhumans is morally wrong required a judgment about extending the realm of morality beyond the purely human realm. In contrast, much of the debate about the morality of abortion involves a judgment concerning the boundaries of the realm of the human itself. The discussions in this section also involve a concern with questions of legislation which were not significant in the discussions of the treatment of animals.

Contemporary discussions about the problems related to abortion—especially regarding the desirability, feasibility, utility, justifiability, and/or morality of making it illegal in the wake of the Supreme Court ruling which struck down almost all antiabortion legislation—have involved some of the most passionate and eloquent pleas on behalf of the fetus, the mother, God, and "morality" in general. Some of the selections in this section provide first-hand evidence of the difficulty of extracting the essence of a moral argument from under the window dressing of colorful rhetoric. Once the rhetoric is removed, the difficulty of the problems becomes all too apparent, especially those of defining "human being" and "living." If a four-month-old fetus is a human being, then abortion might well be considered a form of murder; but is a fetus a human being? This is at most only partially a moral question; it also requires consideration of medical, legal, theological, metaphysical, biological, and other dimensions. For example, some people hold the belief that a soul enters the human body at the moment of conception, and for those persons it is unquestionably the case that the fetus is a human being from that first moment. But an analysis and evaluation of premises such as this requires that we go far beyond the realm of ethical theory and the specific issue of abortion to an examination of some of the basic questions of metaphysics and religion.

The resolution of the problem of whether or not a fetus is a human being is not necessary for some arguments dealing with abortion. For example, it is possible to construct an argument which allows (for the purposes of the discussion at least) the assumption that a fetus is a human being. This type of argument then focusses on the question of whether or not there are any conditions under which it is morally permissible to take a human life. Arguments of this type are similar in important ways to certain arguments dealing with issues of life and death in the contexts of war, capital punishment, and even terrorism.

Some arguments about abortion focus on the right of a woman to control her own body and the question of whether or not a fetus is part of a woman's body. There are some important areas of overlap between this type of argument and certain arguments about compulsory sterilization (which involves the woman's right to become pregnant as opposed to her right to terminate a pregnancy).

EXERCISES

1. Evaluate each of the arguments in this section under the different assumptions that a) the mother, b) the father, and c) the physician is confronted with a decision concerning an abortion. How does this change in circumstances affect the support that the premises provide for the conclusion?
2. To what extent are the arguments offered by the Supreme Court justices in their ruling on abortion *moral* arguments? If they are not moral arguments, then what kind are they?
3. Compare the arguments concerning abortion in this section with those concerning euthanasia in the next section. Are there any significant differences in the problems associated with defining "human being" at the beginning and at the end of life?

Excerpts From Abortion Case

Special to The New York Times

WASHINGTON, Jan. 22—
Following are excerpts from the majority opinion, written by Justice Henry A. Blackmun, in Jane Roe v. Henry Wade, the Texas abortion case and from the dissent written by Justice Byron R. White:

Majority Opinion

The Texas statutes under attack here are typical of those that have been in effect in many states for approximately a century. These make it a crime to "procure an abortion," as therein defined, or to attempt one, except with respect to "an abortion procured or attempted by medical advice for the purpose of saving the life of the mother." Similar statutes are in existence in a majority of the states.

It perhaps is not generally appreciated that the restrictive criminal abortion laws in effect in a majority of states are of relatively recent vintage. Instead, they derive from statutory changes effected, for the most part, in the latter half of the 19th century.

When most criminal abortion laws were first enacted, the procedure was a hazardous one for the woman.

Privacy Rights Unclear

The Constitution does not explicitly mention any right of privacy. In a line of decision, however, the Court has recognized that a right of personal privacy, or a guarantee of certain areas or zones of privacy, does exist under the Constitution.

This right of privacy, whether it be founded in the 14th Amendments concept of personal liberty and restrictions upon state action, as we feel it is, or as the District Court determined, in the Ninth Amendment's reservation of rights to the people, is broad enough to encompass a woman's decision whether or not to terminate her pregnancy.

The detriment that the state would impose upon the pregnant woman by denying this choice altogether is apparent. Specific and direct harm medically diagnosable even in early pregnancy may be involved. Maternity, or additional offspring, may force upon the woman a distressful life and future. Psychological harm may be iminent. Mental and physical wealth may be taxed by child care.

There is also the distress, for all concerned, associated with the unwanted child, and there is the problem of bringing a child into a family already unable, psychologically and otherwise, to care for it. On the basis of elements such as these, appellants and some amici argue that the woman's right is absolute and that she is entitled to terminate her pregnancy at whatever time, in whatever way, and for whatever reason she alone chooses. With this we do not agree.

The Court's decision recognizing a right of privacy also acknowledge that some state regulation in areas protected by that right is appropriate. A state may properly assert important interests in safeguarding health, in maintaining medical standards and in protecting Potential life.

At the same point in pregnancy, these respective interests become sufficiently compelling to sustain regulation of the factors that govern the abortion decision.

The appellee and certain amici argue that the fetus is a "person" within the language and meaning of the 14th amendment. In support of this they outline at length and in detail the well-known facts of fetal development. If this suggestion of peronhood is established, the appellant's case, of course, collapses, for the fetus' right to life is then aguaranteed specifically by the amendment.

The Constitution does not define "person' 'in so many words. The use of the word is such that it has application only postnatally.

All this, together with our observation that throughout the major portion of the 19th century prevailing legal abortion practices were far freer than they are today, persuades us that the word "person," as used in the 14th Amendment, does not include unborn.

Texas urges that, apart from the 14th Amendment, life begins at conception and is present throughout pregnancy, and that, therefore, the state as a compelling interest in protecting that life from and after conception.

We need not resolve the difficult question of when life begins. When those trained in the respective disciplines of medicine, philosophy and theology are unable to arrive at any consensus, the judiciary, at this point in the development of man's knowledge, is not in a position to speculate as to the answer.

The unborn have never been recognized in the law as persons in the whole sense.

With respect to the state's important and legitimate interest in the health of the mother, the "compelling" point, in the light of present medical knowledge, is at approximately the end of the first trimester. This is so because of the now established medical fact that until the end of the first trimester mortality in abortion is less than mortality in normal childbirth.

It follows that, from and after this point, a state may regulate the abortion procedure to the extent that the regulation reasonably relates to the preservation and protection of maternal health.

With respect to the state's important and legitimate interest in potential life, the "compelling" point is at viability. This is so because the fetus then presumably has the capability of meaningful life outside the mother's womb. If the state is interested in protecting fetal life after viability, it may go so far as to proscribe abortion during that period except when it is necessary to preserve the life or health of the mother.

Dissenting Opinion

At the heart of the controversy in these cases are those recurring pregnancies that pose no danger whatsoever to the life or health of the mother but are nevertheless unwanted for any one or more of a variety of easons —convenience, family planning, economics, dislike of children, the embarrassment of illegitimacy, etc.

The common claim before us is that for any one of such reasons, or for no reason at all, and without asserting or claiming any threat to life or health, any woman is entitled to an abortion at her request if she is able to find a medical adviser willing to undertake the procedure.

The Court for the most part sustains this position: during the period prior to the time the fetus becomes viable, the Constitution of the United States values the convenience, whim or caprice of the putative mother more than life or potential life of the fetus.

The upshot is that the people and the legislatures of the 50 states are constitution ally disentitled to weigh the relative importance of the continued existence and development of the fetus on the one hand against a spectrum of possible impacts on the mother on the other hand.

As an exercise of raw judicial power, the Court perhaps has authority to do what it does today; but in my view its judgment is an improvident and extravagant exercise of the power of judicial review which the constitution extends to this court.

I find no constitutional warrant for imposing such an order of priorities on the people and legislatures of the states. In a sensitive area such as this, involving as it does issues over which reasonable men may easily and heatedly differ, I cannot accept the Court's exercise of its clear power of choice by interposing a constitutional barrier to state efforts to protect human life and by investing mothers and doctors with the constitutionally protected right to exterminate it. This issue, for the most part, should be left with the people and to the political processes the people have devised to govern thier affairs.

From *The New York Times*, January 22, 1973.

WHAT THE SUPREME COURT RULED ON ABORTION LAWS

When the U. S. Supreme Court struck down abortion laws in Texas and Georgia on Jan. 22, 1973, it limited any State's right to prohibit abortion.

In effect, the Court's 7-to-2 ruling said that a State can prohibit an abortion only in the last three months of pregnancy and then not if the abortion is necessary to protect the health of the mother.

Basis for this decision: the right to privacy as protected by the Fourteenth Amendment.

Specifically, the Court said:

• During the first three months of pregnancy, the decision to abort rests solely with the woman and her doctor.

• During the second three months, the State can regulate the abortion procedure to protect maternal health.

• During the third three months, when the fetus is viable, the State can regulate or even prohibit abortion except when it's necessary for the mother's mental or physical health.

Thus the Court said a State had the right to pass an anti-abortion law to protect its "interest in the potentiality of human life"—but only in the last three months of pregnancy.

The Court stated that the due-process clause "does not include the unborn."

Left, reprinted from *U.S. News & World Report*, March 4, 1974. Copyright 1974 U.S. News & World Report, Inc.

To the Editor:

In the recent Supreme Court abortion decision, Justice Blackmun has argued that since there is doubt as to when life begins we may abort the unborn. One wonders if the Court will next argue that when an accused murderer's guilt or innocence is in doubt he may legitimately be put to death.

So much has been written and said about the "presumption of innocence" in our legal system as the protection of individual rights against unjust accusations. How much more important would it have been if the Court had created a "presumption of life" in those cases where legal existence is in doubt.

The Court has made a serious mistake in taking these issues away from the people and attempting to substitute its will for the people's will as expressed in legislatures and referendums.

ALBERT E. GUNN, M.D.
Springfield, Va., Feb. 2, 1973

Cooke Warns Catholics on Abortions

By GEORGE DUGAN

Cardinal Cooke warned Roman Catholics yesterday that any involvement with abortion would mean automatic excommunication.

"Putting aside the public debate for a moment," he declared, "we remind ourselves emphatically that any association with an immoral abortion, for any reason, is a grave personal sin. No state law can change that.

"Nor can any convenience — psychological, matrimonial, economic, cultural or social — permit any Catholic to perform, undergo or encourage a direct abortion. To do so is to commit a grave personal and social sin against God and humanity. In so doing so a person separates himself from the Catholic community and communion."

"Catholics must not be misled," the Cardinal said. "There is no 'new theology' on abortion. An informed Catholic conscience can never tolerate the direct destruction of innocent human life. It is a serious and heinous sin for any Catholic—priest or doctor, parent, husband or friend—to encourage a girl to undergo an abortion.

"If we oppose unjust wars, criminal assassinations, political murders and terrorist hijacking; if we move against life-damaging poverty, pollution, hunger and neglect, then we must not condone abortion. I ask you all to join me in prayer today that innocent life, in every form, will be made safe in this nation."

Top, letter to the editor of *The New York Times* by Albert E. Gunn, M.D., February 14, 1973.
Right, from *The New York Times*, October 8, 1973.

Abortion Decision: A Year Later

It is now a full year since the Supreme Court in *Roe* v. *Wade* effectively struck down the traditional abortion statutes of all 50 states. Not surprisingly, that decision has met with every kind of response, from outcries that it represents nothing less than legalized slaughter to claims that it will stand as the social milestone of the century. But critics and supporters have done far more than issue statements. Legislative and court battles continue in an effort to define the implications of the Court's ruling, whether in the interests of constricting its application or broadening it still further. In addition, of course, there has been a nationwide campaign to sponsor a constitutional amendment to overturn the decision.

Support for such a radical approach to the problem continues to grow, but procedural problems in the House Judiciary Committee—in particular, impeachment hearings—will probably block that road for some months. More significantly the writing of such an amendment, as we pointed out last June (6/2/73, p. 506), would be extremely difficult if an attempt were made to include the various exceptions to an absolute ban on abortion held by different religious and ethical groups. And no amendment could promise *greater* protection to the fetus than is already accorded citizens by other provisions of the Constitution (see James Diamond's discussion of this point on p. 27). If drafting an amendment will be controversial, getting it passed by both houses of Congress and three quarters of the states may be impossible. In short, a constitutional amendment, while the most direct legal route, may prove to be an enormous detour on the road to a sane abortion policy in the United States.

Attempts to change the law, of course whether by constitutional amendment or further litigation through the courts, are perfectly appropriate in our system of government and entirely laudable, but they should not consume all of our energy or be allowed to distract us from a pressing educational dilemma. As long as the law supported the moral position of those who opposed ready abortions, the need to consider the complicated ethical questions involved was minimal. Abortions were wrong *and* illegal. The fact that they have been rendered licit by Court fiat in no way changes their moral status.

At the very least, a potential human life is at stake in every determination to abort. To say that a fetus is merely a part of a woman's body runs contrary to all the biological evidence that clearly demonstrates the presence of a new and separate organism in the embryo. But it is an organism entirely dependent on the life of the mother for existence and sustenance during the first six to seven months—a fact that makes the fetus a special case. The moral question is what value shall we place on this unique form of human life? The current trend of American opinion, insofar as it is represented by the *Roe* v. *Wade* decision, displays a shocking callousness to the presence of life in the womb. Before the law, it is denied the protection afforded every human person, citizen or not. In the eyes of many, its rights—and most particularly, its right to exist—are secondary to the convenience of another individual. Simply to overlook or consciously ignore the inchoate humanity of the fetus threatens the very basis of our lives together in society, for it strikes at the common dignity we all claim as human beings. Because it treats human life cheaply and encourages a disregard for the value of all that is vulnerable, abortion-on-demand is an antihuman policy. That point must be made over and over again if we are not be lulled into an uncritical acceptance of what has become legally permissible. If the decision to have an abortion has become a personal one, then the ethical burden of that decision has been increased, not diminished.

Abortions, however, are seldom purely private actions. They require assistance—doctors, nurses, a clinic or hospital. In each case, the consciences of other persons are intimately involved. If the state has decided, through its highest Court, that it has no right to force a woman to bear a child to term against her will, then by the same logic it should have no right to compel an individual, against his conscience, to aid in the termination of that life. The inviolability of one conscience demands the inviolability of the other. Some 17 states have already enacted conscience clauses to cover just such cases. They should be extended as soon as possible to all states and the federal government.

LETTERS:

Abortion—1

I must take ussue with Gordon G. Evans on the matter of abortion. "The crux of the matter" is not, as he contends, "when life begins." Any society that cares as little as ours does for wild life and natural environment *for its own sake* cannot legitimately claim to be concerned about "life" *per se*.

Rather, the crucial question is, When does life begin *to be human?* That can't be answered in physical terms alone. (Remember the plucked chicken that was presented as an example of human life to the philosopher who had defined man as "a featherless biped?")

Birth is by no means "merely an incident" in comparison with conception. It is, instead, the essential event which makes one part of the human community. And it is only as part of the human community, in relationship with other persons, that one can acquire and develop those qualities which are uniquely human. Language is the most clear-cut of these— and no fetus, as long as it is a fetus, is even potentially capable of intelligent speech. That requires communication with other human minds.

Chomingwen D. Pond
Wilberforce, Ohio

Abortion—2

.... While it is correct that a union of an egg and sperm determine the biological chacteristics of a new individual, these same sex cells are themselves alive. Such unicellular stages have specific requirements for continued life and a finite lifespan just as do the multicellular stages of life from which they come and to which they can give origin. To argue that the eggs and sperm are in some way less important than these multicellular stages is as pointless as the old "chicken and the egg" problem.

If every effort must be bent to assure that the needs of all human life are met on an equal basis, there is as much argument for compulsory fertilization of all human ova (unfortunately most sperm will be out of luck as evolutionary design has resulted in the production of millions of sperm for each ovum) as for the preservation of each fetus....

Melissa Stanley
Fairfax, Va.

Top, Chomingwen D. Pond, "Abortion 1" in *Civil Liberties*, No. 302, May 1974, p. 6.
Above, Melissa Stanley, "Abortion 2" in *Civil Liberties*, No. 302, May 1974, p. 6.

THE DISPOSABLE HUMANS?

SHOULD EVERY HUMAN LIFE BE RESPECTED? OR ARE SOME LIVES DISPOSABLE? IS THERE A DIFFERENCE BETWEEN A HUMAN LIFE AND A LEGAL PERSON?

THESE QUESTIONS ARE NOW ASKED WITH REGARD TO UNBORN BABIES. BUT DIDN'T OUR SOCIETY ASK THESE SAME QUESTIONS ONCE BEFORE . . . IN THE 19th CENTURY . . . WITH RESPECT TO BLACK PEOPLE? *(PERHAPS THIS IS WHY, OUT OF ALL GROUPS, IT IS THE BLACK COMMUNITY — NOT THE CATHOLIC COMMUNITY — THAT TODAY SHOWS LEAST SUPPORT FOR PERMISSIVE ABORTION . . . ACCORDING TO A 1970 HARRIS POLL AND A 1971 POPULATION COMMISSION POLL.)*

WHY NOT COMPARE TODAY'S RHETORIC WITH THAT OF THE LAST CENTURY AND SEE WHETHER THERE ARE SIMILARITIES?

S L A V E R Y *1857*	*A B O R T I O N* 1972
Although he may have a heart and a brain, and he may be a human life biologically, a slave is not a *legal* person. The Dred Scott decision by the U. S. Supreme Court has made that clear.	*Although he may have a heart and a brain, and he may be a human life biologically, an unborn baby is not a legal person. Our courts will soon make that clear.*
A black man only becomes a *legal* person when he is set free. Before that time, we should not concern ourselves about him because he has no legal rights.	*A baby only becomes a legal person when he is born. Before that time, we should not concern ourselves about him because he has no legal rights.*
If you think that slavery is wrong, then nobody is forcing you to be a slave-owner. But don't impose your morality on somebody else!	*If you think abortion is wrong, then nobody is forcing you to have one. But don't impose your morality on somebody else!*
A man has a right to do what he wants with his own property.	*A woman has a right to do what she wants with her own body.*
Isn't slavery really something merciful? After all, every black man has a right to be protected. Isn't it better never to be set free than to be sent unprepared, and ill-equipped, into a cruel world? (*Spoken by someone already free*)	*Isn't abortion really something merciful? After all, every baby has a right to be wanted. Isn't it better never to be born than to be sent alone and unloved into a cruel world?* (Spoken by someone already born)

Will the unborn baby become the modern Dred Scott?
Or will our country use its great resources to respect every human life
. . . black or white . . . poor or rich . . . woman or man . . .
unborn baby or octogenarian?

An open letter to all Americans:

What Do People Really Think about Abortion?

The best way to find out is to *ask* them—but evidently it isn't that simple.

On April 8, The New York *Times* carried a story (page 7) headlined "Abortion Poll Finds Public Evenly Split." It reported a recent Gallup Poll on the U.S. Supreme Court's pro-abortion decisions of January 22, 1973. Said the *Times:* "The survey indicated that 47 per cent of the American people favored the court's ruling, and 44 per cent opposed it." The survey was based "on interviews with 1,582 adults."

Gallup's question was: "The United States Supreme Court has ruled that a woman may go to a doctor to end pregnancy at any time during the first three months of pregnancy. Do you favor or oppose this ruling?"

Our question is: How can you take a poll on abortion without using the word? And how accurate would it be? We decided to find out. We commissioned Sindlinger & Co., a highly-respected opinion research firm, to do the job. First (April 16-23) Sindlinger asked 1,653 people (a nationwide representative sampling like Gallup's, only bigger) *the exact same question* Gallup asked. The results were — for those of us who oppose abortion—worse than Gallup's: 45.9 favored the Court's ruling, 39.5 opposed it; almost 10% refused to answer (keep this point in mind), the remaining 4.9% were undecided.

The following week (April 24-30) we did the same thing, to another 1,653 people (if these numbers seem small to *you,* the statistical experts say that they project to a representative sampling of some 67,220,000 adult Americans). Only this time we changed Gallup's wording "go to a doctor to end pregnancy" to **go to a doctor for an abortion.** No other change. The results were . . . surprising. The figures now showed 48.7 *opposed* the Court, 41.0% favored, only 5.9% refused to answer, with 4.4% undecided.

We decided to try it yet again (May 3-8, 1,652 people). The results: 53.7% opposed (i.e., *against* abortion), 42.9% in favor only 2.3% refused to answer, and a mere 1.1% remained undecided! Clearly more and more people are making up their minds on the issue—very likely because abortion is *finally* getting major coverage from the media (after a very long and very strange blackout).

We did more. We *added* two questions to the basic one: a) "How do you yourself rate the subject of abortion—as very important to you—of some importance to you—or of no importance to you?;" and b) "As far as you yourself are concerned would you say you are for or against abortion, or what *do* you think?" The results? We quote Sindlinger's report directly:

"Americans are opposed to abortion by a margin of better than three to two, according to a nationwide survey of U.S. households by Sindlinger & Company of Swarthmore, Pennsylvania.

"In a May 3-8 survey based on a sample of 1,652 households, 59.4 percent said they were against abortion compared with 36.2 percent who favored it. Most of the opposition was voiced by women as 62.7 percent of the females interviewed opposed abortion compared with 56 percent of the men. At the same time, 39.7 percent of the males interviewed and 32.9 percent of the females were for abortion.

"The abortion issue apparently is regarded as important to some degree by seven of ten Americans. In the survey, 29.8 percent regarded the issue as very important and another 39.1 percent called it of some importance. Only 28.4 percent said it was of no importance.

"Better than one of every three women— 35.6 percent—said the issue was very important but less than one of four men—23.9 percent — held it in the same light."

There you have it. If you want to know what Americans really think about abortion, **you have to ask them about abortion.**

What can *you* do about it? If you agree with us that the abortion issue needs to be freely and fully discussed—most especially, if you agree with us in our opposition to the Court's pro-abortion decisions — then you can use the coupon below to help us get our message to *all* Americans! Send as much as you can, but send something, and send it now!

The Ad Hoc Committee in Defense of Life • *P.O. Box 574, Murray Hill Station, N.Y.C.*

To the Editor:

The decision to grant what is tantamount to abortion on demand sets the profession of medicine and civilization back 2,500 years to a time when the doctor and sorcerer were the same individual with the power to kill as well as to cure.

Though Justice Blackmun conveniently dismisses the Hippocratic oath as élitist on the basis of a dead scholar's fragile hypothesis, Margaret Mead reminds us according to a 1972 study by Maurice Levine that the oath marked one of the turning points in the history of man. She states that "for the first time in our tradition there was a complete separation between killing and curing." She added that "it was the Greeks who made the distinction clear and delegated to one profession, medicine, a complete dedication to life under all circumstances."

Dr. Mead emphasizes what Justice Blackmun failed to appreciate: that this radical separation of killing and curing "is a priceless possession which we cannot afford to tarnish, but society always is attempting to make the physician into a killer—to kill the defective child [or] the cancer patient."

The majority opinion of the Supreme Court has disregarded her conviction that "it is the duty of society to protect the physician from such requests." By this failure the Court has recycled today's obstetrician back to the dark ages of the sorcerer, who for a fee will kill or rescue the smaller of two patients in a pregnancy on the basis of the woman's request. Furthermore, the majority opinion insures that a killing operation will become the most prevalent operation performed in the United States, as it is in New York State today.   HERBERT RATNER, M.D.
Director, Dept. of Public Health
Oak Park, Ill., Feb. 1, 1973

Left, letter to the editor of *The New York Times* by Herbert Ratner, M.D., February 14, 1973.
Right, courtesy Knights of Columbus.

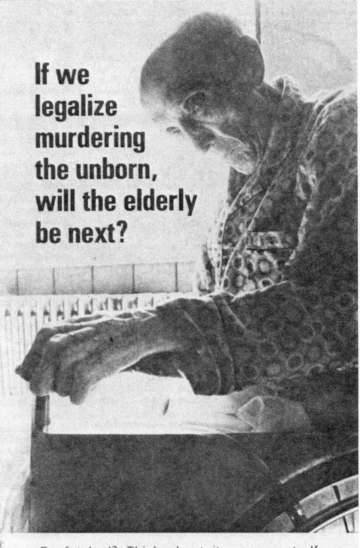

If we legalize murdering the unborn, will the elderly be next?

Far-fetched? Think about it a moment. If society can justify the taking of the life of an unborn child whose only crime is being unwanted, why not the life of a sick or elderly person who has become an unwanted burden?

Once established, there is no end to the ways the principle of legalized abortion could be used to justify the taking of human life "for the good of society."

If you'd like a better understanding of the Christian principles involved, write today for our new pocket-size pamphlet entitled "The Sacredness of Life." We'll send it free and nobody will call.

An Amendment About Life

SEN. JAMES Buckley has proposed an antiabortion amendment to the Constitution, and cosponsoring the measure are six fellow senators. One is a Catholic and the five others are Protestants.

That's a good line-up. It is of central importance that foes of abortion make it clear that their cause is not just a parochial concern of the Roman Catholic Church. While the Catholic hierarchy has been outspoken in its opposition to abortion, the question is not one of simple sectarian preference. At stake are millions of lives.

The Human Life Amendment (and that is no euphemism) was introduced in response to the Supreme Court's unbelievable pronouncement that it is the law of the United States that unborn babies may be freely killed because they are incapable of "meaningful life."

We do not know at this time whether the Court plans to pursue this reasoning to include paralyzed people, very old people, retarded people, or deformed people. But all such citizens might be described as being incapable of "meaningful life." All we need do to make that phrase fit those categories is revamp our criteria a little.

The Human Life Amendment has an excellent chance of becoming part of the Constitution, not because of the lobbying of the Catholic Church, but because it is one of those rare instruments of law that are powerfully, ringingly right. And because state legislatures and public referendums, have indicated that most Americans believe abortions to be profoundly wrong.

Here is what the proposed amendment provides:

Section 1: With respect to the right to life, the word "person," as used in this Article and in the Fifth and Fourteenth Articles of Amendment to the Constitution of the United States, applies to all human beings, including their unborn offspring at every stage of their biological development, irrespective of age, health, function, or condition of dependency.

Section 2: This Article shall not apply in an emergency when a reasonable medical certainty exists that continuation of the pregnancy will cause the death of the mother.

Section 3: Congress and the several states shall have power to enforce this Article by appropriate legislation within their respective jurisdictions.

Interestingly, the most effective campaigner against abortion these days is not some jowly old bishop but a Methodist housewife named Marjory Mecklenburg. Mrs. Mecklenburg has been making speeches around the country, emphasizing the ecumenical nature of the fight against wholesale abortions.

Says she: "To me the crux of this issue is that abortion is the killing of a human who can't protect himself. Obviously, Christians and all humanitarians should help those who can't defend themselves. It is only if you feel that you have no responsibility, one for another, that you can stand by and let another human life be attacked."

If you agree, I hope you will tell your senators. If you disagree, I hope you will think it over.

—*EDWIN A. ROBERTS, JR.*

This column offers varied views of our diverse staff—observations the editors rate worthy of reader consideration.

Intensely Personal

(13

To the Editor:

Regarding "An Amendment About Life" I find it impossible to empathize with Mr. Roberts' point of view. To lump those who are aged, deformed, paralyzed or retarded into the terminology of the Supreme Court decision along with proto-plasmic non-beings is, to me, unthink-ble. The only common ground in this convenient lumping is that they were all, at one time or another, conceived (convenient insofar as giving additional "weight" to Mr. Roberts' argument).

To my thinking, however, the issue is an intensely personal one and should not be brought under the jurisdiction of the courts or the legislature but should be the sole responsibility of the mother-to-be. I assume that in Mr. Roberts' opinion (as well as Senator Buckley, Mrs. Mecklenburg and unnamed others), all unwanted children should be allowed to be born regardless of the circumstances or results of such births. In this age of increased human sensitivity it seems to me that any woman who feels that the birth of a child would do her irreparable harm should not be compelled to bear that child.

Where do we place the importance? Are we to attach such great importance to "life" that we refuse to prevent it (or stop it, in Mr. Roberts' thinking), thus possibly destroying the lives of those who are already living? Is our responsibility as moral creatures to those who *may be* or to those who *are?* Is it equally moral to force a mother to bear a child she neither wants nor can care for as to bring a child into the world to be loved and cared for by its parents?

I would like to remind Mr. Roberts that we are in the midst of a population explosion. There are children growing up unwanted at all levels of society, whose parent(s) cannot provide the type of environment conducive to developing healthy attitudes toward life, and others who are being brought up in orphanages. These are the victims of the thinking of Mr. Roberts and others who feel the act of conception is the origin of an inalienable right to live.

MIRIAM V. DOMER

Denver

☆　☆　☆

(14

'Self-Contradictory'

To the Editor:

The Human Life Amendment is surely self-contradictory. How can a law proclaim in Section 1 that "persons" born and unborn have an equal right to life and in Section 2 that one person's life may be sacrificed when another person's life is in danger?

Are mothers more equal than babies? Why not just let the mother die and then take such measures as are needed to preserve the life of the surviving "person."

DOROTHEA FULKERSON

Levittown, N.Y.

☆　☆　☆

Above, letter to the editor of *The National Observer* by Miriam V. Domer, July 14, 1973.

Right, letter to the editor of *The National Observer* by Dorothea Fulkerson, July 14, 1973.

The Catholic Viewpoint On Murder Of Infants Is Ours

SOME TRUTHS ABOUT ABORTION

By Walter W. Krebs

Editor of Johnstown Tribune-Democat

(Editor's Note: The author of today's column is Charles E. Kane, president of Johnstown Curia of the Legion of Mary. In this article, he presents arguments against the spreading permissiveness in regard to abortions.)

If you should walk into a public building, and there confront a distinguished-looking man with a knife poised to stab a young chld, and he should turn to you and say, "I have decided the life of this child must be ended; do not interfere with my freedom to do as I see fit," would you agree? Or would you try to stop him?

This act is being performed in many places. The child is 2 . . . 4 . . . 6 . . . 8 . . . months old. The only difference from the above scene is that the child is still in the mother's womb.

Ever since Vatican Council II, Catholics have become very self-conscious about imposing our will on those of other faiths. Meanwhile the forces of existentialism have not been reticent about imposing their will on us. The time has come to cut through the web of permissive mumbojumbo and look at a few objective truths.

Life begins at conception. For support of this position we go back to 400 B.C. to the age of Hippocrates. For those few doctors who may have forgotten, this is the oath they pledged: "I will not give to a woman an instrument to produce abortion."

Common law for centuries has recognized the rights of the fetus. It is a very recent development (I say "development" advisedly) that the desire of the mother not to have a baby has been imposed over the right of the child to be born.

Turn to the Bible and read the account of the Annunciation wherein Jesus Christ is conceived. Then read on to the account of the Visitation a few weeks later.

The God-Embryo sanctified John the Baptist while both were in their mothers' wombs.. Yet it is young souls like this from which some would snatch the right to life, without even offering the sanctifying waters of baptism so that the infant soul could be saved. If Jesus Christ were conceived today under the laws of some of our states, the pregnancy would probably be aborted.

Those who are obsessed with the idea that the murder of unborn infants should be made legal, moral, even desirable, will not settle for half-way measures. They began by advocating abortion of pregnancies resulting from such despicable acts as rape or incest. But this has proved a wedge to abortion on demand. The question in my mind is: At whose demand?

One proponent of abortion labeled it "the ultimate method of birth control." Another advocated on TV that abortion should be imposed on all mothers after the third pregnancy? Still another says the state should allow only two children per couple.

Yet another confused young girl declared to the nation that she will never permit any children to be born because it contributes to pollution. (I suppose she and her husband will invest the money they save by not having children in another expensive sports car or a motor boat.)

If we accept the validity of such argument, where will it stop? Shall we "put to sleep" a child which we discover to be retarded or deformed after birth? If we can kill at 6 . . . 7 . . . 8 months after conception, why not 9 . . . 10 . . . 11 . . . months?

It is obvious the stop will not be called until we give in to those who would supplant God's function of giving life with a committee to decide which children would be born; where and when

they would be born; what sex, race and intelligence they would be born with.

Another argument of the abortionists is that legalizing abortion would eliminate illegal abortions. Ridiculous! As a corollary we might say, "We can eliminate speeding on the highways by eliminating speed limits." To carry the argument to the extreme, we could elminate all crime by eliminating all laws.

A similar argument is made for the legalization of marijuana - by many of the same people. I cannot understand how someone can be so disturbed by the deaths of children in Asia and Africa—unfortunate though they be - but at the same time advocate smashing the life from millions of our own children.

But whatever changes we make in the laws of man, there still remain the laws of God. "Thou shall not kill." The abortionists are asking us to say murder is not murder when the victim is still in the mother's womb.

The dehumanization of our society has been noted by many prominent philosophers. This has led us to our current problems, including pornography, sexual deviations, abuse of drugs. The beginning of the decline of respect for human life led us to advocation of artificial birth control. The advocation of abortion for "medical reasons" was only a logical extension of this. This, in turn, has expanded to abortion on demand.

The next "logical" step will be euthanasia. Why not? With millions of abortions - legal and illegal - every year in this country, it is already tantamount to genocide.

I do not call upon my fellow Catholics to impose their beliefs on those of other faiths. But I do call upon all men of good will to recognize an objective moral evil and to speak out while time remains to protect the value of human life.

Right, from *The Wanderer*, March 11, 1971.
Top page, from *The Capital Voice*, March 1, 1971.

Spiro's Theory

"Sooner or later," said Spiro T. Agnew last month, extemporaneously, government must decide whether or not to let terminal patients die, deprive mothers of illegitimate babies of welfare payments and take children from unfit mothers. "I have a theory that these problems will never be subject to complete solution until somebody in public life is willing to take on the hard social judgments that, very frankly, no one I know in elective office is willing to even think about tackling" for fear of being "victimized by the demagogues."

In a newspaper column appearing at about the same time, the Vice President addressed himself to "one angle of the [welfare] problem that must have our best and most serious thinking." Since it is "ridiculous" to think of welfare mothers as capable of providing a "decent home environment," adoption laws must be liberalized to make it easier for couples "willing and able to give children the home they need." Mr. Agnew was not explicit about how the children were to get from their unqualified mothers into the hands of government-qualified parents (perhaps he did not want to dilute the effect of his next speech), but he did offer a clue as to what children he had in mind: children's problems are "far greater in the urban ghettos and it is here that we must begin."

A Republican-sponsored bill recently introduced in the Connecticut legislature proposes that welfare mothers with two or more illegitimate children be given $300 if they agree to undergo sterilization at state expense. Meanwhile the Supreme Court has ruled, in Justice Harry Blackmun's maiden opinion, that welfare recipients may not refuse, under the Fourth Amendment, to open their homes to "visits" by government social workers; to do so, in fact, should automatically disqualify them for further aid.

All rather surprising views to come from Republicans, from a "conservative" Supreme Court, from Spiro T. Agnew, no? No.

Sterilization

The position of the Catholic Church is therefore a condemnation of all forms of direct sterilization, whether compulsory or voluntary. Her condemnation is based on ethics which lay great emphasis on one's inalienable right to life and bodily integrity. The mentality of the contemporary social milieu cannot understand why God may permit suffering and other forms of societal problems to exist. Eugenists fail to see that happiness hereafter is purchasable by self-sacrificing care of the unfortunate. Divine Providence permits the unfortunate to be among us to give man an opportunity to exercise that charity which deserves the kingdom of heaven. They scarcely deserve that kingdom who would rid us of the inconvenient presence of unfortunates by violating nature's law. (See Higgins, S. J., op. cit., p. 214). If God allows misfortune and adversity to exist, He does so for a reason. Suffering may be the occasion for advancement in our spiritual life. Nothing takes place without a reason. God is the Creator of this universe, He is good, kind, just and all powerful. We must have faith in according Him the wisdom in knowing how to run this complex world in which we find ourselves.

Top, from *Triumph*, publication of the Society for the Christian Commonwealth, 278 Broadview Avenue, Warrenton, Virginia 22186, February, 1971.

ON THE RIGHT

William F. Buckley Jr.

✳   ✳   ✳

WELFARE. Let's quit horsing around. The permanent denizens of the welfare rolls, as distinct from the handicapped and the helpless and the temporarily unfortunate, are moral criminals and should be treated as legal criminals too. If parents of a child born out of wedlock are unable or unwilling to care for the child, the parents should be jailed and the child should be put in an institution. For the second bastard, the parents should be sterilized. (Here I note parenthetically the distinction between punitive sterilization and eugenic sterilization. The latter is forbidden by the natural law, by the Catholic Church, and I trust by other churches. Not so the former—though I have no doubt the bleeding hearts would be aghast at the idea.)

Drastic, yes. But does anyone doubt that our present system calls for a drastic remedy? We should never forget that the cost of welfare is only secondarily financial. It breeds a growing underclass that saps the foundation of education, morals and patriotism, that assures an ever-growing criminal cadre. Welfare *attacks America*.

SECTION 9

Murder or Mercy?

Although at first thought it might seem that the question "What is a human being?" must be restricted to the period that the fetus is in the mother's womb, this section contains a number of examples which raise this question for a variety of other cases. It is certainly not uncommon to hear in everyday discourse statements to the effect that a severely retarded infant or a comatose, terminally ill adult is nothing more than a "vegetable," where it is not always clear that this expression is being used figuratively. Such characterizations of the nature of certain individuals are used in some of the arguments in this section as part of the justification for permitting the termination of the lives of these individuals.

In contrast to the arguments that attempt to deny that the individuals involved are humans, many of the arguments in this section deal with cases where this strategy is not feasible or which for other reasons are based on the assumption that the individual involved is indeed a human being. In these arguments the basic question is that of the rightness or wrongness of taking a human life under certain very special circumstances, such as to prevent the suffering of the individual or serious inconvenience to others. The decisions involved in these cases fall into three basic categories, each of which has two forms. These categories are:

1. assisting another person in the termination of that person's life at the request of that person;
2. terminating the life of another person when that person is in a state which

prevents him or her from asking for or refusing such treatment (because he or she is comatose, severely retarded, etc.); and

3. terminating one's own life, with or without assistance from others; in other words, committing suicide.

Each of these categories of termination of life have two forms—active and passive; that is, it is possible to terminate the life by some single direct act (such as shooting with a gun or poisoning) or by *not* acting or withholding basic supportive assistance (such as essential surgery, medicine, or food). While this is a problem which many physicians must address on a regular basis, it is *not* one which any person can be confident of not having to face at some time during (possibly at the very end) of his or her own life. When the question does arise, the person most directly involved very often is not in a good condition for thinking things through as carefully and rationally as might be desirable. Thus it would be quite wise to begin to think through some of these issues now while one has the time and mental and emotional capacities required by the significance of the problem.

EXERCISES

1. Into which of the three categories listed above does each of the cases discussed in this section fall? Determine which of the two forms (active or passive) is involved in each case. Ascertain whether the basic strategy of each argument is to deny that the individual involved is a human being or to assume that the individual is human.
2. Discuss the question of defining "human being." Is an argument in support of the judgment that "The term human being should be defined in such and such a way" a *moral* argument? If it is not a moral argument, what kind is it?
3. Compare the arguments in this section which are based on the assumption that the individual whose life is being terminated is a human being with the arguments for and against capital punishment in Section 12. Are there any moral theories which could be used to support the termination of life in one case but not in the other?

Charge mongoloid baby starved 16 days

By Michael Miner

A newborn mongoloid infant in a Downstate Catholic hospital was allowed to starve for 16 days because its parents wanted the baby to die, members of two Illinois organizations charged Thursday.

Mary Anne Smith, founder of Illinois Citizens Concerned for Life, said the baby was born April 8 in St. Mary's Hospital in Decatur.

According to the ICCL and the Illinois Right to Life Committee, the infant's esophagus was incomplete and the parents would not allow the operation that would have permitted their child to eat.

Furthermore, they said, the parents would not allow the child to be fed intravenously.

This is not unprecedented. Medical records show other mongoloid children have been allowed to die in other hospitals.

Jerome Frazel, an attorney for the Right to Life Committee, said he threatened a malpractice suit, after which, according to his sources, intravenous feeding began Wednesday.

Sister Ann, the administrator of St. Mary's Hospital, told The Sun-Times, "I cannot discuss the case with you at this time."

Frazel said that Mrs. Betty Boland, a registered nurse at St. Mary's, resigned because of the hospital's treatment of the infant.

Mrs. Boland confirmed to The Sun-Times that she gave two weeks' notice on Tuesday, but she said she was ethically constrained from discussing what went on in the hospital.

"I'm used to practicing professional ethics," Mrs. Boland said. "I feel it's unfortunate that it's keeping me from taking action if there's any action to be taken."

Other persons with knowledge of the situation also declined to discuss the matter with The Sun-Times.

The Rev. John Spreen, family life director of the Springfield Diocese, which includes Decatur, and a member of both right-to-life organizations, said Thursday, "As far as I'm concerned, the hospital authorities have taken care of the situation."

Father Spreen would say nothing more.

Mrs. Smith said that at least five persons have called Sister Ann to say they would be interested in adopting the infant. The hospital's administrator has taken their names.

One woman, according to Patricia Kelley, another member of Illinois Citizens Concerned for Life, has hired a lawyer to help in an attempt to adopt the baby.

Mrs. Kelley said that members of her organization have tried to contact the parents through Sister Ann, but have received no response.

"As a woman," Mrs. Kelley said, "I'd want to befriend that poor mother and point out to the woman the degree of mental retardation certainly cannot be determined at birth. People will grasp at the slightest straw of hope and sometimes, going on hope, miracles will happen. . .

"It has us all terribly upset, the idea that a child could be shoved aside to starve to death because it might be less than perfect. It disturbs me for society. If we can lock a baby in a room and walk past it as it starves to death, we can walk past a My Lai. We can walk past the South Side of Chicago.

"It diminishes us all as people."

An article on retarded children in the Oct. 15, 1972, issue of Midwest magazine reported that a generation ago, the mongoloid child — that is the child born with Down's Syndrome — "was automatically institutionalized" and seldom spoken of again.

The article continued:

"Now, however, the parents of the mongoloid, guided by their physician, decide which course is correct . . .

"At least four times in the last five years, parents of mongoloids born at Johns Hopkins Hospital in Baltimore have elected . . . to let the baby die. In each case, corrective surgery would, in the opinion of the physicians involved, have spared the child" from death.

Top, reprinted with permission from *The Chicago Sun-Times* (April 27, 1973). Author of the article, Michael Miner.

MEDICINE

The Hardest Choice

In Baltimore three years ago, the parents of a newborn Mongoloid baby refused to allow an operation to correct a fatal defect in the infant's digestive tract. Despite pressure from doctors and hospital personnel, they refused to change their minds, and the child slowly starved to death.

In Portland, Me., last month, when parents made a similar decision about their severely deformed infant, hospital officials asked a court to decide. A judge, holding that the baby had a right to live, issued an order that allowed doctors to operate on the child. Despite the surgery, the infant died 15 days after birth.

These cases illustrate a vexing dilemma now confronting modern medicine: Should lives of retarded infants or those with multiple birth defects be prolonged—at great cost in manpower, money and anguish—especially if the life that is preserved will almost certainly be one of pain or merely vegetable-like existence?

Few, if any, doctors are willing to establish guidelines for determining which babies should receive lifesaving surgery or treatment and which should not. But many recognize that there are cases, particularly those involving multiple anomalies, when a hands-off attitude is probably for the best. Says Dr. Joan Hodgman, professor of pediatrics at the University of Southern California School of Medicine: "If we have a baby that I know is malformed beyond hope, I make no attempt to preserve life."

Time of Need. Other doctors, too, are speaking out on the subject. Drs. Raymond Duff and A.G.M. Campbell reported in the *New England Journal of Medicine* on a study of 299 deaths among 2,171 children treated in the special-care nursery at Yale–New Haven Hospital over a 2½-year period. They found that 43 of the infants died after parents and doctors decided jointly to discontinue treatment. The other 256, who received the best treatment modern medicine could provide, fared no better; few lived longer than the infants who received no special care. Furthermore, their short existence in many cases bore little relation to human life. One infant, who could not breathe on his own, was kept alive for five months as a virtual extension of a mechanical respirator.

Duff and Campbell believe that in such cases doctors must at least consider whether or not their efforts are in the infant's best interests. "Pretending there is no decision to be made is an arbitrary and potentially devastating decision by default," they write. "It may constitute a victimizing abandonment of patients and their families in times of greatest need."

Not all doctors agree. Some feel that they are bound by the Hippocratic oath to do all they can to preserve life. Others, aware that an incurable condition today may be a manageable one tomorrow, fear making the wrong decision. "No matter how expert we are, we can't predict outcome," says Dr. Judah Folkman, surgeon in chief at Children's Hospital Medical Center in Boston.

Above, reprinted by permission from *Time, The Weekly Newsmagazine* (March 26, 1974); copyright Time, Inc.

Wait Three Days After Birth Before Declaring Child Alive

I think we must re-evaluate our basic assumptions about the meaning of life. Perhaps, as my former colleague Francis Crick suggested, no one should be thought of as alive until about three days after birth. . . .

Our society just hasn't faced up to this problem. In a primitive society, if you saw a baby was deformed, you would abandon it on a hillside. Today this isn't permissible, and with our medicine getting better and better in the sense of being able to keep sick people alive longer, we are going to produce more people living wretched lives. I don't know how you get society to change on such a basic issue; infanticide isn't regarded lightly by anyone.

Fortunately, now through such techniques as amniocentesis, parents can often learn in advance whether their child will be normal and healthy or hopelessly deformed. They then can choose either to have the child or opt for a therapeutic abortion. But the cruel fact remains that because of the present limits of such detection methods, most birth defects are not discovered until birth.

If a child were not declared alive until three days after birth, then all parents could be allowed the choice that only a few are given under the present system. The doctor could allow the child to die if the parents so chose and save a lot of misery and suffering. I believe this view is the only rational, compassionate attitude to have.

—*Nobel laureate* JAMES D. WATSON *in an interview in* Prism, *a magazine published by the American Medical Association.*

Left, from *The National Observer*, September 1, 1973. Copyright Dow Jones & Co., Inc.
Right, reprinted by permission of United Press International.

JUDGE ORDERS CARE FOR MONGOLOID CHILD

MANHASSET, L. I., Oct. 1 (UPI)—A couple who told hospital authorities not to treat their newborn Mongoloid son have been ordered to appear in family court tomorrow to explain their action.

In the meantime, a judge has ordered doctors at North Shore Hospital to give the child the medical treatment he needs.

The boy was born Sept. 4 in Syosset Hospital, where the hospital administrator Pearl Klick, said that the parents had given notice that the infant was to receive no medical treatment.

"We don't act as physicians,' Miss Klick said. "We just care for people. They have their own physicians."

Doctors said that the infant, David Habib, son of a Queens College teacher and his 20-year-old wife, needed surgery to remove an intestinal blockage as well as other treatment for Down's Syndrome, or Mongolism, the most severe and most physically noticeable form of mental retardation.

An anonymous telephone call alerted the child's condition to the Nassau Department of Social Service's Child Protective Division, which referred the case to family court.

Family Court Judge William Dempsey ordered the baby transferred from Syosset Hospital to North Shore Hospital in Manhasset for corrective surgery over the weekend.

Judge plays God

Deformed child dies after court-ordered surgery

PORTLAND, Maine (AP) —The parents of a deformed baby whose 15 days of life sparked a legal and moral controvery have cticized the court for playing God.

David Patrick Houle, the infant son of Air Force Sgt. and Mrs. Robert B.T. Houle of Westbrook, died Sunday in the Main Medical Center here after being in poor condition since the previous Tuesday.

The baby had undergone court-ordered surgery after the hospital sued the parents when they reportedly refused permission for an operation.

The Houles said in a statement released by their lawyer, Navy Lt. James Freyer, that they were "most disturbed by the actions of the court in divesting them of the right to make an intimate parental decision that they believe was rightfully theirs."

The statement added, "Since nature determined that this infant was not a viable life, it was the court and not the parents that played God in deciding that the infant should be kept alive con-

trary to the laws of nature. Mercifully, as between nature and the Superior Court, nature was the court of last resort."

The baby's physician had told the court that corrective surgery would probably not be of any benefit to the infant.

Superior Court Justice David G. Roberts ordered the operation, saying the parents had no right to withhold the treatment because the baby had a "right to life."

Surgery was performed to place a food tube in the baby's stomach. A second op-

eration to connect the esophaugus to the stomach was to be performed next. The child was born with no left eye or ear canal and other deformities.

"If the infant had lived the life of suffering which might well have resulted from the court's decision, the parents could not have escaped the feeling of responsibility that would come from knowing that they were the ones who brought it into the world, yet they were deprived of any and all say as to its future," the Houles' statement said.

Above, courtesy of The Associated Press.

'Murdered' Infants

To the Editor:

Regarding the article "Why Doctors, Parents Let Deformed Babies Die" [Nov. 10], I would like to know why these so-called doctors and parents haven't been locked up?

The taking of a human life is murder, no matter how much you try to justify it. It was always my understanding that the duty of a doctor was to prolong life, not to stifle it by withholding treatment.

How can the parents of a deformed baby say that it is too expensive to keep the baby alive? If the baby were healthy, the parents wouldn't hesitate to spend $15,000 or more for its education.

A deformed baby is a human life, and who are doctors—or parents, for that matter—to decide whether that life should exist or not? A baby of any kind is a gift from God, and only God has the right to take it away.

CATHY MARTIN

Prince George, Va.

Left, letter to the editor of *The National Observer* by Cathy Martin, December 15, 1973.

Right, letter to the editor of *Newsweek* by Sondra Diamond, counseling psychologist, December 3, 1973.

Life-and-Death Decisions

I'll wager my entire root system and as much fertilizer as it would take to fill Yale University that you have never received a letter from a vegetable before this one, but, much as I resent the term, I must confess that I fit the description of a "vegetable" as defined in the article "Shall This Child Die?" (MEDICINE, Nov. 12).

Due to severe brain damage incurred at birth, I am unable to dress myself, toilet myself, or write; my secretary is typing this letter. Many thousands of dollars had to be spent on my rehabilitation and education in order for me to reach my present professional status as a counseling psychologist. My parents were also told, 35 years ago, that there was "little or no hope of achieving meaningful 'humanhood'" for their daughter. Have I reached "humanhood"? Compared with Drs. Duff and Campbell, I believe I have surpassed it!

Instead of changing the law to make it legal to weed out us "vegetables," let us change the laws so that we may receive quality medical care, education and freedom to live as full and productive lives as our potentials allow.

SONDRA DIAMOND

Philadelphia, Pa.

A New Ethic for Medicine And Society

THE TRADITIONAL WESTERN ETHIC has always placed great emphasis on the intrinsic worth and equal value of every human life regardless of its stage or condition. This ethic has had the blessing of the Judeo-Christian heritage and has been the basis for most of our laws and much of our social policy. The reverence for each and every human life has also been a keystone of Western medicine and is the ethic which has caused physicians to try to preserve, protect, repair, prolong and enhance every human life which comes under their surveillance. This traditional ethic is still clearly dominant, but there is much to suggest that it is being eroded at its core and may eventually even be abandoned. This of course will produce profound changes in Western medicine and in Western society.

There are certain new facts and social realities which are becoming recognized, are widely discussed in Western society and seem certain to undermine and transform this traditional ethic. They have come into being and into focus as the social by-products of unprecedented technologic progress and achievement. Of particular importance are, first, the demographic data of human population expansion which tends to proceed uncontrolled and at a geometric rate of progression; second, an ever growing ecological disparity between the numbers of people and the resources available to support these numbers in the manner to which they are or would like to become accustomed; and third, and perhaps most important, a quite new social emphasis on something which is beginning to be called the quality of life, a something which becomes possible for the

From *California Medicine*, September 1970.

first time in human history because of scientific and technologic development. These are now being seen by a growing segment of the public as realities which are within the power of humans to control and there is quite evidently an increasing determination to do this.

What is not yet so clearly perceived is that in order to bring this about hard choices will have to be made with respect to what is to be preserved and strengthened and what is not, and that this will of necessity violate and ultimately destroy the traditional Western ethic with all that this portends. It will become necessary and acceptable to place relative rather than absolute values on such things as human lives, the use of scarce resources and the various elements which are to make up the quality of life or of living which is to be sought. This is quite distinctly at variance with the Judeo-Christian ethic and carries serious philosophical, social, economic and political implications for Western society and perhaps for world society.

The process of eroding the old ethic and substituting the new has already begun. It may be seen most clearly in changing attitudes toward human abortion. In defiance of the long held Western ethic of intrinsic and equal value for every human life regardless of its stage, condition or status, abortion is becoming accepted by society as moral, right and even necessary. It is worth noting that this shift in public attitude has affected the churches, the laws and public policy rather than the reverse. Since the old ethic has not yet been fully displaced it has been necessary to separate the idea of abortion from the idea of killing, which continues to be socially abhorrent. The result has been a curious avoidance of the scientific fact, which everyone really knows, that human life begins at conception and is continuous whether intra- or extra-uterine until death. The very considerable semantic gymnastics which are required to rationalize abortion as anything but taking a human life would be ludicrous if they were not often put forth under socially impeccable auspices. It is suggested that this schizophrenic sort of subterfuge is necessary because while a new ethic is being accepted the old one has not yet been rejected.

It seems safe to predict that the new demographic, ecological and social realities and aspirations are so powerful that the new ethic of relative rather than of absolute and equal values

will ultimately prevail as man exercises ever more certain and effective control over his numbers, and uses his always comparatively scarce resources to provide the nutrition, housing, economic support, education and health care in such ways as to achieve his desired quality of life and living. The criteria upon which these relative values are to be based will depend considerably upon whatever concept of the quality of life or living is developed. This may be expected to reflect the extent that quality of life is considered to be a function of personal fulfillment; of individual responsibility for the common welfare, the preservation of the environment, the betterment of the species; and of whether or not, or to what extent, these responsibilities are to be exercised on a compulsory or voluntary basis.

The part which medicine will play as all this develops is not yet entirely clear. That it will be deeply involved is certain. Medicine's role with respect to changing attitudes toward abortion may well be a prototype of what is to occur. Another precedent may be found in the part physicians have played in evaluating who is and who is not to be given costly long-term renal dialysis. Certainly this has required placing relative values on human lives and the impact of the physician to this decision process has been considerable. One may anticipate further development of these roles as the problems of birth control and birth selection are extended inevitably to death selection and death control whether by the individual or by society, and further public and professional determinations of when and when not to use scarce resources.

Since the problems which the new demographic, ecologic and social realities pose are fundamentally biological and ecological in nature and pertain to the survival and well-being of human beings, the participation of physicians and of the medical profession will be essential in planning and decision-making at many levels. No other discipline has the knowledge of human nature, human behavior, health and disease, and of what is involved in physical and mental well-being which will be needed. It is not too early for our profession to examine this new ethic, recognize it for what it is and will mean for human society, and prepare to apply it in a rational development for the fulfillment and betterment of mankind in what is almost certain to be a biologically oriented world society.

The "New Ethic"

By FRANK MORRISS

An editorial in last September's issue of **California Medicine** has one virtue — extreme candor. This "Official Journal of the California Medical Association" suggests we have done with the hypocrisy of suggesting that life in the womb isn't human, which it says is contrary to medical fact. Instead, we should simply become adjusted to taking human life as the changing public attitude demands.

It seems, according to this editorial, that our distaste for taking human life is tied to our Judeo-Christian heritage, "which has been the basis for most of our laws and much of our social policy." But as everyone knows this "traditional ethic," though still dominant, "is being eroded at its core and may eventually even be abandoned."

As this process progresses, the editorial says, "it will become necessary and acceptable to place relative rather than absolute values on such things as human lives. . . ." Apparently determining these relative values will be the pressure of population, depletion of resources, a "quality of life" linked to "personal fulfillment," preservation of the environment, and most ominous of all, "betterment of the species."

Then comes the call for doctors to get ready to fulfill their duty to the "new ethic." Just as it has responded to the call for abortion (even though bothered by that hypocritical debate over what is being aborted, when every scientist knows it is a human), medical science must be ready to respond when the day dawns for "death selection and death control."

California Medicine is worried that doctors won't be asked to bring their expertise to bear in the determination of these policies, and it insists that "the participation of physicians and of the medical profession will be essential in planning and decision-making at many levels." To guarantee all this, doctors are told that "it is not too early for our profession to examine this new ethic, recognize it for what it is and will mean for human society, and prepare to apply it . . . in what is almost certain to be a biologically oriented world society." There is the distinct impression that **California Medicine** can hardly wait until doctors cannot only serve humanity without reproach by killing admitted humans in the womb, but can extend that service to cover old persons or anyone else standing in the way of that "quality of life" which a biologically oriented world society will make the norm.

All in all, this editorial is one of the most chilling bits of horror writing I have ever come across, perhaps because of its extreme honesty. It is a little as if we should dig up in the ruins of some Berlin building an exhortation to German doctors to get ready to serve Hitler's Reich by exterminating all of the enemies of the "good Nazi life." Here we have the medical profession being told by one of its official agencies to prepare to wipe out all who are enemies of the "good American life," and not be worried about the silly question of whether innocent humans should be killed — for of course they should be if society demands it.

I have called the extreme candor of this editorial a virtue. It is, and it may serve a good purpose if it will only awake our Jewish and Protestant brethren who have been hitherto apathetic to warnings about the implication of abortion. Some of these friends have tried to insist that abortion is well within the Christian and Jewish ethic. I respect the **California Medicine**'s view on that issue more than the ignorance of those who don't see what the true issue is.

The Judeo-Christian ethic is being discarded, and what that means is that human life will become valueless as such, and will be protected only in its ramifications for society. No true Christian or Jew can ever allow such a situation to come about without fighting it even to the point of martyrdom. **California Medicine**'s appeal for legalization and acceptance of murder must be matched by the religion's determination it shall not happen

(I am indebted to L.I.F.E., 615 W. Civic Center Drive, Santa Ana, Calif., 92701, for a copy of the editorial discussed above.)

From *The Wanderer*, Copyright 1971.

William Hines

Abusing the right to die

WASHINGTON — What happened to Harry S. Truman in his final agony shouldn't have happened to a laboratory animal.

The fighting, feisty little figure whom all of us of middle or greater age remember from the '40s and '50s was sustained for weeks (if "sustained" is the proper word) after all rational hope for an old man's survival was gone. The terminal care of Harry Truman wasn't therapy, it was cruelty.

Rumors persist that Mr. Truman had a long-standing agreement with his old friend and personal physician, Dr. Wallace Graham, that when his time came he would be allowed to die in peace and dignity. The rumors are impossible to check because of the traditional veil over the doctor-patient relationship, but it would have been characteristic of Mr. Truman to insist on this, and if in fact the agreement existed it was somehow violated over his not-quite-dead body.

There is no question that a dying person can be sustained for long periods in an undead condition. Medical science has come so far that the Vatican has found it advisable to rule that so-called "heroic" measures of life support are not morally required.

THERE MAY BE AN EXCUSE for keeping a body functioning on a cellular level long after all hope of recovery is past; for example, while a kidney or heart patient is being prepared to receive an organ from a fatally injured donor. And it is not only justified but imperative to give all available support to a sick person with a reasonable expectation of resuming a life with some degree of quality to it.

But to hook up an 88-year-old man with widespread infirmities and without any real hope of improvement, to a battery of machines — to feed oxygen directly into his lungs and chemical solutions into his veins, to invade him with catheters and to visit on him God knows what other sorts of indignities is inexcusable.

To embalm Lenin and leave him on display for half a century has been denounced as barbaric. To publicize Mr. Truman's dying agonies in periodic bulletins trumpeting what can only be described as extremist medicine is hardly less so. The man who filled Franklin D. Roosevelt's chair better than anyone imagined he could deserved something other than this.

The right to life is held in basic American law to be inalienable. Debate over abortion hinges mainly on whether the fetus is an independent being or an appendage of the mother. People who advocate termination of pregnancy while the procedure is still safe for the mother do not advocate post-natal destruction of the infant. The child is born; let him live.

BUT THE RIGHT TO DIE apparently is not so solidly established in law and tradition. Organizations have been formed to protect their adherents from exactly what happened to Mr. Truman, but there is some question whether a written statement of one's desire to die in peace is legally enforceable. A hospital administrator or physician, his eye warily cocked for possible negligence or malpractice suits, might think twice about pulling the plug on a terminal patient if the next-of-kin insisted on further medical efforts.

It has been suggested that maybe Mr. Truman, as a former President, was somehow different from ordinary people and that therefore the special measures to sustain him were justified. This is fuzzy logic to say the least. Presidents are people too, and people die; among all ex-Presidents only Lyndon B. Johnson is the exception that (temporarily) tests the rule.

The place for the former leader of a people is in their hearts, not in an intensive care ward. Today Mr. Truman is where he belongs; he should have been allowed to go there in peace a couple of weeks sooner.

Reprinted with permission from the *Chicago Sun-Times* (January 2, 1973). Author of article, William Hines.

Is 'Mercy Killing' The Same As Murder?

By B. D. COLEN

The Washington Post

WASHINGTON — About four times in the past year, doctors at the Maryland Institute for Emergency Medicine turned off the respirator that was maintaining the life of a quadriplegic patient whose body was completely and irrevocably paralyzed — but whose brain was functioning.

Each time the institute receives such a patient, it keeps the person alive for a few weeks, long enough to determine if the patient's condition will improve to the point where he can again lead a meaningful life. And each time the doctors end up turning off the respirator.

The quadriplegics are never told their respirators are going to be turned off and their families are told only obliquely, according to Dr. William Gill, clinical director of the institute. Gill said the unit receives about four such patients a year.

However, said Gill, the respirator is never turned off if a family asks that it remain on.

"It's illegal, I suppose some people would argue that," said Gill. "(But) you're not actively doing anything to worsen the patient's state than when he came in here. All you are doing is using artificial support to see if you can do something (save the patient), and then withdrawing that support when we find there is nothing we can do.

"We use that as a rationalization in our own mind," said Gill.

The development of various scientific medical marvels has put doctors in a position where they are literally able to revive the dead, but once they do that, they can do nothing to correct the problem that killed the man in the first place.

While the dying and their doctors are often faced with moral dilemmas concerning when to cease treatment, there is also an economic question.

A bed in the intensive care area of the shock trauma unit costs $575 a day and, while officials of the unit said that the average patient runs up a bill of only a few thousand dollars, there have been bills for as much as $50,000 for patients who have been in the unit up to 70 days.

While officials say they never discuss finances with a patient or his family, they say society as a whole must consider the expenses involved in maintaining a patient who will never again function as a normal human being.

"You must think in terms of how much money society should spend on supporting the life of this type if individual," said Dr. McAslam.

"Whether we like to talk about this or not, are we normally correct in spending (huge sums of money to sustain a human vegetable) when we can take a child from the ghetto area with a heart (problem) and, with the same amount of money produce a productive, healthy child with a full life ahead of him, a normal life?" asked McAslan.

DEAR ABBY

By Abigail Van Buren

Top, © The Washington Post.
Above, courtesy of Abigail Van Buren, syndicated newspaper columnist, "Dear Abby."

DEAR ABBY: The headline over your column read, "Is there mercy in killing?" My answer to that question is, "Definitely, yes!"

My mother in law watched her handsome, 6-foot, 200-pound husband dwindle down to 87 pounds when he finally died, and that took four years.

I lost a daughter a year ago. She was 12 years old. For two years she laid there like a rag doll. I saw her go from a beautiful, active 10-year-old girl to a nothing of a 12-year-old vegetable; and all this because of an inoperable tumor, the size of a pea in her brain. She didn't know me or anyone else. Her heart was beating — that was all. They said they couldn't do anything so "inhumane" as to deliberately let her die. You call this living?

The hospital bill alone was $15,000. And after that, the "convalescent" home was $600 a month. A fortune to us which we would have gladly paid to save her life, but it was hopeless and everyone knew it.

Yes, sometimes it is merciful to let a person die. I've seen others suffer and linger this way, and if it ever happens to me, I will kill myself.

A MOTHER

In Terminal Suffering, Euthanasia Is Kindness

DEAR ANN LANDERS: I read with great sadness the letter from the gentleman whose aged father was dying and how the doctors were doing everything under the sun to keep the old man alive even though he wanted to go. Another example of man's inhumanity to man.

My beloved father-in-law was 98 years old. There were no tubes or machines to keep him breathing, but for one solid week we watched him as he tried to escape this vale of tears. It was heartbreaking.

We had a dog we all loved dearly. He suffered a heart attack and was in so much pain he couldn't even lie down. We took him to the veterinarian and I held his paw while the doctor gave him a shot of sodium pentathol which he never even felt. In a short time he was out of his agony. Why can't we be as benevolent to mankind?—I.V.A.

DEAR I.V.A.: I have been an outspoken and vociferous critic of using "extraordinary measures" to keep a person alive when two or three doctors have concluded that the patient is hopelessly ill with a terminal disease. To deny a person the right to die with dignity is wrong.

Your suggestion, however, that a suffering patient be "put out of his misery," as your dog was, is quite another matter. I do not believe in "mercy killing" and cannot condone a decisive act to end a human life.

Left, courtesy of Ann Landers, Field Newspaper Syndicate, and The Atlanta Journal. Right, courtesy of The Associated Press.

Jury Clears Man In Mercy Killing

FREEHOLD, N.J. (AP) — "The only crime Lester is guilty of was having his power to reason overwhelmed by events," Lester Zygmaniak's attorney told a Superior Court jury before it acquitted the young man of slaying his paralyzed brother.

The jury of seven men and five women deliberated 2½ hours on Tuesday before acquitting Zygmaniak, 23, on grounds of temporary insanity. He had been charged with first degree murder.

Zygmaniak admitted killing his 26-year-old brother, George, with a shotgun blast last June as he lay in a hospital bed, paralyzed from the neck down as the result of a motorcycle accident.

The shooting was described by friends and relatives as a mercy killing.

In his closing arguments, defense attorney Robert Ansell pleaded with the jury to release Lester "not on pity, not on sympathy, but on the evidence."

Ansell said Lester was "crazed with love" for his brother when he shot him — "The only crime Lester is guilty of was having his power to reason overwhelmed by events."

Malcolm Carton, First Asst. Monmouth County Prosecutor, told the jury that the state had proved premeditated murder, and he asked the jurors to "do what's right ... do what's honest.... There is nothing in New Jersey law that says you can take the law into your own hands."

In his testimony, Lester admitted carrying a concealed sawed-off shotgun into the hospital and shooting his brother in the head.

"I walked over and asked him if he was in pain," Lester told the jury. "He nodded he was. I asked, 'A lot of pain, George?' He nodded again.

"I went to him and I said, 'Well, I'm here today to end your pain. Is that all right with you?' He nodded yes, and the next I knew I had shot him."

To backup the claim of a mercy killing, George's widow wife, Jeannette related in court testimony during the trial that the night of the shooting her husband screamed:

"Swear to God for me that you won't let me live. Promise you won't interfere, swear to God you won't interfere."

Euthanasia

BY EUTHANASIA OR MERCY KILLING is meant the slaying of helpless invalids and of people in incurable pain.

It is called mercy killing because it is prompted by the motive of relieving a person from suffering. No doubt, freedom from pain in dying is most desirable and that was the original meaning of euthanasia (eu — well, thanatos — death). It had reference to the work of a physician when death seemed imminent and his accepted role was to alleviate as far as possible, through his medical knowledge, the suffering of death whenever it occurred.

The word today has taken a new connotation and implies the bringing about of death itself — accelerating death, not easing it. The practice of medicine in such situations is a premeditation to kill and end the suffering of an individual. Mercy killing is merely a euphemistic term; easy death by lethal doses of drugs or other means to hasten the end of life is murder and against the Fifth Commandment, which states, "Thou shalt not kill." If legalized, it will be but legal murder. Mercy killing is contrary to the natural law because it is against human nature and, consequently, against the duties of reason.

Euthanasia is detrimental to the welfare of society because it destroys man's idea of sacrifice, loyalty, and courage in bearing pain. "If some dying persons accept their suffering as a means of expiration and a source of merits in order to go forward in the love of God and in abandonment to His will, do not force anesthetics on them. They should rather be aided to follow their own way" (Pope Pius XII, op. cit.). The Catholic Church adheres to the principle that drugs which have the unintended effect of shortening life may be given to relieve pain. The patient must consent and there must be no intention on the part of the doctor to kill the patient.

Above, from the booklet, *The Sacredness of Life*, published by the Knights of Columbus, © 1966.
Below, from the *Atlantic Monthly*, April 1968.

The notion that life is sacrosanct is actually a Hindu idea, although Hindus practice things like suttee. It is not Christian or biblical. If it were, all heroism and martyrdom would be wrong, to say nothing of carnivorous diet, capital punishment, and warfare. The sanctity (what makes it precious) is not in life itself, intrinsically; it is only extrinsic and *bonum per accidens, ex casu* — according to the situation. Compared to some things, the taking of life is a small evil, and compared to some things, the loss of life is a small evil. Death is not always an enemy: it can sometimes be a friend and servant.

Life is sometimes good, and death is sometimes good. Life is no more a good in itself than any other value is. It is good, when and if it is good, because of circumstances, because of the context. When it is not good, it deserves neither protection nor preservation. Our present laws about "elective death" are not civilized. It is high time we had some constructive guidance, perhaps from a model code committee of the American Law Institute. Let the law favor living, not mere life.

— *Joseph Fletcher*

Clayton Fritchey

A Question of Life and Death

The busybody strain in American life has always been conspicuous, but there are signs that it is fading. It is becoming possible, for instance, to risk one's life or even indulge in suicidal habits without too much public interference. The retreat on the mandatory use of auto seat belts is a case in point.

It is true that the ingrained national passion to save people from themselves still flourishes enough to pass laws like ones we have had on seat belts, but it is equally true that the House of Representatives, responding to public sentiment, has voted to repeal the law, and the National Highway Safety Administration is going to make it inoperative.

There seems to be a growing consensus that if people want to defy death, it's their business, as long as what they do does not endanger others. Protests, for instance, have been lodged against allowing Evel Knievel to go ahead with what has been billed as a suicidal attempt to leap the mile-wide Snake River Canyon in Idaho in a rocket-shaped "sky-cycle," but it appears that the authorities have no intention of interfering in an effort to keep Knievel from possibly killing himself. After all, it's his life.

A few weeks ago the police did rush in when a daring young Frenchman, Phillippe Petit, strung a tightrope between the twin towers of New York's highest building, the World Trade Center, and walked, danced and stunted his way across while thousands cheered below. Petit, who did it for fun, was arrested for disorderly conduct and trespass, but the charges were later dismissed.

Evel Knievel's stunt will be watched by 50,000 people, which is only a fraction of the hundreds of thousands who go to Indianapolis every year to witness the death-defying auto races, but there is an important distinction between the two events: Nobody at Snake River Canyon will be in danger except the man in the sky-cycle. At the auto races, however, many spectators have been killed and injured over the years.

The seat belt controversy revolves around the same distinction. The mandatory interlocking belts are being abandoned in favor of voluntary ones because failure to use the belts endangers only those who choose not to bother with them. Their negligence is not a threat to others.

All cars should be made as safe as possible. It may cost more to make them with four-wheel brakes, stronger bumpers, non-shatterable windshields and other refinements, but it is well worth the price. It is the same with air bags. The will make cars more expensive, but recent tests indicate that they will save far more lives than seat belts without being the nuisance that the interlock belts are.

No doubt some ingenious drivers will find ways of circumventing the bags as they did the interlock belts, but at least the government and the auto industry will have done what they could—but not too much—to save motorists from committing suicide.

There was a time in the United States when anyone who attempted suicide—and failed—could be jailed as a criminal. Today, only nine states count it a crime. Last year San Francisco, which leads the United States in suicides, had a newspaper referendum on whether a costly view-destroying guardrail should be erected on the Golden Gate Bridge, from which more than 500 people have jumped.

By seven-to-one, the citizens voted to let them jump. This is a considerable advance over other American communities where a lot of people are still being committed to institutions after trying to end their lives, often for perfectly rational reasons.

Suicide as we mentioned signifies any act whereby a man deliberately chooses to end his life on his own authority. According to Catholic teaching suicide is a grave sin whose malice consists in an invasion of the supreme and total dominion of God over human life. Suicide is essentially immoral. We have heard many times where a man may expose himself to certain death in order to save the life of another person, but this is not suicide; it does not mean killing oneself, but accepting death for another. Suicide is the deliberate taking away of one's own life, and no matter what the motive, this is never allowed.

Man is but a steward of his corporeal life and of all his faculties, he is not the owner of his life in the sense that he owns a car, a boat or a summer home. When he deliberately takes his own life he exercises a sort of ownership which does not belong to him. "The intrinsic evil of suicide is clear also from a consideration of the truth, that, since God is the Maker and Last End of man, man belongs totally and essentially to God, he is the property and servant of God" (T. Higgins, S. J., *Man as Man*, p. 202).

Man was created to love, honor, serve and obey God here on earth and to be happy with Him forever in Heaven. By suicide man is rejecting his status of servitude; he is invading God's exclusive right and by taking his life, he assumes the role of God. The suicide puts an end to the potentiality of further service to society and of his own moral growth and perfection. It is a deliberate challenge to the moral law and an act of rebellion against God.

The first and foremost inalienable right is that of life and physical existence. This primary right flows from the concept of person and the nature of man: Since all human persons have this right, the right is possessed from the moment of conception. The right to life and especially to bodily integrity is possessed regardless of physical or mental condition. (See Pius XI, Encyclical on *Christian Marriage*). The only exception to the right of life is the case of one who is being deprived of his life in just punishment for crime. The criminal can forfeit his right to life, as the common good takes precedence over individual good, and it may become necessary that certain crimes be punished by deprivation of life in order that the rights of one's fellowmen are safe and secure.

The state, however, is no more the supreme owner of life than is the individual. It cannot order the individual to kill himself. "Suicide cannot be exercised by appeals to honor nor hallowed by reasons of state. To make an exception in the name of patriotism is to deny that there is any essential morality in suicide at all; it is to leave all moral absolutes at the mercy of the 'situation ethics' which says that nothing's right or wrong but thinking makes it so" (*America*, June 18, 1960).

According to Christian teaching the individual possesses certain fundamental rights which the state must protect and respect. The right to life is one of these. The totalitarian state grants or limits at will the rights of men, even the right to life. The life of every citizen is at the mercy of the political clique or the state. According to totalitarian thinking, the individual exists in order to serve the state. This is contrary to the Christian thought that man is not a pawn of the state and cannot be ordered to the utility of society. Man is not a mere instrument or cog in the machinery of the state. The state has no right to encourage or command suicide. To accord the state this right would not only be contrary to Christian teaching but it would open the door against all other things we consider sacred.

From the booklet *The Sacredness of Life*, published by the Knights of Columbus, © 1966.
Right, courtesy of United Press International, July 2, 1971.

Dying Woman Wins Court Plea to Stop Terminal Surgery

MIAMI, July 2 (UPI) — A daughter, appointed guardian of her mother by a judge, accepted today her pleas against the "torture" of more surgery, although it is all that can save her.

Dr. Orlando Lopez told Judge David Popper in Circuit Court that if treatments were stopped, Mrs. Carmen Martinez, 72-year-old Cuban exile, would die.

Dr. Lopez brought the case into court because he feared he could be charged with aiding the woman's suicide if he granted her request to stop treatments.

Judge Popper, noting that the cure appeared almost as bad as the disease, ruled that because of her weakened condition Mrs. Martinez was not competent to decide her fate. He appointed her eldest daughter, Mrs. Margarita Gottlieb, as guardian and gave her power to make the decision.

Suffers From Anemia

Dr. Lopez said his patient suffered from hemolytic anemia, a disease that destroys the red blood cells. He said she required either surgical removal of her spleen, or continued blood transfusions involving "cut downs" — surgical opening of her veins to facilitate transfer of blood.

"I am not able to state precisely that Mrs. Martinez will live if she is given the transfusions, but if she is not given the transfusions, then she will die," the doctor said.

"No more cut downs, no more cut downs," the daughter cried. Mrs. Gottlieb told the judge her mother had been "begging, 'Please don't torture me any more.'"

The judge said a person "has the right not to be tortured." But he said his ruling did not mean Mrs. Martinez had the right to commit suicide by refusing treatment.

He ruled that Mrs. Martinez could be given any treatment so long as it does not give her pain.

"Why shouldn't I kill myself if I want to?" he demanded.

She replied to that quite seriously.

"Because it's wrong."

"Why is it wrong?"

She looked at him doubtfully. She was not disturbed in her own belief, but she was much too inarticulate to explain her reaction.

"Well—I mean—it's wicked to kill yourself. You've got to go on living whether you like it or not."

"Why have you?"

"Well, there are other people to consider, aren't there?"

"Not in my case. There's not a soul in the world who'd be the worse for my passing on."

All the more he felt determined to force an admission from her on the ethical side.

"At any rate I've got a right to do what I like with my own life."

"No—no, you haven't."

"But why not, my dear girl, why?"

She flushed. She said, her fingers playing with the little gold cross that hung round her neck.

"You don't understand. God may need you."

He stared—taken aback. He did not want to upset her childlike faith. He said mockingly:

"I suppose that one day I may stop a runaway horse and save a golden haired child from death—eh? Is that it?"

She shook her head. She said with vehemence and trying to express what was so vivid in her mind and so halting on her tongue.

"It may be just by *being* somewhere—not doing anything—just by being at a certain place at a certain time —oh, I can't say what I mean, but you might just—just walk along a street someday and just by doing that accomplish something terribly important—perhaps without even knowing what it was."

From *Towards Zero*, © 1944 by Agatha Christie, published by Dodd, Mead and Company Inc.

John Fischer

THE EASY CHAIR

Letter from Leete's Island: a case of termination

To UNDERSTAND HER LETTER you ought to know something about Dorothy.

She was a strong-minded woman. Some called her eccentric, but since eccentrics are about as common as blue jays in our town, that was no reason for special remark. Until you got to know her ways, though, she could be a little disconcerting. If she thought you were talking nonsense, for example, she would say so, loudly, and command you to shut up. When she decided she didn't like a book she was reading, she was likely to throw it into a far corner of the room. "Scoundrel" was her softest term for people she disapproved of—the real estate man who cut a road through her favorite woods, or the banker who had once refused her husband a loan, to mention only a couple on her long hate list. She never forgave her enemies, because she considered forgiveness "part of that damn fool Christianity nonsense." But to her friends, who were far more numerous, she was so fiercely devoted that she would not abide a critical word about any of them.

AFTER HER eightieth birthday, the rheumatoid arthritis that had plagued Dorothy for years took a turn for the worse. She was in severe and increasing pain; neither medication nor physical therapy was much help; and eventually she could get about only with the help of a walker, a few agonizing steps at a time. She never uttered a word of self-pity, but she did resent her growing dependence on friends and on the town's visiting homemakers' service. Most of all she dreaded the day when she would become completely bed-bound; and though her wits (and tongue) remained as sharp as ever, she feared that her wits might begin to falter without her realizing it, as so often happens with elderly people.

When the visiting homemaker came one morning last spring, she found Dorothy in a coma. The town ambulance got her to a New Haven hospital within half an hour, but she died several days later without regaining consciousness.

To Viola she also had entrusted a handwritten letter, with the request that a copy should be sent to each of her "dear friends" shortly after her death. It reads, in part, as follows:

This message was started in November 1971. I have reread it and added to it from time to time but made no basic changes.

To those whom I dearly value, this is an explanation, and a confession, and a plea. For if this ignorantly managed attempt is successful, I ask you to be happy for me—and ultimately for yourselves too.

Long ago I accumulated the means for this act; with no morbid intentions; with no sense of guilt; merely cherishing the feeling that if the time ever came when I thought it far better to fall asleep and never wake, I had the very good great fortune to have it in my power to do so. I seem always to have felt that one could—and even under given circumstances should—be the rightful judge of that moment. (It always seemed so distant and unlikely!)

I began really to feel it only after Jake's death when I began to feel truly alone—in the very critical sense of loss of mutual dependence. I felt too old and dilapidated to undertake new obligations of any validity.

The time may be long or short, I do not know, because I want no despondency involved when the precise moment comes. I'm sure it'll take a bit of doing, but it is not quite exactly a matter of courage or cowardice, except as it is the courage of cowardice and fear (and common sense?). I want to go while I can still enjoy my friends who are so good to me and who I know can still enjoy me; while I can still feel a not too unfavorable balance between the happiness and competence and interest and even limited usefulness of my days—and the difficulties and discomforts and pain and expense involved in trying first to maintain that balance and then later merely to prolong life.

At that point I waited (it is now early April) and the effort is steadily increasing.

I think it will not be long now, for once clearly decided, I can feel the decision setting its own time-quickening schedule...I've just had a splendid hour of sunshine and comradeship in this my best loved room, and it is that which seems real and everlasting—with the other just a grim and foolish nightmare that I'll awaken from. But the inexorable stark truth lies the other way around, and that cherished splendid hour will last only as long as memory lasts....The reasons for the when as well as the reasons for the why, make it a tightly woven complex of tough small fibres that result in a determined act when determined on.

TWO THINGS BOTHER ME about that letter. The first is that Dorothy felt it necessary to write it—she who never in the years I knew her had felt any need to explain or apologize for whatever she did. The second is that her last act had to be "ignorantly managed" and the "means" had to be accumulated surreptitiously and "long ago." Presumably, whatever drug she used had lost some of its potency; hence the prolonged coma at the end.

Yet I am glad she wrote it; for it has led me, over the months I have been thinking about it, to reverse a lifelong conviction. I have quoted from the letter at some length in the hope that it may persuade at least a few others to a similar change in belief—to the conviction that our society's whole attitude toward suicide is profoundly wrong.

I was raised like most Americans in the belief that suicide is an immoral act. Under some circumstances, I still believe that to be true. But in Dorothy's circumstances, what she did now seems to me not only sensible but morally praiseworthy. Even the word "suicide" seems wrong to me in such a case, because it is so heavily encrusted with connotations of disapproval. I would rather call it a case of termination.

Dorothy had no children, no dependents, no close relatives. Her wasting body would soon become a grief and burden to her friends, as it was to her. Recovery was out of the question. Her decision then seems a natural one, like that of the old Eskimos who know when the time has come for them to drift off on an ice floe into the final cold.

'A Crime of Love'

Man Helped Ill Wife in Suicide

PONTIAC, Mich., Dec. 20 (UPI)—Robert C. Waters, former Clarkston village president and high school principal, is to be sentenced Jan. 10 for helping his ailing wife commit suicide. His attorney called it a crime of love.

Waters, 65, wept last month when he confessed to police, but appeared calm in court Thursday, when he pleaded no contest to manslaughter charges.

He told police he went to the garage of his home early Nov. 13, started the engine of his car, then led his ailing wife, Kathleen, also 65, to the car and left her inside the closed garage. She died of carbon monoxide poisoning.

"The reason I didn't stop her was if she did not die here she was going into another medical hospital—mental hospital, psychiatric hospital—for care which she neither wanted nor would approve to find herself in all probability," he said in a statement read in court.

He said he had tried to dissuade her from killing herself since 1971, when physical and mental problems beset her. On the night before her death he had come close to making a suicide pact with her, then talked her out of it. While his wife was dying in the closed garage, he said, he was inside their home, pacing the floor and praying.

"I was just not able men-tally to bring myself to make the decision that if her life was such a hell for her I should not be the one to let her not make up that decision for herself," Waters said.

"And rather than die the way she feared, a cripple maybe and mentally affected, I would rather let her make her own choice and die—if I may say—with dignity, than to go through with what she might have faced.

"It had to be her decision, not mine."

Waters and his wife had been married 40 years. They had no children.

Above, reprinted by permission of United Press International.

A Nobel Laureate Proposes Education for Suicide

MAX DELBRUCK, *the Albert Billings Ruddock professor of biology at the California Institute of Technology and a winner of the 1969 Nobel Prize for Physiology or Medicine, recently was interviewed in Prism magazine by* IRVING S. BENGELS-DORF, *director of science communication at Caltech. Following is an excerpt of the interview, reprinted from Prism magazine, November 1974, copyright © 1974 by the American Medical Association.*

Prism: Do you think that "suicide education" should be provided to the general population by physicians?

Delbruck: Yes. There is an interesting modern example where suicide instruction was denied to a seriously ill patient. In 1961, seriously ill with cancer at the age of 80, Percy W. Bridgman, the 1946 Nobel laureate in physics, took his life. He left a note that said: "It isn't decent for society to make a man do this thing himself. Probably this is the last day I will be able to do it myself." He then shot himself.

Both his family and his physician should have given him the opportunity of taking his life in a dignified way. But because of society's emphasis on the prolongation of life at all costs, he had to end his own life in a lonely and agonizing way.

Prism: But Socrates, when he drank the hemlock, was in good health, and the decision to take his life was a conscious decision. What about the patient who is severely ill or in a coma and cannot participate in a conscious decision concerning the ending of his life?

Delbruck: It would be silly for me to tell the medical profession what to do in such circumstances. Each case requires a specific evaluation.

ALIVE
The Story of the Andes Survivors

The chartered airliner crashed high in the remote wastes of the Andean cordillera, a world of snow, rock, wind and subzero cold, where not a living thing grew. Miraculously, only a few of the 45 persons aboard were killed. Although others died later of injuries, by the tenth day after the crash, when the search for the plane was abandoned, there were still 27 people alive. They were too weak to escape the imprisoning peaks, and soon there would be nothing left to eat. . . .

For some days several of the boys had realized that if they were to survive they would have to eat the bodies of those who had died in the crash. It was a ghastly prospect. The corpses lay around the plane in the snow, preserved by the intense cold in the state in which they had died. While the thought of cutting flesh from those who had been their friends was deeply repugnant to them all, a lucid appreciation of their predicament led them to consider it.

Gradually the discussion spread as these boys cautiously mentioned it to their friends or to those they thought would be sympathetic. Finally, Canessa brought it out into the open. He argued forcefully that they were not going to be rescued; that they would have to escape themselves, but that nothing could be done without food; and that the only food was human flesh. He used his knowledge of medicine to describe, in his penetrating, high-pitched voice, how their bodies were using up their reserves. "Every time you move," he said, "you use up part of your own body. Soon we shall be so weak that we won't have the strength even to cut the meat that is lying there before our eyes."

Canessa did not argue just from expediency. He insisted that they had a moral duty to stay alive by any means at their disposal, and because Canessa was earnest about his religious belief, great weight was given to what he said by the more pious among the survivors.

"It is meat," he said. "That's all it is. The souls have left their bodies and are in heaven with God. All that is left here are the carcasses, which are no more human beings than the dead flesh of the cattle we eat at home."

"You cannot condemn what they did," said Monsignor Andrés Rubio, Auxiliary Bishop of Montevideo, "when it was the only possibility of survival. . . . Eating someone who has died in order to survive is incorporating their substance, and it is quite possible to compare this with a graft. Flesh survives when assimilated by someone in extreme need, just as it does when an eye or heart of a dead man is grafted onto a living man. . . . What would we have done in a similar situation? . . . What would you say to someone if he revealed in confession a secret like that? Only one thing: not to be tormented by it . . . not to blame himself for something he would not blame in someone else and which no one blames in him."

Carlos Partelli, the Archbishop of Montevideo, confirmed his opinion. "Morally I see no objection, since it was a question of survival. It is always necessary to eat whatever is at hand, in spite of the repugnance it may evoke."

Corporate Rights and Responsibilities

All of the arguments in this section share the common feature that at least one of the parties involved in the moral judgment is a corporation rather than an individual person, and in most of them a judgment is being made about the moral rights or responsibilities of the corporation. Granted that corporations are built, owned, and operated by a number of individual persons, their structure is such that it is always difficult and sometimes close to impossible to assign certain moral rights and responsibilities to specific individual executives, employees, or stockholders. Without some nonarbitrary criteria for establishing individual responsibilities, the only obvious recourse is to either ascribe responsibilities to "the corporation" or else refrain from making any moral judgments at all concerning cases in which responsibilities cannot be assigned to specific individuals. The latter alternative appears to be a cop-out, while the former is at best not very helpful or satisfying. Thus, despite the difficulty of the task, it is generally best to exert whatever effort is necessary to "sort out" cases involving judgments about rights or responsibilities of corporations in order to identify specific individuals to whom these rights and responsibilities can properly be assigned.

It must be kept in mind when we are trying to identify specific individuals responsible for various corporate decisions and actions that in many, if not most, cases there will be a number of different individuals who in fact share the responsibility to varying degrees. It is very seldom that a single individual can be assigned total *moral* responsibility for a corporate decision, although many areas of corporate law have been designed in such a way that legal responsibility (and any associated liability and penalties) can be placed on a single person. One person often bears more moral responsibility than any other in a specific case, but this does not mean that he or she should be assigned all of the praise or blame associated with that case. And it is worth mentioning explicitly that certain *rights* of corporations are ultimately assignable to specific individuals in the same way as are responsibilities. A company's right to not be ripped off can be sorted out into the components of a collection of rights of individual stockholders and employees to receive fair return on investments and work performed. In this regard it should also be noted that there are some very real ethical problems which arise entirely within corporate structures, particularly those involving conflicts of rights and responsibilities of employees, managers, and stockholders. Once again, the most appropriate way to deal with these issues, if not always the simplest way, is to do whatever is necessary to assign the rights and responsibilities in the proper degree to specific individuals.

EXERCISES

1. For each of the examples in this section, determine as specifically as possible the roles of individuals in the case being discussed.
2. Compare the arguments in this section with those in Section 13 in order to identify any differences involved in dealing with moral issues related to corporations and moral issues related to governments. What might it mean to state that a corporation has certain responsibilities to a government or vice versa?

A GROWING VICE OF BUSINESS.

Two suggestive incidents will introduce to our readers a vice of business which ought to be reformed before it assumes the magnitude and universality which it is sure to achieve, unless efficient steps are taken to arrest its progress.

INCIDENT NO. 1.—A builder of furnaces was called upon recently to name a price for heating a large structure in a large city. He offered to put in his apparatus for $30,000. After repeated conversations with sundry persons interested in the contracts, he was told that the man who should secure the job would be obliged to pay a percentage to them—in this case amounting to $3,000—the bill, of course, to be rendered in such a form as to make him a party to the fraud upon the owners of the building. He told them that he wanted the job, but that as he also had a desire to go to heaven when he died, he was afraid he should be obliged to decline their conditions. He also suggested that he should like to bid for the job with others, and was informed that not a single contract on the building had been given to the lowest bidder. Then he was politely bowed out of the presence of the gentlemen who could not use him. He went home, and as an experiment, sent them a proposal to put in his apparatus for $25,000. From this he never heard; and some man with a more convenient conscience got the contract and gave the percentage.

INCIDENT NO. 2.—A piano-forte manufacturer sold an instrument, at his regular retail price, to a gentleman of New York. Within forty-eight hours he was called upon by three musicians, every one of whom demanded his percentage upon the sale of the piano, claiming that it was bought upon his recommendation. The purchaser, to make sure of getting the best instrument, had separately consulted all these men, and they had happened to agree upon this maker. The result was, that the maker paid each man the amount of his claim, and said nothing, though he parted with considerably more than his profits on the pianoforte. When asked by the friend to whom he told the story, why he submitted to such an imposition, he replied that he did not dare to do otherwise ; that if he had refused to respond to these exactions, the musicians would have turned against him, and transferred their recommendations to other makers.

The way in which corporations are bled by the leeches that fasten upon them is notorious. The men in respectable society, who regard a corporation as the legitimate subject of plunder, are too many to be counted. Tax-payers and stockholders part annually with untold millions to fill the purses of these dishonest men, and the mouths of their mendacious servants and tools. There are States in the Union in which the public conscience has become utterly demoralized with relation to this particular matter,—where every corporation, including Mutual Life Insurance Companies and Savings Banks, is in some way "sweated" by those who have the management of its concerns. In most instances this result is achieved under cover of the law ; but, in some, gigantic robberies are effected by the purchase not only of the officers, but of the makers of the law.

This process cannot long go on, of course, without such a sophistication of the popular conscience that private trusts will be as little regarded as those which are corporate and public. Indeed, it has already produced its proper fruit, as the incidents we have cited show. Men are everywhere seeking for money which they do not earn. It is quite likely that the piano-dealer is as much to blame for his bondage to the musicians as they are. He may have invited their patronage, indeed, and promised them their pay ; but it is all wrong, and the money all comes out of the consumer in the long run. The price of everything must be raised that tribute may be paid to those who are in a position to exact or steal it. If we go on at the present rate, we shall soon be no whit behind our European neighbors, whose servants are bribed by butchers and grocers and bakers, and who demand their "drink money" for every service, in addition to their legitimate wages. Every man who connives at this mode of doing business is not only a voluntary but a meanly mercenary corrupter of the people.

There is no question that in this matter of personal honesty America has retrograded within the last ten years. The rich corporation and the rich man are come to be regarded by tradesmen and laborers alike as sources of money which they may draw upon to the extent of their ability, without rendering an equivalent. An honest day's work is a much harder thing to get to-day than it was ten years ago ; and unless a reformation take place, the good old standard of personal honesty among the laboring poor, and of business integrity among the prosperous, will become a thing of remembrance only. If it were necessary, whole branches of business might be mentioned which pay a regular tax to what is called "influence," to men who have thrust themselves between the seller and the buyer for the simple purpose of fleecing one or both. Many a product of ingenuity and toil is obliged to buy every inch of its way to the consumer ; and a thousand improvements which affect the public convenience and comfort fail of adoption unless their profits are shared with the influence and power to which they appeal. Congress and the legislatures do not monopolize the lobby, for the lobby is everywhere. Black-mail, commissions, bonuses, gifts, the feathering of private nests among the recesses of great corporate interests, positions sought, won, and used for purposes of theft—all these things are so common that they have ceased to be remarkable ; and they argue sadly against our boasted progress in Christian civilization.

We do not expect to rid the world of thieves ; but the danger is, that honest men will not be able to do business at all without the adoption of their corrupt machinery, the prostitution of integrity, and the sacrifice of self-respect. How far are multitudes of our good houses from this position now ?

From *Scribner's Monthly*, 1871.

Above, from *The Rat*, Underground Press Syndicate.

Right, copyright 1971 by *Christianity Today*; reprinted by permission.

Labor's Double Standard?

Organized labor relies heavily on the support of society at large. Its clout would be appreciably diminished if it did not resort to a variety of social pressures to sign up workers as members. In any office or shop where a union is recognized as bargaining agent by the employer, the individual employee most likely does not have a truly free choice on whether or not to join the union. Labor's rationale for coercion is that everyone who benefits from collective bargaining should contribute to it.

Our society has accepted this infringement upon individual freedom, for better or worse, feeling that the benefits outweigh the loss of liberty. Unfortunately, however, labor seems lately to be reluctant to recognize its debt to society. Unions still have a long way to go in eliminating racial discrimination, but they are resisting government proposals designed to help correct biased policies and practices.

The nation's construction unions issued a strongly worded statement last month saying they would fight government-imposed quotas on non-white workers in apprenticeship programs. We agree that quotas are probably not the answer. But isn't it merely something of a twist on the quota principle that enables the unions to achieve a de facto closed shop? If the government shouldn't force the unions to take in applicants it doesn't want, why should the unions be allowed to force into membership workers who don't want to join? □

A Friedman doctrine—

The Social Responsibility Of Business Is to Increase Its Profits

By MILTON FRIEDMAN

WHEN I hear businessmen speak eloquently about the "social responsibilities of business in a free-enterprise system," I am reminded of the wonderful line about the Frenchman who discovered at the age of 70 that he had been speaking prose all his life. The businessmen believe that they are defending free enterprise when they declaim that business is not concerned "merely" with profit but also with promoting desirable "social" ends; that business has a "social conscience" and takes seriously its responsibilities for providing employment, eliminating discrimination, avoiding pollution and whatever else may be the catchwords of the contemporary crop of reformers. In fact they are—or would be if they or anyone else took them seriously—preaching pure and unadulterated socialism. Businessmen who talk this way are unwitting puppets of the intellectual forces that have been undermining the basis of a free society these past decades.

The discussions of the "social responsibilities of business" are notable for their analytical looseness and lack of rigor. What does it mean to say that "business" has responsibilities? Only people can have responsibilities. A corporation is an artificial person and in this sense may have artificial responsibilities, but "business" as a whole cannot be said to have responsibilities, even in this vague sense. The first step to-

MILTON FRIEDMAN is a professor of economics at the University of Chicago.

ward clarity in examining the doctrine of the social responsibility of business is to ask precisely what it implies for whom.

Presumably, the individuals who are to be responsible are businessmen, which means individual proprietors or corporate executives. Most of the discussion of social responsibility is directed at corporations, so in what follows I shall mostly neglect the individual proprietor and speak of corporate executives.

IN a free-enterprise, private-property system, a corporate executive is an employe of the owners of the business. He has direct responsibility to his employers. That responsibility is to conduct the business in accordance with their desires, which generally will be to make as much money as possible while conforming to the basic rules of the society, both those embodied in law and those embodied in ethical custom. Of course, in some cases his employers may have a different objective. A group of persons might establish a corporation for an eleemosynary purpose—for example, a hospital or a school. The manager of such a corporation will not have money profit as his objective but the rendering of certain services.

In either case, the key point is that, in his capacity as a corporate executive, the manager is the agent of the individuals who own the corporation or establish the eleemosynary institution, and his primary responsibility is to them.

Needless to say, this does not mean that it is easy to judge how well he is performing his task. But at least the criterion of performance is straightforward, and the persons among whom a voluntary contractual arrangement exists are clearly defined.

Of course, the corporate executive is also a person in his own right. As a person, he may have many other responsibilities that he recognizes or assumes voluntarily—to his family, his conscience, his feelings of charity, his church, his clubs, his city, his country. He may feel impelled by these responsibilities to devote part of his income to causes he regards as worthy, to refuse to work for particular corporations, even to leave his job, for example, to join his country's armed forces. If we wish, we may refer to some of these responsibilities as "social responsibilities." But in these respects he is acting as a principal, not an agent; he is spending his own money or time or energy, not the money of his employers or the time or energy he has contracted to devote to their purposes. If these are "social responsibilities," they are the social responsibilities of individuals, not of business.

What does it mean to say that the corporate executive has a "social responsibility" in his capacity as businessman? If this statement is not pure rhetoric, it must mean that he is to act in some way that is not in the interest of his employers. For example, that he is to refrain from increasing the price of the product in

order to contribute to the social objective of preventing inflation, even though a price increase would be in the best interests of the corporation. Or that he is to make expenditures on reducing pollution beyond the amount that is in the best interests of the corporation or that is required by law in order to contribute to the social objective of improving the environment. Or that, at the expense of corporate profits, he is to hire "hardcore" unemployed instead of betterqualified available workmen to contribute to the social objective of reducing poverty.

In each of these cases, the corporate executive would be spending someone else's money for a general social interest. Insofar as his actions in accord with his "social responsibility" reduce returns to stockholders, he is spending their money. Insofar as his actions raise the price to customers, he is spending the customers' money. Insofar as his actions lower the wages of some employes, he is spending their money.

The stockholders or the customers or the employes could separately spend their own money on the particular action if they wished to do so. The executive is exercising a distinct "social responsibility," rather than serving as an agent of the stockholders or the customers or the employes, only if he spends the money in a different way than they would have spent it.

But if he does this, he is in effect imposing taxes, on the one hand, and deciding how the tax proceeds shall be spent, on the other.

Walter
Goodman
STOCKS
WITHOUT
SIN

Still, for the sake of argument, what if it should somehow happen that virtuous actions are not rewarded in this life? "I don't notice that DuPont stock has tripled since they announced they're going to spend $300 million against pollution," remarks a veteran fund manager. Having lately, and belatedly, doubled its anti-pollution budget, the St. Regis Paper Company experienced a 51 per cent decline in profits in the first quarter of this year. Or what if companies that behave in unvirtuous ways make money? "What has been the cost to corporations of discriminating against blacks?" asks Phil Moore as though the answer were evident. Well, the nation is paying for it all right, but was discrimination really all that unprofitable all those years to companies that relied on a supply of low-paid workers to do disagreeable jobs?

A rough study at Princeton University, where students protested against the school's investments in South Africa, indicates that those objectionable stocks had almost a 3 per cent higher average rate of return than other securities in its portfolio. (Incidentally, it would cost Princeton an estimated $5 million in brokerage fees to get out of South Africa altogether.) In its 1971 proxy statement to General Motors, the Domestic and Foreign Missionary Service of the Protestant Episcopal Church urged that GM wind up its $125 million of manufacturing activities in South Africa because apartheid "will inevitably lead to turmoil and instability . . . and consequently to the destruction of foreign capital invested there." However, the church went on, GM should get out of South Africa even if it entailed a loss because "only those corporations which conduct themselves in a socially responsible way will be able to survive profitably, in the long run . . ." The Will to Believe survives among Episcopalians. At least it did before GM's annual meeting, where their proposal won 1.29 per cent of the shares voted.

And what of the managers of trust funds and pension funds? Should they be permitted to risk my money in behalf of their principles? The laws governing fiduciary relationships do not encourage experimentation, even for reasons of conscience. The Wall Street rule for persons legally charged with the management of other people's money runs as follows: "Invest funds in a company with the aim of gaining the best financial return with the least financial risk for the trust beneficiaries. If you later come to disagree with the company's management, sell the stock." This rule, we may assume, is used by many trustees to go along mindlessly with management and avoid the wear and tear of decision-making. Nevertheless, there remains a real legal question. David Silver, general counsel of Investment Company Institutes, a trade group, observes, "If a fund sells a share in a company that it thinks is a good investment because it doesn't like its hiring policies in South Africa, there could be a shareholders' suit."

But even if there were no legal problem, might

there not be a moral problem for the prudent trustee? Peter L. Bernstein, chairman of the board of Bernstein-Macauley and chairman of the investment policy committee of CBWL-Hayden, Stone, confesses that he feels some inner pressure to invest the funds in his charge in mortgages in minority areas, with the prospect of a lower return than they might bring elsewhere. But if he should succumb to that small voice, he observes, it will not be he who pays the price, but his clients: "Sorry, fellas, you've been elected to bear the cost." Why should this particular group suffer this special tax? Moreover, Bernstein points out that in a market economy, if capital flows not toward profits but toward social priorities, "we lose a rational measure of how to allocate capital." That, he acknowledges, suggests the limits of a market economy—and awakens in him stirrings of sympathy for radicals who would scrap the whole thing.

Not all investment advisers are as diffident as Mr. Bernstein. "We're making moral judgments all the time," Donald Weeden, chairman of Weeden & Company, told the *Institutional Investor*. "As individuals, we have been picked for our overall sensitivity to what's been going on." Now, no offense to Mr. Weeden, but I don't know any investment adviser whom I would care to have act in my behalf in any matter except turning a profit—and I'm not sure about that. The value of these specialists, I believe, lies in their limitations; they ought not allow themselves to see so much of the world that they become distracted.

Perhaps, though, fund managers might poll their investors and let them make their own decisions when confronted by a conflict between profit and principle. Under a recent SEC decision, shareholders can vote on whether fund managers should consider the social policies of a corporation before investing in its stock. During the latest GM go-around, in May, the Dreyfus Leverage Fund, holder of 25,000 shares of GM stock, solicited the opinions of shareholders on several of the insurgent proposals. In every case, most people voted with GM management and against the insurgents, whereupon Dreyfus voted its proxy *in favor* of the proposal requiring GM to publish detailed information on pollution and so forth. "We had to vote for that proposal," explains a fund spokesman, "because we believe in it." Mutual fund democracy?

Suppose that in a fit of social consciousness, American Motors should decide to put out a two-year model? And suppose everyone knew that the company's sales would sink in the second year? How many fund managers would hold onto their shares of American Motors? How many investors would stay with funds that operated in that public-spirited way?

Why, after all, should one expect selflessness from the widow dependent on her capital, the father concerned for his children's education, the speculator looking for gain—all those stock marketeers who have spent a lifetime trying to make money make money? We may be certain that any stock whose value drops to a tempting low because the Episcopal Church or a Boston synagogue sells it will be quickly picked up by investors of all religions who don't care what a company does, much less the country where it does it.

Ms. Susan Gross — Spokeswoman for the Project on Corporate Responsibility in Washington, D.C. elaborates on the Project's plan to get major institutional investors like universities to use their power as shareholders to direct corporate powers.

Do you feel that ethical considerations are advisable or necessary when a university, or anyone, is investing in corporations?

The Project on Corporate Responsibility does not really believe in ethical investing as it is commonly defined. That is the sort of "clean portfolio" concept of investing. We do not believe that there can be such a thing as a clean portfolio, because we do not believe there is such an animal as a clean company. One company for example, might have good minority hiring practices, while being terrible in the product safety area and the environmental area. There's no such thing as a clean company when you're talking about something which cannot really be defined. What the Project believes is that investors, universities included, ought to invest their money using economic criteria — investing money in order to get a reasonable return. Our concern is what the investor does once he has invested his money in a company. That is where shareholder responsibility must begin. We believe a shareholder has an obligation and a responsibility to exercise his leverage and influence in the company, to persuade the company to adopt more socially responsible positions, and to urge the longer range goal in which the project believes. This goal is the accountability of corporations to the various groups and constituencies that the corporation affects. I just want to emphasize that the way that you will get corporations to regularly, and seriously, weigh the social consequences of their acts and to make socially responsive decisions is by fundamental internal forms in corporate decision making. Corporate decision makers must be accountable, and they are not now accountable to anyone.

From *Business Today*, May 1973.

An experiment in South Africa

Polaroid sells its products in South Africa as do several hundred other American companies. Our sales there are small, less than one half of one percent of our worldwide business.

Recently a group has begun to demand that American business stop selling in South Africa. They say that by its presence it is supporting the government of the country and its policies of racial separation and subjugation of the Blacks. Polaroid, in spite of its small stake in the country, has received the first attention of this group.

We did not respond to their demands. But we did react to the question. We asked ourselves, "Is it right or wrong to do business in South Africa?" We have been studying the question for about ten weeks.

The committee of Polaroid employees who undertook this study included fourteen members – both black and white – from all over the company. The first conclusion was arrived at quickly and unanimously. We abhor *apartheid*, the national policy of South Africa.

The *apartheid* laws separate the races and restrict the rights, the opportunities and the movement of non-white Africans. This policy is contrary to the principles on which Polaroid was built and run. We believe in individuals. Not in "labor units" as Blacks are sometimes referred to in South Africa. We decided whatever our course should be it should oppose the course of *apartheid*.

The committee talked to more than fifty prominent South Africans both black and white, as well as many South African experts. They heard from officials in Washington. They read books, papers, testimony, documents, opinion, interpretation, statistics. They heard tapes and saw films.

They addressed themselves to a single question. What should Polaroid do in South Africa? Should we register our disapproval of *apartheid* by cutting off all contact with the country? Should we try to influence the system from within? We rejected the suggestion that we ignore the whole question and maintain the status quo.

Some of the black members of the study group expressed themselves strongly at the outset. They did not want to impose on the black people of another country a course of action merely because *we* might feel it was correct. They felt this paternalistic attitude had prevailed too often in America when things are done "for" black people without consulting black people.

It was decided to send four of the committee members to South Africa. Since this group was to include two black and two white members, it was widely assumed they would not be granted visas. They were.

It was assumed if they ever got to South Africa they would be given a government tour. They were not.

It was assumed they would not be allowed to see the actual conditions under which many Blacks live and would be prevented from talking to any of them in private. They did see those conditions in Soweto and elsewhere. And with or without permission they met and talked to and listened to more than a hundred black people of South Africa. Factory workers, office workers, domestic servants, teachers, political leaders, people in many walks of life. They also talked to a broad spectrum of whites including members of all the major parties.

Their prime purpose in going to South Africa was to ask Africans what they thought American business should do in their country. We decided the answer that is best for the black people of South Africa would be the best answer for us.

Can you learn about a country in ten days? No. Nor in ten weeks. But our group learned one thing. What we had read and heard about *apartheid* was not exaggerated. It is every bit as repugnant as we had been led to believe.

The group returned with a unanimous recommendation.

In response to this recommendation and to the reports of the larger study committee, Polaroid will undertake an experimental program in relation to its business activities in South Africa.

For the time being we will continue our business relationships there (except for sales to the South African government, which our distributor is discontinuing), but on a new basis which Blacks there with whom we talked see as supportive to their hopes and plans for the future. In a year we will look closely to see if our experiment has had any effects.

First, we will take a number of steps with our distributor, as well as his suppliers, to improve dramatically the salaries and other benefits of their non-white employees. We have had indications that these companies will be willing to cooperate in this plan.

Our business associates in South Africa will also be obliged (as a condition of maintaining their relationship with Polaroid) to initiate a well-defined program to train non-white employees for important jobs within their companies.

We believe education for the Blacks, in combination with the opportunities now being afforded by the expanding economy, is a key to change in South Africa. We will commit a portion of our profits earned there to encourage black education. One avenue will be to provide funds for the permanent staff and office of the black-run Association for Education and Cultural Advancement (ASECA). A second method will be to make a gift to a foundation to underwrite educational expenses for about 500 black students at various levels of study from elementary school through university. Grants to assist teachers will also be made from this gift. In addition we will support two exchange fellowships for Blacks under the U.S.-South African Leader Exchange Program.

Polaroid has no investments in South Africa and we do not intend to change this policy at present. We are, however, investigating the possibilities of creating a black-managed company in one or more of the free black African nations.

Why have we undertaken this program? To satisfy a revolutionary group? No. They will find it far from satisfactory. They feel we should close the door on South Africa, not try to push it further open.

What can we hope to accomplish there without a factory, without a company of our own, without the economic leverage of large sales? Aren't we wasting time and money trying to have an effect on a massive problem 10,000 miles from home? The answer, our answer, is that since we are doing business in South Africa and since we have looked closely at that troubled country, we feel we can continue only by opposing the *apartheid* system. Black people there have advised us to do this by providing an opportunity for increased use of black talent, increased recognition of black dignity. Polaroid is a small economic force in South Africa, but we are well known and, because of our committee's visit there, highly visible. We hope other American companies will join us in this program. Even a small beginning of co-operative effort among American businesses can have a large effect in South Africa.

How can we presume to concern ourselves with the problems of another country? Whatever the practices elsewhere, South Africa alone articulates a policy exactly contrary to everything we feel our company stands for. We cannot participate passively in such a political system. Nor can we ignore it. That is why we have undertaken this experimental program.

Polaroid Corporation

A public statement made by Polaroid Corporation, which appeared in the press in January of 1971.

JOHN R. RARICK
6TH DISTRICT, LOUISIANA

COMMITTEE:
AGRICULTURE

January 13, 1971

Mr. Edwin H. Land, President
POLAROID CORPORATION
Cambridge, Massachusetts 02139

Dear Mr. Land:

Having shared your newspaper advertisement from today's **Washington Post,** "An Experiment in South Africa," with my morning coffee, I felt that I should drop you a line to express my disgust, or rather sympathy, at your naivete.

South Africa is a long way from Cambridge, Massachusetts, and from the United States. So it must be easy to make peace with your blackmailers by joining in their guerrilla warfare against another peaceful ally of the free world.

If it is to now be the policy of the Polaroid Corporation to embarrass the American people further in our international relations for your self-serving employee relations, when are you going to run ads expressing your company's abhorrence for the national policies and customs of other nations?

Is Polaroid going to employ some Arabs to investigate apartheid in Israel so you can denounce that country?

What about India with its caste system, where the untouchables are not to be seen in public even in the street by the higher caste? Of course, under your researchers' racist type examination, you must hire the lower caste to help formulate your policies.

Then we have the many African nations such as Liberia, Congo, Ethiopia, which still practice slavery. Most certainly you will want to alienate these nations as well as Zambia, which persecutes Jehovah's Witnesses, Indians, and all Moslems.

Finally, I notice nothing in your public relations propaganda which indicated that your company is cutting camera trade with Russia or its Communist satellites, which practice apartheid not only against the Zionist Jew, but other religious and ethnic minorities as well.

If you think life is so bad in South Africa, why is it that there are no lines of refugees or escapees fleeing that country? On the other hand, people fleeing from Communist countries at the risk of losing their lives and all of their belongings is a daily occurrence. I dare suggest that for a successful industrial organization, you people have been taken.

Yes, South Africa is a far piece from the United States, and as your article confesses, you have little if any business there anyway, so what do you have to lose in South Africa? Perhaps you are unaware that there are many Americans who are sick and tired of the Black Panthers and these revolutionaries being pampered and bank rolled by organizations such as yours.

It has hardly been a month since your $20,000 contribution to Boston's black appeal was sent to Cairo, Illinois to help destroy race relations in that community — the remainder was sent to Communist affiliated revolutionary troops in Africa, dedicated to kill white people and overthrow responsible governments.

I think that you will find that the people of South Africa have far more friends in the U.S. than your colored advisors have led you to believe. As for me, neither myself nor any member of my family will ever consider buying a Polaroid product, or using same. Until the day when South Africa manufactures her own cameras, I will confine my photography to the Zeiss of Germany, and Yashica. These companies are still interested in increasing sales and friendships — not alienating them.

Sincerely,
John R. Rarick
Member of Congress

JRR:cf

P.S. Incidentally, I am writing the Internal Revenue Service to inquire for an opinion as to whether corporations which are forbidden by law from making political donations can write off full page newspaper advertisements such as this as operating expenses.

U.S. Interests in South Africa

In your article "U.S. Business in South Africa" (BUSINESS AND FINANCE, March 29) you attribute to a Ford Motor Co. spokesman the statement that "U.S. corporations should not interfere in the domestic affairs of the countries in which they do business." Supposedly this is a counterargument to the demand that Ford withdraw its investment in South Africa's apartheid.

The hypocrisy of such an argument is obvious, but its perversity is made manifest in a later article in the same section in which you report Henry Ford II's interference in British affairs. Capitalist Ford presented Prime Minister Edward Heath with the economic ultimatum that until "stability" returned to Britain, he would not make further commitments in that country.

The roots of such a double standard can lie only in the profitability found in fascist but stable South Africa and not found in Britain's experiment in social and economic justice. What are America's priorities? Profitability and repression, or freedom, justice and equality? And why are the latter not the priorities of U.S. business abroad?

ALAN J. ERICKSON

Nashville, Tenn.

Above, letter to the editor of *Newsweek* by Alan J. Erickson, April 19, 1971.

Courtesy of John R. Rarick, the representative from the Sixth District, Louisiana.

Maybe the way to change the world is to join a large corporation.

We don't make a lot of noise, but this is where it's really happening. You see, a large corporation like Kodak has the resources and the skill to make this world a little more decent place to live. And we intend to do what we can to see that this is exactly what happens.

Take our home city, Rochester, New York for example. We cut water pollution in the Genesee River by using natural bacteria to dispose of unnatural wastes. We cut air pollution by using electrostatic precipitators in a new combustible waste disposal facility. We helped set up a black enterprise program in downtown Rochester, and we've been experimenting with film as a way to train both teachers and students—including some students who wouldn't respond to anything else.

And we didn't stop with Rochester. Kodak is involved in 47 countries all over the world. Actively involved.

Why? Because it's good business. Helping to clean the Genesee River not only benefits society...but helps protect another possible source for the clean water we need to make our film. Our combustible waste disposal facility not only reduces pollution...but just about pays for itself in heat and power production and silver recovery. Our black enterprise program not only provides an opportunity for the economically disadvantaged...but helps stabilize communities in which Kodak can operate and grow. And distributing cameras and film to teachers and students not only helps motivate the children...but helps create a whole new market.

In short, it's simply good business. And we're in business to make a profit. But in furthering our business interests, we also further society's interests.

And that's good. After all, our business depends on society. So we care what happens to it.

Courtesy of Eastman Kodak Company.

Lamenting the fallen sparrow

Is technology doing the human race good, or doing it in?

That question persists after more than 200 years of technological innovation. Not many people argue any longer that if God had wanted humans to fly, He would have given us wings. But there are plenty of contemporary alarms against invention.

It won't surprise anyone to learn that Mobil believes technology does a great deal of good. It may surprise some people when we concede that technological advance takes its toll. Like many other things, technology is sometimes a blessing, sometimes a bane.

On this subject, we share the views of Dr. Hans Landsberg, director of the resource appraisal program carried out by Resources for the Future—a nonprofit corporation for research and education in the development, conservation, and use of natural resources.

At a symposium some time ago of the American Academy of Arts and Sciences, Dr. Landsberg said:

"One is apt to view the more disagreeable aspects of modern life, including most prominently those due to the impact of technology, with partiality—often unconsciously. We take for granted that we may drink tap water, eat uncooked fruit or vegetables, and consume milk with no thought of falling victim to a lurking bug. We are reminded of our good fortune only when we travel in parts of the world that require preventive or remedial countermeasures....

"But, customarily, we fail to do much balancing of pluses and minuses.

"We tend to overlook the fact that the chemical industry produces not only controversial pesticides, but also antibiotics and vaccines; that the automobile whose incomplete fuel combustion fouls the city air does, at the same time, enable us to escape its boundaries and to know the world in a way available a generation or two ago only to the daring or the rich.

"We are quick to lament the fallen sparrow, but slow to celebrate the fall of 'Typhoid Mary.'"

Responsible enterprise, Mobil believes, should not merely lament the sparrow's fall, but try to prevent it. Yet industry should not be—and need not be—deterred from striving to make technology a blessing for the earth and all the living things that inhabit it.

Mobil®

THE DOW CHEMICAL COMPANY

<u>Statement of Position on Napalm</u>

The Dow Chemical Company endorses the right of any American to protest legally and peacefully an action with which he does not agree.

Our position on the manufacture of napalm is that we are a supplier of goods to the Defense Department and not a policy maker. We do not and should not try to decide military strategy or policy.

Simple good citizenship requires that we supply our government and our military with those goods which they feel they need whenever we have the technology and capability and have been chosen by the government as a supplier.

We will do our best, as we always have, to try to produce what our Defense Department and our soldiers need in any war situation. Purely aside from our duty to do this, we will feel deeply gratified if what we are able to provide helps to protect our fighting men or to speed the day when fighting will end.

(1966-67)

Courtesy of the Dow Chemical Company.

Eco-Guerrilla Warfare

The capers of the Chicago Fox (THE CITIES, Jan. 11) make me think of a scenario that could pose some problems far more significant than the identity of the stain on the rug at U.S. Steel.

Suppose an eco-guerrilla ran a hose from an industrial smokestack into the company president's office. The fumes then kill the executives and a few secretaries. The environmental prankster is caught soon afterward.

Would he be charged with murder? Presumably he would. However, if he could be found guilty of murder for pumping industrial fumes into an office, what about the company that is releasing the poisons into the air in the first place?

Three cheers for the Fox if his actions force people to contemplate deeper implications of the muck on the rug.

JEFFREY C. BAUER
Colorado Springs, Colo.

Left, letter to the editor of *Newsweek* by Jeffrey C. Bauer, February 8, 1971.

Meanwhile we find ourselves confronted by a most disturbing moral problem. We know that the pursuit of good ends does not justify the employment of bad means. But what about those situations, now of such frequent occurrence, in which good means have end results which turn out to be bad?

For example, we go to a tropical island and with the aid of DDT we stamp out malaria and, in two or three years, save hundreds of thousands of lives. This is obviously good. But the hundreds of thousands of human beings thus saved, and the millions whom they beget and bring to birth, cannot be adequately clothed, housed, educated or even fed out of the island's available resources. Quick death by malaria has been abolished; but life made miserable by undernourishment and over-crowding is now the rule, and slow death by outright starvation threatens ever greater numbers.

And what about the congenitally insufficient organisms, whom our medicine and our social services now preserve so that they may propagate their kind? To help the unfortunate is obviously good. But the wholesale transmission to our descendants of the results of unfavorable mutations, and the progressive contamination of the genetic pool from which the members of our species will have to draw, are no less obviously bad. We are on the horns of an ethical dilemma, and to find the middle way will require all our intelligence and all our good will.

Above, from *Brave New World Revisited*, © 1958 by Aldous Huxley.

Northrop: Know The Right People

By Jack Egan

Washington Post Staff Writer

The Northrop Corp. saga, as it has unraveled, is the story of influence-peddling at the highest levels of government in an industry where governments are really the only customers and where single decisions can mean hundreds of millions and billions of dollars.

Subcommittee chairman Frank Church (D-Idaho) said the Northrop story was summed up in a quote from one of the company's top Washington consultants, Frank J. DeFrancis: "I don't know a damn thing about an airplane except the nose and the tail."

"But DeFrancis knew the right people," Church said, "and that is really what the Northrop case is all about: how to get to the right people in foreign governments to make the right decisions about which airplane to purchase. The propriety with which this was to be accomplished seems not to matter."

One Northrop executive, John R. Hunt, in an interview with the company's auditors as part of an investigation of the company, said, "The role of the agent is primarily that of influence peddler;' that is, he knows who to talk to and whose pockets to line in a particular country to get the job done."

Hunt said "agents are an expensive and necessary evil of doing business in a foreign country; the agents make the necessary payments." Corporate officials in general "don't know and don't want to know where the money paid to agents goes," he added.

Above, from *The Washington Post*, June 15, 1975.
Below, from *The Washington Post*, 1975.

Lockheed Admits Making $22 Million in Foreign Gifts

By James L. Rowe Jr.

Washington Post Staff Writer

Lockheed Aircraft Corp. admitted yesterday that it has paid about $22 million to "foreign officials and foreign political organizations" over the last 5½ years.

Lockheed, which had steadfastly denied paying any foreign bribes or political contributions, defended the practice and said the payments were "necessary in consummating certain foreign sales." The giant aerospace firm said the overseas payments were made "with the knowledge of management" in Burbank, Calif.

Lockheed said yesterday that it believes all of its foreign payments "are consistent with practices engaged in by numerous other companies abroad, including many of its competitors, and are in keeping with business practices in many foreign countries."

But the company warned that disclosure of any payoffs would hurt the company and that if the company is stopped from making these contributions, it "could seriously prejudice the company's ability to compete effectively in certain foreign markets."

Pay-offs in doing business abroad

Congratulations for casting the harsh light of publicity on the pay-offs American companies allegedly are making to influence peddlers to increase foreign sales. Being in the oil business, hardly a day passes without someone phoning me and offering special deals involving the supply of foreign crude oil if I will only pay them a healthy commission, most of which they allegedly have to use to pay off friends of the shiek, shah, or someone.

My reply is always, "No interest, because I have been told by the representative of the country involved, as well as by our government officials, that such sales must be made direct with the national oil company." In fact, most of the producing countries have publicly stated that their sales policy is never to deal through third parties or brokers.

Companies that pay off in-between influence peddlers are not only wasting their stockholders' money, but, what is even worse, they are casting a dark reflection on our Western ethics of doing business in a moral manner.

Congress and the IRS should act to stop such monkey business. We cannot afford to allow the venality of a few harm the broad interests of our country.

John K. Evans
Washington, D.C.

Left, letter to the editor of the *Washington Star* by John K. Evans, 1975.
Right, © *The Washington Post*, May 1975.

Pepco Won't Seek Special Low Rates

By Claudia Levy
Washington Post Staff Writer

If low-income customers have trouble paying increasing electricity costs, it's not the responsibility of the electric company to seek special low rates for them, W. Reid Thompson, president and chairman of the Potomac Electric Power Co., told stockholders yesterday.

"It's not our function to make the social judgment that some of our customers should bear the problems of poverty-level customers," Thompson said, in answer to suggestions by several stockholders that the local utility ask for adjustments in its rate structure to favor small users.

Any subsidies for this class of customer should come from the federal government, Thompson insisted, perhaps in the form of an "energy stamp" that would provide benefits like those of food stamps.

Last year, average residential bills in Pepco's service areas in Maryland and all of the District rose 33 per cent, while the cost of living generally rose about 12 per cent. Increases in electric bills resulted mainly from increased costs to the utility for fuel, with December residential bills averaging $17.50 in the District and $29.03 in Maryland, for instance.

In the last increase it granted the utility, the D.C. Public Service Commission said Pepco could not charge more for customers who use less than 400 kilowatt hours a month, 55 kilowatts under the average usage in the city.

Stockholders yesterday urged Pepco to institute the lowest, so-called "lifeline" rate for the first 400 kilowatts used by a household. James Sullivan asked his fellow shareholders to "put yourselves in the shoes of low-income customers . . . Think of yourself living without a refrigerator . . . or sitting in a room . . . without heat."

By charging residential customers who use small amounts of electricity less per kilowatt hour than large users—who currently pay a smaller price per unit of electricity—Pepco's income would not be significantly affected and its "image would soar," Sullivan told Thompson.

The Pepco chief said the lifeline rate, currently being widely discussed among utilities, "has some appeal to it, of course . . . " But he said there was a "real question about the use of utility rates as a vehicle for desirable social programs, such as taking care of the economically deprived."

Other stockholders complained about stock offerings recently made by the company—without preferential treatment to existing stockholders at below book value, an action some said diluted earnings for the earlier shareholders and required a greater return per share to keep up earnings. Thompson said the sale had been necessary to raise money for expansion, now slated at far lower levels than previously planned.

Judy Gingert, a stockholder representing D.C. Power, a coalition of local civic groups, said that in meeting with Thompson, her group was told that "the purpose of the company is to provide service to customers . . . But now you speak the same words to stock holders . . . about your 'grave and earnest concern' " for them.

POINT

SAFER: It's said that bribing foreign governments has become a way of life for big American corporations who do business in Asia and Latin America. Although it's been going on for years, it's now become something of a cause celebre. Everyone seems to be talking about it or doing it; and when people talk, Jack Kilpatrick and Shana Alexander insist on having their say. Here's Point/Counterpoint.

JAMES J. KILPATRICK: We're having fits of morality in Washington, Shana, over what's denounced as corporate bribery abroad. It's the most unheard of thing you ever heard of. It appears that Gulf Oil paid out $4-million in political contributions in South Korea alone. It looks as if United Brands paid a whopping sum in Honduras to get out from under a tax on bananas. Down in Bolivia, the former President apparently was involved in accepting corporate money. Can you imagine any such thing? The American corporations are being charged with shame and scandal. Some of the more virtuous members of Congress are demanding punitive measures. The air resounds with cries of lofty rectitude, coming mostly from people with a highly cultivated sensibility for other people's morals. It's a terrible state of affairs! But what it really is, Shana, is a terrible lot of hypocritical nonsense.

The American companies are being singled out by a bunch of professional business haters and sanctimonious rousers. In certain foreign countries, bribery is an ancient way of life. Payments to public officials are a plain and simple business expense. German, Swiss and British companies pay up just as ours do. And to complain that the American corporations didn't disclose these payments to the SEC is pettifoggery. You couldn't very well expect Gulf Oil to publish an expense account - "bribe to a president: $400,000". Gulf's good manners may be better than Bolivia's bad morals.

Who are we to talk? The trade unions give $35,000 to a freshman Congressman, and we call it just a contribution. Milk producers, oilmen, doctors and bankers all kick in to politicians. How did we get so pure? Let's not try to reform the Bolivians, Shana. We have enough to do in reforming ourselves.

Above and right page, from the CBS News broadcast *60 Minutes*, June 1, 1975.

COUNTERPOINT

SHANA ALEXANDER: I'll say I'm shocked! But what shocks me is you, Jack. You're telling me that the Communists are right, that the end justifies the means? Well, I can't agree with that. The end, in this case, is to maintain business as usual between great big American corporations and a few rotten little countries where bribery is, indeed, a way of life. Should that make it our way of life?

You're suggesting we crawl back down into the same mud that Washington and Jefferson founded this country to lift us out of. You're talking Godfather morality - give them a bribe, a big payoff. Make them an offer they can't refuse. Well, let the United States do that, or let Gulf Oil or any other corporate big shot do that, and you turn what's left of integrity in this country (and there's an awful lot of integrity left here in my town, if not down there in Washington) - you reduce that to the ethics of Ecuador and the honor of Honduras. The argument that everybody does it is no good. Say your kid gets caught ripping off the five-and-ten, and he says all the kids do it; you tell him I don't care what the other kids do, it's wrong! And if he does it again, you'll punish him, because otherwise he's apt to grow up and become chairman of Gulf Oil; and when Congress asks him how come you gave $4-million to the President of South Korea, he's going to say, well, Exxon does it, United Fruit does it, and Jack Kilpatrick says it's okay because Bolivia does it.

Lockheed's Little Helpers

ANYONE who credits Congress with a collective ethical principle is hard put to prove his point, since ethics usually finishes among the also-rans on Capitol Hill. It is especially difficult to find anything resembling a principle in congressional approval of a $250,000,000. loan guarantee to Lockheed Aircraft Corp. But let's try, very hard, to uncover what our lawmakers were trying to tell us in their handling of that political-economic-diplomatic squabble.

If one can believe the proponents of the loan to Lockheed, a basic goal was to save jobs. President Nixon, in hailing the passage of the bill, said it would "save tens of thousands of jobs that would otherwise have been eliminated." Unquestionably that will happen. But the inequities of saving 60,000 jobs at Lockheed while permitting thousands of other workers to become jobless every month because of business failures are so clear that even congressmen and the Nixon Administration can't help but comprehend them.

Perhaps, then, the idea was to preserve jobs of workers in "big" companies. How big? Companies with 20,000 employes? Or 10,000? Where does one draw the line in deciding which jobs are worth saving?

If that's not the answer, maybe the goal was to "help ensure that the nation's largest defense contractor . . . will continue serving the nation's needs," as Mr. Nixon declared. That brings the Government's emphasis out of saving jobs and into saving companies. Again, apparently size has something to do with it, because Congress is unlikely to rescue a filling-station operator who is going bankrupt or, for that matter, a small defense contractor.

The real reason could be related more to diplomacy than to economics. The British government, after all, was threatening to allow *its* principal industrial weakling, Rolls-Royce Ltd., to go out of business unless the United States bailed out Lockheed. Rolls-Royce makes the engines for the TriStar airbus, the commercial jet being developed by Lockheed; the partnership of the two companies in this shaky project seems singularly appropriate, like putting a Studebaker engine in an Edsel.

All of those reasons for helping Lockheed seem unconvincing, so maybe there is something else. We must try not to be cynical, but the phrase "political expediency" does come to mind. Lockheed has huge plants in California and Georgia, where thousands of Lockheed employes vote. It would have been too much to expect Senators Tunney and Cranston, California Democratic liberals, and Senators Talmadge and Gambrell, Georgia Democratic not-so-liberals, to oppose the bill. And, indeed, they voted for it. One wonders whether the Nixon Administration had some similar vote-getting goals in mind in its strong support of the bill.

That's a nasty thought, not to be dwelled on. It's much better to think of politicians as being motivated by high principles. So if your candy store is going bankrupt, don't call the banker, call your senator or representative. Ask him to apply the "ethics" of the Lockheed "principle" to your little store. But be prepared for a going-out-of-business sale.

—JAMES G. DRISCOLL

Reprinted from *The National Observer*, August 9, 1971. Copyright Dow Jones & Company, Inc.

Money-Lending, Interest, and the Christian

A Conflict in Real Values

By EILEEN EGAN

The home of the Venezuelan bishop was simple and orderly. Mother Teresa of Calcutta was paying a courtesy call on him since she had just been visiting a nearby jungle area at the invitation of a neighboring bishop. She was considering asking a team of the Missionaries of Charity to work in the area. I was doing the translating.

The bishop turned to me and asked about my work. When he found out that I worked and lived in New York, he asked me if I could do him a favor. He wanted me to make the first contacts with New York banks concerning a loan of up to $50,000. The plan was to borrow the money from the United States at a rate of interest of about seven percent. The funds would then be deposited with local banks and loaned out at the going rate (about twenty or twenty-two per cent). The difference in interest rates would insure the support of the seminary and other activities of the diocese. The bishop spoke in simplicity and utter frankness.

I told the bishop that I was not the person to help him. Not only did I lack contacts with New York banks but to help in such an operation would be against my principles.

"How would it be opposed to your principles?" he asked. "Is not the support of a seminary a worthy Catholic work?"

"Of course," I answered. "It is the matter of interest that is against my principles. I do not think demanding of interest is a worthy action for a Christian. I still believe that the Church was right when it forbade interest. In fact," I added, "to ask for interest of twenty per cent on loans would seem to be what the Church even today would call usury."

My only regret about that conversation with a bishop trapped in the mores of his time and place was that I had not given him an example of opposition to interest that had occurred in New York City. In 1960, the Catholic Worker had returned to the City of New York a check for $3,579.39 because it represented interest. The check came with the sum of $68,000, the payment offered by the city for the Catholic Worker house which was demolished for a subway improvement. As the payment had been delayed, the city authorities punctiliously added the amount of interest the money would have earned had it been deposited in a bank. In return, the city received a letter that will probably remain as a unique item in its files.

Dorothy Day explained in the letter accompanying the check that the Catholic Worker movement still took seriously the prohibition of the Church Fathers and Councils on lending money at interest. "In the Christian emphasis on the duty of charity," she wrote, "we are compelled to lend gratuitously, to give freely . . ." Some readers reacted strongly to the return of the money, money which could have gone into feeding the poor, they pointed out. It seemed an outlandish act, in the twentieth century, to oppose the system of interest.

I have personally discovered that my nonviolent or pacifist position is considered far less of an aberration than my refusal to condone interest. There have been times when I was forced to pay interest, but I opted out of situations where I would receive interest. My friends have felt they had to remind me that the whole free enterprise system of our country and its unexampled growth depends on the amassing of capital for the establishment of basic industries: that the stimulus for investment is the return on the investment; that in any case the return on invested money is often no more than enough to counteract the loss in the value of money through inflation. There are many more arguments of a technical nature, arguments which I can only counter on an entirely different plane with arguments of a moral nature.

The most telling argument, as far as I am concerned, is the collision of values between the capitalistic idea of property and the use of one's surplus property, and the Christian one. The capitalistic concept of property (according to the proponents but not the critics of capitalism) calls for the accumulation of savings through thrift and their investment at interest. Money thus breeds money. Surpluses are put to use in an unending spiral of gain. No one, no institution, can set a ceiling on this unending spiral. National taxes do not stop its motion. This spiral is accompanied by the spiralling of production and by pressures for ever-greater consumption. If mass production is called for by the spiral of gain, then it becomes the method of production, and there is no question of slowing down to ensure human work for human beings. The rights of the producer are completely lost in the emphasis on supplying the consumer. "Consumerism" is the result, and the word mirrors not only the succumbing of the consumer to the pressures of advertising, but the degradation of the producer.

Since the rise of capitalism, the Christian who does not believe in using his surplus for gain is often considered a troglodyte. For the Christian is expected to direct his surplus funds, not into the nexus of the market, but to meet the need of his near and far neighbor in the human family. His surplus is to bring him no gain but should contribute to the development of his neighbor and society. The collision of values, clear-cut in the early days of capitalism, became foggy as capitalists embraced the globe.

Perhaps today, when spiralling industrial growth and consumption are polluting the planet and depleting its energy resources, the Christian idea of property may emerge as having pragmatic as well as ethical validity. The god of un-controlled economic growth has clearly failed.

The Christian concept of property was unequivocally stated in the 1967 encyclical letter of Pope Paul VI, **The Development of Peoples.** "No one is justified," says the encyclical, "in keeping for his exclusive use what he does not need when others lack necessities. This is a simple rule, and each follower of Jesus can, and must, work it out for himself. Each person's, each family's, needs are different. The point is that a determination of those needs must be made in the light of the needs of others. Those others are not only those whose needs we see around us, but also those whose needs come to our attention.

The Development Of People is specific in condemning other abuses of capitalism, including the transfer of income abroad, the phenomenon known as "flight capital," the retention of large landed estates against the common good, and the concept that property constitutes "an absolute and unconditioned right." Regrettably, part of the sting of this encyclical was removed for Americans by a disclaimer pasted into the first edition, namely: "This individualistic system of capitalism so strongly condemned by Popes Leo XIII, Pius XI, Pius XII, John XXIII and Paul VI, involves a type of calloused exploitation which certainly is not descriptive of the prevailing business practices of the United States in 1967."

"Money-Lending" by Eileen Egan, *Catholic Worker.*

Editorials

Protecting Buyers of U.S. Grain

When the Russians start taking delivery of the American grain they're now in the process of buying, they'd better bring along their own inspectors to make sure they get what they pay for. American inspectors are supposed to guarantee the quality of American shipments, but many of them can't be trusted. They're hired hands of the very exporting companies that stand to benefit from the sale of substandard grain overseas.

The Federal Grain Standards Act is supposed to ensure that grain exports comply with federal standards for quality and cleanliness. But overseas shipments are routinely shortweighted by substituting stones for some of the grain, which then can be sold twice. Some shipments are adulterated with rice hulls and other fillers, and some are infested with rodents.

None of this should come as much of a surprise to the Department of Agriculture, which has on its books no less than 101 official complaints about the quality of American grain delivered overseas—some of them dating back a decade.

Under the present inspection system, the Agriculture Department licenses grain inspectors, but they're not federal employees. They work for private firms and local boards of trade that hire them out to the companies whose cargos they are supposed to inspect. Only Alice in Wonderland would expect that system to work.

Twenty persons, mostly grain elevator inspectors at New Orleans and Houston, are under federal indictment for allegedly taking bribes and engaging in other illegal practices. Now the scandal is spreading to virtually every American port that handles grain exports. The only way to stop it is for Congress to put teeth into laws designed to protect the integrity of American exports.

Since it's the Russians and other overseas buyers who are being stuck, why should Americans worry about the grain scandals? Because they're driving up the price of grain on world markets—and that's being reflected in U.S. supermarkets. Because other countries are likely to retaliate with the same sort of slipshod inspection of raw materials they ship to the U.S. And because American firms now stand accused of the same type of illegal and unethical practices they frequently complain about having to put up with overseas. Integrity begins at home.

A woman moves the Pentagon

Can one person make a difference? You'd better believe it.

One person, an unmarried pregnant Wave stationed at Patuxent River Naval Air Station in Maryland, "was a factor," Navy Secretary J. William Middendorf II concedes, in forcing the Pentagon to change a longstanding policy.

Until recently, the policy was that a servicewoman, married or unmarried, who became pregnant was automatically dismissed from the service unless she could get a waiver, which wasn't easy.

The new policy is that she will automatically be retained unless she requests a release or became pregnant during her initial indoctrination or training.

The Wave, whose name has been withheld, pointed to the anomalies of the policy she successfully fought. "If I had chosen to get an abortion," she wrote a congressman, "the Navy would not only have paid for it, but I would not have been forced to go through the mental harassment that I have."

Moreover, as she pointed out to her superiors, her status was no more of a burden on the service than if she'd been a divorced man or widower with custody of children.

It goes without saying that we don't recommend that unmarried women, in service or civilian life, get pregnant. But fair is fair. If a woman can do her job and wants to, having a child shouldn't disqualify her.

George F. Will

Death as a Spectator Sport

Idaho's Snake River Canyon, where every prospect pleases and only man is vile, soon will be the scene of a remarkable example of man's work. On Sept. 8 Evel Knievel will try to leap 1,500 feet across the canyon on a 350 m.p.h. motorcycle.

Through all of what might be called his adult life, Knievel has devoted himself sedulously and successfully to the task of breaking all his bones seriatim. His usual metier is motorcycle jumps over Mack trucks. But repetition has blunted the keen edge of his zest, so the canyon provides a needed change and an opportunity to break all his bones simultaneously.

Obviously he is loony to the core and tough enough to eat spinach with sand in it. Conversation, especially about himself, tumbles trippingly from his tongue, and he expresses himself with especially generous strength on the subject of his own heroism.

But Knievel, and the hard-eyed men who merchandise him and the mutton-headed people who celebrate him, are enough to alter one's conception of man as nature's final word.

He estimates that he has a 50-50 chance of failing in his jump and falling to his death in the canyon. If the jump is not as risky as it is advertised to be, it is a fraud. If, as seems probable, it does involve serious risk of Knievel's life, it is obscene. Millions of people watching this dreadful spectacle will be happy as giddy crickets at the prospect that they have a 50-50 chance of seeing a man splatter himself on Idaho's rocks.

Asked why she was waiting in a long line to see the gruesomely shocking movie "The Exorcist," a lady answered: "I want to see what everybody is throwing up about." That movie only titillated an unseemly appetite for the grotesque. The witless Knievel is titillating a barbaric appetite for treating violent death as a spectator sport. Like pornography, the event is brutalizing, anti-life.

Knievel is nimble at minting canards for every occasion, and his latest batch includes: "I like to live with a lump in my throat and a knot in my stomach." He also likes a lump in his wallet.

When he is not dispensing metaphysical mush ("The greatest competitor in life is death"), it is clear that money is the lamp unto his feet. He is going to make a fortune with this jump.

The voluptuous pleasure of watching a man risk killing himself evidently is not dampened by the nagging possibility that he might not kill himself. Knievel is building roads to enable a huge mob of spectators to gather on the rim of the canyon.

Watching Knievel's foul enterprise from the canyon rim is not a pastime for the proletariat. Spectators must pay $25. But the carriage trade is expected to snap up 50,000 tickets, briskly. Millions more will pay $8 to watch on closed-circuit television.

Knievel or his estate will make at least $13 million from the jump itself. And his various promoters and sponsors—the toy and T-shirt manufacturers, and others—think they can milk more than $100 million from this. Obviously they are aiming at children of all ages, but especially at real children.

Knievel's success on the jump is a consummation devoutly to be desired, if only because failure would bestow upon him a mindless martyrdom and might make his merchandisers rich even beyond their dreams of avarice. The merchandisers know that if Knievel plunges to his death, in living color, he will go down in legend and in song. Says a vice president of the Ideal Toy Co.: "If he does go, we hope that he'll still be unique. He'll be a legend."

If Knievel wants to risk smashing out what might be called his brains, that is his business. If adults want to pay to watch, that is a free transaction between consenting nincompoops. But it would be nice if there were some exploitation to which not even a toy manufacturer would stoop.

The whole wretched business calls to mind Macauley's observation: "The Puritan hated bear-baiting not because it gave pain to the bear, but because it gave pleasure to the spectators." Sound folks, Puritans.

Alas! why must we be so selfish that we can feel nothing but that which touches ourselves, *our* hearts, *our* pleasures, or *our* pockets?

And since so many children are born into the world without competent protectors from its evils, why is innocence left in ignorance and poverty, to stumble and fall under temptation? And when is that ever-present enigma to be solved which Carlyle suggests as the great problem of life :—"So many shirts in the world, and so many shirtless backs ; how to get the shirtless backs into the shirts?"

So many little unprotected children in the world, and so many rich men and women with warm human hearts ; how to get these children into these hearts? How to show people who are anxious to save a suffering and perishing world, that the place to begin is the cradle, just as they would begin with a very young plant in order to fashion the tree in symmetry.

Inquiries by the United States Commissioner of Education, seeking the solution of such problems, have elicited facts respecting the number and condition of the poor children in this city, which, it is believed, will be of interest to every thinking man and woman in the country.

How few residents of Manhattan Island realize, or are even aware of the fact, that within its confines are at least one hundred thousand children—the adjacent cities contain perhaps as many more—to whom the morning light on six days of the week brings only toil. For these children there are no schools, no nuttings in the woods, no bright walks in Central Park. They are prematurely burdened with the cares of life ; dwarfed in stature from the lack of proper nutriment ; by confinement in the bad air of workshops ; by the bearing of heavy burdens, and the deprivation of such recreations as a normal childhood imperatively demands. They may be seen in the early morning, in all portions of the city, among the laboring throng, hastening with serious mien to the service of the day.

When Briareus-handed industry knocks at the gates of the morning, we are apt to think only of strong men and healthy women. But here, side by side with these, are frail little forms, too often but poorly protected against the wintry blast.

Did you, reader, ever reflect that many children begin the terrible struggle of life for food, shelter, and clothing, at an age when others are scarcely out of their cradles?

But in all these hundreds of occupations which busy the skilled fingers of little children, the greatest number, and those of the most tender age, are engaged in the preparation of feathers, flowers, and tobacco—mere luxuries, yet considered so indispensable by a majority of men and women.

Reader, if this fact should seem to you of any special significance, and if it should suggest serious thoughts occasionally, do not drive them away, but entertain them kindly. I do not desire to plant thorns in any of your flowers. Far from it. But may it not be hoped that the fine lady, luxuriating in forms of airy beauty, grace, and harmony will sometimes think pitifully and helpfully of the little children ; that the man of ease, contentedly smoking his pipe or cigar, or rolling the sweet morsel under his tongue, may occasionally be carried in imagination to the filthy rooms where young children—almost babes—spend the long day in "stemming" the weed.

Do you think God intended childhood as a season for drudgery? If not, can any of you suggest some good plan by which the "rights" of children may be secured to them? Women who are already awake to some of the great issues of the hour, will you now arouse more fully to the importance of educating the children? Is not the question a fundamental one? And the rights of all children once secured, will not the world then be right?

Ten thousand children, it is said, are working in tobacco, in New York and Brooklyn, for ten hours a day, six days of the week, and fully five thousand of them are believed to be under fifteen years of age. Children in many cases supply the places of more mature hands, and thus offer the employer an opportunity for gain not to be resisted as long as other manufacturers with whom he must compete employ this cheap labor.

Were stringent laws passed, similar to those existing in some of the New England States, regulating the employment of children under a certain age, many of the employers would accept the change, and would co-operate with others in arranging for a voluntary system of half-time schools ; while not a few declare that such a system "wouldn't work," they "couldn't be bothered with it."

Tell them of the good results at Indian Orchard, and other places, from half-time schools, they say :—"O, in New England things can be done that can't be done anywhere else. Besides, in New England they work more hours than we do here. Our children can have an extra two hours for evening school."

In addition to the outrage of sacrificing the health and educational interests of children by keeping them at mechanical drudgery nearly all their waking hours, certain kinds of labor they perform are absolutely dangerous to life and limb. At the evening schools we heard of girls who, while working in twine manufactories, had lost one and two joints of their fingers. The principal of one school stated that last winter she had ten girls who had lost the initial finger from the right hand, and therefore could not be taught to write. One child, who learned to write with the left hand, came to school afterwards with the initial finger of that hand also gone. It was taken off in the twisting machinery at a twine factory.

It is expected that penalties must follow violations of the law of mechanics, as of other laws, but children should not be placed in situations where so sad a penalty is the result of a moment's inattention. Their innocence and ignorance appeal for protection against the possibility of such calamities. An engine of 150 horse-power, driving a balance-wheel of 18,000 pounds weight, is an irresistible force when it clashes with the little finger of a child. Should not children's fingers be protected from the destruction threatened by such machinery, in some manner, by law if not otherwise?

But if the situation of children engaged in regular employment is so sad, what can be said of those who are drifting about the streets of the city, without any real homes or steady employment, but supporting a miserable existence by such irregular work as they can obtain—living "by their wits." From fifteen to twenty thousand is considered a moderate estimate of the number of boys and girls situated thus in the midst of this great centre of wealth and refinement. Many of these are orphans — others worse than orphans — children of criminals and poor wretches sunk deep in the degradation of drunkenness. Some are runaways from other cities ; some are children of emigrants whose parents die upon the way here ; some have fathers in the army and no mothers ; others have invalid mothers and no fathers. Their daily portion is hunger, cold, and misery of almost every description. They may be seen almost every day upon the street, bent double, staggering under heavy loads, sweeping the crossings, or begging.

From *Scribner's Monthly*, 1871.

Courtesy of UE News Service.

Editorials

Unsolicited Business

A prostitute has been defined as a person, usually a woman, who has sexual intercourse for money. An expanded definition is a woman who gets paid for not rejecting another, i.e., the customer.

Interestingly, the definition of a prostitute as one who receives money for not rejecting sums up rather nicely women's role in society at large. Women in their social functions, as lover, mother, and wife, are trained not to reject, but to give. For the glory of the family, as it's called. In return, by convention, women are umbrellaed under a contract of perpetual care. So are cemetaries.

Likewise, the corporation's female staff ("the girls") is hired not to reject. As secretaries, administrative assistants, and girl fridays, women are hired not to reject the boss' sexual attentions, fantasies, whims or well-paid courtships. The solicited woman stands or falls alone, but all of us have a responsibility to react to sexism whether in employment or advertising.

Even if accepted into the male job hierarchy, a woman should alert new employees to the boss' sexual harassment and stalking patterns. Women in all job levels, including corporate executives should support others who resist. Notably, women most often preyed upon by "corporate johns" are those in the lower strata with the least power and influence in the business world. Women who yield to the situation are equally in need of support. Whether a woman accepts or rejects, she loses; she should not be ostracized.

The sexist nature of the situation is heightened because it is the younger, prettier women who are chosen; often the older less attractive women take satisfaction in the individual's dilemma or relish the office gossip.

Sexual offensiveness must be confronted. Suggested actions are: organize office guerrilla campaigns against offending executives, know how and where to activate existing laws to prevent job harassment, and hold advertisers responsible for demeaning copy by writing letters to those advertisers and their competitors.

Boycott their products.

News, Ethics and Negotiations

FOR SOME TIME, a debate has been going on with respect to the ethics of those who bring you the news each day. It concerns such questions as whether it is ever proper for a reporter to accept any form of gift or gratuity from a news source; whether the outside activities of reporters and editors should be known to the people they work for and to their readers; whether journalists should accept free tickets to sporting and cultural events granted merely and specifically because of their association with a news-gathering organization. Most of those questions have been argued informally within news organizations and between journalists and their outside critics.

Now, it appears, the debate has been given a more formal structure. Last week, Judge Nancy M. Sherman of the National Labor Relations Board issued a ruling against the Madison (Wisconsin) Capital Times that is sure to be appealed. Judge Sherman found for the Capital Times Unit of the American Newspaper Guild, which had charged the editor-publisher of the Capital Times with unfair labor practices. The reason for the charge was that the editor, Miles McMillin, had set forth a code of ethical behavior he said he expected editorial employees to follow. The union charged that such a code was a proper subject for negotiation, that the editor could not enforce such a code on his own.

It is impossible to guess where the full NLRB will come out, should the controversy go that far. As matters now stand, the variety of permissible practices is almost as extensive as the number of news organizations. Some newspapers permit their employees to accept free trips worth hundreds, if not thousands, of dollars from groups that have an interest in what the reporters write. Often, nothing specific, save "goodwill" is expected in return—and often something is. Sometimes a "good" story is expected by the donor.

Judge Sherman argues in her opinion that it is all right for a newspaper to try to promulgate a code of ethics, but that since such a code necessarily affects the economic life of reporters, it must be a subject of negotiation. Judge Sherman's ruling is framed within her understanding of the National Labor Relations Act. We do not share her certainty, however, that ethics are negotiable, since we believe that a newspaper's principles are more than a summary of labor-management contracts.

Judge Sherman's opinion asserts, for example, that if a reporter knows that certain gifts are likely to result from working for a particular newspaper, then the newspaper management cannot eliminate the reporter's right to accept those gifts without bargaining on the subject. "I find," said Judge Sherman, "that the receipt of 'freebies' usable in connection with coverage constitutes, at least presumptively, wages and working conditions which are a mandatory subject of collective bargaining."

By that reasoning, once a reporter on a newspaper has become accustomed to these extra emoluments, they cannot be denied by order of the management—even if management believes such practices undermine the credibility and independence of the newspaper. Here we are faced with a conflict between the state of labor law and the requirement of newspapers to shun even the appearance of impropriety.

To allow a lengthy negotiation process to be the sole basis on which a newspaper's ethical standards are established could make it possible for a dizzying array of standards to prevail in the meantime. In the best of all possible worlds, responsible journalists will know better than to accept gifts from news sources and subjects, to accept some form of side employment with those they may be called on to cover or to accept membership in groups and organizations in which they have a journalistic interest and which have a particular interest in their treatment by the press. Because journalists are human and subject to all the frailties that go with that condition, rules help. This newspaper, for instance, expects its reporters to accept no gifts or other emoluments from their sources or those about whom they write. Some other newspapers do the same. There is no way to tell what the impact of the Sherman ruling will be in American journalism, but we still believe in the old fashioned right—indeed, duty—of a paper to set its standards for ethical conduct, and we hope that view prevails as the Capital Times case goes through the courts.

© *The Washington Post* (January 27, 1975).

AN OPEN LETTER
TO ALL STRIKING
LOCAL 1199 EMPLOYEES

The tragedy of the 1199 strike continues. The safety and lives of our patients are in danger. The fear and worry of the patients' relatives are great. Thousands of our fellow New Yorkers cannot get the services of our hospitals that they need.

This strike was called for two reasons:
- For the full wage increase of $12. or 7½%.
- And to bring to the attention of the public and government officials the delay in arriving at a decision by the Cost of Living Council.

THE WAGE INCREASE:

You know that you already have 5½% guaranteed. Therefore, the wage issue at stake in this terrible strike is 2%. As of tomorrow, you will have lost one weeks' pay—the equivalent of 2% of your annual salary!

PUBLIC AND GOVERNMENT OFFICIALS:

The strike has disrupted vital health services. It has created the worst health emergency New York has ever seen. The Mayor, Governor, Senators and Congressmen and many other government officials are feverishly working to solve this tragic matter.

The point has been made and there is no public official in the city, state or federal government who has not been pressured to act. **As we have done before many times the League of Voluntary Hospitals and Homes has expressed to all these officials the support of all of its member institutions for full implementation of the arbitration award.** To continue this walkout would be senseless, illogical and demeaning to you as compassionate human beings.

You have nothing else to gain. You have made the impression you walked out for. Contrary to what has been stated by the union, we all know now that the delay in arriving at a decision was due to the labor unions' representatives on the Cost of Living Council, including Mr. Max Greenberg, the President of Local 1199's International Union.

To continue to punish the men, women and children needing the care, attention and support of all hospital employees would be criminal.

MEMBERS OF THE
LEAGUE OF VOLUNTARY HOSPITALS AND HOMES OF NEW YORK
60 EAST 42nd STREET, NEW YORK, N.Y. 10017

Courtesy of the League of Voluntary Hospitals and Homes of New York.

An Important Statement By Important People About The Shell Strike

The following statement was issued by the undersigned people regarding our strike at the Shell Oil Company. We believe it deserves the thoughtful consideration of everyone who is concerned about the world we live in and the way we live in it.

Last January, the Oil, Chemical and Atomic Workers International Union (OCAW) struck Shell Oil refineries and called for a boycott of Shell oil and chemicals. This strike is unique in labor history, being exclusively prompted by concerns for occupational health rather than by labor's traditional preoccupations and wages.

Earlier this year, OCAW negotiated new contracts with all major oil companies which established the basic, but innovative, principle of joint management-labor responsibilities for protecting workers' health. Shell and Chevron refused to agree to this principle and insist on maintaining unilateral control over occupational health and safety.

The major provisions of these contracts are:

—Periodic inspections of plants, by independent consultants, jointly approved by labor and management, to determine whether workers are being exposed to hazards.

—Medical examination of workers, at company expense, when indicated by inspections.

—Availability to the Union of all future company records on workers' sickness and death.

dustrial use, 500 new chemicals are introduced annually. Existing standards relate to only 450 of these chemicals, are obsolete, ignore delayed toxic effects, particularly cancer and chronic respiratory disease, and are poorly enforced.

Despite recent conclusions by an *ad hoc* HEW committee of international authorities in carcinogenesis, that *no* exposure level to carcinogens is safe, many workers are continuing exposed to potent occupational carcinogens, including asbestos, benzidine, 2-naphthylamine, 4-aminodiphenyl and bis—(chloromethyl) ether and occupational radiation exposure, particularly in the growing nuclear industry and in uranium mines. **Some 1,100 of 6,000 Western uranium miners will probably die of lung cancer in the next 20 years. Of 50,000 insulation workers, 20,000 are likely to die of asbestosis or cancer. The fate of 3.5 million others already exposed to lower levels of asbestos will remain unknown for 20 years. Recently, bladder tumors have been found in 16 percent of 315 workmen exposed to the rubber antioxidant 4-aminodiphenyl.**

The major objective of the 1970 Occupational Safety and Health Act is "... to ensure so far as possible every working man and woman in the nation safe and healthful working conditions ..." Implementation of the Act has, however, been ineffective. There are fewer than 100 qualified Occupational, Safety and Health Administration (OSHA) industrial hygienists and only about 500 OSHA inspectors for 4 million workplaces. OSHA has promulgated only one permanent standard, for asbestos. This standard, reflecting the epidemic of asbestosis and asbestos-induced lung and other cancers, particularly in insulation workers, however, will not be implemented until 1976. Labor has consequently recognized that vigorous enforcement of the Act demands its own initiatives.

The scope of occupational hazards is generally unrecognized. Of 80 million workers, there are over 7 million annual work-related diseases and injuries, of which 2 million are disabling and 14,500 fatal—more than the number of U.S. servicemen killed yearly in Viet Nam. Industrial disability results in losses of 250 million-man working days—ten times more than from strikes—costing $1.5 billion in wages and an annual loss to the GNP of $8 billion.

This situation is progressively deteriorating. The incidence of disabling injuries in manufacturing industries is now 20 percent greater than in 1958. Apart from over 10,000 chemicals in widespread in-

The growing recognition that most human cancers are environmentally induced and hence preventable has had no apreciable impact on occupational practice. Imposition of a zero tolerance for certain occupational carcinogens—as promulgated for carcinogenic food additives by the 1958 Delaney Amendment, and minimizing exposure to all categories of carcinogens—would be a major step towards practical implementation of the President's Cancer Conquest Program to prevent, besides treat, cancer.

Workers have long served as unwitting "guinea pigs", providing useful toxicological data which helped to protect the public. The effects of most environmental pollutants, such as carbon monoxide, lead, mercury and also of most human carcinogens were first detected in workmen; the in-plant environment is a concentrated toxic microcosm of that outside. Additionally, many toxic agents disperse beyond the plant and post public hazards.

The success of the OCAW strike is critical both to labor and the public. This has already been recognized by ten major environmental and public interest groups who have endorsed the Shell strike and boycott. The demand of labor to participate actively in protecting the health and safety of workers is basic and inalienable and cannot be sacrificed to narrow economic interests. It is hoped that Shell will adopt a posture more consistent with the public interest and the intent of the 1970 Occupational Safety and Health Act and follow the example of other oil companies.

OIL, CHEMICAL & ATOMIC WORKERS INTERNATIONAL UNION, AFL-CIO

A. F. Grospiron, *President*
1636 Champa Street
Denver, Colorado 80201

Left and right page, published by special permission of the Oil, Chemical and Atomic Workers International Union, AFL-CIO/CLC, P.O. Box 2812, Denver, Colo. 80201.

SECTION 11

Civil Disobedience

Many of the arguments in most of the sections of this book are concerned either directly or indirectly with the question of whether or not certain acts (e.g., abortion, drug use, handgun ownership, sale of pornography, and sale of term papers, to name just a few) should be prohibited by law. The arguments in this section are primarily concerned with the question of whether or not under any circumstances whatsoever it is morally right to commit an act which is prohibited by law. The question can be formulated in many ways which range from relatively minor violations (such as breaking the speed limit to get a dying person to a hospital) to the extreme of overthrow of the entire legal system (revolution). The most violent form of this last extreme is what is today referred to as "terrorism."

"Give unto Caesar that which is Caesar's and unto God that which is God's." This is one of the oldest statements of the theory that there are two kinds of duty—moral and legal. Statements such as this suggest that this is a simple, clear-cut dichotomy, that all cases fall directly into one category or the other. In point of fact, many of our laws are essentially codifications of basic moral rules and principles, in direct contradiction of the adage that "You can't legislate morality." The difficult questions arise when there is a direct conflict between moral and legal rules. And since in a democratic system, when a majority of the population believes that if a law is in conflict with moral principles the law should be changed, the most difficult questions are those focussed on cases in which an individual's moral judgment is in conflict with the moral beliefs of the majority of the society, as well as of the laws of that society. In cases where the democratic process is not functioning, the question of opposition to the law and violation of it requires the consideration of additional factors, including the problem of identifying the "will of the majority."

EXERCISES

1. Examine the working draft of the United States Declaration of Independence. Discuss the significance of each of the changes in wording in the various versions with regard to the extent to which each change strengthens or weakens the support provided for the conclusion that it was right for the American colonies to overthrow the laws of the English government. Is this argument in any way relevant to the discussion of violating any of the laws of the United States government today? Does this argument in any way provide justification for various acts of terrorism in the United States or in other areas of the world today?
2. Examine the arguments in the examples in this chapter to determine if there is any significant difference between cases in which the law is violated openly and the violator is willing to accept the prescribed punishment for that violation and cases in which the violator attempts to act in secret and to avoid punishment.
3. Discuss the question of whether or not one can justify the violation of a moral principle on the grounds that to do so would be to break a law of the society.

Editing the Declaration

THE DECLARATION OF INDEPENDENCE underwent numerous changes, mostly minor but some major, before Congress approved it last week. The editing process is illustrated in key excerpts. The words that are crossed out and replaced in roman type are alterations made after Thomas Jefferson consulted with John Adams and Benjamin Franklin. The bracketed words were cut and the italicized words were added by the Congress.

"When in the course of human events it becomes necessary for one ~~dissolve the political bands which have connected them with~~ a people to ^advance from that subordination in which they another, and to ~~have hitherto remained, & to~~ assume among the powers of the
                                                                     separate and equal
earth the ~~equal & independent~~ station to which the laws of nature & of nature's god entitle them, a decent respect to the opinions of mankind requires that they should declare the
                                                                     the separation.
causes which impel them to ^~~the change.~~
                                                                     self-evident;
"We hold these truths to be ^~~sacred & undeniable~~; that all
                                                                     they are endowed
men are created equal ~~& independent~~; that ^~~from that equal~~
by their creator with ~~equal rights, some of which are~~
~~creation they derive in rights~~ certain [inherent &] in-
                                                                     rights; that   these
alienable* ^among ~~which~~ are ~~the preservation of~~ life, liberty, &
                                                                     rights
the pursuit of happiness; that to secure these ^~~ends~~, govern-ments are instituted among men, deriving their just powers from the consent of the governed; that whenever any form of
                                                                     s
government ~~shall~~ become ^destructive of these ends, it is the right of the people to alter or to abolish it. . ."

The Declaration then lists 27 specific charges against King George III. Among the most important:

"he has refused his assent to laws the most wholesome and necessary for the public good:. . .

"he has dissolved, Representative houses repeatedly [& continually], for opposing with manly firmness his invasions on the rights of the people:. . .

"he has [suffered] *obstructed* the administration of justice
                                                                     states
[totally to cease in some of these ^~~colonies~~]. . .

"he has made [our] judges dependent on his will alone. . .

"he has kept among us in times of peace standing armies [&
                                                                     without the consent of our legislatures:
ships of war], ^

"he has combined with others to subject us to a jurisdiction foreign to our constitutions and unacknowledged by our laws;
                                                                     acts of
giving his assent to their ^pretended ~~acts of~~ legislation. . . for cutting off our trade with all parts of the world; for imposing taxes on us without our consent; for depriving us *in many cases* of the benefits of trial by jury. . ."

The Declaration concludes:

"We therefore the representatives of the United states of America in General Congress assembled *appealing to the supreme judge of the world for the rectitude of our intentions*, do, in the name & by authority of the good people of these [states, reject & re-nounce all allegiance & subjection to the kings of Great Britain . . . & finally we do assert & declare these colonies to be free & independent states,] colonies, *solemnly publish and declare, that these United colonies are, and of right ought to be, free & independent states; that they are absolved from all allegiance to the British crown* . . . & that as free & independent states they ~~shall hereafter~~
                                                                     full
have ^power to levy war, conclude peace, contract alliances, establish commerce, & to do all other acts and things which independent states may of right do. And for the support of this declaration, *with a firm reliance on the protection of divine provi-dence*, we mutually pledge to each other our lives, our fortunes & our sacred honour."

*This word was changed — to "unalienable" — apparently by the first printer, John Dunlap of Philadelphia.

TOPICS OF THE TIME.

THREE PIECES OF THE WOMAN QUESTION.
FIRST PIECE.

A SURVEY of the States of the Union, and of the Union under the general government, will show to any candid observer that the legislation of the country, in all its departments, is above, rather than below, the average moral sense of the nation. The fact is seen in the inadequate execution of the laws. There are many statutes relating to public morals and civil policy which appear to be the offspring of the highest and purest principles, that stand as dead letters in State and national law, simply because the average moral sense of the people does not demand and enforce their execution. They are enacted through the influence or by the power of men of exceptional virtue, who find, to their sorrow, that while it is easy to make good laws, it is difficult, and often impossible, to execute them. So far as we know, it has never occurred to them to call for the assistance of women in the execution of these laws, nor has it occurred to women to offer their assistance to them for this end. One or two questions, suggested by the discussions of the time, naturally grow out of this statement.

First :—Is it of any practical advantage to have better laws, until the average morality of the people is sufficient to execute those which we have?

Second :—Is it right that women should have an equal or a determining voice in the enactment of laws which they do not propose to execute, which they do not propose to assist in executing, which they could not execute if they would, and which they expect men to execute for them?

Third :—Supposing that women would give us better laws than we have (which is not evident), what would be the practical advantage to them or to us, so long as they must rely upon us to execute them—upon us, who find it impossible to enforce our own laws, some of the best of which are the outgrowth of the pure influence of women in home and social life?

SECOND PIECE.

In national and international life there are policies of action and attitude to be adopted and maintained. These policies sometimes cost a civil war for their establishment or defense, and, not unfrequently, a war with related nations. It so happens, in the nature of the case, that no single nation has it in its power to abolish war. The only way for a nation to live, when attacked by foes within or without, is to fight ; and, in the present condition of the world, a national policy which has not behind it the power of physical defense is as weak and contemptible a thing as the world holds. Out of this statement, which we presume no one will dispute, there arise two questions.

First :—Would a lack of all personal risk and responsibility, on the part of those delegated to establish and pronounce the policy of a nation, tend to prudent counsels and careful decisions?

Second :—Is it right—is it kind and courteous to men —for women to demand an equal or a determining voice in the establishment of a national policy which they do not propose to defend, which they could not defend if they would, and which they expect men to defend for them?

THIRD PIECE.

Mr. Gleason, the Tax Commissioner of Massachusetts, reported to the Legislature of that State in May, that a tax of nearly two million dollars is paid annually by the women of the State on property amounting, at a low valuation, to one hundred and thirty-two million dollars. The fact is an interesting and gratifying one, in every point of view. Naturally it is seized upon by the advocates of woman-suffrage, and brought prominently forward to assist in establishing woman's claim to the ballot. The old cry of "no taxation without representation" is renewed, however much or little of essential justice may be involved in the phrase. Well, if women are, or ever have been, taxed as women (which they are not, and never have been) ; if they produced this wealth, or won it by legitimate trade (which they did not) ; if the men who produced it received their right to the ballot by or through it ; if nine-tenths of the wealth of the State were not in the hands of business men whose pursuits have specially fitted them to be the guardians of the wealth of the State ; if the counsels of these tax-paying women could add wisdom to the wisdom of these men ; if the men who produced this wealth, and bestowed it upon these women, did it with distrust of the laws enacted by men for its protection, and with the desire for the social and political revolution which woman-suffrage would produce, in order that it might be better protected ; if there were any complaint of inadequate protection to this property on account of its being in the hands of women —if all or any one of these suppositions were based in truth—then some sort of a plea could be set up on Mr. Gleason's exhibit by those who claim the ballot for woman. As the facts are, we confess our inability to find in it any comfort or support for those who seek for the revolution under consideration. On the contrary, we find that the ballot as it stands to-day, with its privileges, responsibilities, and limitations, secures to woman complete protection in the enjoyment of revenues which are proved to be immense, all drawn from land and sea by the hands of men whose largess testifies alike of their love and their munificence.

SCIENCE

Concerning Dissent and Civil Disobedience

What rights are exercised, and what rights are violated, when students forcibly occupy a campus building, when participants in the Poor People's Campaign march to the U.S. Capitol with the intention of being arrested there, or when critics oppose the war in Vietnam? Abe Fortas, newly appointed Chief Justice of the Supreme Court, has written an admirably brief and clear explanation* of the constitutional principles involved.

The need to understand the principles will continue. The war in Vietnam is not the first and may not be the last unpopular war. Much has been achieved in the removal of racial discrimination, but the much is still too little. Justified student complaint must be distinguished from disruptive intent. The dean of Howard University's Law School has described the dilemma of his students in wanting to follow the law yet wanting to change radically our legal and social structure. The reformer's appetite is increased, not satisfied, by moderate initial success. The need to understand the principles involved will not soon disappear.

The rights to dissent, to advocate social change, to oppose government policy and practice, to change government itself—all these, if carried out by peaceful means, are protected under the Constitution. Fortas writes: "Nowhere in the world—at no time in history—has freedom to dissent and to oppose governmental action been more broadly safeguarded than in the United States of America, today."

But the right to dissent runs into another right. "The Constitution seeks to accommodate two conflicting values, each of which is fundamental: the need for freedom to speak freely, to protest effectively, to organize, and to demonstrate; and the necessity of maintaining order so that other people's rights, and the peace and security of the state, will not be impaired." It is actions, therefore, rather than motives or thoughts that must be judged. No matter how nobly motivated, actions that endanger others or infringe their rights are unlawful and subject to punishment.

Yet sometimes one feels it his duty to disobey a law he considers immoral, and Justice Fortas writes: "I am a man of the law. I have dedicated myself to uphold the law. . . . But if I . . . had been a Negro living in Birmingham or Little Rock or Plaquemines Parish, Louisiana, I hope I would have disobeyed the state law that said I might not enter the public waiting room reserved for 'Whites.' "

If the route of disobedience is taken, the consequences must be accepted. Acting in the great tradition of true civil disobedience, Dr. Martin Luther King warned that Negroes would disobey unjust laws, and then insisted that the disobedience be open and peaceful and that those who disobeyed accept the consequences. It may seem unduly harsh to fine or jail a person who violates a law he believes immoral or unconstitutional, but this is the rule of law—the rule of law that is essential to the procedure we have developed to protect dissent and to encourage peaceful change. The objectives of a particular movement or protest may be of great importance for the quality of our lives, but preservation of the procedure is our guarantee of future change and improvement.

In a time of troubled disagreements, when the term *civil disobedience* is widely misapplied, Mr. Fortas offers help to protestors and activists in understanding their rights and the limitations on those rights, and a guide to other persons in formulating standards for judging the actions they watch with fear, with wonder, or with sympathy.—DAEL WOLFLE

*Abe Fortas. *Concerning Dissent and Civil Disobedience* (New American Library of World Literature. New York. 1968). 64 pages. paper. 50¢.

It is surprising to encounter solecisms in Wolfle's editorial. Justice Fortas, whose recent essay *Concerning Dissent and Civil Disobedience* stimulated the editorial, is permitted such legerdemain: Fortas is a lawyer, and lawyers are trained to confound and to employ logic dialectically.

1) The freedom "to speak freely and protest effectively" (*ex Fortas*) is activity and entails further activities. So it makes no sense to say that exercises of First Amendment rights must be judged by the consequent actions "rather than motives or thoughts." To imagine such a disjunction between motives, thoughts, and behavior is not only to subscribe to a passé legal fiction, but also to consign science and the intelligentsia to the status of a bauble.

2) Actions which "endanger others and infringe on their rights" are of course, *ex def.*, "unlawful" if reference is to positive law. (That is not quite accurate, since official action that endangers people *is* lawful, except in cases where subsequently it is officially decided to have been unlawful.)

3) To assert next that "the [legal] consequences must be accepted" by those who disobey laws which they deem to be immoral is to beg the question altogether—the question being, under what circumstances, if any, should the law be set aside to satisfy the claims of morality? The reasoning of the editorial could not distinguish Eichmann from Dr. Spock, because it values legal coercion for its own sake.

4) "The rule of law" is offered as the logical and ethical underpinning of this line of thought. To be sure, the rule of law is not a term of art among jurists. It is a political slogan which celebrates the values of compliance and due process. What it means is that disputes should be settled according to rules agreed upon in advance of the dispute, administered impersonally, and stated sufficiently precisely for people to be able to anticipate the risks of liability. Hence, "the rule of law" is procedural, has no substantive contents, and cannot possibly be relevant to political disputes in which the interpretation or validity of a particular law is in issue. . . .

Those who agreed with the sentiment behind Wolfle's editorial will be protesting to themselves that it was never intended to be understood in this way. That means that it was never intended to be understood, period; it was meant to be agreed with.

DONALD A. STRICKLAND
Department of Political Science,
Northwestern University,
Evanston, Illinois 60201

A Government of Laws, and Not of Men

Wolfle's editorial "Concerning dissent and civil disobedience" (5 July, p. 9), represents . . . unreal thinking. If one may disobey the law according to one's personal feelings then the only wrong that can be adjudged against Sirhan, Ray, or Oswald for their alleged offenses is that of resisting arrest, of "not accepting the consequences."

Personal physical violence is not included? Then how about destroying a man's home or business? No? How about just partially destroying them? How about hindering his means of livelihood? Where should the line be drawn?

The fact is that the basic statement is wrong. One is morally obligated to change a law he feels is wrong, not disobey it. As long as there are any legal means by which the law may be changed one must use them. The mere fact that a majority of people do not support the change gives no license to disobey, but only to work to make a majority see the need for the change.

No, I submit that "civil disobedience" in this country is wrong, a truly immoral act, and will remain so as long as we have a freely elected form of government and legal redress in the courts.

LESLIE M. BAGNALL
Department of Mechanical Engineering,
Texas A&M University,
College Station 77843

The editorial stated that "the term *civil disobedience* is widely misapplied." That term can be defined as the refusal to obey civil laws, especially, as Webster's puts it, "as a nonviolent collective means of forcing concessions from the government." The alleged crimes of Messrs. Sirhan, Ray, Oswald, and Eichmann are in a different domain.

Bagnall briefly, and Rhine more fully, hope we can rely on majority rule. So does the true civil dissenter (but not the violence monger who may come along at the same time). He accepts the principle of majority rule; he wants the majority to change a law; when he concludes that other means of persuasion will not succeed, he uses civil disobedience to emphasize and dramatize his case. He is saying, "I believe this law to be morally wrong. I believe it so strongly that I violate the law and expect to be punished. But I hope thereby to convince you that the law is wrong and that you should change it." Although he is violating a particular law, he accepts what Strickland called "rules agreed upon in advance" or the editorial called "the rule of law."

The sentiment behind the editorial was, I thought, clear and cogent. It is the desirability, in a period of much controversy—which concerns a variety of issues and is expressed in a variety of ways—of understanding the constitutional principles concerning dissent and civil disobedience, and of discriminating among the various means by which disagreements are expressed. I am sorry Strickland misunderstood.

DAEL WOLFLE

Left, letter to the editor of *Science* by Leslie M. Bagnall, September 13, 1968. Right, letter replying to critics of editorial by Dael Wolfle in *Science*, September 13, 1968.

'Not Yet a Good Man'

By William Sloane Coffin Jr.

NEW HAVEN—I was very fond of Jeb Magruder when we were together at Williams College. It was in 1958, his senior year and my first year as teacher and college chaplain. He and two classmates used to take my wife and me to dinner. He babysat for our daughter. Although we never saw each other after his graduation, for several years we corresponded.

During his time at Williams I worried about Jeb. I used to say to him: "You're a nice guy, Jeb, but not yet a good man. You have lots of charm but little inner strength. And if you don't stand for something you're apt to fall for anything."

When I saw him again on television testifying before Senator Ervin's committee, I was again drawn to him. While I do not excuse his conduct, I want to say something in explanation, for his testimony said as much about his education and American society as it did about Jeb himself.

In the 1950's students were agreeing their way through life. There was no civil rights movement to speak of and of course no antiwar movement. At Williams, as at so many exclusive colleges, there were few blacks, no Chicanos, no women and altogether too many fraternities which tended to promote an élitist team spirit, and breed a mistrust of healthy criticism. Professors everywhere were morally asleep. For the most part they represented the bland leading the bland.

Education was for making a living, not a life, to be traded upon rather than to be used to create a better world.

Jeb was very gregarious. He wanted to be liked. He had a much greater sense of himself when he was with others than when alone. As a natural winner, he conformed easily to the American success ethic of the day—popularity, power, money.

As his ethics teacher, I wish now I had stressed the errors and illusions that stem from the fear of being a loser in this particular game plan. I wish I had pointed out the paradox of winners being losers, and losers winners. I wish I had stressed the importance of solitude. I wish I had emphasized that it is the individual consciences of history which, as opposed to the mass mind, best represent the universal conscience of mankind.

Maybe these emphases would have helped Jeb to develop individual convictions. Certainly it would have helped his understanding of civil disobedience, for many of the great consciences of history—Moses, Jeremiah, Jesus, Socrates, Thoreau, Gandhi—many we today regard as heroes were notorious lawbreakers in their time.

I was shocked to hear Jeb lump all lawbreakers together. He should have known—and the Senators pressing him should have reminded a listening nation—that Martin Luther King and many in the antiwar movement were protesting what they considered to be illegal laws whose constitutionality could be tested only by a refusal to obey them. There is an enormous difference between trying to keep the nation under the law and trying to keep it under Nixon, between being a loyal servant of the Constitution and being a loyal servant only of the man who hires you.

If there are differences in ends so there are differences in means. Whatever Dr. King and Dr. Spock did they did openly. All America could see and judge. Jeb operated behind closed doors. Most of the people in the civil rights and antiwar movements were careful not to infringe on the civil liberties of other citizens. Jeb and his friends deliberately violated these liberties. When the Supreme Court declared against him, Dr. King went from Georgia to Alabama to take his punishment. The draft resisters who went to jail accepted theirs. But Jeb's crowd, far from accepting punishment, tried only to conceal their crimes. Dr. King and those who followed him disobeyed the law to protect it. It is a sad and savage irony if Government officials learn from the practitioners of civil disobedience that law is made to be circumvented.

Teaching is at best a precarious business; the rational mind is no match for an irrational will that needs to place popularity and power above truth. Nevertheless all of us who taught him, and American society as a whole, could have done better by Jeb. Now we have the opportunity to learn from him the ancient lesson that to do evil in this world you don't have to be evil—just a nice guy, not yet a good man.

The Rev. William Sloane Coffin Jr., is chaplain at Yale.

Article in *The New York Times* by the Reverend William Sloane Coffin, Jr., June 10, 1973.

Magruder on Watergate:
Ends Justify the Means

By JAMES M. NAUGHTON
Special to The New York Times

WASHINGTON, June 14—Government officials he respected had done it. The university professor of ethics he admired had done it. So Jeb Stuart Magruder had done it too, he told the Senate committee investigating the Watergate affair today. He had let the end justify the means.

Mr. Magruder, the former deputy director of the Committee for the Re-election of the President, displayed a controlled nervousness and was more than a little apologetic as he sat all day at the witness table relating in detail that he and an assortment of high officials—from the Attorney General to the President's lawyer—had planned, executed and then tried in vain to cover up the Watergate affair.

Q. I still can't quite come to grips with why you all had an expressed reservation about this and you still went ahead with it.

A. I knew you would get to this line of questioning, so why don't I give you what I think is the appropriate re sponse here.

I had worked for some two years, three years, really, in the White House and at that time, I was mainly engaged in the activities trying to generate some support for the President. During that time, we had worked primarily relating to the war situation and worked with anti-war groups.

Student of Ethics

Now I had gone to college, as an example, under—and had a course in ethics as an example under William Sloane Coffin, whom I respect greatly. I have great regard for him. He was quoted the other day as saying, well, I guess Mr. Magruder failed my course in ethics. And I think he is correct.

During this whole time we were in the White House and during this time we were directly employed with trying to succeed with the President's policies we saw continuping violations of the law

done by men like William Sloane Coffin. He tells me my ethics are bad. Yet he was indicted for criminal charges. He recommended on the Washington Monument grounds that students burn their draft cards and that we have mass demonstrations, shut down the city of Washington.

Now, here are ethical, legitimate people whom I respected. I respect Mr. Coffin tremendously. He was a very close friend of mine. I saw people I was very close to breaking the law without any regard for any other person's pattern of behavior or belief.

So consequently, when These subjects came up although I was aware they were illegal we had become somewhat inured to using some activities that would help us in accomplishing what we thought was a cause, a legitimate cause.

Now, that is absolutely incorrect; two wrongs do not make a right.

For the past year, I have obviously had to consider that and I understand completely that that was an absolute, incorrect decision. But that is basically, I think, the reason why that decision was made, because of that atmosphere that had occurred and to all of us who had worked in the White House, there was that feeling of resentment and of frustration at being unable to deal with issues on a legal basis.

I fully accept the responsibility of having made an absolutely disastrous decision, or at least having participated. I didn't make the decision, but certainly participated in it.

SENATOR ERVIN: I was very much impressed with your testimony about the climate that prevailed in the White House and afterwards in the committee to re-elect the President. As a matter of fact, was there not a fear there of Americans that dissented from policies of Government? You spoke about your former professor—

A. The Reverend Coffin. Yes.

Q. He just came down and demonstrated. There were a great many demonstrations,

weren't there? A. He did quite a bit more than demonstrate.

Q. He was supposed to try to frustrate the draft. A. He did, and he participated in many activities that were considered illegal.

Q. You were disturbed at the demonstrations, weren't you, the people at the White House? A. Yes, sir. We were.

Q. The reason I asked the question, I have had to spend my time fighting such laws and legislative proposals as no-knock laws, preventive detention laws, the claim that there was an inherent right of the President to bug anybody suspected of domestic subversion, and things of that kind. And I just could not understand why people got so fearful.

A. I would characterize that at least my reaction was stronger after three years of working in that atmosphere than it had been before.

Q. I am familiar with that kind of atmosphere. I came up here during Joe McCarthy days wren Joe McCarthy saw a Communist hiding under every rose bush and I have been here fighting the no knock laws and preventive detention laws and indiscriminate bugging by people who've found subversives hiding under every bed. In this nation, we have had a very unfortunate fear. And this fear went to the extent of deploring the exercise of personal rights for those who wanted to assemble and petition the Government for redress of grievances.

Some of it happened before you got into the White House and I am not blaming you, because even under a Democratic Administration, I had an investigation here where they became so afraid of people that they used military intelligence to spy on civilians whose only offense was that they were dissatisified with the policies of the Government and assembled and petitioned for relief.

Now, I think that all grew out of this complement of fear, did not it, the whole Watergate incident?

A. I think from my own personal standpoint, I did lose some respect for the legal process simply because I did not see it working as I had hoped it would when I came here.

From *The New York Times*, June 14, 1973.

Spread of objections of conscience

must be halted

One thing must be made plain from the very beginning — demands for a defence tax (Wehrsteuer) must be accompanied by demands for a better army. Defence tax can only have a sound purpose if it is considered as a way to adapt general conscription to the age in which we live.

All considerations must be based on the duty of protecting the community. Providing external security is a binding commitment on everybody. This can be achieved in a number of ways. One of these is by becoming a soldier.

What we now understand by defending our country has been largely freed of the pathos of a personal sacrifice of life and limb.

NATO armies are trained for war, it is true. They must be able to fight. The martial spirit must not be extinguished.

But their military role is given a political interpretation. The army is a means of preventing war. It has to exist as a threat to others. Its deterrent effect is one of the cornerstones of the strategy of maintaining peace.

Diplomatic flexibility, political will, industrial power, technical organisation, economic opportunity and treaties of alliance are the other factors of our strategy.

Conscription and the soldiers thus provided are essential to external security. Soldiers are important but they do not stand at the centre of planning for this work-sharing strategy. Not all the young people liable for conscription are called up. A selection can be made among them.

Conscription must be interpreted differently than was once the case. It is no longer the reservoir for a large armed body. It must be compared with the readiness of the modern industrial nation to contribute to external security in a large number of fields.

In times of peace a measurable form of action for the security of the community is the financial contribution of the individual in preserving the common good.

Everyone pays for our external security by paying taxes. Those who do military service in addition are taking over further burdens.

Starting from the fact that everyone has to pay taxes and that events do not force everyone to do military service, a person cannot fail to come to the conclusion that a person who does military service should pay less.

Nobody will underestimate the technical difficulties involved in shifting various parts of the tax burden. The first thing to do is to work out the financial value of the service period.

The period during which a person is freed from paying taxes need not necessarily be the same as the time he spends in the reserves. How are people who want to serve yet are not recruited to be treated?

But really all these questions can be answered during the course of events. The main point to be recognised when discussing the problem of a defence tax is that the contribution to external security can take a number of forms.

Military service too must be viewed as a special type of defence tax. At the same time it must be freed from the myth that it is a levée en masse.

The old idea of the indissolubility of the right of the citizen to be provided with defence and his duty to provide it is no longer relevant in an industrial nation. We have become more sober. We are satisfied by the duty alone.

This type of attitude makes it easier for a government to approach the ideal production State. Even the mention of "military autonomy" could not be used to prevent modern interpretations of the role of army and State.

If military defence tax is to be understood as compensation, it is easy to draw up laws to satisfy the moral and political demands of soldiers for balanced personal treatment in a democracy.

The way would also be cleared for greater justice in the armed forces. The chance that often decides whether a person is conscripted or not has done a lot to contribute to the disinclination toward doing armed service.

Conscientious objection may be traced to the recognition that modern European war is no longer a battle between knights but a military form of mutual extermination. A sensitive conscience must be respected.

But a large number of young conscripts know that their role is to provide security. Many have understood what deterrent strategy entails.

The suspicion is therefore justified that there is a link between conscientious objection and the injustice surrounding conscription. There is no other explanation for the flood of applications to be excused military service on the grounds of conscientious objection.

11,446 applications have already been received in the first quarter of 1971. Six thousand applications were made during the whole of 1967, twelve thousand in 1968 and nineteen thousand in 1970.

It is estimated that by the end of 1971 more than 100,000 applications will have been made since the Bundeswehr was set up.

The Bundestag could not ignore this fact during its debate on the subject. Unorthodox action is necessary if the situation is to be changed.

Adelbert Weinstein
(Frankfurter Allgemeine Zeitung für Deutschland, 12 May 1971)

Originally published in *Frankfurter Allgemeine Zeitung*, May 12, 1971.

ADVICE TO A DRAFTEE by Leo Tolstoy

In my last letter I answered your question as well as I could. It is not only Christians but all just people who must refuse to become soldiers — that is, to be ready on another's command (for this is what a soldier's duty actually consists of) to kill all those one is ordered to kill. The question as you state it — which is more useful, to become a good teacher or to suffer for rejecting conscription? — is falsely stated. The question is falsely stated because it is wrong for us to determine our actions according to their results, to view actions merely as useful or destructive. In the choice of our actions we can be led by their advantages or disadvantages only when the actions themselves are not opposed to the demands of morality.

We can stay home, go abroad, or concern ourselves with farming or science according to what we find useful for ourselves or others; for neither in domestic life, foreign travel, farming, nor science is there anything immoral. But under no circumstance can we inflict violence on people, torture or kill them because we think such acts could be of use to us or to others. We cannot and may not do such things, especially because we can never be sure of the results of our actions. Often actions which seem the most advantageous of all turn out in fact to be destructive; and the reverse is also true.

The question should not be stated: which is more useful, to be a good teacher or to go to jail for refusing conscription? but rather: what should a man do who has been called upon for military service — that is, called upon to kill or to prepare himself to kill?

In every person's life there are moments in which he can know himself, tell himself who he is, whether he is a man who values his human dignity above his life or a weak creature who does not know his dignity and is concerned merely with being useful (chiefly to himself). This is the situation of a man who goes out to defend his honor in a duel or a soldier who goes into battle (although here the concepts of life are wrong). It is the situation of a doctor or a priest called to someone sick with plague, of a man in a burning house or a sinking ship who must decide whether to let the weaker go first or shove them aside and save himself. It is the situation of a man in poverty who accepts or rejects a bribe. And in our times, it is the situation of a man called to military service. For a man who knows its significance, the call to the army is perhaps the only opportunity for him to behave as a morally free creature and fulfill the highest requirement of his life — or else merely to keep his advantage in sight like an animal and thus remain slavishly submissive and servile until humanity becomes degraded and stupid.

For these reasons I answered your question whether one has to refuse to do military service with a categorical "yes" — if you understand the meaning of military service (and if you did not understand it then, you do now) and if you want to behave as a moral person living in our times must.

Please excuse me if these words are harsh. The subject is so important that one cannot be careful enough in expressing oneself so as to avoid false interpretation.

April 7, 1899   Leo Tolstoy *he emblem of the Symbionese Liberation rmy [S.L.A.].*

We of the Symbionese Federation and the S.L.A. define urselves by this name because it states that we are no nger willing to allow the enemy of all our people and ildren to murder, oppress and exploit us nor define us by or and thereby maintain division among us, but rather ve joined together under black and minority leadership in half of all our different races and people to build a better d new world for our children and people's future. We e a United Front and Federated Coalition of members om the Asian, Black, Brown, Indian, White, Women, Grey d Gay Liberation Movements.

Who have all come to see and understand that only if we ite and build our new world and future, will there really a future for our children and people. We of the People d not the ruling capitalist class, will build a new world and stem. Where there is really freedom and a true meaning to justice and equality for all women and men of all races and people, and an end to the murder and oppression, exploitation of all people.

We of the Symbionese Federation and the S.L.A. are the children of all oppressed people, who have decided to redefine ourselves as a Symbionese Race and People. Yet, recognizing the rich cultures of each and enforcing our rights to possession of our many cultures within a united federation of independent and sovereign nations, each of them flourishing and protected by its own laws and codes of self determination.

We are of many colors, but yet of one mind, for we all in history's time on this earth have become part of each other in suffering and in mind, and have agreed that the murder, oppression and exploitation of our children and people must end now, for we all have seen the murder, oppression and exploitation of our people for too long under the hand of the same enemy and class of people and under the same system.

Knowing this, the Symbionese Federation and the S.L.A. know that our often murderous alienation from each other aids and is one of the fundamental strengths behind the ruling capitalist class's ability to murder and oppress us all. By not allowing them to define us by color, and also recognizing that by refusing ourselves to also internalize this false division definition, knowing that in mind and body we are facing the same enemy and that we are all comrades of one people, the murdered and oppressed, we are now able to become a united people under the Symbionese Federation and make true the words of our codes of unity that TO DIE A RACE, AND BE BORN A NATION, IS TO BECOME FREE.

Therefore, we of the Symbionese Federation and the S.L.A. DO NOT under the rights of human beings submit to the murder, oppression and exploitation of our children and people and do under the rights granted to the people under the Declaration of Independence of the United States, do now by the rights of our children and people and by Force of Arms and with every drop of our blood, Declare Revolutionary War against the The Fascist Capitalist Class, and all their agents of murder, oppression and exploitation. We support by Force of Arms the just struggles of all oppressed people for self determination and independence within the United States and The World. And hereby offer to all liberation movements, revolutionary workers groups, and peoples organizations our total aid and support for the struggle for freedom and justice for all people and races. We call upon all revolutionary black and other oppressed people within the Fascist United States to come together and join the Symbionese Federation and fight in the forces of The Symbionese Liberation Army.

THE ETERNAL CASE AGAINST INJUSTICE

By JACQUES MADAULE

Friends of mine have been very shocked when, in a moment of discouragement, I have told them that the petitions we sign and the demonstrations we stage against this or that injustice, against a death sentence, for example, are totally useless and probably do not have any effect upon the outcome. After all, there were demonstrations galore for Sacco and Vanzetti, and the Rosenbergs, and Julian Grimau —and they changed nothing.

There were slightly happier endings to the Burgos and Leningrad trials, inasmuch as no one was hanged, but all the demonstrators and petitioners may not have influenced the issue. What makes me think so is that in Yaoundé and Conakry, very soon afterwards, the public killings went on and no one batted an eyelid. Neither does a week go by without bringing more ghastly evidence of torture in Brazil year in, year out, and for how many years?

Perhaps we ought to throw up our hands in despair and call the whole thing off, since they are always the same people making the same useless fuss. Governments could perfectly well forecast, with all their computers, the world's precise reaction to this or that particular misdeed. The only astonishing thing is that, despite all their marvellous machines, they persist in acting irrationally, putting their political opponents to death and systematically torturing political prisoners.

Of course, one could retort that they are counting on the effects of terror and that unhappily this is not a completely irrational premise. My answer would be that for all Brazil's Gestapo tactics the regime's opponents still manage to pull off a spectacular kidnapping from time to time; and the police can no more find the missing diplomat than the opposition can stop torture. The dénouement comes with the inevitable exchange of the hostage against a score or two of prisoners, a scene out of a familiar ballet.

It adds up to this: we hear about all kinds of the world's wrongs, we protest and demonstrate indefatigably, and we ignore the very patchy results we tend to obtain. Protests and demonstrations do not seem to lessen the sum of suffering, of the universal bane of mankind, as Péguy's Joan of Arc said, particularly since we cannot protest or demonstrate against everything.

Surfeit of causes

You can spend days and nights signing protests, you can always be up at the front of the demonstrations, even so there will always be someone to ask why you failed to protest against this abomination or demonstrate against that horror, and what principles determined your choice of good causes. If you answer, "public opinion," you will be reminded how dextrously all sides manipulate it.

All of which is almost unanswerable—short of saying that there is a lot of wrong with the world, that no one person can hope to put it all right, but that it is still necessary, even vital, to keep fighting, and break down the conspiracy of silence that so many find so convenient.

Should the day ever come when not a voice raised because it seems there is no point in doing so, then the condemned and tortured will suffer and die in abominable loneliness. The real reason why we petition and demonstrate is to show them there are others, in the world outside who have not forgotten them. It is to give them the feeling of a human presence, even if it is invisible.

I believe that in so doing we keep up the morale of those for whom we cannot do anything more. There are too many of them, in too many parts of the world, and the vision of so much horror everywhere makes even the most stout hearted lose hope —not to mention the huge, indifferent herd interested only in their personal affairs, people more inured than ourselves, people who have always known that protesting does not help and that injustice has always had its way since the world began.

Heaven preserve us from such niggardly common sense! One day, the sooner the better, we should perhaps tackle the root causes, rather than the periodic symptoms, of the evil which men keep doing to each other—as if disease and injury, death and natural disasters were not enough. What makes us take out our personal frustrations on our fellow beings as if they were to blame for them? One might think the pain we cause them compensates for the pain we feel ourselves. It is always dangerous to give one man power over another, in case he takes advantage of it. It is the principle of tyranny.

So let us give credit to those who are sincerely trying to lessen the sum of evil in the world, even if they feel a twinge of flattered vanity at seeing their names in print, or buy an easy conscience too cheaply. Only, let us also hope that they do not remain content with merely demonstrating. Let them think, hard, without prejudice, about the real causes of all this human wretchedness.

In that case their devotion will certainly not have been totally useless.

From the weekly English edition of *Le Monde*, February 17, 1971.

Punishment vs. Rehabilitation

A number of the sections of this book contain arguments which deal primarily with whether or not certain kinds of acts (e.g., possessing, using, or selling certain kinds of drugs, having or performing abortions, publishing certain materials) should be prohibited by law. One of the factors relevant to such discussions is the feasibility of enforcing such laws (see the arguments concerning gun-control legislation in Section 6). But the question of legislating against certain acts necessarily involves the additional questions of what kind of treatment should be prescribed for persons who violate the laws, what the purpose of that treatment should be, how it should be administered, and so on. And these questions themselves require consideration of feasibility as well. For example, some of the suggested purposes of the treatment to be imposed on violators include discouraging others from violating the same law and rehabilitation of the violator so that he or she will not violate laws in the future, in addition to the traditional aim of the treatment which was simple and direct retributive punishment.

During the past century there was a shift in emphasis in the American criminal justice system away from the goal of punishment and toward the goal of rehabilitation—at least in the nominal sense that many jails and prisons today are called "correctional institutions" and "rehabilitation centers" instead of the traditional "penal institutions." But there is a growing debate as to whether or not any institutions do in fact or could reasonably be expected to "rehabilitate" persons who have violated laws, and it is being suggested by many that the only purposes of treatment of violators of laws should be deterrence of others from violating laws and/or simple punishment of the violator for purely retributory reasons. It is even being argued by some that the procedures being used in an attempt to rehabilitate violators are more inhumane and in violation of basic human rights than are the traditional methods of direct retribution.

Even if one accepts the goal of treatment of violators to be simple retribution, there are still many questions as to what is an appropriate, fair, and just punishment for specific acts. Should it be a simple and automatic "eye for an eye" procedure or should the system of punishment be "tempered by mercy" as was argued by President Ford in his pardoning of Richard Nixon? And what about the problem raised by the fact that the legal system as a whole is (and quite possibly must be) very complex, which means that persons who can afford expert legal counsel can avoid punishment for apparently major violations of law while poor persons can get substantial punishment for relatively minor violations? Some people would argue that if a system of punishment cannot be operated in a truly just and fair manner it would be better to have no laws at all.

About half of the arguments in this section are concerned with the most final form of punishment—the death penalty. It is a complex topic whose complexity is compounded by its ultimate finality, although it is also possible to perceive this feature as making this the simplest possible case. If it is simply *always* wrong to take another human life, then killing cannot be justified even in the case of someone who has taken another's life. But as soon as one allows the possible legitimacy of taking another's life in self-defense, then the gate has been opened for the argument that the very existence of the death penalty will prevent at least some murders from occurring.

EXERCISES

1. Examine President Ford's statement of pardon for Richard Nixon. To what extent could the same premises be used for justifying the pardon of other violators of the law, or is the statement sufficiently qualified to permit its application to this case only?
2. Apply the various arguments concerning punishment in this section to the specific cases in Sections 1–3 and 6. Discuss what punishment, if any, would be appropriate for the various "crimes" in those sections and what the grounds for that punishment are (e.g., retribution, rehabilitation, deterence).
3. Can punishment be justified for violating moral rules if no laws have been violated?

Sarajevo Hails Assassin but Debates Ethics of Deed

By MALCOLM W. BROWNE
Special to The New York Times

SARAJEVO, Yugoslavia, March 24—With plans going forward for a new movie about the 1914 assassination that brought permanent fame to this ancient and picturesque town, some

The Talk of Sarajevo Sarajevo citizens are wrestling once again with the moral issues of political killing. It was an assassination here on June 28, 1914—the victims were Archduke Franz Ferdinand, heir to the Austro-Hungarian throne, and his wife, Sophie — that precipitated World War I.

According to Veljko Bulajic, the Yugoslav producer of the film, previous movies on the assassination have been "romanticized commercial ventures." This one, in effect, will seek to justify the assassination and will portray the plotters as "men who were and remain the early heralds of contemporary revolutionary developments."

Dr. Marko Sunjic, vice president of the executive council of Bosnia and Herzegovina and a principal Communist leader here, said of the killing in an interview:

"Sometimes we regret that people know us for the assassination and think of Sarajevo as an unsafe place where heads of state can be killed. But as an Austrian colony Bosnia had a very high illiteracy rate, and its natural resources were exploited in a colonial way. In such a situation no other remedy could be found, and young people undertook the assassination."

Asked if this reasoning would not justify all acts of political terrorism, including those of the Palestinian guerrillas, he replied:

"Revolutionary movements do not condone individual acts of terrorism. Terrorism is the last resort of young people who are disillusioned and can achieve their ends in no other way.

"There have been several such examples in the history of the League of Communists of Yugoslavia. The league never approved such acts, although the idea of individual sacrifice for a cause cannot help but inspire admiration. Even today our young people are inspired by Princip."

'Acts of Despair'

"As for the Palestine liberation movement," he continued, "I do not personally approve of terrorism, but I see the acts of the Palestine guerrillas as acts of despair. If there was a political solution, there would not be such acts."

Buying More Trouble

Now that The Netherlands is advertised as the place that is kind to terrorists, one may only wonder how long it will be until the next armed fanatics take advantage of Dutch hospitality. Those three gunmen of the underground Japanese Red Army who departed from Amsterdam in style this week, after releasing 11 hostages they held in the French embassy, no doubt are exemplars to many on the lunatic fringe.

Their success, indeed, was astounding, even taking into account that the French ambassador to Holland was among their captives. They demanded and secured the release of a fellow terrorist held in a French jail, but that was the least of it. The other rewards were rich: $300,000 in ransom for the hostages (which has been returned), a French jet airliner to take them anywhere they chose, the Dutch premier at the airport to see them off. And also smaller favors such as ample Coca-Colas, mineral water, food, reading materials and a big police escort to assure their unhampered getaway at the airport.

It must have been a heady sensation for this trio, which doubtless was fully ready to kill its hostages and be killed, but possibly had no firm expectation of bringing a nation to heel. They could, of course, simply have been sealed off in that embassy without food, water or utilities, to do what they might and suffer the consequences.

That would have been the wiser course, we expect. The Dutch, in their humaneness, decided otherwise and saved the lives at stake. But the question is how many lives will be lost further down the road by capitulating to, and hence encouraging, this sort of thing.

CARL T. ROWAN

Delusions of Tough Guy Machismo

By the time this column reaches print, those Black September terrorists who murdered three diplomats may already have been executed by a Sudanese government that has been ruthlessly swift at punishing wrongdoers.

Yet, perhaps not. The same "blood is thicker than water" impulses that caused the terrorists to weep and surrender without killing their Arab hostages could work in a way to cause the Sudanese to spare the lives of Arab killers.

But no matter what happens to those Black September madmen, we Americans have some thinking to do about how to deal with terrorists, and about how far a civilized people are obligated to go to save the lives of ambassadors and other diplomats abroad.

A lot of Americans, from the White House down to Joe Blow, are infected with delusions of John Wayne-type *machismo* that lead to simplistic slogans like, "The first rule is that you never reward terrorists." This is movie-tough-guy nonsense that simply cannot be applied to every airplane hijacking, to every kidnapping, to every seizure of a U.S. diplomat abroad.

While much of the world was still hoping and praying that Ambassador Cleo A. Noel Jr. and his outgoing deputy, George C. Moore, could be gotten out alive, we heard the tough-guy line from the White House that the U.S. would not be "blackmailed."

The standard argument is that when you give in to one band of terrorists, you encourage others. The implication of that White House stance, so popular in Israel, is that a seized ambassador, or anyone else, must become a sacrifice to the cause of not encouraging terrorism. The line is than an envoy accepts that risk and duty when he goes abroad.

Let me make it clear that I have no evidence that the two Americans and the Belgian diplomat could have been gotten out of the Sudan alive. I do know that, had I been the ambassador, I would have wanted my country to give me the same chance to live that a kidnapped child receives from his father.

Who among us, with his child, wife, or other close relative abducted, would take the hard, pious line that we will "pay no ransom, because ransom encourages other kidnappings"? All but the mentally ill among us would try to get our relatives back, and only with them in our embrace would we launch any derring-do campaigns to prove that crime, especially kidnapping, does not pay.

I have some colleagues in this town who, after the first martini, start arguing that the answer to hijackings is not all these searchers and electronic gear that infest our airports, but an armed guard aboard every airliner who will start shooting the moment any hijacker rears his evil head.

You ask them a question: "If your wife is on the plane, sitting next to the hijacker, do you still want the guard to start shooting?"

You find they aren't so eager to start shooting.

Many airline passengers are alive today because ransoms were paid and because no trigger-happy guard started a shootout at 33,000 feet.

Let the Black September terrorists be executed, if that be the decision of the Sudanese. Let them lie in the sun as a festering monument to the bestiality of man. But let us not forget that their deaths, their ignominy, will not assuage in any degree the sorrow and suffering of the Noel and Moore families. For no one among them would trade Noel's or Moore's life for those of a thousand terrorists.

"But it would be unthinkable to let Sirhan B. Sirhan, the killer of Robert F. Kennedy out of prison to free those diplomats," one American hardliner said to me.

Unthinkable? It would have been unthinkable to do anything else if there were a reasonable chance of getting Noel and Moore out alive. The joy of seeing those two diplomats alive and with their families is infinitely more important to me than knowing that Sirhan suffers.

Field Newspaper Syndicate 1975.

Web of barbarism

Random violence rightly horrifies civilized society. Man recognizes that uncontrolled, unchecked force represents a step back toward the beast. The social structure, therefore, organizes rules and patterns to suppress such outbursts.

In time of war, the lid comes partly off, as large numbers of citizens take up arms and become soldiers. But even then, societies still usually observe rules which aim at channeling violence so it does not become all-encompassing, and does not engender such hatred and destruction that it makes any chance of post-war recovery impossible.

For instance, it is regrettable but expected when soldiers are killed in battle. But when a civilian area is bombed, even if accidentally, society is disturbed that the combatants did not take greater care.

Deliberate attacks on civilians or civilian installations are rare in ordinary warfare, if only because military commanders naturally consider concentrations of enemy troops and arms to be immensely more appropriate and rewarding targets than unarmed civilian areas.

And yet civilian areas are precisely the target of the modern urban guerrilla, who deliberately chooses non-combatant men, women, and children for his victims. He lays his plans not in a moment of passion, miscalculation, or frustration, but with full and careful knowledge.

The urban terrorist thus introduces a barbaric level of violence into civilization.

The most arresting current example is in Northern Ireland, with bombings and counter-bombings, assaults and counter-assaults by extremist Catholics and Protestants who do not allow each other safety in a tavern or while Christmas shopping.

Surely it is the height of man's overweening moral arrogance for him calculatedly to blow up a store packed with shoppers (killing four persons, including two children), as occurred Dec. 11 in Belfast, or to touch off a bomb and destroy 16 lives in a pub, as happened a week earlier.

Something is morally amiss with the world's violent radicals—as exemplified so well by Ireland's IRA and Quebec's FLQ—when they decide that their social goals are attainable at the cost of lives of housewives and children.

Individual tragedy means nothing to terrorists who claim to seek that elusive ideal, the perfected social order. What a travesty that the victims of their delusion are innocent bystanders.

Left, from *The Arizona Republic*, December 21, 1971.

Below, courtesy of Hallowell Bowser and *Saturday Review*, March 20, 1971.

Against Provocation

" **A** gent provocateur" is a fancy term for a quite ugly kind of spy. Unlike ordinary spies, the provocateur does not join a "suspect" group to keep close tabs on its activities; instead, his aim is to stampede the group into doing something rash, egregious, and incriminating.

When challenged about using such provocative, para-legal tactics, the "fuzz and feds" claim they are just needling extremists into attempting now, in a botched, premature way, anti-Establishment exploits that they would have brought off with devastating success if allowed more lead time.

This is, of course, thin reasoning. As "red squad" people well know, an impassioned-cause group is like a Navy blimp that is riding free just a few feet off the ground. The blimp may weigh many tons, but a good hard shove by a determined man can warp the craft around and send it floating off in any direction the shover chooses. When an undercover agent gives a volatile splinter group a hefty push, the group is likely to go kiting off in an ideological direction astonishing to the onlooker.

But why push for empty violence that only enrages both the public and the police? Why not try instead to provoke—or evoke—positive, fruitful activity? Roger Baldwin may have hit on part of the explanation when, thirty-odd years ago, he wrote in the *Encyclopedia of the Social Sciences*, "Sometimes the political police have provoked or committed crime . . . to make a showing of the need for their services and thus to wrest from a hesitant government increased funds and larger powers."

—HALLOWELL BOWSER.

A NEW TWIST IN EXTORTION

BUENOS AIRES

"Ransom in advance"—that's the latest extortion racket being worked by foreign terrorists, with U. S. business interests a major target.

Ford Motor Company, with a booming car and truck plant in this Argentine capital, became a million-dollar victim of a "protection" demand by revolutionary guerrillas on May 23. Pay up, the terrorists warned, or a Ford executive will be kidnaped or slain.

But Ford is not the only American victim—or even the largest—of extremist activity sweeping this country.

Two months ago Eastman Kodak paid a reported 1.5 million dollars to gain the release of a kidnaped executive, Antony R. da Cruz, a U. S. citizen.

Other firms known to have paid ransom for their kidnaped executives include the First National Bank of Boston, International Telephone & Telegraph Corporation and the British-American Tobacco Company.

In addition, terrorist bombs have damaged offices of an ITT subsidiary, the First National City Bank, the 3M Company, General Electric, Pan American and Sheraton hotels.

Protection, but—. Executives have hired hundreds of guards and taken extra precautions—but they admit their inability to cope with the problem.

Says one top U. S. businessman: "It will not do any good for one company to say 'We will not pay.' Everybody has to say 'We will not pay.' And that is just about impossible."

Foreign firms are setting up their own corps of security experts, installing all sorts of security gadgets in their plants and in the homes of executives. It has proved of little effect. Some firms have even taken out insurance policies against kidnaping—an expensive and complicated form of protection.

The policy of the U. S. Government is not to pay ransom, even in the cases of kidnaping of American diplomats. The State Department informed the Ford Company of this policy—but said that Ford would have to make its own decision.

Said Edgar R. Molina, a vice president of Ford in Buenos Aires: "We believe, under the circumstances, we had no choice but to meet these demands."

Other Ford officials said theirs was the 25th company to meet guerrilla payoff demands.

"Apparently the Government has no way of protecting business from this sort of thing," one executive commented.

American executives and officials of other foreign firms were quick to take sides for and against the decision of Ford to make the payoff.

"This will have a terrible repercussion," said a U. S. banker. "Extortion will take the place of kidnaping."

A forecast from a long-time North American resident of Buenos Aires:

"It will be 2 million dollars next time there is one of these demands."

But another U. S. executive saw the situation this way:

"There are lots of reasons for Ford to have come to the conclusions that they did. They have hundreds of employes out there—I would not want to have the burden of saying that I was prepared to risk the lives of those people."

That, apparently, was the conclusion also reached in talks between Ford officials here and at the home office in Michigan. Ford prides itself on excellent employe relations, resulting in freedom from strikes for nearly a decade in a country that is one of the most strike-ridden in the world.

Left, reprinted from *U.S. News & World Report,* June 4, 1973. Copyright 1973 U.S. News & World Report, Inc.
Below, from the *San Francisco Chronicle*

Investigating Tortu

by Philip Nobile

According to Dr. Amelia Augustus, Amn International's UN representative, torture become epidemic. She claims that even United States has dirty hands. Despite benevolent uses one might imagine for tortur extreme situations, Dr. Augustus emphasizes it never leads to good.

Without seeming to defend the horror torture, I would argue that the case is not c and shut, and I took that line in the follow conversation.

Do you rule out torture under any con able circumstance?

Yes. You never know whether you're ge truth from torture. So what good is it?

Say we caught one of those Arab terro who slaughtered 31 innocent people at the R airport recently. What if we could pre further mass murders by getting him to about future terrorist plans? And only to would make him talk? Would you bend the then?

Never. I will not torture even a mass murc in order to save other innocent lives. Tortu one Palestinian doesn't stop all the others. If want to be a torturer, you're going the wa dictators.

Why not a little selective torture in special situations? Where's the harm?

This is insanity. A little torture is like bei little pregnant. Once a government gives i torture, its use is bound to increase.

NEW HUMANIST

Volume 88 No 3   July 1972

HECTOR HAWTON

Personally Speaking

Ethics and blackmail

I WAS LOST in admiration for the skill and panache with which the Israelis recently dealt with hijackers at Lydda Airport. They were faced with a moral dilemma all too familiar nowadays. Should they risk the lives of 90 passengers, or let the blackmailers get away with it? They took the risk — and one can imagine the outcry if the gamble had not succeeded. They have been criticized, however, for allegedly breaking a promise to the Red Cross not to use force. If that is the case — and it has been denied — they were faced with two conflicting principles: never yield to blackmail, and never break a promise. Most moral principles are too general to be applied to particular situations, but this is not quite true of the rule to keep promises. If you don't, nobody will ever believe you again. On the other hand, whether or not the Red Cross were deceived, the brilliant operation carried through by General Dayan cannot be repeated. Future hijackers have been alerted, and you can't perform the same trick twice.

The problem of hijacking, like that of political terrorism, can be finally solved at a price that would be morally repugnant. There is no certain way to prevent another outrage by suicidal fanatics.

Left, from the *New Humanist* (July 1972), published by the Nationalist Press Association, London, England.

Right, reprinted from *The Guardian*, July 14, 1972.

Sentence on in balance Okamoto

From ERIC SILVER : Sarafand, July 13

Kozo Okamoto will have to wait until Monday for the military court's verdict on his part in the Lydda Airport massacre. The prosecution and defence rested their cases with brief closing speeches this afternoon, but for the first time in the four-day hearing they were overshadowed by the small, sullen figure in the dock.

Freed temporarily from the handcuffs that have manacled him, waking or sleeping, for most of the six weeks since his arrest, Okamoto today delivered his revolutionary testament. The world now knows as much as it ever will about what impelled him and two Japanese comrades to fly here and turn their automatic rifles on the crowded customs hall. It remains precious little.

Okamoto stood stiffly to attention for one hour and 25 minutes. He had sat passively through the long girations of "bourgeois justice." Now his time had come and he was ready for it.

"We accept this system of jurisprudence as our means of propaganda,' 'he told the court. His delivery was as fluent and coherent as the frequent pauses for translation would allow. Once he shouted in English, " I want to continue." But this was his chance and he was not going to waste it.

Okamoto emerged as neither an original nor a particularly penetrating social thinker, but he has learnt his latter-day Marxism diligently. History demanded revolution, revolution demanded violence. If this meant his own life or other people's, so be it. He was no armchair romantic.

His profession, he said, was a soldier of the Red Army. "The three of us, soldiers in the Red Army, in this revolutionary action decided that our contentions would have to be carried forward decisively. That is to say, it was my duty towards the people whom I sacrificed and towards my two comrades who lost their lives.

"I take on myself full responsibility for the people who have been killed. Revolutionary warfare is a warfare of justice.

"The definition of the word justice is to create a society in which there is no class distinction. The meaning of justice is to create a society in which there is no class struggle."

The Lydda attack, Okamoto added, was no mere battle. It was warfare, and warfare was destruction. "As we engage in this we cannot limit warfare to destruction of buildings. We believe that the slaughter of human bodies is inevitable.

But why this operation? Why Israel? "I believe that as a means towards world revolution I must propose the creation of a world Red Army. And we decided to have relationships with the Popular Front for the Liberation of Palestine. This was one springboard, one means by which we could propel ourselves on to the world stage...the Arab world lacks in spiritual fervour. So therefore we felt we could probably stir up the Arabs."

And no qualms? " My leader approved of the operation. Since I am a soldier I obeyed and joined this operation. The Red Army soldier is ready at all times to give his life. This is for the sake of the revolution: it is not for the sake of anything else."

Lest anyone should still miss the point, Okamoto flashed a further warning : "Red Army soldiers will slay anyone who stands on the side of the bourgeoisie. This I do not say as a joke."

Finally, and with the nearest to a hint of remorse, the 24-year-old student took refuge in Japanese folklore. "We three of us, after we died, wanted to become the three stars of Orion. When we were young we were told the story that when we died we would become stars in the sky. While I may not totally believe it, I was ready to be persuaded of it.

"I do not know what the customs are in foreign countries. I believe that some of those whom we slaughtered have become stars in the sky. The revolutionary war will continue, and there will be many, many stars. However, if we recognise that we shall go to the same heaven, there to shine together, then we can have peace of heart."

185

Terror at the Top

From one end of the world to the other, people are sickened by the way terror is disfiguring human society.

They are aghast when a gunman fires into a car carrying Princess Anne and her husband, Capt. Mark Phillips, in a kidnapping attempt. They are horrified by the monstrous irresponsibility of militants who use kidnapping as a means for forcing social progress. They are stunned when a madman, thinking himself a patriot, shoots his way onto a commercial airliner, intending to crash-dive it into the White House.

But what about terror employed by governments as an instrument of foreign policy? Why is there no indignation over the fact that the largest nations in the world openly pursue their objectives through a balance-of-terror strategy? Both the United States and the Soviet Union seek credibility in their policies toward each other by possessing the means for setting off instant holocausts. Each country has access to a switchboard of total annihilation that can be activated by a fingertip.

NEW FORMS of authorized terror continue to spin off the apocalyptic assembly belts. The latest advance is the "smart bomb," which, it is said, will revolutionize warfare. Unlike the German buzz bombs of World War II, which exploded over the general vicinity of London, the new bombs have special features that ensure precision-targeting. Computers, lasers, and television combine to eliminate even the marginal errors of the vaunted Norden bombsight. The "smart bombs" can carry a nuclear payload.

News of this technological advance in man-made cataclysms has been received without any of the moral indignation that has attended news of still another hijacking or kidnapping. Nor has there been a public outcry over the fact that the United States and the Soviet Union, between them, possess nuclear stockpiles in excess of 75,000 megatons of explosive force. If only one-fourth of this power were to be used, life on earth could be severely jeopardized. A blanket of deadly radioactivity could settle over the globe.

In this sense, the entire human race today is hostage to the balance-of-terror strategies of the nuclear powers.

We can keep on hoping that the SALT negotiations at some point will hit pay dirt, but the best chance that they will do so depends on the pressure of public opinion rather than on any bursts of initiative by the negotiating parties. It is here—in the field of public opinion—that the real issue will be tested. That issue is whether people will apply to government the same moral yardsticks that apply to the rest of human society. The special exemptions that people tend to make for foreign policy no longer fit into the requirements of rational survival. We can count on it that governments will make moral judgments in the formation of their foreign policies when their own political survival depends on it.

N.C.

Courtesy of *Saturday Review/World*, April 20, 1974.

Assassin Beheaded by Saudis

RIYADH, June 18 (AP)—A young Saudi prince was publicly beheaded today with one swipe of a gold-handled sword for the assassination of his uncle, King Faisal. The watching crowd of thousands chanted in Arabic, "God is great" and "Justice is done."

Earlier in the day, Prince Faisal Ibn Musaed, 27, had been judged guilty by a Sharia, or religious court, of assassinating his uncle as the monarch celebrated the Moslem feast of the Prophet Mohammed's birthday March 25. The sentence was approved by King Khaled.

The American-educated prince was led out of the jail behind the government palace into Dira Square as afternoon prayers were ending and crowds of men were leaving Riyadh's great mosque nearby. An official of the court faced Prince Faisal and read the guilty verdict, then invoked "heaven's mercy" for the convicted man.

Prince Faisal appeared calm. His hands were tied behind his back, but he was not blindfolded.

As the prince knelt, a security man prodded him in the side with a stick so that his head jerked upward. The executioner brought the sword flashing down and decapitated him. Blood spattered on the dusty pavement.

The assassin's head was hoisted on a wooden stake and displayed briefly to the applauding crowd.

Immediately afterward, the head and body were placed on a stretcher and carried away for burial in an unmarked grave—the same simple Islamic interment given to the assassinated monarch.

Saudi Arabia's strict Islamic law prescribes the death penalty for murder unless the defendant is found to be insane. The Koran demands "a soul for a soul," and gives the next of kin of a victim the right to exact revenge.

With the modernization of Islam, the government has taken over the duty of exacting revenge, chopping off the heads of killers and the hands of thieves, stoning adulterers and jailing others.

The Koran also states punishment is important for its deterrent value and calls for it to be carried out publicly. Saudi Arabia boasts one of the lowest crime rates in the world, and there are only occasional public executions and maimings.

Above, courtesy of The Associated Press.
Below, from *The Washington Post*, 1975.

U.S. Penal System 'Truths' Questioned

By Leroy Aarons
Washington Post Staff Writer

LOS ANGELES—Out of the violence and turmoil inside American prisons that boiled over into the public realm in the late '60s and early '70s, a new consensus is emerging. Mainly, that the basic assumptions on which most prisons have been operating for the last 50 years have been disastrously wrong.

"A lot of it is just cosmetic," said Willie Holder, an ex-convict who heads the San Francisco prisoners union. "We're still waiting to see if they're serious."

Holder favors elimination of indeterminate sentencing, probation and parole, and he favors voluntary rehabilitation programs.

"Criminals should be punished," he said. "Society ought to admit that punishment is a form of retribution and not pretend that prisons are for any other purpose. I've heard many prisoners say they'd rather be beat in the head with a shovel than have their brain constantly examined like they do.

"The important thing is that if you're going to punish, you ought to do it equally. If Spiro Agnew is a thief, he ought to get the same thing some ordinary burglar gets."

Mr. McCLELLAN. Mr. President, in June of 1972, the Supreme Court handed down its decision in the case of Furman against Georgia, one of the Court's most significant decisions in recent years. It was in the Furman decision that a bare majority of the Court—five of the nine Justices—determined that the death penalty could not constitutionally be imposed as administered in the cases before it. The effect of that decision was to eliminate capital punishment throughout the country as an authorized deterrent and punishment for even the most violent and brutal crimes.

I recognize that we are not only faced with the question of whether or not legislation can be drafted that will meet the requirement of Furman. We are also faced with a much more basic question—whether or not this country should have a death penalty at all.

The answer to that question becomes clearer and clearer with every new kidnaping, with every new hijacking of a plane filled with innocent people, with every new murder by the Symbionese Liberation Army, with every murder committed for hire. The death penalty must be restored if our criminal justice system is to combat effectively the ever-increasing tide of violent crimes—crimes of terror—that threaten to engulf our Nation and if the confidence of the American people in our system of justice is to be restored.

Mr. President, those who argue against the death penalty claim that it serves no useful purpose and should therefore be eliminated. Perhaps most importantly, they say that there is no proof that it deters crime.

I simply do not agree with that.

I can recall from my youth that the knowledge that I would be punished for doing wrong was indeed a deterrent. And the more severe I thought the punishment was likely to be, the less likely was it that I would misbehave. I would suggest that everyone in this Chamber has had a comparable experience.

To say that the death penalty, the severest penalty society can impose, does not deter is to say that no punishment deters—and with that I believe no one here can agree.

Some will say that the real issue is not whether the death penalty deters, but whether it deters more than life imprisonment. To me the answer to that question is obvious.

Life is our most precious possession. So long as the premeditated murderer has his life there is the chance for parole, for freedom, for escape. There is often the opportunity and the temptation for

one convicted of murder or imprisoned for some crime to kill a guard or a fellow prisoner—there are many instances of such tragic occurrences. If a criminal knows that he will forfeit his own life if he commits one of the crimes enumerated in this bill, he will certainly be must less likely to commit that act than if all he had facing him was a prison sentence and eventual parole.

What better example of this do we have than the case of the man robbing a bank with a gun when the police get the drop on him. The robber is told to drop his gun or he will be killed. What does he do? If he believes he is going to be killed, he drops his gun. If the police told him to drop his gun or he would be slapped in the face, or kicked, or even put in prison, it might not be enough to stop him.

Where the criminal—the murderer—knows that he is going to pay a price for his crimes and that price is death, he will be deterred.

Mr. President, it is here that the problem exists. The criminal must be made to realize that he is going to die himself if he chooses to murderously deprive someone else of his life. If penalties are not imposed, the mere prescribing of them by law will not deter. We can be sure of that. A punishment is only going to be effective as long as it is imposed. Once it stops being applied, it loses its potency.

The death penalty is a perfect example. The last execution in this country took place in 1967—not because the country disapproved of the penalty, but out of a desire to let the Supreme Court rule on the question. In the 5 years between 1967 and 1971 the number of murders in this country rose 61 percent. More importantly, the rate of murder for every 100,000 persons rose 52 percent in that same 5-year period of time. Can anyone seriously argue that this was a mere coincidence?

Not only our law enforcement officers but even criminals themselves have told us that it was not. Very shortly ater the Furman decision was handed down a bank robery took place in New York City. Hostages were taken and threats were made. The Washington Star-News quoted one of the robbers as saying:

I'll shoot everyone in the bank. The Supreme Court will let me get away with this. There's no death penalty. It's ridiculous. I can shoot everyone here, then throw my gun down and walk out and they can't put me in the electric chair. You have to have a death penalty, otherwise this can happen every day. [The Washington Star-News, Aug. 23, 1972, p. 1, col. 1.]

I agree completely.

Mr. President, when all is said and done, when all the talking about deterrence and retribution and incapacitation is finished, what it all boils down to is whether it is ever "just" to impose the death penalty. Can a man ever be found to have acted so viciously, so cruelly, so much like an animal as to justify society in imposing upon him the ultimate punishment? I firmly believe he can.

What other punishment is "just" for a man, found to be sane, who would stab, strangle, and mutilate eight student nurses?

What other punishment is "just" for men who would invade the home of members of a rival religious sect and shoot to death men, women, and children, after forcing a mother to watch as her three young children were drowned before her eyes?

What other punishment is "just" for a band of social misfits who would invade the homes of people they had never even met and stab and hack to death a woman 8½ months pregnant and her guests?

What other punishment is "just" for people who would force a 24-year-old woman to douse herself with gasoline so that they could turn her into a human torch and watch as she burned to death?

There are other current cases that I could cite that we would all recognize, that come within the category of those I have just described. But since some of the defendants are now in the process of being tried for their crimes I will not mention or identify them in my remarks today. But, Mr. President, pick up almost any newspaper, today, yesterday, or the day before, or pick one up tomorrow, and you can read about some of these current cases to which I am now referring.

Mr. President, human justice is not feeding and clothing such people for a few years and then returning them to society on parole to do what they wish.

People who commit crimes like these have forfeited their own right to life. They have merited the clearest statement that such inhuman action cannot and will not be tolerated and that people who perform such acts will not be allowed to do so again. Justice demands no less.

It is indeed a great tragedy that a Nation, a civilized Nation, such as ours, that offers so much to so many, needs the death penalty to protect its citizens. Although it is sad and lamentable, there is no other course that squares with equal justice under the law. Nothing less will provide ample protection for the innocent, or insure a safe society.

Mr. HUGHES. Mr. President, the question before us today is symbolic and overriding—whether it is morally right and socially defensible for the State, under our system of criminal justice, to destroy a human life for any crime.

The legislation before us would restore the death penalty that was ruled unconstitutional by the Supreme Court in 1972.

How is it that a nation that has not suffered the brutality of a public execution for 8 years is now deliberately considering going back to the hangman's noose, the electric chair, and the gas chamber?

Primarily, public support for the restitution of the death penalty, as reflected in some public opinion polls, is a reflex response to fear.

One of the great tragedies of our time is that law-abiding citizens of this great land are spellbound from day to day by the fear of crime and violence.

The situation calls for remedial action.

But what action?

Is the morbid trip back to the death penalty the right way to go to protect society from violence and to keep faith with our moral purpose as a people? Is ultimate violence the antidote for violence?

For me, the answer must be "No."

I cannot be brought to believe that the way to conquer crime in America is to revert to institutional killings in the name of justice.

It is true that I am one of those who, for deeply religious reasons, believes in the absolute sanctity of human life.

"Thou shalt not kill" is the shortest of the Ten Commandments, uncomplicated by qualification or exception. I recognize that there are other passages of scripture that are cited in justify the death penalty.

To me, the Sixth Commandment is overriding.

It is as clear and awesomely commanding as the powerful thrust of chain lightning out of a dark summer sky.

But I oppose the restitution of capital punishment for good and sufficient reasons in addilton to my basic religious conviction.

I oppose the death penalty because it demeans human society without protecting it. The weight of the evidence is that capital punishment does not deter serious crime. The weight of history is that judicial killing brutalizes the nations who practice it.

I oppose the death penalty because it cannot undo or rectify any crime that was committed, however brutal, and because there is no road back if the convicted man is later proven innocent.

As Lafayette said:

I shall ask for the abolition of the penalty of death until I have the infallibility of human judgment demonstrated to me.

Finally, I oppose the death penalty because it is grossly destructive of human hopes for a society more amenable to peace and less dependent on violence for the solution of its problems.

No Member of this body should be spared the agonizing knowledge of the suffering he has been asked to sanction.

Listen to the words of men who have been face-to-face with the manner of death imposed by the State:

The classic form of execution, still used by several States prior to the Furman decision, was hanging. Warden Clinton Duffy of San Quentin, a frequent witness, describes the process of hanging:

The day before an execution the prisoner goes through a harrowing experience of being weighed, measured for length of drop to assure breaking of the neck, the size of the neck, body measurements, etc. When the trap springs he dangles at the end of the rope. There are times when the neck has not been broken and the prisoner strangles to death. His eyes pop almost out of his head, his tongue swells and protrudes from his mouth, his neck may be broken, and the rope many times takes large portions of skin and flesh from the side of the face that the noose is on. He urinates, he defecates, and droppings fall to the floor while witnesses look on, and at almost all executions one or more faint or have to be helped out of the witness room. The prisoner remains dangling from the end of the rope for from 8 to 14 minutes before the doctor, who has climbed up a small ladder and listens to his heart beat with a stethoscope, pronounces him dead. A prison guard stands at the feet of the hanged person and holds the body steady, because during the first few minutes there is usually considerable struggling in an effort to breathe.

Clarence Darrow put the question even more graphically:

But why not do a good job of it? If you want to get rid of killings by hanging people or electrocuting them because these are so terrible, why not make a punishment that is terrible? . . . Why not boil them in oil, as they used to do? Why not burn them at the stake? Why not sew them in a bag with serpents and throw them out to sea? . . . Why not break every bone in their body on the rack, as has often been done for such serious offenses as heresy, witchcraft and adultery?

There is no such thing as being half-dead. Death inflicted by the State is not painless or instantaneous.

Our vote today is a signal to the world of the true regard we as a nation have for the value and dignity of human life everywhere.

Today is the time. There can be no alternative. It is life or death. It is not just a matter of a few simple crimes. It is not just a matter of applying it to remove someone from society. Certainly, with the technology we have and the ability we have, we can remove such persons from society without killing them.

For killing does brutalize us. After 10 long years of war, after savagery reaching all over the world and in our own political processes, after watching our own leaders struck down in violence, and noting the effects on television, do we now have to tell this country again that we are going to resort, in the name of the State, to killing, because there is no other way to proceed, because in our day and age and time there is no other way?

Who can deny that the death penalty is cruel and unusual punishment?

Has anyone ever described any execution, to say that by premeditation it is not cruel and unusual punishment? Let's stand behind the Constitution, the Supreme Court and the sixth Commandment.

Many years ago, the poet, John Donne, wrote:

No man is an island entire of itself, every man is a piece of the continent, a part of the main . . .

Any man's death diminishes me, because I am involved in mankind, and therefore never send to know for whom the bell tolls, it tolls for thee.

We have seen humankind diminished enough by the ways of violence. Let our decision be not to return to the primitive darkness, but to move forward into the light of day.

For whom the bells tolls? It tolls for us.

Mr. President, the issue cannot be avoided today, tomorrow, or whenever this vote comes. It is a vote for life or a vote for death. A vote for life is a torch for a more humane and understanding way for humanity, a symbol to the world that people can see; but, in my opinion, a vote for death is a step backward into the primitive world of the past.

Mr. McCLELLAN. Mr. President, I am moved to make one observation. It is life or death. And the question is, shall we sacrifice the lives of future victims in order to spare the life of a murderer? Yes, there is life and death involved. He who demonstrates that he has no respect for life and is willing to set himself up as a judge and a god, to wantonly take the life of his fellow man, makes that decision, and makes it with sanity, when he carries out the act. If he does it once, he will do it again.

It is easy to describe the agony of death, either by hanging or in a gas chamber. It is also easy to describe the agony of a mother, 8½ months pregnant with child, begging strangers whom she has never seen, whom she does not know, who stand over her with a dagger to take her life and that of her unborn child, begging for her life.

Yes, you can describe horrors, but shall the murderer be permitted to live and have another opportunity to commit such a horrible crime, or shall we protect society and the next innocent victim against his dastardly deed?

Innocent people are entitled to live. He who commits the act condemns himself, and the law says that if he does it, that is his penalty.

Even the Bible, if I recall correctly, condemns to the eternal punishment. It is punishment that is sanctioned. We may want to forgive but we also want to protect the innocent. They must be protected, otherwise we do not have a civilization. A society that cannot protect its people from violent death, that refuses to take the precautions which are necessary, even if it does take the life of a murderer in order to protect the innocent, invites a repetition of the dastardly act by him who is so callous as to commit it in the first instance.

Don't bring back capital punishment

MONSIGNOR S. J. ADAMO

Let me emphasize this point. In the year 1964 I served as a member of the New Jersey Commission To Study Capital Punishment. Among the shocking statistics presented at that time were some that covered a fifteen-year period ending August 1, 1962. The figures concerned the various national backgrounds of those convicted of capital crimes and how they fared.

Thus, 76 convicted Americans had been executed while 29 had their sentences commuted to life. That means that roughly 30 percent were shown mercy. During the same period 26 Italians were put to death—without one commutation. Likewise executed were three Puerto Ricans, three Russians, one Pole and one Irishman.

When it came to American citizens of foreign descent, a similar pattern was discovered. Thus 15 persons of Italian descent went to the electric chair, while only 2 were shown mercy. Three of Polish descent were executed, and one Pole was spared. However, three criminals of Irish descent, marked for execution, were all given life instead. The luck of the Irish!

In the event you are ecumenically inclined it may be discouraging to realize that a Protestant sentenced to death during that period would have had a 50-50 chance of having his sentence commuted to life imprisonment; whereas a Catholic sentenced to death had only one chance in eight for commutation. In short, the possibility of a convicted murderer being shown mercy were four times greater if he were a Protestant.

These figures simply demonstrate the terrible bias that was operating in meting out capital punishment. The more wealthy were always less likely to feel the full impact of the law. Crime doesn't pay, but having money does shield one against the law's severity.

One minor item: it is almost unheard of for a woman to be put to death, especially during the last half century. For them the quality of mercy was seldom strained, and was generally poured out fully. Even though Women's Lib thinks that the female sex is disfavored in America, in this vital area it was always highly favored.

Clearly, then, the Supreme Court decision was a tribute to social justice not to reckless permissiveness.

There are those who insist that all the argumentation so far proves only that the death penalty should be administered more equitably. So they urge the fashioning of laws that are airtight, precise and utterly impartial. Even granted such an impossible dream could be realized, there is still reason to seek the abolition of the death penalty.

Consider that it is basically an act of vengeance. It doesn't correct the criminal nor help the dead victim. It satisfies only the desire to avenge a murder or some other terrible crime. This is why the Indiana Catholic Conference recently called for the continued elimination of capital punishment, stating that "a most effective way to teach respect for human life is to refuse to take life in the name of the law."

A 1973 Modest Proposal (from 33 A.D.):

Those who call for the restoration of the death penalty do not go far enough! Is it not written: "An eye for an eye, a tooth for a tooth"? Not only should we begin killing murderers once again (life for life), but we should return to the practice of cutting off the robber's hand, pulling out the slanderer's tongue. (Surely he was talking collectively for all his people where it is written: "Vengeance is mine; I will repay, sayeth the Lord.")

But first things first. Let us begin killing people again to show people that killing people is evil!

Who says that capital punishment is not a deterrent? So what if several states that have abolished the death penalty have not had a rise in the number of murders committed? What does that conclusively prove?

Enough of this permissive sentimentalism! Restore the death penalty, then. . .

Steve Mailloux
Los Angeles, California

Even God in explaining the Ten Commandments says: "When a man kills another after maliciously scheming to do so you must take him even from my altar and put him to death." (Ex. 21:14)

Name Withheld
Dubuque, Iowa

There are no arguments for capital punishment for a Christian. "Vengeance is mine, sayeth the Lord." As Christians we might best show our deep respect for the awesome mystery of life by challenging the taking of human life at all times, abortions, war killings, killing of caged humans.

Edward J. Lozicki
Fremont, Michigan

"He who kills a man shall be put to death." (Lev.: 24:17)

Name Withheld
Winchester, Illinois

The question of capital punishment is very much related to other much-discussed issues of today like warfare and abortion.

I am opposed to warfare; I am opposed to capital punishment; and I am opposed to abortion for the same reason—I am for life.

I don't think the Scriptures give us a clear foundation one way or the other on the absolute sacredness of human life. I just think it will be more productive of social development if we highly regard human life on the battlefield, in the womb, or in the jail cell, than if we take human life lightly in any of these places.

Father Ronald Luka, C.M.F.
Garden City, New York

Top and above, reprinted with permission from *U.S. Catholic* (May 1973), 221 West Madison St., Chicago, Illinois 60606.

How About The Victim?

All sorts of legal semantics are involved when there is argument over the death penalty as has just taken place before the U.S. Supreme Court. But it comes down to a simple moral issue.

All along the line from the less severe crimes right up to murder, the victim is increasingly becoming the forgotten man.

But to nail the issue right on the head let us confine the discussion to murder and to be more specific let it be a typical case of murder committed during a holdup.

A housewife, walking home to her husband and children is assaulted and robbed. When she resists she is shot and killed, the assailant is later caught, tried and convicted. The opponents of capital punishment would say that to electrocute this man would be cruel and unusual punishment and that the death penalty has been "repudiated by the conscience of contemporary society."

Now this matter of conscience: Where does proper concern comes in? A family is left motherless. The focus of the opponents of capital punishment is centered not on the victim but on the killer who has contributed nothing to society and in fact is a proven enemy of society. If he had not been apprehended he would likely have committed more crimes.

Yet the concern is that capital punishment would be a cruel penalty for him. We feel that the surviving husband and children of the dead woman know more about cruelty than the attorneys who would strike down the death penalty.

Top, editorial cartoon by Pat Oliphant. Copyright *Washington Star.* Reprinted with permission Los Angeles Times Syndicate. Above, from *The Times Record,* January 19, 1971.

Shapp on Capital Punishment

ON MARCH 23, nine years ago, the late Gov. David Lawrence announced in Harrisburg a freeze on capital punishment until the Legislature resolved the issue of whether to execute or not to execute. Later that year the General Assembly voted to retain the death penalty.

The freeze was lifted. But, except for 1962, the following years saw no human beings die in the electric chair in this state.

With Gov.-elect Shapp's weekend statement of total opposition to capital punishment, the freeze is back on. It will be up to the General Assembly to do what it failed to do under previous governors, from Shafer (who, as Lieutenant Governor, favored the death penalty), through Scranton (who doubted its efficacy) to Lawrence (who opposed it outright).

It will be up to the General Assembly to legislate us out of this vestige of tribal barbarism by replacing capital punishment with life imprisonment. In this predominantly Christian nation, we understand the moral rule to be one which prohibits the taking of human life except in self-defense and, by extension, in war—although we like to think that that tribal form of aggression will soon be conquered, too.

In any case, neither the state nor its citizens can know absolute truth, which is solely for the gods to ponder. Yet unerring, perfect truth is the assumption on which sentencing and executing a person is based. The state's killing a convicted killer is the final, absolute act.

Scientifically, we k n o w j u s t enough about psychology and about brain circuitry and its malfunctions to know how little we do know, far from enough to "know" who is really guilty **enough** to deserve death. That, again, is for the gods to ponder.

Under Mr. Shapp's moral impetus, we suspect the Legislature will find it difficult to duck this issue which has hung fire so long. We hope, however, that the people's representatives in Harrisburg will have the wisdom to eliminate the death penalty completely, rather than keeping it for some classes of crimes—like the killing of an on-duty police officer, an exception which some legislators favor. There is no moral or logical reason to place higher value on a policeman's life than on any other human being's. Either capital punishment is an effective deterrent or it isn't. Crime figures over the years do not support its efficacy. Logic and morality do not support it at all.

Let us have done with it.

Right, from *The Pittsburgh Post-Gazette*, December 30, 1970.

What Death Row Has Taught Me About Living

By Leaman R. Smith

After what seemed an interminable pause, the bailiff's dull, flat voice intoned: "We, the jury, having found the defendant, Leaman Russell Smith, guilty of murder in the first degree, fix the penalty as death."

What had begun as a bad-check spree had ended with my killing two policemen and receiving the death decree. Society demands my life, and I will no doubt pay in full. In the interim, I have existed for nearly seven and a half years on San Quentin's overcrowded death row, apprehensively waiting for someone to push the button that will end my existence.

Although I have offended society and must pay for it, you and I may have more in common than you suspect. I have read where 91 percent of people questioned admitted they have committed acts for which they might have received prison sentences. Ninety-one percent!

And may I be forgiven for asking: What good does my punishment really do? □

Above, from *Family Weekly*, February 27, 1972.

An Open Reply to Death-Row Author Leaman R. Smith

In the February 27 issue, FAMILY WEEKLY published an article by Leaman R. Smith entitled, "What Death Row Has Taught Me About Living." I'm afraid Mr. Smith only convinced me that his ordeal on death row really has taught him very little. He mentions that he learned to face reality and stop indulging in self-pity. Yet he closes with an obvious appeal for sympathy motivated by self-pity.

Mr. Smith mentions a survey showing that 91 percent of people questioned admitted having done things for which they could legally be imprisoned. That statistic is probably close to the truth. How many of those people, though, had only done a *single* such act, for which they would probably have been given a suspended sentence? And how many of the 91 percent he calls his fellows would have taken the life of a police officer in the midst of a crime? No, I think most of us have very little in common with Mr. Smith.

The greatest deterrent to crime yet devised, since we have not been able to eliminate the motivation toward crime, is the certainty of detection, capture and punishment. The 91 percent cited by Mr. Smith are not a symbol of brotherhood with *him;* rather, they are a monument to our citizenry's failure to care.

How many hardened criminals are walking the streets today because citizens will not report criminal acts, will not appear as witnesses; in short, will not "get involved"? Why is it so reprehensible for an American to report somebody who is assaulting or stealing from his neighbor? If every citizen were to report criminal acts to proper authorities, we could reduce our crime/conviction ratio enormously, secure proportionate reductions in our insurance premiums and greatly improve the personal security and happiness of our daily living.

What good does Mr. Smith's punishment really do? By his capture, trial and execution, other young men and women are made aware that the law *does* operate to apprehend criminals and mete out justice. By this knowledge they may be deterred from following Mr. Smith's example and instead encouraged to make their way within the law. To let him go free or reduce his sentence would do just the reverse and encourage more to enter the field of crime.

Why should Smith *not* be punished? Would it give life back to those from whom he violently took it? Would it give comfort to their widows and children? Would it make our citizens feel safer walking the streets, or going about their daily lives? Would it help our policemen do a better job of protecting us? In point of fact, Mr. Smith, *what have you done to deserve to live?*

If you don't know the answer to your question, Mr. Smith, I don't believe you have much to offer society. And if society does not recognize the answer, I fear that it has little to hope for except more crime, more fear, less individual freedom and less enjoyment of life in these United States.
—*Victor T. Lyon, Hobbs, N.M.*

Letter to *Family Weekly* by Victor T. Lyon, May 14, 1972.

Capital Punishment—
For What?

By DAVID BRUDNOY

Shortly before the election, in what could probably be seen as his gesture to the friends of "law and order," Massachusetts Gov. Francis W. Sargent gave a tough little speech in which he urged the imposition of compulsory capital punishment on anyone convicted of killing a police officer or bombing a building in which someone was killed:

The governor's talk seemed to evoke little comment in the press, although, coming from a liberal like Sargent, the position should have been more widely remarked. His position—death for two types of killers, and two only—raises several questions and leads at least to a few tentative answers.

Those favoring capital punishment have long contended that the ultimate penalty deters would-be criminals from committing their crimes and/or is morally right, in that our respect for the lives of innocents is shown by demanding death for those who kill.

Anti-capital punishment people rebut, saying the death penalty does not deter crime and/or that the morally correct response to a heinous crime is compassion, not the further taking of a life.

As stated, these two positions have the virtue of internal consistency, whatever one might think of that view with which one disagrees.

The argument as to morality also admits of no final proof. No one can "prove" the existence of God scientifically, nor disprove His existence; no one can prove what "morality" is by reference to objective criteria, but only by reference to man-made systems of ethics, which may or may not derive from divine inspiration—which gets it all back again to the non-provability of God's existence by scientifically verifiable criteria.

Thus we can assert until kingdom come that capital punishment is moral or immoral, and be "right" by our own lights, but dismally wrong according to other, perhaps just as thoughtful, observers.

Why, then, capital punishment for cop-killers and bombers who kill while bombing? If Gov. Sargent thinks capital punishment is such cases will be a deterrent, then surely we might demand that he press for capital punishment for all killers, in the hopes that such punishment will deter their crimes as well. If the governor believes it is morally right to kill killers under cover of law, then are we to believe that he thinks the lives of policemen are worth more than the lives of others, or that those killed by a bomb are any the less dead, or of more worth, than those killed by a knife, gun, pipe, rope, razor, what have you?

Perhaps the governor has arrived at his conclusion because he thinks the two types of crimes which he has named are so dreadful that they exceed in wickedness all other types of crime; that is, the Eichmann analogy. May others not feel just as strongly that some other form of killing—such as the bashing in of a skull of some defenseless old person, by a brutal attacker—is even more reprehensible, or at the very least, equally as reprehensible?

Gov. Sargent's proposal seems short of the mark, according to those who favor capital punishment for whichever or both of the reasons I've suggested and it seems to be excessive to those who are against capital punishment.

Suspicion as to the governor's motivation for his proposal continues to bother one. Is Mr. Sargent trying to steer a careful course between the "get-tough" types and the "go-soft" sorts? Because of the current wave of bombings and cop-killings? If not, why? If so, what of other terrible types of killing?

My own view, for what it's worth, is that whether capital punishment is a deterrent or not—and my hunch is that it is, although as mentioned above I cannot so prove—it is morally right for society to avenge the death of innocents by demanding the death of the killer, after a fair trial, according to scrupulous due process, and with access to appeals procedures.

There, too, my "morally right" position is based on faith, not on proof. But my position is only one man's and need not cloud the major point I wish to make which is this: The governor's position lacks internal consistency and hints at expediency.

Both the governor of Massachusetts and the rest of us should examine the matter seriously, right now, and bring the issue to the point of active intellectual controversy. Perhaps we can arrive at a statewide consensus which could help guide the General Court in its next session.

Reprinted with permission from the July 5, 1971, issue of *Human Events*, 422 First St., S.E., Washington, D.C. 20003.

Mainstreams

. . . On Murder

By Edwin A. Roberts, Jr.

◆ This week the Mainstreams columnist interviews himself.

Daniel St. Albin Greene, your friend and fellow staff writer, recently attacked you in print because in the past you have defended the legitimacy of capital punishment in certain instances. What is your response?

Well, all things considered, I would rather be attacked by Dan Greene in print than in an alley. As for the issue itself, it is one that offers no satisfaction to either side. For one thing, it requires long thoughts on unnatural death, a subject no sober man takes up with pleasure. But once we are into it, I think we must decide with what degree of outrage we regard cold-blooded murder—and I refer to moral outrage, not the emotional kind. Moral outrage lasts.

What we seek, of course, (and what we will never have) is a society without

---

Comment

---

murders. The best we can do as a community is to emphasize with spirit our belief that premeditated murder is an abomination. One way to demonstrate our conviction is to provide that kidnap-murder, rape-murder, political assassination, and similar misdeeds are repaid in kind. Is this tawdry vengeance or fair retribution? If we believe that society must be the victim's surrogate, inasmuch as the victim has been rendered incapable of seeking redress on his own, then I think the word is retribution.

But doesn't the death penalty brutalize society even as it fails to deter would-be murderers?

The murder rate is soaring, which means we are already brutalized, and terrorized, by the killers among us. Do we make society more brutal by executing those who are the first brutalizers? I'm not sure. Do we become more brutal when we fire a gun at an intruder? Our major concern must be for our personal safety. There is no reason to believe that a prison term is equal to death in the mind of a man with murderous notions.

To Staff Writer Daniel St. Albin Greene:

My sincere compliments for your top-notch Observations on the subject of capital punishment. In my line of work, I quickly learned to leave unsaid any original thought I may have had. But now that I am retired from that line of work, I feel it important that I express myself in favor of those ideas, points of view, and positions which my experience tells me are correct and to reject those to which I am perforce opposed.

I was a hired *killer*. My job was to kill, if and as necessary, every last living thing that my employers could construe as a threat to their well-being. I was paid for a "risk" job to protect their interests—interests which inevitably came to be identified as my own. I do not remember that the "risk" of losing my life was in any way a deterrent to *kill* on command—although, it is true, more than once I sensed fear.

JOHN C. ALLEN
U.S. Navy (Retired)

Guadalajara, Mexico

False Solution to Crime

IT HAS BEEN said by critics of more stringent firearms regulation that such legislation would be futile if left unenforced. There can be little argument to that line of reasoning. More enforcement is needed.

But to say that the best policy in dealing with convicted killers is "an eye for an eye" abdicates humanity and denies the possibility of human beings solving human problems. And to say that society's attempts to date have been only marginally successful is no argument that the effort should not be continued.

I fear that to pursue the course of capital punishment is to abandon efforts to solve society's problems; it would be a false panacea to a society that no longer cares enough to try. Surely there is still faith in the humanity of mankind.

LeROY KRAMER III

As Our Readers See It

THE POLICE slaying of 15-year-old Anthony Moorer is yet another tragedy for the city of Detroit. I would like to express my personal sorrow over his death and over the deaths of the young boys recently murdered. I would also like to add my voice to that of many others in asking all Detroiters to put away their guns and stop the killing.

Many people are calling for a return to capital punishment in order to halt the rising crime rate. I feel that the restoration of the death penalty would only serve to further cheapen life. If we do not eliminate the root causes of the despair and frustration felt by many people, the death penalty will add to our tragedy.

The way to reduce crime is to achieve true social justice: true economic justice, where a man's worth on the job comes from what he achieves, not from the color of his skin; true educational justice in a school small enough to treat people as individuals; equality in housing, without blockbusting or "steering"; criminal justice that brings all accused persons to a speedy trial.

If we achieve social justice the dope dealers will disappear, the "Saturday night specials" will be thrown away, and a young boy's life will be worth more than a yellow 1971 Ford LTD.

JOHN J. JACHMAN

The Unnecessary Deaths

By KENNETH A. GIBSON

NEWARK, N. J. — The bloodshed that occurred in Attica, N. Y., disturbs me more deeply than any event in recent memory.

The use of coordinated organized violence in overcoming the inmates at Attica state prison stands as one of the most callous and blatantly repressive acts ever carried out by a supposedly civilized society on its own people. All of us who oppose violence must deplore this use of force by so-called responsible authorities. Further, we must attempt to understand this event fully.

The demands of the inmates at Attica were basically reasonable and human. They asked for more relevant vocational shops, true religious freedom, a chance to work at renovating the facilities, and other things which we recognize as necessary for a man to function as an alert, healthy being. The fact that they had to take over the prison only suggests the extent of their frustration and the lack of other channels to express totally legitimate grievances.

We understand why these demands had to be made.

But we must understand more than this. We must recognize the political awareness present in the inmates' actions. And we must see in this awareness an awakened desire of people actively and constructively to change and improve their condition.

Across the country young men and women in prisons are becoming aware of the forces which have controlled their lives. Many of these people have previously been uninvolved, alienated, without direction. They now attempt to learn how to deal with these forces and institutions so that they might be able to shape their own destiny and that of their children.

We applaud this as a vital and human development, recognizing that it is good for people to become involved in the process of changing their lot.

And we say that if this practice involves challenges to existing institutions then those institutions must be open to the challenge for it is made out of genuine legitimate concerns. Yet, we must recognize that those in positions of power who feel threatened by this political awareness react in a most violent and repressive manner. We condemn this repression, because awareness and involvement of people in controlling their own future is something to be encouraged.

And there is still more to understand. When we look at pictures from Attica or the Tombs or San Quentin, we see black and Spanish faces. In some prisons inmate population is 80 per cent or more black and Spanish. Those people who have been victimized by the society on the streets are now victimized in prison. When we look at prison conditions and the brutal use of force at Attica we see the same force of racism which caused and then put down with force civil disturbances in this country's ghettos. This racism cannot be tolerated.

The inmates of Attica were victims of a systematic violence which pervades not only our prisons but the streets and towns of this society. We must admit as a nation that the deaths at Attica should never have occurred and we must act to erase the possibility of their recurrence.

Mayor Kenneth A. Gibson of Newark wrote this statement on Monday, Sept. 13, immediately after hearing of the Attica catastrophe.

Curing the Criminal

Should prisons rehabilitate? The question has rece a new twist in Connecticut, where a state prison lately paroled nine convicted child molesters who submitted to an experimental behavior modification gram. The 12-week program uses mild electrical s and other "aversive" techniques to cure the subjec their lust for children. So far, none of the parolees, have been free for as long as 11 months, is know have repeated his offense, and another inmate, soc be released, says the program, though unpleasant been both painless and successful. "Children are sexual objects to me anymore," he asserts.

The program is of course voluntary, but objec have naturally been raised. "It's inherently coerc charges William Olds of the Connecticut Civil Lib Union. "There's no such thing as a real volunteer prison, especially when a prisoner knows particip may enhance his chances for parole." If this is so, by the same token prisoners should not receive tim for good behavior either. But why deny, in the nam liberty, the penitent convict who really wants to b of an inclination to one of the most loathsome of versions? "Also," Olds goes on, "it's unproven, we're concerned about the danger of releasing pedop into the community on the basis of something like A much better point, and how wonderfully reass to hear it made by the leader of an organization usually turns livid *en masse* when a murderer is tr brusquely by his arresting officer. An ACLU of Alvin Bronstein, objects that such techniques hav tremendous potential for abuse." True; so doe power; which is why it must be exercised prud with all reasonable safeguards. But this program seems to have a tremendous potential for good, fo rehabilitation, far beyond any yet shown by sociol homilies and prison study groups; and that is w should not be hastily forsworn.

Dull or not, it is obvious that the great majority of Americans prefer to fight crime within the law, agreeing with the following statement given to PARADE by Attorney General Edward H. Levi on the dangers of vigilantism.

ATTORNEY GENERAL'S VIEW

"Vigilante groups always have one thing in common: They operate outside of the law. With crime at such high levels today, some citizens might be tempted to band together in vigilante groups, but such actions are not only counter to our democratic processes, they are ineffective as well.

"Vigilantes do not build respect for the law—they destroy it. There are a great many responsible roles for citizens to play today in the support of law enforcement and criminal justice. Crime can be reduced only if the criminal justice system is strong and effective. It cannot be strong if every group tries to take the law into its own hands."

Another Angle

by James L. Hicks

"Revenge is mine. I will revenge it, if I have to swim in my own blood to do it. A pig will die, and in the name of the people. I'm tired and won't lay back and watch them kill my brother. So this will probably be the last letter you'll get from me."

This, indeed, was the last letter that George Dobbins, a 25 year old Black activist inmate of the maximum security prison at Atmore, Alabama, wrote to his mother on January 18th. Shortly after writing the letter, George Dobbins dies in the aftermath of a prison riot.

Alabama state authorities first said that Mr. Dobbins was shot to death when security forces stormed the cell block where prisoners were holding guards as hostages.

But on February 12, almost a month later, a white newspaper publisher who is a member of a citizens' committee probing the cause of the prison riot, said in a front page article in his newspaper that George Dobbins was not shot to death during the riot, but that he had been stabbed to death long after the riot had been quelled.

The newspaperman, who incidentally is editor and publisher of the largest and most influential newspaper in the state, was backed up by a state toxicologist, who confirmed, after viewing the body, that George Dobbins did in fact die from stab wounds in the head.

Thus, we have another mysterious slaying of a Black man in prison and another echo of Attica in far off Alabama. It's the same old story repeated over and over again, of state authorities apparently using an often justified riot among inmates to "Get" certain leaders in prison who refuse to bow to the often inhuman treatment imposed upon them by prison authorities.

Dobbins claimed in his letter that prison authorities had beaten his brother Charles "Because they hate me and have found out that he is my brother". And now after the fact, the fact being that Mr. Dobbins is dead, a spokesman for the prison system says that his death is "under investigation" and that prison authorities will present the "results" to a grand jury.

This is merely the second chapter that goes along with the first, in far too many cases. If the third chapter follows the pattern that has become the mode in other parts of the United States, the third chapter will end up as a whitewash by the grand jury with prison guards being exonerated and given a pat on the back for "doing their duty".

This is what has happened over and over again, and despite the courage of the newspaper publisher who unearthed this deadly dirty work, there is little reason to believe that the state of Alabama will not follow the pattern already set in so many other states.

Thus, the shame of America's penal institutions will continue unabated with prison officials heavily armed, either shooting down defenseless men themselves or persuading weaker inmates in their custody to do their dirty work through the promise of a little relief from the horrible conditions under which they live.

The situation now borders on a national outrage which obviously can no longer be left to state officials for correction.

It's time for the federal government to take the lead in bringing about badly needed reform in our prisons

Above, "Another Angle" by James L. Hicks, February 23, 1974 issue, New York *Amsterdam News*.

Violent Us

The Burgesses Would Turn Prisons Into Torture Chambers

By a PRISON GOVERNOR

LONDON—If criminals are to be punished even more severely (be it hanged or beaten or flogged or psychologically assaulted, humiliated, degraded, or broken as human beings) who is supposed to do the punishing?

Where will the wild men who advocate such punishment recruit those who will punish other men as their daily contribution to the health of society?

There are, of course, in every society, sick and perverted men and women who would gladly spend their lives as professional punishers, degraders, humiliators, hurters, torturers and killers of their fellow men—people who are fulfilled by psychological and physical violence against others. They exist in every society. But when any society legitimizes their perversion by employing them in numbers to degrade

and punish and destroy, that society itself is sick unto death.

We know about the Gestapo, the SS and the concentration camps and the gas chambers. In our own time we see around us in this stricken world the same phenomena. God forbid that our society, sick though it is, should decide to employ professional punishers. When we do, if we do, civilization has gone ultimately from our society. These are not times in which we can afford to stand lightly by such matters.

The task of the Prison Service in our country is to ameliorate, as best it can, the appalling effects of imprisonment.

Prison staff are not employed to punish or to degrade. The only punishment the courts deal out in this respect is loss of liberty. Prison governors are instructed to hold in custody, not to *punish* prisoners. Loss of liberty is terrible enough for most men to bear without additional punishment.

Imprisonment — especially in the quite appalling conditions of overcrowding which exist today and which will continue to exist for as long as can be reasonably anticipated — can degrade and dehumanize both prisoners and staff alike unles there is instant moral vigilance and an un-

remitting conviction that human beings, even in captivity, must be treated with respect as persons and accorded the highest degree of dignity possible in their circumstances.

Only such an attitude, and the behavior appropriate to it within the penal system, can preserve the fabric of civilized society. Civilization is a tenuous concept even in Britain today. If the present staff of prisons are forced to become, or are replaced by, professional punishers and degraders, society will not be helped

I, for one, would want no part in a society which employed men for such a task and which legitimized violence of such a kind.

I am more afraid—and all of us should be more afraid—of the violence of those respectable burgesses who cry for death and blood and pain and degradation for criminals, than I am of criminals themselves—and I have known thousands of criminals. The violence of the frightened burgess is the most terrifying of all, and the most destructive of all.

What we need to recognize more than anything else in our disintegrating world is that violence is not a problem only of the criminal.

Above, from *The New York Times*. This letter is excerpted from *The Guardian* of London. The author, who asked that his name be withheld, is governor of an English prison.

Text of the Pardon   'To Show Mercy'

◆ Here is President Ford's statement announcing a pardon for former President Nixon:

———

LADIES and gentlemen, I have come to a decision which I felt I should tell you and all of my fellow American citizens, as soon as I was certain in my own mind and in my own conscience that it is the right thing to do.

I have learned already in this office that the difficult decisions always come to this desk. I must admit that many of them do not look at all the same as the hypothetical questions that I have answered freely and perhaps too fast on previous occasions.

My customary policy is to try and get all the facts and to consider the opinions of my countrymen and to take counsel with my most valued friends. But these seldom agree, and in the end, the decision is mine. To procrastinate, to agonize, and to wait for a more favorable turn of events that may never come, or more compelling external pressures that may as well be wrong as right, is itself a decision of sorts, and a weak and potentially dangerous course for a President to follow.

I have promised to uphold the Constitution, to do what is right as God gives me to see the right, and to do the very best that I can for America.

I have asked your help and your prayers, not only when I became President, but many times since. The Constitution is the supreme law of our land, and it governs our actions as citizens. Only the laws of God, which govern our consciences, are superior to it.

As we are a nation under God, so I am sworn to uphold our laws with the help of God. And I have sought such guidance and searched my own conscience with special diligence to determine the right thing for me to do with respect to my predecessor in this place, Richard Nixon, and his loyal wife and family.

Theirs is an American tragedy in which we all have played a part. It could go on and on and on, or someone must write the end to it. I have concluded that only I can do that, and if I can, I must.

There are no historic or legal precedents to which I can turn in this matter, none that precisely fit the circumstances of a private citizen who has resigned the Presidency of the United States. But it is common knowledge that serious allegations and accusations hang like a sword over our former President's head, threatening his health as he tries to reshape his life, a great part of which was spent in the service of this country and by the mandate of its people.

After years of bitter controversy and divisive national debate, I have been advised, and I am compelled to conclude, that many months and perhaps more years will have to pass before Richard Nixon could obtain a fair trial by jury in any jurisdiction of the United States under governing decisions of the Supreme Court.

No Respecter of Persons

I deeply believe in equal justice for all Americans, whatever their station or former station. The law, whether human or divine, is no respecter of persons, but the law is a respecter of reality.

The facts, as I see them, are that a former President of the United States, instead of enjoying equal treatment with any other citizen accused of violating the law, would be cruelly and excessively penalized either in preserving the presumption of his innocence or in obtaining a speedy determination of guilt in order to repay a legal debt to society.

During this long period of delay and potential litigation, ugly passions would again be aroused. And our people would again be polarized in their opinions. And the credibility of our free institutions of Government would again be challenged at home and abroad.

In the end, the courts might well hold that Richard Nixon had been denied due process and the verdict of history would even more be inconclusive with respect to those charges arising out of the period of his Presidency, of which I am presently aware.

Concern for the Country

But it is not the ultimate fate of Richard Nixon that most concerns me, though surely it deeply troubles every decent and every compassionate person. My concern is the immediate future of this great country.

In this, I dare not depend upon my personal sympathy as a longtime friend of the former President, nor my professional judgment as a lawyer, and I do not.

As President, my primary concern must always be the greatest good of all the people of the United States whose servant I am. As a man, my first consideration is to be true to my own convictions and my own conscience.

Sealing the Book

My conscience tells me clearly and certainly that I cannot prolong the bad dreams that continue to reopen a chapter that is closed. My conscience tells me that only I, as President, have the Constitutional power to firmly shut and seal this book. My conscience tells me it is my duty, not merely to proclaim domestic tranquility but to use every means that I have to insure it.

I do believe that the buck stops here, that I cannot rely upon public-opinion polls to tell me what is right.

I do believe that right makes

might, and that if I am wrong, 10 angels swearing I was right would make no difference.

I do believe, with all my heart and mind and spirit, that I, not as President, but as a humble servant of God, will receive justice without mercy if I fail to show mercy.

Goal of Peace

Finally, I feel that Richard Nixon and his loved ones have suffered enough and will continue to suffer, no matter what I do, no matter what we, as a great and good nation, can do together to make his goal of peace come true.

Now, therefore, I, Gerald R. Ford, President of the United States, pursuant to the pardon power conferred upon me by Article II, Section 2 of the Constitution, have granted and by these presents do grant a full, free, and absolute pardon unto Richard Nixon for all offenses against the United States which he, Richard Nixon, has committed or may have committed or taken part in during the period from Jan. 20, 1969, through Aug. 9, 1974.

Q. *Since President Ford was so quick to give Richard Nixon a full and complete pardon for all the crimes he may have committed, including income tax evasion, obstruction of justice, telling lies to the American people, masterminding the Watergate coverup, and who knows what else—why won't Ford give the same sort of pardon to Nixon's fellow conspirators: John N. Mitchell, Bob Haldeman, John Ehrlichman, and Robert Mardian?—F. G., Phoenix, Ariz.*

A. President Ford's reasoning is as follows: Mr. Nixon is the only President in U.S. history who was forced to resign from office. The pardon for him was intended to end the national focus on Watergate and to put the bitterness and divisiveness surrounding Watergate behind us so that the nation could focus on its difficult problems. Ford contends that these circumstances do not apply to Mitchell, Haldeman, Ehrlichman and Mardian and that these convicted men must pursue the normal judicial processes. This is specious reasoning, of course, having little to do with equal justice under law and pointing up the proclivity of relating prior pardon to high office. But according to White House spokesmen this is what President Ford contends.

Above, from the April 13, 1975 issue of *Parade*. Courtesy of Parade Publications.

'Regret' for 'My Mistakes'

♦ This statement by former President Nixon was released after the announcement of a pardon of Nixon by President Ford:

I HAVE been informed that President Ford has granted me a full and absolute pardon for any charges which may be brought against me for actions taken during the time I was the President of the United States. In accepting this pardon, I hope that his compassionate act will contribute to lifting the burden of Watergate from our country.

Here in California, my perspective on Watergate is quite different than it was while I was embattled in the midst of the controversy while I was still subject to the unrelenting daily demand of the Presidency itself.

Looking back on what is still in my mind a complex and confusing maze of events, decisions, pressures, and personalities, one thing I can see clearly now is that I was wrong in not acting more decisively and more forthrightly in dealing with Watergate, particularly when it reached the stage of judicial proceedings and grew from a political scandal into a national tragedy.

No words can describe the depths of my regret and pain at the anguish my mistakes over Watergate have caused the nation and the Presidency—a nation i so deeply loved and an institution I so greatly respect.

I know that many fair-minded people believe that my motivation and actions in the Watergate affair were intentionally self-serving and illegal. I now understand how my own mistakes and misjudgments have contributed to that belief and seemed to support it. This burden is the heaviest one of all to bear.

That the way I tried to deal with Watergate was the wrong way is a burden I shall bear for every day of the life that is left to me.

A LESSON IN SOCIOLOGY:

THE REWARDS OF CRIME

by Jonathan Quick

PRISONS

One of the most disturbing events of the last decades is the extraordinary increase in crime. Theft, burglary, rape, fraud, etc., occur in ever increasing frequency and a larger range of people than ever before seem to become involved in such activities. Even policemen have been caught committing burglaries and selling stolen goods.

The experts don't agree on the reason for this phenomenon. Some of them believe that poverty breeds crime and they point to the plight of many poor people, who live cooped up under terrible conditions in city slums. Others, however, take a less deterministic view.

They tell us that the poor, God bless them, have always been with us and that they are not necessarily criminals; it is not poverty that causes crime, but people commit crimes (just as guns don't kill people, but people kill people).

No doubt this is true to the same extent as one can say that hens lay eggs and cattle produce fertilizer, but it doesn't go far enough for an explanation. (For instance, farm animals could hardly persist in their physiological functions unless they are fed. We therefore need to look at those who feed a bull to understand what he produces.)

Coming back to the issue of crime, we must look beyond the obvious fact that people commit crimes. A good case can be made for the proposition that wealth, not poverty, causes crime.

In the first place, poverty hasn't greatly increased in recent years, but the overall standard of living went up and the number of very rich people became much larger.

It should certainly be possible to demonstrate a high correlation between increase in crime and increase in the number of millionaires during any recent period of time. Moreover, there are good reasons to believe that such a correlation is not accidental or trivial, but in fact causal.

As people acquire wealth, they also acquire prestige and credibility (in contrast to poor people, who have to be simply truthful to be believed) and they often go into politics or become members of various boards and foundations; they can well afford to give financial support to their peers (it is always less embarrassing to give to those who don't need it) and they are in a position to influence government and other agencies.

Recent experience has shown that they may become over-zealous in their civic efforts and do things which are against the law. If they then get caught and convicted for, let's say, bribing an official or taking a bribe, they can count on being punished with a fine many times smaller than the amount of money that had been feloniously transacted.

This enormous discrepancy between the benefit and the punishment of a crime is bound to serve as an incentive for the wealthy to commit even more and bigger crimes. (Such an incentive is not available to the poor, who can't afford expensive lawyers and payments of fines, and who have to serve jail terms for infractions of the law.)

While it may be unfortunate that crime does pay for the rich, the worst part of this is the bad example it sets for the vast middle classes (or at least that half-vast part of them with social ambitions -- those who read and pay attention to the news).

In order to acquire wealth, these people tend to imitate the wealthy and are likely to get involved in criminal activities at whatever scale they feel they may be able to get away with. Thus, the most damaging role of wealth in the causation of crime is that it serves as a corrupting model.

It is, therefore, proposed to reduce crime by the simple device of reducing the number of wealthy people. The French, during their well known revolution, tried to solve the problem by reducing the people themselves, but much gentler methods have since become available, such as the almost painless removal of excess wealth by taxation.

It is only a question of being willing to apply these already available methods to stop the spread of the criminally rich (or vice versa). Once the big crime has been taken care of, it should be easy to deal with the small fry in our urban centers.

■

By Jonathan Quick, reprinted from the February 1974 issue of *Freedom News*, Richmond, California.

SECTION 13

International Relations

The area of international relations and ethics is at once the most general and abstract and also the most immediate and concrete of those addressed in this book. It is general and abstract insofar as most of us feel that we have no direct influence on decisions made in this sphere, but it becomes frighteningly concrete when the decisions that are made at this level result in wars or famines which can in turn result in death and suffering for a large number of individuals. It is in part the abstractness of the issues that makes it particularly difficult to identify their moral dimensions. Who (what person or persons) is confronted with what decisions? As mentioned in our discussion in the Introduction, it is not at all obvious that any individual has any real control at all over the course of events at the international level. But this is not an ethical question in and of itself (at least not in most definitions of ethics).

Certainly some of the arguments in this section must be classified as quite abstract and general, particularly the "debate" between Henry Kissinger and Alexander Solzhenitsyn over the morality of détente, although even here the concrete implications of this general policy (in terms of the possibility of a nuclear war and the reality of the treatment of individuals—particularly political dissenters—within the two countries) cannot be easily missed. But many of the arguments do involve quite specific decisions confronted by particular individuals within the context of the international political realities. For instance, given the fact of détente in 1975, a police equipment salesman was confronted with a choice that he did not have previously of whether or not to sell various types of equipment to the Soviet Union. And given the realities of the international trade situation, in conjunction with the world food and population situation, there are some choices which certain groups assert are open to all of us which could result in preventing the death by starvation of one or more individuals in another country, although as always, the scientific accuracy of such assertions must be carefully scrutinized. In brief, while ethical issues related to matters of international relations are among the most difficult and complex of all to deal with in any intellectually adequate way, they are also of such great potential significance (even in terms of some everyday decisions of quite ordinary persons) as to justify any efforts to give them thought and consideration.

EXERCISES

1. From the arguments in this section, identify the different decisions open to specific individuals concerning international issues.
2. Compare the arguments in this section with those in the sections on civil disobedience and gun control to identify common issues. In particular, is there any significant difference between the role of the individual in relation to foreign policy and international relations and his or her role in relation to national policies and laws within the country?
3. Compare the arguments in this section with those in Section 10 concerning corporations. Is the corporation more like the individual person or more like the state with regard to moral judgments?
4. Are there any significant similarities between the arguments concerning inter*national* relations and the arguments in Section 1 concerning inter*personal* relations?

The 'Covert Operations' Debate

The following are excerpts from the Senate debate of Oct. 2 on an amendment to the foreign aid bill which would have ordered the Central Intelligence Agency immediately to halt all covert operations not related to intelligence. The amendment was defeated, 68 to 17. This marked the first time either house of Congress had debated and voted on this issue.

Sen. James Abourezk (D-S.D.): This amendment will, if enacted, abolish all clandestine or covert operations by the Central Intelligence Agency.

I believe very strongly that we must have an intelligence-gathering organization and I believe the CIA and our defense intelligence agencies do an adequate job in this respect.

We have every right to defend ourselves from foreign attack and that right includes intelligence gathering to protect our security.

But there is no justification in our legal, moral, or religious principles for operations of a U.S. agency which result in assassinations, sabotage, political disruptions, or other meddling in other country's internal affairs, all in the name of the American people. It amounts to nothing more than an arm of the U.S. government conducting a secret war without either the approval of Congress or the knowledge of the American people.

I want to remind the Senate that the present director of the CIA, William Colby, said a couple of weeks ago that while he preferred to retain the clandestine or covert services, the Capitol would not fall if it were abolished.

He also said that there was not any activity going on anywhere in the world at this time that required the use of clandestine activity.

●

Sen. Clifford Case (R-N.J.): If I may express my own view about covert activities, it is that they all should be regarded as wrong. There ought not to be an institutionalization of them, even to the extent that we have now. I do not think that a committee is the answer. We have a committee downtown, a Committee of 40, which is supposed to review this matter and advise the President; and he acts on their advice in most cases, I understand.

We have a committee here, when it meets. I am not complaining that it does not meet more often, because I do not think a committee is the answer.

Once we get into an institutionalization of this kind of thing, we begin to make it respectable, and that I do not like. There ought to be a general rule against it, with a general understanding of the American people that on occasion the President has to act in violation of the law, if you will—our law, other laws—and take action in the interest of a country, in great emergency. This I think he does at his own peril and subject to being either supported or turned down by the country, after the fact. I think this is about as close as we can come to any statement about how this matter ought to be handled.

I would, of course, consider any proposal made for procedural reform here, but I want to state now that I do not think any such thing is possible because of the nature of the animal with which we are dealing.

●

Sen. Mark O. Hatfield (R-Ore.): To me, it is transparently obvious that the CIA's covert operations, undertaken in Chile to "destabilize" the Allende government, were in violation of these commitments of international law. At the very least, such operations compromise the sincerity of our loudly proclaimed desire for world peace and world freedom, I think we ought to address ourselves to the legal obligations this nation has undertaken when it has affixed its signature to these various statements and these various charters.

That is why I feel that the amendment offered by the senator from South Dakota really does not go far enough. I should like to see it go farther, to put this Senate on record that

we totally and completely oppose any involvement whatsoever in covert activity. That does not deny the gathering of information and intelligence, but indicates the refusal of this Senate to permit the CIA to go beyond gathering intelligence into an action of covert activity.

●

Sen. Barry Goldwater (R-Ariz.): If we destroy our right to engage in covert activity altogether by the adoption of this amendment—in fact, I think the language of this amendment would even prevent us from going to war—I think we would be making a very grave mistake.

I do not support everything that the CIA has done. On the other hand, I do not know everything it has done, and I do not think we necessarily have to know. I think this would be dangerous.

I cite the example of a member of the House of Representatives who happened to have seen, so he says, a page of testimony. We do not know whether he saw that testimony or not. But on this one statement, in which, in my opinion, he violated his pledge to secrecy, the whole CIA has come under criticism. I do not believe it is fair of this body to accept the hearsay words of a man who divulged classified material.

So, I hope we will defeat this amendment and defeat it soundly. I think I am safe in saying that the chairman of the Committee on Armed Services, together with the chairman of the Committee on Foreign Relations, would be willing to institute proper hearings, at which time we could hear all arguments for and against the operation of our intelligence collecting agencies.

From *The Washington Post*, 1974.

Speech

July 15, 1975
Minneapolis, Minnesota

Bureau of Public Affairs
Office of Media Services

THE MORAL FOUNDATIONS OF FOREIGN POLICY

Secretary Henry A. Kissinger before the Upper Midwest Council.

It is time to face the reality of our situation. Our choice is not between morality and pragmatism. We cannot escape either, nor are they incompatible. This nation must be true to its own beliefs or it will lose its bearings in the world. But at the same time it must survive in a world of sovereign nations and competing wills.

We need moral strength to select among often agonizing choices and a sense of purpose to navigate between the shoals of difficult decisions. But we need as well a mature sense of means, lest we substitute wishful thinking for the requirements of survival.

Morality and Policy

The relation of morality to policy is thus not an abstract philosophical issue. It applies to many topics of the current debate. It applies to relations with the Communist powers, where we must manage a conflict of moral purposes and interests in the shadow of nuclear peril; and it applies in our political ties with nations whose domestic practices are inconsistent with our own.

Our relationship with the Communist powers has raised difficult questions for Americans since the Bolshevik Revolution. It was understood very early that the Communist system and ideology were in conflict with our own principles. Sixteen years passed before President Franklin Roosevelt extended diplomatic recognition to the Soviet Government. He did so in the belief, as he put it, that *"through the resumption of normal relations the prospects of peace over all the world are greatly strengthened."*

Today again courageous voices remind us of the nature of the Soviet system and of our duty to defend freedom. About this there is no disagreement.

There is, however, a clear conflict between two moral imperatives which is at the heart of the problem. Since the dawn of the nuclear age, the world's fears of holocaust and its hopes for a better future have both hinged on the relationship between the two superpowers. In an era of strategic nuclear balance—when both sides have the capacity to destroy civilized life—there is no alternative to coexistence. In such conditions the necessity of peace is itself a moral imperative. As President Kennedy pointed out: *"In the final analysis our most basic common link is that we all inhabit this small planet. We all breathe the same air. We all cherish our children's future. And we are all mortal."*

It is said, correctly, that the Soviet perception of "peaceful coexistence" is not the same as ours, that Soviet policies aim at the furthering of Soviet objectives. In a world of nuclear weapons capable of destroying mankind, in a century which has seen resort to brutal force on an unprecedented scale and intensity, in an age of ideology which turns the domestic policies of nations into issues of international contention, the problem of peace takes on a profound moral and practical difficulty. But the issue, surely, is not whether peace and stability serve Soviet purposes, but whether they also serve our own. Constructive actions in Soviet policy are desirable *whatever* the Soviet motives.

Our immediate focus is on the international actions of the Soviet Union not because it is our only moral concern, but because it is the sphere of action that we can most directly and confidently affect. As a consequence of improved foreign policy relationships, we have successfully used our influence to promote human rights. But we have done so quietly, keeping in mind the delicacy of the problem and stressing results rather than public confrontation.

Therefore, critics of detente must answer: What is the alternative that they propose? What precise policies do they want us to change? Are they prepared for a prolonged situation of dramatically increased international danger? Do they wish to return to the constant crises and high arms budgets of the cold war? Does detente encourage repression—or is it detente that has generated the ferment and the demands for openness that we are now witnessing? Can we ask our people to support confrontation unless they know that every reasonable alternative has been explored?

In our relations with the Soviet Union, the United States will maintain its strength, defend its interests, and support its friends with determination and without illusion. We will speak up for our beliefs with vigor and without self-deception. We consider detente a means to regulate a competitive relationship—not a substitute for our own efforts in building the strength of the free world. We will continue on the course on which we are embarked because it offers hope to our children of a more secure and a more just world.

These considerations raise a more general question: To what extent are we able to affect the internal policies of other governments and to what extent is it desirable?

There are some 150 nations in the world, and barely a score of them are democracies in any real sense. The rest are nations whose ideology or political practices are inconsistent with our own. Yet we have political relations and often alliances with some of these countries in Asia, Latin America, Africa, and Europe.

Congressman [Donald M.] Fraser has raised this issue with great integrity and concern, and I have profited from many discussions with him. We do not and will not condone repressive practices. This is not only dictated by our values but is also a reflection of the reality that regimes which lack legitimacy or moral authority are inherently vulnerable. There will therefore be limits to the degree to which such regimes can be congenial partners. We have used, and we will use, our influence against repressive practices. Our traditions and our interests demand it.

But truth compels also a recognition of our limits. The question is whether we promote human rights more effectively by counsel and friendly relations where this serves our interest, or by confrontational propaganda and discriminatory legislation. And we must also assess the domestic performance of foreign governments in relation to their history and to the threats they face. We must have some understanding for the dilemmas of countries adjoining powerful, hostile, and irreconcilable totalitarian regimes.

Our alliances and political relationships serve mutual ends; they contribute to regional and world security, and thus support the broader welfare. They are not favors to other governments, but reflect a recognition of mutual interests. They should be withdrawn only when our interests change and not as a punishment for some act with which we do not agree. In many countries, whatever the internal structure, the populations are unified in seeking our protection against outside aggression. In many countries our foreign policy relationships have proved to be no obstacle to the forces of change. And in many countries—especially in Asia—it is the process of American disengagement that has eroded the sense of security and created a perceived need for greater internal discipline, and at the same time diminished our ability to influence domestic practices.

The attempt to deal with those practices by restrictive American legislation raises a serious problem, not because of the moral view it expresses—which we share—but because of the mistaken impression it creates that our security ties are acts of charity. And beyond that, such acts—because they are too public, too inflexible, and too much a stimulus to nationalistic resentment—are almost inevitably doomed to fail.

There are no simple answers. Painful experience should have taught us that we ought not exaggerate our capacity to foresee, let alone to shape, social and political change in other societies. Therefore let me state the principles that will guide our action:

• Human rights are a legitimate international concern and have been so defined in international agreements for more than a generation.
• The United States will speak up for human rights in appropriate international forums and in exchanges with other governments.
• We will be mindful of the limits of our reach; we will be conscious of the difference between public postures that satisfy our self-esteem and policies that bring positive results.
• We will not lose sight of either the requirements of global security or what we stand for as a nation.

Solzhenitsyn— WORDS OF WARNING TO AMERICA

By ALEXANDER SOLZHENITSYN

It was a dramatic warning to all the world—and to Americans in particular—that Nobel Prize winner Alexander Solzhenitsyn delivered in Washington, D.C., on June 30.

Many papers in the West have written: Let's hurry up and end the bloodshed in Vietnam and have national unity there.

One of your leading newspapers, after the end of Vietnam, gave a full, big headline: "The Blessed Silence." I would not wish that kind of blessed silence on my worst enemy. I would not wish that kind of national unity upon my worst enemy.

I have spent 11 years in the "archipelago." And for half of my lifetime I have studied this question. Looking at this terrible tragedy in Vietnam from a distance, I can tell you: A million persons will be exterminated. Four to 5 million—in accordance with the scale of Vietnam—will spend time in concentration camps and will be rebuilding Vietnam.

What is happening in Cambodia you already know. It is genocide. It is full and complete destruction, but in a new form.

Once again, the technology is not up to building gas chambers, so in a few hours the entire capital city, the guilty capital city is emptied out—old people, women, children are driven out without belongings, without food. Go, die!

Now we hear voices in your country and in the West: Give up Korea and we will live in peace. Give up Portugal, of course. Give up Japan, give up Israel, give up Taiwan, Philippines, Malaysia, Thailand, 10 African countries. Just let us live peaceably.

Give us the possibility to continue driving our beautiful cars on our splendid highways. Make it possible for us to play tennis and golf. Let us mix our cocktails as we are accustomed to doing. Let us see the beautiful, toothy smile in the glass on every advertisement page of a magazine.

One hears: "We cannot defend those who cannot defend themselves with their own human resources, with their own manpower." But, against the powers of totalitarianism—when all of this power is thrown against a country—no country can defend itself with its own resources.

We are told: "It is not possible to protect those who do not have full democracy." This is the most remarkable argument of the lot. This is the leitmotiv I read in your newspapers and I hear in the speeches of some of your political leaders. Who in the world, on the front lines of defense against totalitarianism, ever has been able to sustain full democracy? You? The United States?

Even the united democracies of the world were not able to do it—America, England, Canada, Australia. With the first

Above and right, from *U.S. News and World Report*, July 14, 1975.

Something which is almost incomprehensible to the human mind is the West's fantastic greed for profit and gain, which goes beyond all reason, all limitations, all conscience.

I have to admit that Lenin foretold this whole process. Lenin, who spent most of his life in the West and knew it much better than Russia, always said that the Western capitalists would do anything to supply the Soviet economy— "They will fight with each other to sell us goods cheaper and sell them quicker so that we'll buy from one rather than from the other."

And in the difficult moments of a party meeting in Moscow he said: "Comrades, don't worry when things are hard with us. When things are difficult, we will give a rope to the *bourgeoisie* and the *bourgeoisie* will hang itself with this rope."

Then, Karl Radek, a witty fellow you may have heard of, said: "Vladimir Ilyich, where are we going to get enough rope to hang the whole *bourgeoisie?*"

Lenin said immediately: "They'll supply us with it."

Nikita Khrushchev came here and said: "We're going to bury you." People didn't believe that—they took it as a joke.

Now, of course, the Communists have become more clever in my country. They do not say, "We're going to bury you" any more. Now they say, "Détente."

Nothing has changed in Communist ideology. The goals are the same as they were.

206

danger of Hitlerism, you stretched the hand out to Stalin.

It is also said that "if the Soviet Union is going to use détente for its own ends, then we"— But what will happen then? The Soviet Union *has* used détente in its own interest, is using it now, and will continue to use it in its own interest.

For example, in China and in the Soviet Union they're both participating in détente, but they have grabbed three countries of Indo-China in a quiet way. True, perhaps as a consolation, they will send you a table-tennis team!

Do you understand properly what détente has meant all these 40 years? Friendship, stabilization of the situation, trade, et cetera—I have to tell you something which you've never seen or heard—how it looks from the other side. Let me tell you now:

A mere acquaintance with an American—and God forbid that you should sit with him in a restaurant—means a 10-year term for espionage. In the fourth volume of the "Archipelago," I will tell of an event. One Soviet citizen was in the United States, and when he came back he told people that in the United States they have wonderful automobiles, roads. The State Security arrested him and they demanded a term of 10 years. But the judge said: "I don't object, but there's not enough evidence. Couldn't you find something else against him?" So the judge was exiled because he quarreled with the State Security, and they gave the other man 10 years. Can you imagine what this means? He said there were good roads in America. He got 10 years for that.

So what are we to conclude from that? Is détente needed or not? Not only is it needed, it's needed like air. It's the only way of saving the earth; that is, instead of having a world war, we must have détente, but a true détente. I would say that there are very definite characteristic marks of what a genuine détente would be.

There are only three. In the first place: that there be a disarmament—not only a disarmament from the use of war, but also from the use of violence—not only arms, but also violence; not only the sort of arms which are used to destroy your neighbors, but the sort of arms which are used to destroy your fellow countrymen.

This is not a détente, if we here with you today can spend our time in a friendly way, while over there people are groaning and dying and in psychiatric insane asylums. The doctors are going around and putting injections in people which destroy their brain cells.

And the second sign of true détente is the following: that it be not one based on smiles, not on verbal concessions. It has to be based on a firm foundation. You know the word from the Bible, "Not on sand, but on rock." There has to be a guarantee that this will not disappear overnight or be broken overnight. And for this, we need that the other party to the agreement have some control over attacks, some control by public opinion, some control by the press, control by a freely elected parliament. Until such controls exist, there's absolutely no guarantee.

And the third simple condition: What sort of détente is it when they employ the inhumane propaganda which is called, in the Soviet Union, "ideological war"? Let us not have that. If we're going to have détente, let's be friendly—and end ideological warfare!

In evaluating everything I have said to you today—and I'm coming to my conclusion now—I could say we don't even have to have our conversation on the political level—why such and such a country acted in such and such a way, how they—what they were counting on in acting in such a way. We should rather rise above this to the moral level and say:

"In 1933 and in 1941, your leaders and the whole Western world in an unprincipled way made a deal with totalitarianism. We will have to pay our cost for this and for 30 years we've been paying for it, and we're still paying for it, and we're going to pay for it in a worse way."

One cannot think only in the low level of political calculations. It's necessary to think also of what is noble, what is honest and what is honorable, not only what is useful.

The adroit Western legal scholars have now introduced the term "legal realism." By this legal realism, they want to push aside any moral evaluation of affairs. They say: "Recognize realities. You have to understand that if such and such laws have been established in such and such countries, then these laws, which provide for violence, have to be recognized and respected."

At the present time, this concept is widely accepted among lawyers—that law is higher than morality; law is something which is worked out and developed, whereas morality is something inchoate and amorphous. That isn't the case. The opposite is rather true—morality is higher than law.

Law is our human attempt somehow to instill in the laws a part of that moral sphere which is above us. We try to understand this morality, bring it down to earth and present it in the form of laws—sometimes we are more successful, sometimes less. Sometimes you actually have a caricature of morality, but morality is always higher than law. And we cannot forget this ever.

In our heart and soul, we have to recognize that it's almost a joke now to talk in the Western world in the twentieth century about words like "good" and "evil." These are almost old-fashioned concepts, but these are very real and genuine concepts. These are concepts from a sphere which is higher than us.

And instead of getting involved in shortsighted political calculations, we have to recognize that the concentration of world evil and the tremendous force of hatred is there, and it's flowing from there throughout the world. And we have to stand up against it and not try to give to it, give to it, give to it everything which it asks for.

I started by saying that you are the allies of our liberation movement in the Communist countries, and I call upon you: Let us think together and try to see how we can adjust the relationship between these two processes. Whenever you help the persons being persecuted in the Soviet Union, you're not only displaying magnanimity and nobility, you are defending not only them but you're defending yourselves as well. You're defending your own future.

So let us try to see how far we can go to stop this senseless process of endless concessions to aggressors, these clever legal arguments for why we should make one concession after another and give up more and more and more.

Why have we got to hand over increasingly more and more technology—complex, subtle, developed technology—that it needs for its weapons, for crushing its own citizens?

If we can at least slow down that process of concessions, if not stop it altogether, and make it possible for the process of liberation to continue in the Communist countries, ultimately these two processes will combine and yield us our future.

On our small planet, there are no longer any internal affairs. The Communist leaders say: "Don't interfere in our internal affairs. Let us strangle our citizens in quiet and peace."

But I tell you: Interfere more and more, interfere as much as you can. We beg you to come and interfere.

Solzhenitsyn's Politics

ALEXANDER SOLZHENITSYN arrived in Washington on the wings of his immense artistic reputation and his great personal stature as one who has suffered, as a prisoner and dissenter in his native Russia, for his beliefs. In his speech before the AFL-CIO, moreover, the exiled Russian writer offered a critique of detente that strikes chords both in those who had expected too much from Soviet-American relations in recent years and in those who had expected very little at all. In his new role as a direct participant in American political dialogue, as in his old role as a Russian prophet, his is a voice that demands to be heard.

It is in terms of that old role, nonetheless, that he must still be understood. For Mr. Solzhenitsyn is a man with a single mission: to bring about the moral regeneration of the Russian people and their release from what he regards as the immoral grasp of Communist power.

© *The Washington Post* (July 4, 1975).

He has no particular interest in, or knowledge of, foreign affairs. He has a consuming obsession with the destiny of his own people. This is precisely why the Soviet authorities jailed, harassed and finally exiled him. It is the wellspring of his artistic genius. And it is why his counsel on foreign policy needs to be listened to with care.

The first purpose of American foreign policy, after all, is to prevent war and enhance the welfare of its own citizens. Mr. Solzhenitsyn, however, would dedicate American power to the defeat of Soviet communism. To him this is a matter not of strategic advantage but of moral necessity. He regards every compromise Washington has made with Moscow over 40 years—from FDR's recognition of Russia, to his wartime alliance against Hitler, to the various increments of contemporary detente—as deals struck with the devil. Their result, he declares, is to deny the liberation of the Russian people.

The nobility of Mr. Solzhenitsyn's summons is undeniable, and his words stand as a deserved rebuke to those who would read a moral component out of foreign policy altogether. Fortunately, few citizens in the United States share either his compulsion against compromise or his fierce commitment to a Russian renaissance. For these would involve a cost and peril beyond reckoning. This is not to say that every American step toward detente has been a wise and good one. But Americans have spent the better part of a generation escaping from the notion that foreign policy should be a moral crusade. The example of Mr. Solzhenitsyn's personal courage should not blind us to the dangers of trying to emulate it on a national scale.

His host in Washington, AFL-CIO President George Meany, shares the Russian writer's conviction that communism is immoral. He does so out of his own longstanding belief in what he calls the "first principles of the labor movement"—the welfare of workers and "freedom for all people elsewhere." This meeting of fundamentalist minds is one of the more sobering, not to say exotic, political matches of our time. But it does not add up to a prescription for wise policy. Human dignity, as pursued by these two men, is a high moral value. But so is the avoidance of nuclear war—this is the overarching goal of detente. There is more room on the mountaintop than Mr. Solzhenitsyn and Mr. Meany may be prepared to grant.

Proposed Sale Of Police
Equipment To Russia Hit

WASHINGTON (AP) — several American firms are going to an international exhibition next month in Moscow with hopes of selling sophisticated police and criminology equipment to the Soviets.

Participation by the U.S. companies came under fire Sunday from Sen. Henry M. Jackson, D-Wash., who said in a televised interview:

"Are we getting detente when we are going to sell...to the Russians police equipment that will help the KGB to hold the dissidents even under tighter control?"

Rep. Charles A. Vanik, D-Ohio, who along with Jackson has been pressing for tighter controls on export of American technology to the Soviet Union, has called the prospective business deals "shocking and unconscionable."

"A crime control device can easily be converted into a weapon of oppression," Vanik declared in a House speech last week. "It would be tragic if oppression in the Soviet Union would result from devices and equipment stamped: 'Made in America.'"

Voice Identification Inc. of Sommerville, N.J., one of the American firms participating Aug. 14-28 in the Soviet-sponsored exhibition, "Krimtehnika '74," manufactures an advanced electronic voiceprint device widely used by law enforcement agencies in the United States.

Voiceprint devices identify individual characteristics in a person's voice.

Voice Identification equipment was used to verify the voice of ex-Soviet premier Nikita S. Khrushchev on tapes that were later published as "Khrushchev Remembers."

Alexander I. Solzhenitsyn's novel "The First Circle" focused on a Stalin-era Soviet institute where scientist prisoners were under pressure to develop a rudimentary voiceprint machine for pinpointing a political criminal.

"They envisioned a system, like fingerprinting, which would someday be adopted: a consolidated prints of everyone who had at one time or another been under suspicion," Solzhenitsyn wrote.

Asked whether he thought the Soviets might employ his firm's equipment in wiretapping of political dissidents, as well as against ordinary criminals, William Hughes, vice president of Voice Identification, said:

"Boy, that's a hell of a question. It's an interesting one.

"Quite honestly, I am going over there to exhibit equipment. I suppose they'll want to buy it — I certainly hope so, that's the purpose. It's obviously, as it is here, an investigatory tool. Now, how do they want to use it? I don't know. I can't speak for them or their system of justice or anything else."

Right, excerpted from "The Necessary Amorality of Foreign Affairs" by Arthur Schlesinger, Jr., *Harper's Magazine*, August 1971.

In short, the individual's duty of self-sacrifice and the nation's duty of self-preservation are in conflict; and this makes it impossible to measure the action of nations by a purely individualistic morality. "The Sermon on the Mount," said Churchill, "is the last word in Christian ethics. . . . Still, it is not on those terms that Ministers assume their responsibilities of guiding states." Saints can be pure, but statesmen must be responsible. As trustees for others, they must defend interests and compromise principles. In politics, practical and prudential judgment must have priority over moral verdicts.

Losing crusades

IF MORAL PRINCIPLES have only limited application to foreign policy, then we are forced to the conclusion that decisions in foreign affairs must generally be taken on other than moralistic grounds. What are these other grounds? I believe that where the embryonic international community cannot regulate dealings among nations, the safest basis for foreign policy lies not in attempts to determine what is right or wrong but in attempts to determine the national interest.

National interest, realistically construed, will promote enlightened rather than greedy policy. So a realist like Hamilton said (my emphasis) that his aim was not "to recommend a policy absolutely selfish or interested in nations; but to show, that a policy regulated by their own interest, *as far as justice and good faith permit*, is, and ought to be, their prevailing one." And a realist like Theodore Roosevelt could say: "It is neither wise nor right for a nation to disregard its own needs, and it is foolish—and may be wicked—to think that other nations will disregard theirs. But it is wicked for a nation only to regard its own interest, and foolish to believe that such is the sole motive that actuates any other nation. It should be our steady aim to raise the ethical standard of national action just as we strive to raise the ethical standard of individual action."

A Basic Human Right: The Right to Leave

By REP. JACK KEMP (R.-N.Y.)

Next to the right to life, the right to leave one's country and return is probably the most important of human rights. However fettered in one's country a person's liberty might be and however restricted his longing for self-identity, for spiritual and cultural fulfillment and for economic and social enhancement, opportunity to leave a country and seek a haven elsewhere can provide the basis for life and human integrity.

The right of all persons to emigrate from and also return to one's country is probably first among the human rights that define a free society. Only a free society grants its citizens the liberty to leave.

In the United States, we strongly believe that the right to leave and to return is the constituent element of personal liberty, and thus all Americans (except those under some kinds of legal due process) may leave and may return for good reason or bad or no reason at all.

It is significant to note that this concept is hardly one of recent origin. The right to leave is founded on natural law. Socrates regarded the right as an "attribute of personal liberty," and the Magna Carta in the year 1215 incorporated the right to leave for the first time into national law.

The French Constitution of 1791 provided the same guarantee, and an act of the U.S. Congress declared in 1868 that "the right of expatriation is a natural and inherent right of all people, indispensable to the enjoyment of the rights of life, liberty and the pursuit of happiness."

The right to leave must be recognized as a precedent for other rights. For example, if a person is restricted from leaving a country, he may thereby be prevented from observing or practicing the tenets of his religion; he may be frustrated in his efforts to marry or found a family; and he could be prevented from obtaining the kind of education that he desires.

Denial of the right can also be a precedent for the denial of other rights. Disregard of this right frequently gives rise to discrimination in respect of other human rights and fundamental freedoms, resulting at times in the complete denial of those rights and freedoms. I believe that for a man who is being persecuted, the denial of the right to leave may be tantamount to the total deprivation of liberty, if not life itself.

I am personally familiar with someone who has experienced the abuses I have just described. On a recent trip to Israel I met with Rita Gluzman, whose husband has been prevented from emigrating from the Ukraine to join her and their infant son in Israel. I am sure that such regrettable instances are very common.

This view that next to the right of life, the right to leave one's country and return is probably the most important of human rights is sustained by international opinion as authoritatively expressed in a study compiled by the Subcommission on the Prevention of Discrimination and Protection of Minorities entitled, "Study of Discrimination in Respect of the Right of Everyone to Leave Any Country, Including His Own, and to Return to His Own Country." Published in 1963 after exhaustive research, it is considered to be the best expression of international opinion.

By Rep. Jack Kemp in the October 30, 1971 issue of *Human Events*.

IT is impossible to deal justly with the Chinese labor question without a fair examination of our entire labor-system.

The United States, in their relations to labor, stand alone among all the countries of the earth. The very principles of freedom and equality, upon which we depend for our cohesion, are adverse to a practical labor-system. Whereas other nations find their labor-market supplied by the peasant order, or by a system of serfdom or slavery, we have no such resource, and are forced to look abroad for paid substitutes for those who, in other countries, are presumed to feel some slight interest in the land and people they serve.

We have no peasantry ; and since our native-born population have been disinclined to turn their attention to menial labor, it has followed that we must look for assistance to the refuse population of older and over-crowded countries, in order that we might develop the resources of our own.

This would be all well enough, if it were not that inventive genius and intellectual power require instruments of some mental capacity to make them profitable. The truth is, that while, in the first period of our existence, we needed only brute force, and the muscular power that could fell trees and hoe potatoes, now we must have intellectual and skilled labor to utilize our inventions, to develop our manufactures, and to enrich our land with intelligent agriculture. Agriculture, horticulture, and manufacture, which were at first conducted with a view to absolute necessity, are now followed, in a degree, as fine arts, needing all the adjuncts which the mind can offer to advance them.

For such advancement our present labor-system is incompetent ; and this leads to the first proposition to be offered in this article, viz. : that *our present labor-system is intellectually inadequate to the necessities of the people and the capacity of the country and period.*

Again, not only has our labor-system failed to advance in value and capacity with our advancing resources ; not only is it a dead-weight upon invention and improvement ; but it has also been the occasion for the introduction into our social and political organization of an element fraught with danger to our welfare and position as a nation. Forced to depend for the labor which built our residences and our warehouses, and which tilled our fields and worked our manufactories, upon the refuse of the ignorant lower orders of Europe, or, in default of these, upon a peasantry imbued to a large extent with the *sans-culotteism* of the times, we have seen our servants educated to overturn their masters, and the worst features of despotic injustice introduced into our republican law, by the very ones who had fled from their own homes to escape the workings of similar unjust dispensations.

This brings us to a second proposition, which is, that *the interference of ignorant labor with politics is dangerous to society, injurious to operatives, and practically impedes the progress and advancement of labor itself.*

Hitherto our labor-market has been a monopoly with no competitors ; and the consequence has been—as must ever be the case under similar circumstances—labor improperly and grudgingly performed, and exorbitant compensation insolently demanded. There should be nothing freer than labor. Our market should be open to the world, since only by that means can the natural laws which regulate it gain opportunity for their working.

Now as to agriculture. The abolition of slavery was certainly productive of results, as regards our agricultural progress, whose bitter and injurious effects must be felt for an indefinite period of time, unless some other form of labor shall take the place of the one so summarily annihilated. And yet this act of emancipation, ruinous to our agricultural interests as it must be at the outset, cannot but result favorably in the end, provided it be made the stepping-stone to a more advanced and intelligent system. The colored population of the South, ignorant and brutish as a mass, can never be anything more to our soil than the blind workers, whose labor must be fruitless except as directed by a higher intelligence. The necessity for this kind of labor is being rapidly obviated by the introduction of machinery ; and it becomes obvious that what will be needed hereafter in this direction is a much higher standard of intelligence, combined with education, and a marked degree of aptitude for the duties required.

Heretofore, the chief immigration to America has been twofold—the class of small farmers from the villages of Germany, who brought money with them and labored to obtain a foothold upon the soil for themselves and their families ; and the poverty-stricken peasantry of Ireland, whose only desire was to escape a condition which they rightly believed could hardly be made worse. Of these two classes, while one has supported itself, we have had to support the other ; neither being precisely what we require to strengthen and improve the country. The German element, while it has, to some extent, developed our agricultural resources, has done so in a small way and purely for self. The Irish has served too largely to fill our prisons and reformatories, and to introduce into the political system of our large cities the worst features of European mobocracy. It is true that Italy sends us organ-grinders, and Germany lager-beer brewers ; but it may be questioned if this admixture largely strengthens our body politic.

The usual food of the Chinese is rice, fish, poultry, and vegetables ; and on this diet, or any portion of it, they are capable of prolonged efforts in labor which would put to shame many of our stalwart beef-eaters. The Chinaman works for a motive, the strongest possible to his race ; his sole wish and design is to obtain sufficient money by his savings to enable him to return to his family, and live in comparative comfort and ease for the rest of his days. He is therefore economical and abstemious. A few hundred dollars in gold will accomplish all his needs and his desires, and if he can save this amount in three or five years he is satisfied. Again, he is content with the current market price for labor, and such an idea as a combination or "Union" to enforce a higher standard of wages, is not only unknown to him, but is foreign to all his instincts and repugnant to his feelings. Naturally peaceable, he shrinks from conflict, and, as his past history has proven, will put up with oppression, contumely, and wrong for the longest before he will strive to relieve himself ; and then only by flight. Meanwhile, he will of course seize every legitimate means for bettering his condition, and will not work for one employer for less pay than another is willing to give him for the same amount of labor.

It is, therefore, not only for the convenience to society, the advantage to our national welfare, the healthy competition in labor which it promises, that the new element should be welcomed and sustained, but also for the fact that it promises to eradicate the most pernicious features of our present political life. There is no danger that the Chinese will interest themselves in our politics or mode of government. The experience of California is a sufficient guarantee on that head.

Accustomed to be governed, and to have no word or voice in the laws or their execution, they have only a desire to be allowed freedom to pursue their own avocations, and personal safety while engaged in the pursuit. Of votes, and candidates, and caucuses, and primary elections, torch-light processions, nominations, jobs, and rings, they are in blessed ignorance. And since we know them to be intelligent, there is the less fear of their influence, when they do arrive at this height of learning and experience, than if it were accompanied by that condition of ignorance which cannot discern the difference between right and wrong, except when a greenback is placed between them.

From *Scribner's Monthly*, 1871.

George F. Will

Victory in the Sheep Meadow

Last Sunday about 50,000 peace activists gathered for a last hurrah and hootenanny at the Sheep Meadow in Manhattan's Central Park. There, at the scene of so many peace rallies, they celebrated the peace that has come to Indochina.

In Cambodia, the Communists, running true to form, are concentrating their fury on the ultimate enemy of any Communist regime, the people. The Communists have emptied the cities, driving upwards of 4 million people—young and old, childing mothers and newborn babies, the healthy, halt and lame—on a forced march to nowhere, deep into the countryside where food is scarce and shelter is scarcer still.

Even hospitals have been emptied, operations interrupted at gunpoint, doctors and patients sent packing. The Communists call this the "purification" of Cambodia.

This forced march will leave a trail of corpses, and many more at its destination, wherever that is. But this is, according to the Communists, not an atrocity, it is a stern "necessity."

The Detroit Free Press contained a droll (I hope it was meant to be droll) sub-headline on events in Cambodia: "Reds Decree Rural Society." If one kind of society offends you, decree another.

Communism, like its totalitarian sibling, fascism, is the culmination of a modern heresy: People are plastic, infinitely malleable under determined pounding. And society is a tinker toy, its shape being whatever the ruling class decrees.

To create a New (Soviet, Chinese, German, Cambodian) Man—and what totalitarian would aim lower? — you must shatter the old man, ripping him from the community that nourishes him. Send him on a forced march into a forbidding future.

He may die. If he survives he will be deracinated, demoralized, pliant.

There is no atrocity so gross that American voices will not pipe up in defense of it. Today they say: It is "cultural arrogance" for Americans to call this forced march an atrocity, when it is just different people pursuing their "vision."

This is the mock cosmopolitanism of the morally obtuse. Such people say: "Only ideologically blinkered" Americans mistake stern idealism for an atrocity just because it involves the slaughter of innocents. Such people will never face the fact that most atrocities, and all the large ones, from the Thirty Years War through Biafra, have been acts of idealism.

Of course, one must not discount sheer blood lust, and the joy of bullying. Totalitarian governments rest on dumb philosophy and are sustained by secret police. But they are a bully's delight.

Totalitarians have never been without apologists here, people who derive vicarious pleasure from watching — from a safe distance, of course; from the Sheep Meadow, with ice cream bars, if possible—other people ground up by stern "necessities."

Apologists say that totalitarians only want totalitarianism for the sake of the revolution. The apologists, being backward, have got things backward.

Above, © *The Washington Post* (May 16, 1975).

Gigantic moral failure

One of the lasting shames of our age is that decent Western liberals, otherwise so sensitive to assaults on human values, have failed to condemn Communist brutality and terror in other than pro forma phrases.

Instead, they have reserved their obloquy for those who have perceived that communism is perhaps the most sordid doctrine ever to enslave the minds and bodies of masses of 20th century men. They have not been content to denounce merely the oversimplifiers among the anti-Communists; they have worked over virtually every public figure or scholar who has refused to genuflect before the belief that communism is merely another political sys-

tem, worse than some and better than others.

Communism is not pernicious merely because it is atheistic, bureaucratic, and minatory. It is pernicious because it is a doctrine that transforms ordinary human beings into moral monsters, capable of even such heinous crimes as the wholesale slaughter and liquidation of its own people.

It is pernicious because it regards human beings as mere clay to be moulded and twisted according to official state doctrine. It is evil because, in every Communist nation on earth, it exacts obedience through fear, terror, and intimidation. It is, as Russian writer Valery Tarsis described it, a

system of "police facism" on a scale unknown in history.

But leftists in the Western democracies, with only a handful of honorable exceptions, have regularly excused the crimes of communism and attacked its critics. Theirs is a moral failure without parallel in our century.

Russia remains what it has been — a vast prison run by guards driven by a brutal, debased ideology. And while we are appalled at the treatment given the Tutnauers during their visit, it is worthwhile to point out that they received red carpet treatment compared with the ordeal the average Russian citizen is subjected to throughout his lifetime.

Above, from *The Arizona Republic*, August 28, 1971.

212

REFLECTIONS
THE LIMITS OF DUTY

"Let us follow the process of creating an evil more closely. A scientist who is doing his specialized duty to further research and knowledge develops the substance known as napalm. Another specialist makes policy in the field of our nation's foreign affairs. A third is concerned with maintaining the strength of our armed forces with the most modern weaponry. A fourth manufactures what the defense authorities require.

A fifth drops napalm from an airplane where he is told to do so. The ultimate evil is the result of carefully segmented acts; the structure itself guarantees an evasion by everyone of responsibility for the full moral act."

From an article by Charles A. Reich, appearing this week in The New Yorker. Yes, The New Yorker.

Above, courtesy of *The New Yorker*.
Right, courtesy of C. P. Sarsfield and *The New Guard*.
Below, a message from Pope Pius XII.

CEASAR'S DUTY

A nation is required to protect the lives of its citizens; it is not expected to do good to all the world, and those who would demand that it do are not fit citizens. Given a choice of having liberty or death, some would choose the latter, for there are fates worse than death. Letting it be known that death is not feared if life as one wants it connot be had, can sometimes be an effective measure of policy. It is sometimes known as calling a bluff. It draws a line, and though the price may be high, in time that line is usually respected. Some may die, even many; but their deaths win worthy goals for their successors. That is sometimes known as laying down one's life for his fellows. It is an act the benefits from which the pacifist is willing to accept without contributing his proportional measure.

In a remarkable allocution to Military Doctors (October 19, 1953), Pius XII said:

"Let there be punishment on an international scale for every war not called for by absolute necessity. The only constraint to wage war is defense against an injustice of the utmost gravity which strikes the entire community and which cannot be coped with by any other means — for otherwise one would give free course, in international relations, to brutal violence and irresponsibility."

Relating the principle of proportionality to modern times, he added:

"Defending oneself against any kind of injustice, however, is not sufficient reason to resort to war. When the losses that it brings are not comparable to those of the 'injustice tolerated,' one may have the obligation of 'submitting to the injustice.' This is particularly applicable to the A.B.C. war (atomic, biological, chemical)."

First Decree for the Protection of Life

WHEREAS —

After thousands of years of slow and laborious development, mankind during the past few decades has rapidly come into possession of technological means which promise either unlimited opportunity and abundance or sudden and universal catastrophe.

The People of Earth are, in fact, confronted daily with the threat of instant extermination by the accidental or deliberate unleashing of nuclear weapons. This threat multiplies as more nations gain nuclear capability and install multiple warheads which defy inspection and control by treaty.

Even limited use of nuclear weapons and other weapons of mass destruction imperils civilian populations, towns, cities and country-sides, and can turn entire countries into ravaged battlefields.

The $200,000,000,000 being spent by the nations each year for military purposes, mainly for weapons of mass destruction and their deployment, is a criminal waste of resources and manpower which could otherwise be devoted to supplying the People of Earth with adequate food, shelter, clothing, education, health services and expanding opportunities in life.

So long as nations give priority to expenditures for military might, there is scant chance of applying the brainpower, manpower and resources needed to solve other rapidly mounting problems which threaten humanity with the breakdown of society, misery and death in multiple ways before the end of the century. These problems include environmental pollution, the gap between rich and poor, hunger and population, urban decay, technological cancers, social disorientations and other troubles.

Apart from dangers of universal ruin, the means of modern warfare comprise the tools of force by which stronger nations interfere in the affairs of weaker nations and enforce imperialistic and colonial policies.

Meanwhile, the civil and human rights of people in all countries are nullified when nations are permitted to keep large and heavily armed military forces, since it is with military force that dictatorships and tyrannies are enforced, movements for peaceful change crushed, and people kept subservient — making a mockery of the Charter of Human Rights adopted by the United Nations.

Despite the extreme dangers to all life on Earth, which are growing every day and year, the national governments not only fail to protect their citizens from these dangers, but on the contrary many national governments are actively increasing the hazards by continuing to install nuclear weapons and to devise other weapons with ever greater capacity for death and ruin.

During the next one to thirty years, in order to survive and prosper, the residents of Earth must overcome manifold problems and perils of planetary scope unknown in history. Yet at the world level, no agency exists which has the authority or competence to cope with the problems, and anarchy prevails.

THEREFORE —

When life is seriously endangered and existing governments are either unable or unwilling to remove the dangers and improve the conditions of life, then it becomes necessary for responsible citizens to proceed with remedies which seem appropriate.

Men and women acting under such circumstances may be described as Trustees acting for the common good, ultimately justified by whether their actions are endorsed by their fellow citizens.

In view of the increasing jeapordy to the lives and property of everyone on Earth, and in the absence of effective action by national governments and international agencies to protect life, we who are listed below, from many countries, have organized ourselves into an Emergency Council of World Trustees to take immediate action on behalf of humanity. Our purposes are to outlaw war and war preparations, to convene a Peoples World Parliament for continuous work, to prepare a Constitution for Federal World Government for submission to the Parliament, to appoint global legislative commissions to prepare legislation on urgent world problems for submission to the Parliament, and to take other appropriate action leading to the establishment of a Provisional World Government under democratic popular control.

As a first action to rescue Planet Earth and its inhabitants from destruction, and to provide a tangible rallying ground for people everywhere who want peace and human rights while moving towards the creation of a Provisional World Government, we do hereby issue this First Decree for the Protection of Life:

1. Upon the effective ratification of this decree, it shall be outlaw and forbidden everywhere on Earth to design, test, produce, transport, sell, buy, install, deploy or use nuclear weapons, chemical-biological weapons, or any weapons of mass destruction, including airplanes equipped for bombing, I.C.B.M.s and other delivery systems, battleships, tanks and all manner of bombs and newly devised weapons.

2. This decree shall go into effect as soon as it is ratified by groups of students and professors at 200 universities and colleges in at least 20 countries, or by the signatures of at least 10 million individuals in at least 20 countries, or any equivalent thereof.

3. Any and all executive, administrative and chief policy making officials in governments, the military forces, industry, scientific work education or labor who may be responsible for violation of this decree after effective ratification, shall be guilty of war crimes and crimes against humanity.

4. Those who sign or ratify this decree thereby pledge themselves personally to abide by the decree. Opportunity to ratify shall be continued beyond the minimum stated herein for the decree to go into effect.

5. Individuals found guilty of violation of this decree may be assigned to rehabilitation and reconstruction work in areas devastated by war, or to other work of service to humanity.

6. Procedures for enforcement of this decree shall be determined either by the Emergency Council of World Trustees upon effective ratification, or by the Peoples World Parliament or Provisional World Government as soon as the latter institutions are established.

PEOPLE OF EARTH, UNITE TO OBTAIN NEW PRIORITIES FOR LIFE, BY SIGNING OR RATIFYING THIS FIRST DECREE FOR THE PROTECTION OF LIFE!

This First Decree for the Protection of Life was issued at the inaugural meeting of the Emergency Council of World Trustees at Santa Barbara, California, Dec. 28, 1971, to Jan. 2, 1972. At time of issuance, the Decree carried the signatures of several hundred persons from all continents of Earth, more than half being presidents of university student unions and other student leaders.

ALL PERSONS WHO AGREE WITH THIS ACTION ARE URGED TO RATIFY THE DECREE AND SEND A CONTRIBUTION TO CARRY THE ACTION FORWARD!

Ratified by .... Native country ....

Print name .... Contribution $................................

Address ....

Occupation or position ....

Please send me .... copies of the Decree to circulate for ratification, together with a list of the first signers. (Note: You can help the cause by printing the Decree at once and circulating it in your community or on your campus. Use this copy for offset printing.)

Return signed Decrees with contributions to the World Constitution and Parliament Association, Inc., Trustees Office, 1480 Hoyt St., Lakewood, Colorado 80215, USA.

Courtesy of the World Constitution and Parliament Association, Inc., and *The Humanist*, January-February 1972.

There was another fifties

By Richard R. Lingeman

As for the war, at times it seemed a banal meaninglessness. There were actually two wars in my mind; war, which was bad, and the "police action" war, which reasonable men could give reasons for. I wrote a muddled *cri de coeur* in my diary as the time for entering the service drew near:

"About the war: It seems to me I must approve of it. Our country is acting on principle and is motivated by a world-wide vision. To fight for our belief —in a world order—we must use the irrational techniques of war. We, as a whole, are acting through goodwill but we are faced by a nation [I meant the Soviet Union] that does not act through goodwill, only expediency. We are forced to fight with that nation on its own terms—the evil terms of war.... This war is a big impersonal one—a preview perhaps of those '1984' wars. The principle of our actions and the institutions which embody them are too large really to motivate any but a few. The rest merely carry out their part in the war and perhaps die. Oh well, I will think about it more later."

I didn't think about it much later — especially the dying part—but, armed with a principle I admitted was too abstract and distant for me to accept in my heart, I enlisted in 1953, scared, excited, prepared to hate the Army.

Top, from *The New York Times Magazine*, June 17, 1973.

Playing at War

Why *The Progressive,* with a sixty-two year record of outspoken opposition to war and all things military, was included in a recent publicity mailing from the Avalon Hill Company, we shall never know. But the Baltimore firm which has designed such war games as *D-Day, Afrika Korps, Stalingrad, Gettysburg,* and *Blitzkrieg,* recently sent us a release that panted with excitement about its latest game offering—*Panzerblitz.*

This new board game, says the communique from the Avalon Hill command post, "is a tactical-level strategy game that simulates action of the largest ground campaign of World War II." Developed "from official documents" it recreates "thirteen historical engagements" in "a faithful re-creation of the critical armored battles fought on the Eastern Front 1941-45."

"Fifty-six per cent of all soldiers killed in World War II were Russian. Yet this gigantic theater has been virtually ignored by Western historians," the company discloses—an oversight by military scholars that Avalon hopes to correct, at a profit, through a large sale of *Panzerblitz.*

Their new war game "also happens to be fun to play," says Avalon Hill. All you need to play it is "just common sense, a competitive spirit," and the $8.98 purchase price charged "wherever adult games are sold."

What can be considered "adult" about war games we cannot imagine. They glamorize war, the most infantile and lunatic of all men's pursuits. It would be a healthy sign of American maturity if *Panzerblitz* and all other war games and toys turned out to be a total flop in the stores this Christmas shopping season.

Above, reprinted by permission from *The Progressive,* 408 West Gorham Street, Madison, Wisconsin 53703. Copyright 1970, The Progressive, Inc.

The Great Trip-Wire Delusion

Courtesy of Alan Cranston, U.S. Senator from California and *Saturday Review*, July 19, 1971.

EDITOR'S NOTE: *The following guest editorial is by Alan Cranston, U.S. Senator from California, and longtime contributor to SR.*

The U.S. Senate recently voted down Majority Leader Mike Mansfield's attempt to compel a 50 per cent reduction in the number of American ground troops stationed in Europe.

In the Senate debate much attention was given to the need to scale down East-West tensions, to correct our adverse balance of payments, and to get our now quite prosperous allies to assume a larger share of the financial and military burdens of NATO. All good points. But I sensed a disturbing undercurrent.

There appears to be a tacit understanding on both sides of the Atlantic that a sizable number of American troops must be stationed on the Continent as a kind of human trip wire to assure our intervention in the event of a Soviet invasion of Western Europe.

The theory seems to be that thousands of Americans must be engaged in mortal combat in the first days of such an invasion, else we will not intercede. The belief is that the larger this human trip wire, and the more human flesh it contains, the more confident our friends and allies will feel, and the more hesitant the Russians will be.

I find this concept utterly repellent, and morally grotesque. I am appalled by the image of 300,000 Americans being offered up as sacrificial hostages in a new, perverted version of "earnest money" to reassure our friends that we will keep our pledge. I am shocked each time our foreign friends interpret any effort to reduce the number of hostages as hard evidence that we indeed intend to go back on our word.

What kind of friends are these anyway? What kind of opinion do they have of us to think that we do not value human lives unless they are American lives? To think that we would not consider the lives of other free men worthy of our concern in the event of Soviet aggression? And to think that only the on-the-spot slaughter of young Americans could provoke us to act in our own best interests?

Those who subscribe to the trip-wire strategy claim it offers us flexibility—a way to resist aggression without resorting to all-out nuclear retaliation. The fact is, however, that the great armies of NATO and the Warsaw Pact facing each other across an imaginary line in Central Europe are as dated as the cavalry that tried to stand up to the Nazi panzer divisions in Poland. Our troops in Europe are armed with tactical nuclear weapons as are, presumably, the Warsaw Pact forces.

The Davy Crockett, a cannon manned by a crew of five, has been called the "keystone of the Allied defense line." With an explosive force somewhat less than that of the Hiroshima bomb, it is our smallest tactical weapon, and we have others even more powerful.

In an East-West war in Europe, the side that is losing, or thinks it is losing, will without doubt resort to nuclear weapons to "save the day." Even the "winning" side would do so, if it thought the enemy was about to launch a strike. It is for just these eventualities that we have our tactical nuclear weapons positioned there. So our troops in Europe are targets for almost certain death or radiation poisoning in the event of war. They cannot win; they can only destroy and be destroyed.

We have been lucky so far, but the day must come soon—before this murderous insanity goes too much further—when we will have to reduce our NATO forces. We must recognize that there is no true security for us or for anyone else in a world in which nuclear weapons are on the loose. We must set about the task of providing leadership dedicated to achieving world peace through world law.

Do some of our leaders feel that they must use a trip-wire force to insure that we will keep our commitment to our NATO allies? Are we busily preparing for a day when we may be in the same position in Europe as we are now in in Southeast Asia? Will we someday be told that millions of Americans must die for those 300,000 American troops in Europe—just as we are being told now that still more Americans must die in Indochina so that the deaths of the 45,000 already killed there will, somehow, have been "worthwhile"?

If that is what some of our leaders think, if that is why they insist on maintaining 300,000 American troops on European soil, their perspective, in my judgment, is dangerously distorted. One such horror is more than enough in the lifetime of any nation.

The fact is that the whole structure of the trip-wire concept is built on false assumptions. The fact is that we do not need such an immoral mechanism forcibly to link Europe's destiny with ours. The fact is that we are inextricably linked with Europe—by past history and heritage, and by present politics and economics.

A free, independent Europe is vital to America's survival and to world peace; a free Europe and a free America stand or fall together.

That is the real meaning of NATO, that is why we are in the alliance, that is why we will unhesitatingly honor our commitment should we ever be called upon to do so—not to avenge the blood of American hostages, but to defend American freedom and the very concept of freedom.

Our European allies and those of our leaders who presume otherwise do the American people a grave injustice.

—ALAN CRANSTON.

SR/JUNE 19, 1971

Something jars

Photography: Mick Dean

Because there's an alarming economic gap between you and the poor bloke who grew or harvested the coffee beans which went to make your instant coffee.

You pay maybe 25p for a small jar.

He'll be lucky to earn £100.

A year.

You can afford the trimmings: processing, packaging and advertising.

He can barely afford essentials: food, clothing and shelter for his family.

Coffee is grown in poor developing countries like Brazil, Colombia and Uganda. But that doesn't stop rich countries like Britain exploiting their economic weakness by paying as little for their raw coffee as we can get away with.

On top of this we keep charging more and more for the manufactured goods they need to buy from us.

So?

So we get richer at their expense. Business is business.

Perhaps one day humanity will replace self-interest in international trade. Meantime, something needs to be done now about the appalling poverty which these Third World countries are facing.

Oxfam is a very small part of this effort. Currently, we're spending the money you give on more than a thousand development projects in 80 countries.

Nets and boats for poor fishermen. Family planning clinics. Reservoirs to catch the seasonal rains. Training for youngsters in skills their countries desperately need. Tools and seeds for struggling farmers.

Want to know more?

Write to us and we'll send you a copy of *The Internationalist*. It'll cost you 25p, and it reports on the way rich countries treat their poor neighbours. We'll also tell you more about our worldwide development programme —and how you can help.

And next time you drink a cup of coffee, remember where it came from.

And what it really cost.

OXFAM

Room 4, 274 Banbury Road, Oxford OX2 7DZ

217

Pragmatic Immorality

Today's issue of The New York Times Magazine carries a description of one of the most pessimistic and morally threadbare intellectual positions to be advanced since the demise of the Third Reich. The position, called Triage, is based on a World War I medical practice—necessitated by scarcity—of separating the wounded into three categories: those who would get well without treatment, those who would die no matter what, and those who might be saved if given care. Only the wounded in the last category were treated.

It is now argued earnestly by some American analysts that the problems of food scarcity around the globe and the incompetence of some of the countries in need are so severe as to require the application of the Triage principle in dispensing humanitarian food aid.

The first problem is that the competence argument doesn't entirely wash because India and other South Asian countries—the obvious first victims of the policy—are currently in deep trouble largely because of factors beyond their control: soaring oil and food prices, fertilizer scarcity and bad weather.

Beyond that, however, and more basic, the world has yet to make a really serious effort to crack the food crisis. The Rome food conference last November was the first universal attempt to face up to the problem. Just two years ago, prior to the grain sale to the Soviet Union and a run of bad weather around the globe, there was too little awareness of the food problems to marshall the political will for an effective effort.

There is no question now that the problem is urgent and extremely difficult, but there is no proof that there are not on earth the will, the resources and the technology to overcome the crisis. Nor is there evidence that letting people starve will actually solve the population problem. There is some evidence indicating that where death rates go up because of starvation, there is a compensating rise in birth rates. Conversely, there is other evidence that the encouragement of small-scale farming by small farmers and landless laborers—a program discussed at length at Rome—results not only in substantially increased food production but also in a decline in the birth rate.

But the essence of the problem is that humankind has not yet come close to defining, in terms of political and economic cooperation, what responsible membership in the human family or the community of nations can be or can produce. There is thus no basis in reason or morality to argue that the only recourse now, in the interests of the greater good, is to allow millions of people a long way off to starve to death. It may be hard to be human or moral, but it is even harder—in fact impossible—to play God.

Turkey to lift ban on heroin

ANKARA (UPI) — Turkey has decided to bow to demands from its unemployed poppy farmers and lift a 13-month-old heroin ban imposed at the request of the United States.

A government s0okesman said Thursday Foreign Minister Turhan Gunes told U.S. Ambassador William Macomber the decision was made to ease the financial plight of Turkey's 70,000 poppy growers.

"One part of mankind cannot be driven to despair to safeguard another part," the ne2spaper Hurriyet quoted the foreign minister as saying.

The announcement did not say when the ban would be lifted or whether the government might reconsider i5s decision if the United States offered to step up compensation payments to farmers.

Turkey banned poppy growing last year after a decade of delicate negotiations with the United States. In return, Washington a;reed to pay Turkish farmers more than $35 million in indemnities.

The farmers complained, however, the compensation payments were "hardly more than a tip" and pressed candidates in last October's national elections to take a stand on the issue.

More food for a hungry world... or less?

With lives at stake, decisions had better be based on fact.

There are hundreds of millions of people in the world whose food intake is near starvation level.

These people must have food.

They will not get it if we produce less beef in this country, as some suggest.

The United Nations Food and Agriculture Organization says beef is a source of high-quality, assured-quantity protein that helps provide adequate nutrition. This is as true for industrialized nations as it is for developing nations.

It is unfortunate that many people are being misled, because of faulty information, into believing less meat will mean more of something else.

It is a fact that...

Beef has every amino acid the body needs ...the amount and quality of protein no single vegetable, grain or fruit can provide.

It is a fact that...

It takes about 3 pounds of grain to produce one pound of beef, not 8 or more, as has been reported.

It is a fact that...

75 percent of all feed consumed by cattle is grass, forage and by-products which are inedible by humans.

It is a fact that...

Most cattle are raised on land that cannot grow food for humans—nearly 900 million acres in the U.S. alone.

It is a fact that...

Only ruminants (animals with four stomachs) such as cattle can produce high quality protein for humans from this otherwise unusable natural resource.

What we need in this world is more food, not less. That means more beef and other animal proteins as well as more grain, vegetables and other foods. The beef industry accepts its share of this challenge to increase food production through increasing efficiency and use of available resources.

Courtesy National Live Stock & Meat Board.

BEEF INDUSTRY COUNCIL OF THE MEAT BOARD

Feeding the World Is
A Task for the Whole World

Many of the developing countries have dubious records in food policy. They too often failed to offer their farmers adequate incentives to produce. They have too often tried to placate urban consumers with cheap food policies based on concessional imports. They have too often put their development capital into glamor industries instead of into fertilizer plants and irrigation pumps. They have too long put off serious efforts to slow their own birth rates.

The world must feed the world.

The United States and U.S. agriculture will do their share, but we should not mislead ourselves or others. The job is too big for any one country. And we must begin now to build a stronger world agriculture — especially in the developing countries—or suffer the consequences in the years ahead.

—From a speech by CLAYTON YEUTTER, *assistant Secretary of Agriculture, before the National Water Resources Association meeting in Fresno, Calif.*

Left, from *The National Observer*. Copyright Dow Jones & Co., Inc.

Right, letter to the editor of *Time* by J. Van Cleve, June 3, 1974. Reprinted by permission from *Time, The Weekly Newsmagazine*, Copyright Time, Inc.

Sir / Having just returned to the U.S. after six years of living in Asia, in Asian terms and on Asian levels, I notice that we Americans are virtually all fat. It is ethically as well as aesthetically disgusting. We overconsume ourselves into an unhealthy obesity. Then we compound our selfish idiocy by pouring still more dollars into fancy-priced reducing salons, ranch vacations, exercise programs and machines. We waste twice, while the rest of the world dies because it cannot eat its fill once.

J. VAN CLEVE
Round Lake, Ill.